A Short Course in Writing

A Short Course in Writing

Composition, Collaborative Learning, and Constructive Reading

Fourth Edition

Kenneth A. Bruffee

Brooklyn College, City University of New York

With Foreword by
John Trimbur and Harvey Kail

PEARSON
Longman

New York • San Francisco • Boston
London • Toronto • Sydney • Tokyo • Singapore • Madrid
Mexico City • Munich • Paris • Cape Town • Hong Kong • Montreal

Acquisitions Editor: Lauren A. Finn
Senior Marketing Manager: Sandra McGuire
Production Manager: Bob Ginsberg
Project Coordination, Text Design, and Electronic Page
   Makeup: Pre-Press Company Inc.
Cover Design Manager/Cover Designer: Wendy Ann Fredericks
Cover Photo: © Jeff Greenberg/PhotoEdit
Senior Manufacturing Buyer: Dennis J. Para
Printer and Binder: RR Donnelley & Sons Company, Crawfordsville
Cover Printer: Phoenix Color Corporation

Visit us at www.ablongman.com

ISBN 0-321-43267-3

12345678910—DOC—09 08 07 06

Brief Contents

Detailed Contents

PART FOUR   189

Reaching Out to Members of Other Communities

PART SIX   293

A Course for Writing Peer Tutors

ANTHOLOGY OF STUDENT ESSAYS   **319**

ANTHOLOGY OF PROFESSIONAL ESSAYS 343 ———

Foreword

Kenneth A. Bruffee's *A Short Course in Writing* provides a good occasion to ask what makes a textbook in rhetoric and composition a classic. The fact that Bruffee's book is among the first to appear in the Longman Classics in Rhetoric and Composition series cannot be attributed, after all, to its commercial success. In his review of the original manuscript of *A Short Course*, Richard Beal, the most prominent English editor at the time, told Paul O'Connell, who published the first edition at Winthrop in 1972, that Bruffee could either alter the book and sell a lot of copies or publish the book as is and make history.[1] What Beal predicted has indeed come to pass. As *A Short Course* appeared in subsequent editions (the second from Winthrop in 1980; the third from Little, Brown in 1985; and the fourth from HarperCollins in 1993), it has influenced, far out of proportion to its sales, the actual practices of writing instruction and, more broadly, of educational reform in U.S. college composition.

If anything, it is the professional appreciation of Bruffee's distinct combination of practical rhetoric and collaborative learning that has made *A Short Course* a classic. A generation of writing teachers, writing center directors, writing program administrators, and writing theorists, not to mention other textbook authors, have affirmed the value of *A Short Course* as not just another textbook but instead a way of thinking about writing and liberal education. *A Short Course* belongs to a subgenre we might call the "short rhetoric," a guide to writing with a point of view, poised precariously between a professional book and a textbook. Peter Elbow's *Writing Without Teachers*, William E. Coles's *The Plural I*, and Ann Berthoff's *Forming, Thinking, Writing* are good examples. These books

---

[1]Beal's review can be found in the National Archives of Composition and Rhetoric at the University of Rhode Island, which includes extensive collections of both Beal's and Bruffee's papers. We thank Robert A. Schwegler for pointing us to Beal's review of *A Short Course*.

make no pretense to being comprehensive, like the full-service rhetorics such as James McCrimmon's *Writing With a Purpose* or the multi-author *The St. Martin's Guide to Teaching Writing*. Instead, the short rhetorics are meant to be edifying, to offer a lesson about how writing might be taught and learned.

Without the apparatus, manuals, and ancillaries of the long rhetoric, *A Short Course* addresses students and teachers simultaneously and transparently, as joint participants and necessary components of educational change in the composition classroom. The task that *A Short Course* took on in the early 1970s was defined by a nearly visceral sense that traditional forms of teaching writing were in crisis because they are hierarchical, atomizing, authoritarian, disabling, and just plain ineffective. For Bruffee, the problem was one not just of jettisoning the worn-out models of the past but more important of designing more adequate and enabling forms of classroom life. The task, as Bruffee begins to develop it with the first edition of *A Short Course*, involves resituating the participants in writing classrooms by redescribing the authority of the teacher and reorganizing the way students work together with texts. Like the other short rhetorics, *A Short Course* is a partisan book, a call to change the social relations of reading and writing—to materialize new meanings for literacy in the first-year composition course.

Recognition of *A Short Course* can be seen quite concretely in the way Bruffee's characteristic devices have been assimilated into writing pedagogy—short forms of writing based on propositions and reasons; descriptive outlines; reading aloud; sequenced exercises in written peer evaluation. Part of the appeal of *A Short Course* (and consequently one of the sources of its influence) is the ease with which the assignments and exercises can be lifted and put into practice. Many writing teachers have read *A Short Course*, learned from it, and used its materials, whether they ever actually assigned the book or not. In its thirty-five-year history, *A Short Course* has circulated in a variety of contexts—in the classrooms and syllabi of individual teachers, to be sure, but also, more programmatically, in the meetings of City University of New York (CUNY) writing faculty during open admissions in the early 1970s, the Brooklyn Plan as a model of peer tutor training, the Brooklyn Institute in Training Peer Tutors of the 1980s, the collaborative learning workshops Bruffee has done at conferences and at colleges and universities, and the professional networks of writing teachers and theorists who read Bruffee's articles in *College English* and *Liberal Education* as an indispensable departure point in understanding the connections between collaborative learning and composition. In writing center circles, where it originated, *A Short Course* has become a standard manual for training peer tutors. To put it another way, the status of *A Short Classic* as a classic in rhetoric and composition can be traced to its uses, its infiltration of practice, and its influence on the underlying theories that enable writing instruction, peer tutoring, and writing program design.

This did not happen all at once. It is important to see the editions of *A Short Course* as a work in progress, a part of Bruffee's larger project to understand the potentialities of mutual aid and associated learning and to link this understanding to the development of rhetorical judgment. The activities, assignments, and exercises in *A Short Course* have remained remarkably consistent over the four editions. What can be seen unfolding rather is Bruffee's clarification of the meaning of collaborative learning for the teaching of writing. As we will see, *A Short Course* provided Bruffee with a laboratory to codify his experiments with peer group learning and a forum to explain and disseminate the model of collaborative learning he advocates.

The genius of *A Short Course in Writing* is in the unique relationship it establishes between formal writing exercises and rigorous peer review tasks. When students move together through these collaborative exercises, they become better writers by learning to help others in the class become better writers. Of course this is an easy claim to make but not necessarily so easy to accomplish. Teaching students to earn trust and critical judgment from each other is complex and fraught. However, in the clarity and purposefulness of its writing and reading tasks and in its accumulated wisdom about collaborative learning, *A Short Course* comes as close to a curricular machine for producing educational mutual aid among students as we have ever seen. Although specific *Short Course* exercises can and frequently have been lifted out of the text for other purposes, *A Short Course* is best used by following the sequence of assignments that unfold over time in order for students to learn not only the standard forms of academic and public discourse but also to learn them by becoming competent readers of each other's prose and articulate, tactful critics of each other's writing.

The joining of a practical rhetoric with a collaborative learning pedagogy is an interesting story in itself, one that is both specific to Bruffee and germane to higher education reform in the late 1960s and early 1970s. Students and faculty were experiencing at the time the drama of the anti-Vietnam War and civil rights movements on their own campuses, as grassroots movements were seeking to democratize higher education through open admissions. Bruffee became director of first year composition at Brooklyn College in April 1971. In June, against a backdrop of city-wide student protests, the City University of New York opened its doors to all New Yorkers who had earned a high school diploma. Seemingly overnight students who had never had the opportunity for higher education—or the educational preparation and academic success traditional to the highly selective Brooklyn College campus—were streaming in the door. Enrollments jumped from 14,000 to 34,000 in just three years (Hawkes 3). Faced with 108 divisions of Freshman English and a staff as unprepared as he was for the task, Bruffee acknowledges, "We just muddled. We didn't know what we were doing. That's the truth. We didn't know" (Interview 3/03). Researching, writing, and revising the early editions of *A Short Course* became Bruffee's way out of this educational and cultural muddle.

The innovative notion that students should and could play a systematic role in each other's education as writers and thinkers came into *A Short Course* at just this time of ferment and change in American higher education. One of the most important early influences on the development of *A Short Course* came from a student on Bruffee's own Brooklyn College campus. Peter Amato, an undergraduate, was running a peer counseling service to help other students resolve personal problems related to finances, housing, health care, and other issues that affected their matriculation. Bruffee remembers that "there was something about this that began to muddle in my head" (Interview 3/03). If students could help other students with serious life issues such as financing their college educations or getting their health needs addressed, surely, he reasoned, they could help other students write a paper that makes a point and defends it. Thus inspired and instructed by a student, Bruffee began training undergraduates at Brooklyn College to tutor their peers in writing, teaching the first peer tutor training course in writing in the United States.

Bruffee adapted an early, mimeographed version of *A Short Course* for the purpose, incorporating the brief argument forms that he had been experimenting with since the 1960s as the foundation and practical rhetoric of his course. Proposition and two reasons, strawman and one reason, Nestorian Order, concession—these are the infamous *Short Course* forms that appear in the text as schematic hook and ladder diagrams, outlining the shape that the argument should follow: proposition here, reasons there, three paragraphs, no conclusion. Bruffee has stood by these argument forms steadfastly through all the editions of *A Short Course* not only because they are "basic, useful and variable forms" of public discourse but also because they "make collaborative learning easier to organize" (*Short Course* 6). In the course of a semester's study and writing, *Short Course* forms do, indeed, create a communal, intellectual space within which collaborative learning can be experienced. Through their repetition and evolving complexity, their clarity and rigor, they become the scaffolding by which students master the tricky demands of learning together rather than apart.

The peer review assignments Bruffee developed over the course of the early editions of *A Short Course* call on students to help each other by writing and conversing in terms of the unity, coherence, development, mechanics, and style of their writing, a method of workshopping writing that Peter Elbow would later call "criterion-based feedback" (240). The difference is that in Bruffee's peer tutor training course, the students were not simply giving each other "feedback"; they were immersing themselves in the complex experience of learning composition together. As the formal writing tasks in *A Short Course* become more complex and more challenging, the collaborative learning exercises in turn become more thorough and evaluative, moving students together from description and analysis of form, to evaluation of the strengths and weaknesses of argument, and finally to making and explaining practical suggestions for revision. The entire progression calls not only for increasing competence in analytical precision and judgment but the development of tact and diplomacy, as well— the kind of conversation that teaches students "the skills and partnership" of interdependence.

By 1972, when the first edition of *A Short Course* was published, Bruffee had come to the "tentative but not very original conclusion" that it was necessary to "redefine the roles of teacher and student" in order that young people might "recapture themselves" from the "docility and dependence bequeathed to them by American schooling" (*Short Course* xii). Bruffee found a model by which to reorganize this vital relationship between "those that want to learn and those whose calling it is to teach" (Interview 3/03) at Columbia University's Graduate School of Social Work, where he enrolled in classes in the early 1970s to investigate more systematically the way people learn in groups. At Columbia he studied with William Schwartz, a leading theorist and practitioner of mutual aid groups. The predominant model of social work in the 1960s and 1970s assumed the social worker as a case manager who worked one-to-one with individual clients helping them solve individual problems. Schwartz was proposing and documenting a model that focused instead on the social worker as a mediator interacting with small groups, rather than with individuals, to help the group develop mutual aid. Schwartz and his colleagues were committed to extending the value of small group social work to settings such as prisons, hospitals, and union halls where the notion of mutual aid might find fertile ground.

Bruffee began constructing a role for the teacher in the composition classroom similar to that assigned to the social worker in the small group paradigm. Rather than the teacher instructing the class as an aggregate of individuals, addressing each student on a one-to-one basis (even when that one-to-one relationship is embedded in a lecture or classroom discussion), the teacher in *A Short Course* becomes a task designer, a community organizer, a referee of difference and dissent, a mediator among the students and between the students and the academy. Rather than an occasion for lectures or class discussion, the class itself becomes an alternative social structure within the institution, constructing a transitional subgroup of peers that students can rely on as they go through "the risky process of replacing dependence on the teacher's authority with confidence in their own authority as writers and critical readers" (Instructor's Manual 9).

Throughout the 1970s, Bruffee was reading the work of educational theorists and practitioners who were also engaged in organizing people to learn from each other, and he was synthesizing and incorporating their ideas into *A Short Course*. What is striking about Bruffee's sources and his thinking at this early stage of *A Short Course* is how much they prefigure themes in his later work. Bruffee began to conceptualize collaborative learning by drawing on John Dewey's interest in reforming the atomized, asocial character of traditional education and his retrospective critique that progressive education had abandoned the traditional authority of teachers and the school without devising an alternative enabling structure to replace it. From *Anatomy of Judgment*, M. L. J. Abercrombie's study of small groups learning diagnostic skills in medical school, Bruffee picked up the idea that peer learning is best suited not so much to learning new material but instead to developing evaluative judgment and intellectual maturity. Another early influence was Edwin Mason's *Collaborative Learning*, where Bruffee found the term for his new writing pedagogy, along with an early suggestion that was to occupy his work more and more, the idea that not only learning but knowledge itself was social. Lev Vygotsky's notion of thought as "inner speech," the internalized conversation with others, pointed further, for Bruffee, to the inescapably social character of writing and learning.

By the time the third edition of *A Short Course* was published in 1985, Bruffee had consolidated a theoretical grounding, and, in a telling move, he brought his explanation of collaborative learning forward from the back of the book, where it had been residing, to the very front, where it appeared in a revised and significantly expanded version as the doorway to the text, to "writing as a collaborative and social act." Two new and, in some measure, interdependent influences now seem crucial to this development of *A Short Course*. The first was Bruffee's invention of the Brooklyn College Summer Institute in Training Peer Writing Tutors. With support from the Fund for the Improvement of Postsecondary Education and the City University of New York, the Institute brought together fifteen writing center directors in both 1980 and 1981 to disseminate the Brooklyn Plan, Bruffee's model for training and using peer tutors. The idea was to train a cohort of thirty young college and university writing instructors to return to their home institutions and use *A Short Course* to train peer writing tutors.

Lisa Ede notes that composition history has often neglected the role institutes and seminars such as Bruffee's Brooklyn Institute, Richard Young's National Endowment for the Humanities seminar, and Janice Lauer's Rhetoric Seminar have played in shaping the intellectual life of the field through the formation of professional networks and individual careers. As part of the first group of fifteen in the Brooklyn Institute, and relatively new to writing centers and to composition studies in 1980, we can attest to how this works. For five weeks we followed the syllabus for training peer tutors in the second edition of *A Short Course*: we explored topics through structured conversation; wrote descriptive outlines, peer reviews, and author's responses; read drafts aloud; turned our papers in to Bruffee for his commentary; and revised. Sessions led by Alex Gitterman, a colleague of William Schwartz at Columbia, met twice a week to introduce Institute fellows to social group work theory and practice and to examine the Institute itself as a working experiment in developing a mutual aid group. The intensity we experienced as peers in a rigorous collaborative learning environment generated struggles with our feelings and attitudes toward the authority of the teacher and the intimacy and frustrations of small group learning. It also produced new articulations of what it might mean for teaching composition in the academy if writing tasks were systematically immersed in the social relations of peers. Bruffee takes up these themes that so stirred the Institute, presenting them in new and clarified terms in the introduction to the third edition of *A Short Course*.

The second, related influence that shaped the third edition was Bruffee's synthesis of social constructionist thought and his application of its nonfoundationalist assumptions to the teaching of writing. Bruffee had for some time been reading in the history of science, anthropology, psychology, composition, and literary theory, trying, in his own interdisciplinary way, to find a language to help him explain collaborative learning and its unsettling relationship to knowledge. In the Brooklyn Institute, we came to think of this synthesis of ideas as the triad Kuhn/Fish/Rorty. From Thomas Kuhn's *The Structure of Scientific Revolutions*, Bruffee gleaned the idea that scientific knowledge was a social construct, not the discovery of what is really out there but instead what can be ratified by a consensus of knowledgeable peers.

From Stanley's Fish's *Is There a Text in this Class?*, Bruffee found confirmation of the notion that knowledge is more of a process of acculturation to an "interpretive community" than an individual encounter with an unmediated reality or rationality. These, and other related writers and ideas, which Bruffee described in a series of influential articles in the early 1980s (see our Suggestions for Further Reading), all came into bold relief for Bruffee when he discovered Richard Rorty.

As Bruffee tells the story, he was enrolled in Professor Reuben Abel's course in epistemology at the New School (it is typical of Bruffee to enroll in a course or courses when he is researching something, testimony to his willingness to educate himself in public) when "some guy came in [to the class] waving this green book and saying to the professor 'What about this?'" (Interview 3/03). The book was *Philosophy and the Mirror of Nature*. From Rorty, Bruffee discovered the language through which he could at last respond to the criticism that collaborative learning, while useful perhaps as a means of social support, amounted, as a matter of intellectual development, to the blind leading the blind. The problem, Bruffee learned by reading Rorty, was with the way we think about knowledge. In the metaphor of the "Mirror of Nature" that has dominated Western philosophy, Rorty holds, knowledge is conceived of as a reflection of the world inspected by the "Inner Eye" of the knowing self. In Rorty's view, however, we should drop the optic metaphors and their claim to establish the foundation of knowledge in the relation between the individual mind and the world. Instead, Rorty says, we can better "understand knowledge when we understand the social justification of belief, and thus have no need to view it as accuracy of representation" (170). Accordingly, for Bruffee, if knowledge is constructed by the discursive practices of communities of people and learning thereby involves joining new communities, then we can stop worrying about the blind leading the blind. Collaborative learning makes sense precisely because it provides the conditions to negotiate the terms of understanding and the changes in social allegiances and affiliations involved in learning.

For Bruffee, the writing classroom has always been a forum for educational change, and *A Short Course*, with its elaborate pedagogy of collaborative learning, is the first composition text to develop the value of peer influence over an entire semester course. Nonetheless, for some writing teachers in the 1970s and 1980s, at the height of the process movement, Bruffee's short forms of writing and his reliance on propositions and reasons looked like nothing so much as the current-traditional rhetoric of Sheridan Baker and the five-paragraph theme. The boxy visual representations of the short forms seemed damning evidence of a formalism that threatened individuality, creativity, and inventiveness. By the early 1980s, however, with the "social turn" in composition, Bruffee's work took on new dimensions as a widely cited instance of "social-constructionist" theory (Faigley) and "social-epistemic" rhetoric (Berlin) and an exemplary pedagogy for writing teachers and theorists seeking alternatives to the personal essay in the public reasoning of academic discourse. Not surprisingly, Bruffee's nonfoundationalist rhetoric was seized on by the social wing of composition as a conceptual counter to expressivist and cognitivist currents in composition.

Still, for all its well-recognized influence on the composition theory of the 1980s, Bruffee's practical rhetoric cannot be neatly folded into the debates of the day, for it grows as much out of Bruffee's understanding of the aims of liberal education. Bruffee's nonfoundationalist rhetoric abandons Enlightenment epistemologies, to be sure, but holds, in crucial aspects, to the liberal tradition of enlightened citizen-rhetors who have freed themselves from what he calls the "allure of the status quo," the unwillingness to question and to change. Inspired by Dewey and the movements of the late 1960s and early 1970s, Bruffee's practical rhetoric is meant to teach the "way out" of docility, obedience, and unexamined dependence on authority through the use of reason in public. This is the "undefined work of freedom" that remains, for Foucault, the enduring legacy of the Enlightenment, as exemplified by Kant's essay "What Is Enlightenment?": the active sense, as Foucault puts it, that the "process that releases us from the status of 'immaturity'" involves "a modification of the prevailing relations linking will, authority, and the use of reason" (305). The achievement of the practical rhetoric in *A Short Course* is how it enacts such a "modification" by linking standard forms of writing—reasoning in public—to the desire to participate in the "undefined work of freedom" where individuals enable each other, collaboratively, to make up their minds through rhetorical interaction.

Far from being a pressure to conform, as process advocates claimed, Bruffee's practical rhetoric is intended rather to precipitate a crisis of authority in order to overcome immaturity and dependence. Nowhere in *A Short Course* is this more clear than in what Bruffee calls the "crunch." "The writing course crunch," Bruffee says, "is the moment when you face the question, 'Am I going to control my words and my ideas, or am I going to go on letting my words and ideas control me?' To choose to control your words and ideas, you may have to undergo a disturbing change. This change involves a change in the way you think about yourself. You may have to become less passive, dependent, and self-deprecating, and instead become more autonomous, self-possessed, and self-controlled" (143). The autonomy, self possession, and self control that Bruffee envisions for students should not be confused with what he calls "rampant individualism" or "isolated, self-directed enterprise." For Bruffee, the point of the "crunch," of successfully navigating the inevitable crisis of authority involved in learning—the freedom that one can achieve—is the "recognition of human interdependence" ("Way Out" 470). This vision, which has animated the four editions of *A Short Course*, as well as Bruffee's larger project of educational change, affirms the development of the individual as a fully socialized human being engaged in reciprocal relations with others. The lasting contribution of *A Short Course* is that it provides teachers and students alike with the conceptual framework and the tools of rhetorical exchange to make this happen.

WORKS CITED

Bruffee, Kenneth A. *A Short Course in Writing: Composition, Collaborative Learning, and Constructive Reading,* 3rd ed. Boston: Little, Brown, 1985.
———. Interview with Harvey Kail. 21 March 2003. On file at the Writing Centers Research Project at the University of Louisville.
———. Instructor's Manual, *A Short Course in Writing,* 4th ed. Boston: HarperCollins, 1993.
———. "The Way Out: A Critical Survey of Innovations in College Teaching." *College English* 33 (1972): 457–70.
Ede, Lisa. *Situating Composition: Composition Studies and the Politics of Location.* Carbondale, Ill.: Southern Illinois University Press, 2004.
Elbow, Peter. *Writing with Power.* New York: Oxford University Press, 1981.
Foucault, Michel. "What is Enlightenment?" *Ethics: Essential Works of Foucault 1954–1984.* Ed. Paul Rabinowitz. London: Penguin, 1994.
Hawkes, Peter. "Open Admissions and Vietnam Protests: Tracing the Politics of Kenneth Bruffee's Collaborative Learning." Thomas R. Watson Conference. Louisville. 11 October 1993.
Rorty, Richard. *Philosophy and the Mirror of Nature.* Princeton, N.J.: Princeton University Press, 1979.

SUGGESTIONS FOR FURTHER READING:
SELECTED BIBLIOGRAPHY OF KENNETH A. BRUFFEE

"The Way Out: A Critical Survey of Innovations in College Teaching." *College English* 33 (1972): 457–70.
"The Brooklyn Plan: Attaining Intellectual Growth through Peer-Group Tutoring." *Liberal Education* 64 (1978): 447–68.
"Liberal Education and the Social Justification of Belief." *Liberal Education* 68 (1982): 95–114.
"Collaborative Learning and the 'Conversation of Mankind.'" *College English* 46 (1984): 635–52.

"Social Construction, Language, and the Authority of Knowledge: A Bibliographic Essay." *College English* 48 (1986): 773–90.

Collaborative Learning: Higher Education, Interdependence, and the Authority of Knowledge. 2nd ed. Baltimore: Johns Hopkins University Press, 1999.

"Binge Drinking as a Substitute for a 'Community of Learning.'" *The Chronicle of Higher Education* 5 Feb. 1999: B8.

"Taking the Common Ground: Beyond Cultural Identity." *Change* 34.1 (2002): 11–17.

"Cultivating the Craft of Interdependence: Collaborative Learning and the College Curriculum." *About Campus* 7.6. (2003): 17–23.

JOHN TRIMBUR
HARVEY KAIL

Preface

The fourth edition of this book appears exactly twenty-one years after the first (1972). It is heartening that during that period many members of the teaching profession have begun raising some of the questions that this book has raised. The basic question, as the preface to the first edition puts it, is how can we "redefine the role of student and teacher." That is, how can we redefine the role of "people who want to learn and people whose calling is to help them learn," in order to meet the needs of education in a modern, diverse democratic culture?

I have tried to refine my answer to that question in each successive edition. In the third edition (1985) I was able to say three things with some confidence. First, redefining the role of student and teacher requires students to gain "authority over their knowledge and...independence in using it." Second, "a necessary intermediate step on the way to effective independence is effective interdependence," which in turn depends on learning what I call the craft of interdependence. And third, writing is "the major element in [a] liberal education framed on these principles."

Since the early seventies, the profession at large has undergone profound changes in philosophy. In one way or another many of us have been trying to shake off foundations and foundationalisms. To that end, teachers have pursued interests of several poststructuralist kinds. Some of these interests have been political and critical. Others have been influenced by one or the other of the two most prominent nonfoundational thinkers of the past quarter-century, Jacques Derrida and Richard Rorty. The work of Rorty and Derrida is complementary; they do the same sort of thing in different philosophical systems. Derrida calls into question the foundations of phenomenology, variously called *presence* or *being*. Rorty calls into question the foundations of epistemology, particularly cognition and other supposed mental processes and entities. In the past decade I have found that this non-foundational thought provides language for talking coherently about collaborative learning, just as I had found earlier that the discipline of social group work provides expertise for practicing collaborative learning effectively.

In this edition of *A Short Course in Writing*, therefore, I hope that I have come still closer to the book's original goal: to help students learn to write better by working collaboratively.

NEW IN THE FOURTH EDITION

Readers familiar with earlier editions will find that the basic format of the book remains the same. There are a few changes, however, and I hope that both long-time users and new users will welcome them. I have expanded and clarified explanations throughout this edition and addressed them more directly to students. I have also included many new collaborative learning tasks and a more thorough and detailed explanation of descriptive outlines. I have shown the relationship between reading and writing by including the explanation of descriptive outlines along with several related issues (such as reading aloud and peer review) in a new section on constructive reading (Part Three). This section is designed to help students write better by becoming better readers of their own writing and better readers of assigned texts.*

The fourth edition emphasizes an aspect of writing that earlier editions implied but did not make explicit: explanatory subordination. The new, long-overdue section on Reasons in Notes for Part Two describes how writers generate reasons from examples. It also explains why they do so: When writers turn examples into reasons, they do not just make their writing more concrete, they also interpret and synthesize their experience.

Finally, long-time users may notice two new conceptual developments. First, at the suggestion of several colleagues I work closely with on collaborative learning, in particular Mara Holt (Ohio University) and John Trimbur (Worcester Polytechnic Institute), I have addressed

---

*Some long-time users will notice that in this edition I have reversed the order of *says* and *does* statements in the descriptive outline format. I did this on the basis of experience and the recommendation of students. I put the *does* section first in earlier editions in order to emphasize it, because most students can paraphrase a passage before they can describe its organization. But more recently I have noticed that many students gain confidence in attacking the more difficult and unfamiliar task of describing organization if they paraphrase the passage first. The change is a minor one. Teachers can ignore it if their experience and preference differ from mine.

the role that diversity and dissent play in collaborative learning. Second, I have responded to the increasing interest among writing teachers in social constructionist thought by adding to the Introduction a description of the relationship between language, writing, teaching, and social construction, and their relevance, taken together, to the larger issue of change in higher education.

I have addressed these two issues as a means of pursuing the larger question raised in the book's first edition, how to meet "the growing need for change in American education, and . . . what kinds of change ought to be made."Those interested in a more general treatment of this issue may consult my *Collaborative Learning: Higher Education, Interdependence, and the Authority of Knowledge,* Johns Hopkins University Press.

DEBTS

Over the years, this *Short Course in Writing* has continued to benefit from conversation, formal and informal, with the group of colleagues I first met, and who first met each other, at the Brooklyn College Institute on Collaborative Learning and Peer Tutoring in the early 1980s. Members of that group also formed the faculty of an institute on collaborative learning at the Bard College Institute in Writing and Thinking in the summer of 1990, and at Pennsylvania State University in the summer of 1992. Almost every page of the book has felt the impact of this long, gratifying conversation.

Improvements in this edition are also due in great part to careful review by several long-time users. Luisa Fels (Califronia State Polytechnic University-Pomona) in particular has patiently and intelligently reviewed and reviewed again all the revisions done for this edition, giving me the benefit of her long and varied experience with the book. Both she and John Trimbur have helped me unpack the issues addressed in Reasons. I am grateful also for astute critical reading done by several other HarperCollins reviewers: Lisa Lebduska, University of Rhode Island; Lisa McClure, Southern Illinois University; S. Michael McCully, Bakeless Center for Humanities, Bloomsberg University of Pennsylvania; George Meese, Foundations, St. Petersburg; and for the thoughtful ministrations of my editor at HarperCollins, Jane Kinney

I must thank several colleagues for particular help: Mary Rowan of the Brooklyn College Modern Language Department for so kindly and astutely guiding me on the style and content of a new example essay on trading peer tutoring in English for peer tutoring in foreign languages; Elmer Sprague of the Brooklyn College Philosophy Department for his early encouraging suggestions about how collaborative learning might be used in other disciplines; Peter Hawkes (East Stroudsburg State University), Mara Holt, and Luisa Fels for offering several new student-written example essays and other material; and Jackie Eubanks of Brooklyn College's Gideonese Library for once again revising the section on bibliographic resources for the "review of reviews" research exercise.

I am grateful also to those whose work on using collaborative learning in a variety of situations and under a variety of conditions has come to my attention, such as Bechtel on reorganizing libraries and reorienting librarians to encourage collaborative learning; Cooper and Selfe on increasing and enhancing collaboration through computer networks; Lunsford and Ede on collaborative writing; Borresen on teaching mathematics; Glidden and Kurfiss on teaching philosophy; Hawkes on teaching literature; Miller and Cheetham on teaching biology; Rau and Heyl on teaching sociology; and Steffens on teaching history. I would also like to call attention to Goodsell, Maher, and Tinto's collaborative learning source book; Johnson, Johnson, and Smith's compendium of practical advise; and Wiener's indispensable article on evaluating teachers who organize their classes for collaborative learning. These and other valuable contributions are listed in the Bibliography at the end of the book.

I continue to be grateful to the following students whose work has appeared in earlier editions and appears again in this edition: Jay Blickstein, Andrew Boyle, Hung Chan, Anita Forman, Eleanor Gaffney, Frederic Garsson, Harold E. Grey, Christopher Guardo, Vladislav Kats, Terry Hayes, Roslyn Kestenbaum, David Lepkofker, Dana Wenger Morris, Carol James Mullings, Gail Olmstead, Sharon Owens, Lucille Tornatore Orlando, Antonio Rambla, Eric Raps, Barbara Pleener Sackrowitz, Thomas Seghini, Anette-Marie Skjerdal, Joyce Bresnick Slevin, Jeffrey Sonenblum, Gregory Suarez, Chris Taylor, Kathleen Wilson, and Joyce Yager.

I am especially grateful also to the following students who have allowed me to add their essays and other written material as examples to this edition: Eugene Benger, Annette Brill, David Bugayer, HyunSoo Cha, Annemarie Edwards, Daniel W. Foley, Karen Dickman Friedman, Christina Hartmann, Elan Katz, Eric Leibowitz, Eric Miller, Theresa Montoya, Kelly Quintero, Joyce S. Theroux, Chris Varney, Michele C. Watts, and Kerri Weiss.

Research tools and procedures have vastly changed during the past fifteen years. As a result, the research section of this book needed thorough revision. Colleagues and friends helped with that revision in many ways. Miriam Deutch and Irwin Weintraub of the Brooklyn College Library and Philip Napoli of the history department contributed source titles. Jane Stafford Salwen graciously agreed to manage the revision, track down sources, and edit the results—a more demanding task than either of us had expected—and carried it out with patience, accuracy, intelligence, and tact. And Mariana Regalado, a superlative research resource librarian, translated premillennial research tools and procedures into fluent Internet search engine terms.

Harvey Kail and John Trimbur put aside many personal and professional demands to write the introduction to this updated edition. As Peer Tutoring Institute members, they themselves spent five weeks writing the essays and enduring the peer critiques. In many respects they understood better than I what we were all up to, collaboratively, so many years ago. I am grateful to them beyond expression. It is a rare and moving privilege to have such generous, understanding friends.

KENNETH A. BRUFFEE
APRIL, 2006

INTRODUCTION

Writing, Collaboration, and Social Construction

The purpose of this short course in writing is to help students learn to read and write better through collaborative learning. Collaborative learning assumes that reading and writing are not solitary, individual activities, but social and collaborative ones. When we read and write we are never alone, although we may seem to be. We are always in the company of communities of other readers and writers whose language and interests we share.

Collaborative learning places this social nature of reading and writing at the center of college and university education. This book, based on collaborative learning principles, turns writing classrooms into collaborative classrooms by making them active, constructive communities of readers and writers and by making students' own writing the most important text in the course.

To make collaboration practical in teaching writing, the book applies one of the well-worn tenets of writing itself: selection and emphasis. It focuses on writing well-planned, well-developed essays, and it organizes a writing course the way good writers organize such an essay: it selects a single important issue in writing for primary emphasis and relates all other writing issues to it. First, it asks students to master two of the most important aspects of essay writing: organization and coherence. To do this, it assigns essays with clear, basic formal requirements. Then it focuses students' attention on other major aspects of writing such as reasoning and style as they relate to organization and coherence.

COLLABORATIVE LEARNING AND CLASSROOM PRACTICE

The book provides two kinds of tasks for students to work on collaboratively. One kind is designed to be done in a single class hour and concentrates on the most important "work points" in writing well-planned, well-developed essays. The book contains a great variety of these tasks—more than fifty of them. They help students work collaboratively on issues such as invention or topic choice, generalization, paragraph development, unity, coherence, and style. All of these class-hour collaborative learning tasks are listed at the end of the book in the **Index of Collaborative Learning Tasks**.

The other kind of collaborative task that the book provides requires more than one class hour to do: sixteen essay exercises. These concentrate on a large, central issue in essay writing: the organization and coherence of whole essays and of paragraphs within essays. Each essay exercise asks students to do three things: (1) write a short essay of a particular kind, a position paper; (2) collaborate by reading their own essay constructively, that is, by writing a descriptive outline of the essay, paraphrasing it, and explaining how it is organized; and (3) collaborate by exchanging essays with another student in the class, writing a descriptive outline of their partner's essay, and then conferring with their partner in a systematic way about each other's outlines and essays.

1. **Each essay exercise asks students to write a position paper, a whole essay that involves all of the most important aspects of writing.** These essay exercises do not involve collaborative writing. Every student writes his or her own essay. **The book makes writing collaborative by helping students talk with each other about writing every step of the way:** finding a topic; deciding on a position to take on that topic; developing material to defend or explain that position; reading, describing, and evaluating what has been written; and rewriting.

2. **Students learn to read constructively in increasingly complex ways as they work their way through the series of essay exercises.** They begin by sketching the overall organization of their own and each others' essays in basic descriptive outlines. Next, in learning to write detailed descriptive outlines they also learn to describe the internal organization of paragraphs. Finally, based on this careful constructive reading, they learn to evaluate each other's essays and offer tactful, acceptable, concrete, practical suggestions for revision.

3. **Student peer conferences also develop progressively, because these conversations about writing are based on constructive reading that students learn by doing descriptive outlines.** At first, students negotiate the differences between the way they have described their

own essay and the way their partner has described it. Later, they talk through the evaluation each one has written of their partner's essay and negotiate the suggestions for improvement that their partner has offered. Finally, in some courses (such as advanced composition courses, discipline-dedicated writing courses, and tutor-training courses) students evaluate each other's peer reviews.

These exercises help students learn to engage in constructive conversation about what interests them and about writing itself, conversation both face-to-face and in writing with members of their own community, their peers. The book assumes that if students converse constructively with peers about their own and other people's writing, they will internalize the language of that conversation. They will then be able to carry on the same conversation with themselves about their own writing internally when they are working alone. Learning to talk constructively about writing enables students to think constructively about it.

HOW THIS BOOK IS ORGANIZED: A SKETCH OF THE CONTENTS

Every essay assignment in the book asks writers to

- take a position on a topic that interests them and explore, explain, or defend their position,
- describe their essays with a descriptive outline,
- read their essays aloud to their peers, who are their fellow writers in the class,
- exchange their essays with other students and write peer reviews of each other's essays,
- and then confer, comparing the way they have read their own and each other's essays and negotiating their differences.

To support these essay assignments, the book divides into two parts the process of taking a position and exploring, explaining, or defending it in a short position paper. **Part One: Remembering, Questioning, Generalizing** helps students learn how to discover a topic, generalize it, and take a position based on that generalization. The exercises and collaborative learning tasks in Part One are about *invention*, or generating topics. They show students how to explore their own experience, both personal and academic: what they have done and what they have read. These exercises help students learn how to discover a topic and formulate a generalization that states a position on that topic. In short, students learn in Part One that they really do have something significant to say.

That experience in itself can be new and rewarding.

Part Two: Writing Position Papers helps students write well-planned, well-developed essays that explore, explain, or defend a position. In particular, they learn the conventions of explanatory subordination: how to arrange what they have to say so that other people can read it easily and understand it. Students learn one simple, reliable form for doing that. The form is certainly not the only one to use in expository writing. But it is a sound, adaptable, frequently used one. Students will find right away that they can use it when they write exams and term papers, and that they can vary it, expand it, and extend it in many ways. They will also find that learning to control this basic essay form by writing short essays will help them develop the control they need in order to write still longer essays and write in more sophisticated expository forms.

Following Part Two, the **Notes for Part Two: Critical Issues in Writing Position Papers** discuss the main work points of any well-planned, well-developed position paper. These work points are

1. the *introduction*, which prepares readers to entertain the position taken in the essay,
2. the *proposition*, or thesis statement, the position that the essay will explore, explain, or defend and to which everything else in the essay will be subordinated,
3. *reasons*, the elements that the essay subordinates in ways that explore, explain, or defend that position, and
4. *transitions*, the signposts of explanatory subordination that create unity and coherence between paragraphs and within them.

There are also notes in this section on

- topics,
- introductions,
- paragraph development,
- style,
- assumptions,
- conclusions,

and on how learning formal organization may affect students' writing and attitudes toward writing in the short run:

- the *Short Course* crunch.

Part Three of the book, **Constructive Reading,** focuses on the relation between reading and writing. It assumes that since writers are always their own first readers, the better they can read, the better they can write. So this part teaches students two related kinds of constructive reading: descriptive reading (reading to figure out how an essay is put together—what it *does*), and substantive reading (reading to figure out what an essay *says*).

Students learn constructive reading by learning to write descriptive outlines. A *descriptive outline* helps students become constructive readers of their own writing, their peers' writing, and professional writing. A descriptive outline helps students gain some distance on their writing and learn to regard writing as a craft. The book's reading can easily be adapted to courses in which students read selections in an essay anthology or reader, even though the book assumes that the most important texts in a writing course are the students' own essays.

The last three parts of the book and accompanying notes introduce students to some of the more sophisticated and complex issues they may encounter in writing position papers. **Part Four: Reaching Out to Members of Other Communities** shows how writers can enter a conversation already under way by showing that they "speak the same language" as those who may read the essay. The **Notes for Part Four: Putting Position Papers to Good Use** deal with three practical adaptations: writing essay exams, writing long papers, and business and professional writing.

Part Five: Research and Research Writing assumes that research is part of this conversation. It shows how writers can enter the conversation by finding out what other contributors to the conversation, other writers, have said. That is, Part Five translates research and research writing from a sterile task into a social process and an intellectual challenge. It teaches research writing as discovering and synthesizing the unfamiliar ideas of other writers and synthesizing those ideas with the writer's own reading and experience. The book's new *Instructor's Manual* also contains a section on research. This section, called **Organizing Independent Study Research,** explains how other research procedures, especially some other basic kinds of writing done in research, such as proposal writing and accounts of work done, also contribute to the conversation among readers and writers.

Finally, **Part Six: A Course for Writing Peer Tutors** presents an aspect of collaborative learning that remains "essential to the book's history and identity," as one teacher who has used the book a long time puts it. Following these instructional sections of the book are two short anthologies. The **Anthology of Student Essays** supplements the example essays offered throughout the book with writing on a variety of topics.

The **Anthology of Professional Essays** exemplifies the form that the book teaches and provides sources of information and models of reasoning.

WHY SHORT COURSE *FORM?*

The issue in essay writing that this book emphasizes is organization, or **explanatory subordination.** The book deals foremost with the decisions that writers have to make over and over again: What should I say first? What should I say second? How do I show how what I'm saying second is related to what I said first? And *then* what should I say?

In answering these questions, inexperienced writers tend to write "from the top down," from beginning to end. They write whatever comes to mind as it comes to mind. This procedure works wonderfully well for prewriting and other idea-generating procedures, but it doesn't produce focused, coherent, readable essays.

To write essays like that, experienced writers do not normally write from the top down. They write "from the inside out." This does not mean that they always write a detailed outline ahead of time of what they are going to say. It means that, once they have done some unstructured idea-exploration and prewriting, they begin the actual essay writing with a tentative structural concept, a mental picture that sketches out roughly where things belong.

This book presents this basic structural concept in the form of hook-and-box diagrams. These diagrams guide students' thinking by mapping out roughly what goes where in an essay. The book's essay exercises, a series of "finger exercises" in essay form, help students learn that one basic essay form and several useful variations. And it asks students, after they have written a draft based on the formal mental picture, to write a descriptive outline of the essay and use it as a tool for revising.

This three-paragraph form was chosen for this set of essay exercises not only because it is a basic, useful, and highly flexible and variable form, but also because it makes collaborative learning easier to organize. A consistent essay structure focuses students' conversation as they learn to read constructively. It helps them know what to look for and where to look for it. By keeping overall essay form relatively steady, the exercises allow students to pay closer attention to transitional elements, reasoning, stylistic details, and so on.

One of the most important issues raised by the three-paragraph essay exercise form is organization. It requires students to explore, explain, or defend the position they have taken in more than one paragraph. That means that they have to learn how to synthesize more than one element or reason to support a single generalization.

Obviously they could do that just as well in ten or a dozen paragraphs, and they could do it just as well by inventing their own distinctive formal structure for each essay they write. But writing long essays and inventing expository forms take lots of time, both for students writing essays and for students and teachers reading them. Time is at a premium in teaching writing. Semesters are short. Trimesters and quarters are even shorter. Since organizational issues remain the same whether students write two paragraphs or ten, or write in a standard form or make one up, this book requires two-paragraph development on grounds of efficiency. Two paragraphs is the smallest unit in which students can learn most of what they need to learn about expository organization and coherence so that they can write well-planned, well-developed essays.

Focusing students' attention in this way, two-paragraph development affects both the quality and substance of students' writing in two ways. It helps students develop their ideas more fully than they have been doing, and it helps students make connections among ideas that they might not otherwise have made. Learning this formal control in writing gives students a kind of leverage for learning. It helps them move more conceptual weight than they would otherwise be able to move.

While students are learning to use this basic essay form effectively, some of them may begin to feel that it limits their creativity and leads them to write thoughtless, unimaginative essays. They are overwhelmed by the temptation to fill in the form mechanically instead of formulating positions based on their own experience that they can become engaged with intellectually and emotionally and therefore write well about.

In that case it may help students to realize that carpenters also use hammers and saws mechanically and unimaginatively sometimes, building dull, repetitive, poorly built houses. And plenty of poets have written mechanical, unimaginative sonnets, another highly restrictive writing form. But poorly built houses and poorly built sonnets satisfy no one— neither those who build and live in the one, nor those who write and read the other. A poorly built house is almost sure to leak. It may even collapse. Mechanical essays and sonnets leak too. Their arguments don't hold water. What is more, in spite of the ever-present temptation to write sonnets mechanically, after some four-hundred years of writing them, poets are still writing fresh, imaginative sonnets and saying new things in them. Some poets have even claimed that writing sonnets helped them say things that they didn't know they wanted to say. Students have been known to say the same thing about writing in *Short Course* form. Formal writing can be one of writing's most powerful and reliable heuristics.

One of the writing problems that this book is designed to help students solve, in fact, is mechanical writing. The book limits form rather than content because it assumes that no one can learn anything by trying to learn everything at once and that one of the first things to try to understand about any object is how it is put together.

So the book gives students some frank, constructive, above-board direction in how to organize their ideas. It teaches them to walk as writers before they run, without compromising their knowledge and intelligence. The book assumes that, given the opportunity to explore their experience in liberating ways ahead of time, formal limitation in essay writing—a simple, firm, clearly defined scaffolding—can help college students master their thinking as thoroughly as free, experimental, trial-and-error exploration of verbal forms can, and a lot more quickly and easily.

WHAT SOCIAL CONSTRUCTION MEANS IN THIS BOOK

All of the book's collaborative learning exercises make the social constructionist assumption that sense, meaning, perhaps even minds and selves are things we construct through a social process of conversation, negotiation, and collaboration. In particular, the book's collaborative exercises make this assumption about reading and writing, which it regards as socially constructive activities.

READING AND WRITING AS CONVERSATION

According to this social constructionist way of thinking, every time we read and write we join a conversation already in progress. One reason that reading and writing are socially constructive activities is that both involve language, and language itself is a social construct. In conversation with each other, human beings make and remake, learn and relearn language all the time.

Another reason reading and writing are socially constructive activities is that whenever we have something to write or say, we are responding to what other people have written and said. Other people write, and sooner or later we read what they have written and write back. Then, with any luck at all, someone reads what we have written and writes back to us. Reading and writing are slow, displaced versions of conversation. When one of us decides to sit down and put our position on some topic or other into writing, the conversation slows to a creep while we try to deepen our thinking by gathering and arranging the arguments and ferreting out the nuances. (See Reasons, p. 96.)

Then we go back to that faster, more direct version of conversation, talking, because we have more to talk about now: what we have been reading and what we have written.

POSITION PAPERS AND CONSTRUCTIVE CONVERSATION

The essay exercises in this book are called *position papers* because writing a position paper is one way to join a conversation already in progress or begin a new one. In a position paper we try to get other people to join us in thinking about the position we have taken on an issue or "sharable concern." We want to explore our own thinking on that issue and convince other people that it is worth their while to consider it. What we want from the people who read a position paper we have written is not agreement. What we want is more conversation.

That is, a position paper assumes that there is almost certainly another point of view than ours on the issue. Another writer may well take another position. All of the essay exercises in this book acknowledge different points of view. Some of them do so only implicitly (exercises 5 and 6). Others acknowledge different points of view explicitly by asking students to take issue with one such alternative (exercises 7 and 8). And one exercise acknowledges different points of view by asking students to concede that the topic can be approached in another way that may be just as reasonable and legitimate as the position they are taking (exercise 9).

All of these essay exercises, furthermore, ask students to formulate a position and explore, explain, or defend it in a conventional, widely accepted essay form. There are several reasons for making this request, but one of the most important from a social constructionist point of view is that an agreement on form is an agreement on expectations. People engaged in conversation certainly don't have to agree on the issues they are discussing, but they do have to agree what their expectations are and what they have to do in order to fulfill those expectations. They have to agree, as Richard Rorty puts it, on what counts as an acceptable question and what counts as a reasonable answer. When writers control what they say with formal conventions, they adapt their (socially constructed) inner thoughts and feelings to the (socially constructed) expectations of the community of people they are addressing. (See Paragraph Development, p. 111, and Unity and Coherence, p. 116.)

Conversation in which people succeed in understanding and meeting each other's expectations is likely to be a **constructive conversation.** One purpose of the essay exercises in this book is to help students learn to engage in constructive conversation with each other about their own interests and, especially, about writing. The book assumes that if students can converse constructively about the position papers they write, they can internalize that conversation. That is, they can carry on the same sort of conversation with themselves, thinking constructively about their writing when they are working alone. (See Constructive Reading, p. 147.)

The book engages students in constructive conversation about writing in several ways. For example, *descriptive outlines* set up a workshop relationship among students. Reading descriptive outlines of essays that writers have written, along with the essays themselves, lets readers look over writers' shoulders as they work. Then readers and writers can talk about a position paper as something quite literally "under construction."

Similarly, regular *peer review* of student essays fosters constructive conversation by helping students learn the kind of talk that goes on all the time among experienced writers, between writers and constructive readers, and among all kinds of well-trained readers.

DISCOURSE COMMUNITIES

Most constructive conversations necessarily involve recognizing and negotiating differences among discourse communities. *Discourse communities* are groups of like-minded people who "speak the same language." Members of a discourse community talk with each other about the same sorts of things in the same sorts of ways, ways that differ from the ways that the members of other discourse communities talk with each other. Because people socially construct values and expectations in the terms that constitute the discourse community that they belong to, members of different discourse communities maintain different values and expectations.

The language used by members of a discourse community constitutes that community in much the same way that, for example, the language of the U.S. Constitution constitutes the large and otherwise enormously diverse and complex community we call the United States. The different ways we talk with other people, and therefore the different ways we think, constitute all of the layered, overlapping, and nested discourse communities that each of us belongs to. Negotiating differences among these diverse communities is unavoidable, not only negotiation between individuals in conversation with one another, but also negotiation at the boundaries between the community languages that we have internalized to think with.

We are of course more strongly committed to membership in some of the communities we belong to than others. Our strongest commitments are the longest standing, most familiar ones, the ones we may be least self-consciously aware of: the particular familial, ethnic, religious, and cultural communities that we were brought up in. The constituting language of those communities is, so to speak, our cultural mother tongue. Other members of those communities are the people we are most likely to turn to first when we need help and support and are most likely to understand, agree with, and trust.

But most of the people we meet outside our home, our neighborhood, our hometown, our church, temple or mosque, are not members of those familiar discourse communities. They belong to communities that are quite different from our own, and therefore they maintain values and expectations that are quite different from our own. When students first arrive at college, they are likely, perhaps for the first time, to meet people who belong to discourse communities that they do not belong to, and who therefore talk about different things in different ways and maintain different expectations and values.

One of the implications of social constructionist thought for college and university education is that it addresses these inevitable differences by revealing the role that interdependence plays in learning.

NEGOTIATING COMMUNITY BOUNDARIES

Of course, new college and university students are likely to find plenty of fellow students who come from the same communities that they themselves come from, or strikingly similar ones. They can talk to these students easily and be understood right away. So long as they all stick together, difference as an issue is not likely to arise among them. In fact, they are likely to suppress differences of any kind that do threaten to arise. But new college and university students will also encounter other students who seem strange, whom they don't understand, and with whom they can't seem to carry on a sensible conversation. These differences tend to silence students with regard to each other. As a result, everyone loses.

For conversation to occur between members of different discourse communities, everyone involved has to learn how to **negotiate differences** at the boundaries of the communities they belong to. This means that for many college and university students today, the most important educational issue they face is finding what they have in common with the other students they meet, and how to use those common elements to bridge the community boundaries that separate them.

Negotiating community boundaries is an important educational issue because members of different discourse communities think in different—sometimes vastly different—ways, and the ways we think are a result of the ways we converse with each other. Of course, no one thinks only what other people write or say, and all of us think some things that we don't write or say to anyone. But we all think, talk, and write in ways that we have learned at some time in our lives in conversation—written, spoken, or in gesture—with other people. We know no other way. And when we talk to each other, write to each other, and read what each other has written, we return the internalized conversation we call thought to its native element, human social interaction carried on in the socially constructed conventions of language.

The educational issue of negotiating boundaries among the discourse communities that students bring with them onto a college or university campus, then, is how to negotiate socially constructed linguistic conventions—the terms that people use, in Clifford Geertz's phrase, to represent themselves to themselves and to one another—at the boundaries between the communities they constitute, so as to help students begin to understand how each other thinks. Research (by Kurt Lewin, among others) suggests that these negotiations cannot usually occur without establishing temporary transition, or support, groups in which students develop a new conversational history dedicated in part to boundary negotiation and thus to the kind of change that they are undergoing.

Understanding the process of **boundary negotiation** is important for college students to learn because most students begin college as discrete entities in an aggregate crowd. They make very little sense to each other because they are members of different language communities. Knowing something about boundary negotiation can help them become a cohesive new community of people who speak the same language. By negotiating, translating, and making conversational adjustments at the boundaries of the communities they normally belong to, they change the way they use words. As their language changes, their relationships change. They develop a conversational history in terms of a new composite language common to their new conversational group.

Several parts of this book help students in various ways to understand and learn boundary negotiation. Part One helps students discover the differences between their own interests, ideas, and background and other people's interests, ideas, and backgrounds—that is, differences between their own language and other people's—that they were never aware of before.

Part Four suggests some of the ways that the boundaries of discourse communities may be negotiated by learning to speak other people's language. It shows students how to package their position papers so as to induce readers to put aside their normal way of understanding something and consider the writer's way of understanding it. To do that, students have to inform themselves about their readers' normal, everyday ways of thinking about things, what their readers are likely to know, are likely to be interested in, and are likely to be feeling, so that they can find points where the position they are taking may be related to their readers' experience, interests, or knowledge.

Part Five of the book, on research, shows students how to become more actively and productively engaged in boundary negotiation. In research, students get the pleasure and satisfaction of contributing to conversations going on in disciplinary communities they haven't been members of before by learning how the members of those communities talk with each other and behave.

The languages that disciplinary communities require students to learn (for example, sociology, philosophy, or chemistry) are new to most students. Because it is used in many, if not all, disciplinary communities, one of the most important of these new languages is the one that people use to converse constructively about reading and writing. Learning how to talk constructively with each other about reading and writing changes the relationships among students. They learn to respect each other's evaluative judgment and assume responsibility for each other's improvement as writers. That is, they begin to turn to each other for help and support, and they begin to understand, agree with, and trust the members of this entirely new community, this transition, or support, community of readers and writers made up of their student peers. (See Accepting Authority in Evaluative Peer Review, p. 176.)

Learning to trust each other's judgment in this way may come hard at first for some students. They find it hard to believe in their own authority to evaluate another student's work and in another student's authority to evaluate theirs. But that redistribution of authority, like formal control in writing, is a social construct too. People authorize themselves and authorize each other through conversation, negotiation, and collaboration. This process lies as close as anything I know to the core of a liberal education.

PART ONE

Remembering, Questioning, Generalizing

he essay exercises in this book ask you to write essays, but they do not tell you what to write those essays about. They give you a form, but not a topic. For each essay exercise you have to come up with something to write about on your own.

That may be a disturbing prospect. It may even seem unfair. You may wonder "What have I got to write about?" and you may find yourself answering "Nothing."

If so, then this book chooses not to believe you. It believes that you do have something to write about. In fact, it believes that you have a lot to write about and have a lot to say. The purpose of Part One is to prove it to you. Part One is about *invention*. That means inventing topics to write about and inventing what to say about them. If you already know what you want to write about, you can skip exercises 1 and 2 and begin with exercises 3 and 4. If you already know what you want to write about *and* what you want to say about it, you can skip Part One entirely and begin with exercise 5 in Part Two.

Exercises 1, 2, and 3 ask you to write about yourself in different ways: to reminisce about old times, tell family stories, describe changes in yourself and your life, and recall things you have learned in school and elsewhere. Exercise 4 explains how to discover what may be worth writing about from the material you produce in exercises 1, 2, and 3.

What you write in these invention exercises is not an essay. It is raw material. It is like oil when it first comes out of the ground—an unclear, undifferentiated mass that is potentially very valuable, however unpromising it may look. To make that raw material valuable, you have to analyze it.

When you do that, you wind up with general observations, judgments, or statements of opinion based on your raw material. These generalizations can become the main point, or proposition, what some people call the thesis statement, of any essay in Parts Two to Five (exercises 5 through 11).

There are many other kinds of invention exercises you could do besides the ones suggested in this section. But these alone, if you worked through them carefully, could give you enough interesting topics to keep you busy writing essays for years.

The best way to use these invention exercises is to combine them with essay exercises 5 through 9. When you set out to do exercise 5, for example, begin by using exercise 1, 2, or 3 to generate raw material and then use exercise 4 to discover some of the issues implicit in that material. When you do that, your essay is sure to be about a topic that interests you, because it grows out of your own experience. Some of that experience may be experience reading. The topic you settle on in any case will probably be one that you know something about, will like writing about, and can explore, explain, or defend in your essay with a good deal of feeling.

In short, the invention exercises in this section can help you learn to explore your ideas through writing. They may even help you discover ideas you never knew you had. A few of these ideas may be entirely your own, because no one has experienced exactly what you have experienced. These ideas will probably be the hardest to get across to people. Other ideas will be more familiar to people who share some of your experiences and background. These ideas will therefore be easier to explore, explain, and defend in writing.

Discovering issues in this way is the first thing to do in learning to write. If you start by discovering issues based on your own experience, including your experience reading, your writing will help you understand yourself better. It will also make your readers more willing to consider what you have to say and maybe even agree with you. These are two of the most important uses of writing.

▷ EXERCISE 1   MINING THE PAST

You can do this exercise in one or more of the following three ways:

REMINISCENCE

Write a true story about something that happened to you once that deeply moved you, upset you, or made you angry.

Write in language that fits the experience. Tell the story in the most forceful way you can, explaining how you felt about what happened.

Give plenty of details, but write only as much as you need to in order to tell the story as you feel it must be told. Don't pad it. And for this exercise, don't worry about spelling, punctuation, usage, or grammar. Don't worry about being correct or "proper" in any way.

Just begin at the beginning and tell the whole story: what happened, in the order that it happened, and how you felt about it. Finally, when you have completed the reminiscence to your satisfaction, skip to exercise 4 to discover issues based on your reminiscence and write a generalization you can use in writing an essay.

☐ EXAMPLE REMINISCENCE ─────────────────────────

Arnie and the FBI

A few years ago while we were sitting at the dinner table one night an awful thing happened. The whole family was there, my mother and father and I, and my three sisters, my younger brother, and also my older brother Arnie. Arnie was there because he had run away from the Army. He was AWOL—absent without leave.

Arnie joined the Army on his eighteenth birthday, just as soon as he could. They sent him to basic training right away and we didn't see him for a couple of months. We didn't hear much from him, either. He called once or twice, but he didn't say much. He sent a couple of postcards. Everything seemed okay.

But one day he turned up home. He said they'd given him leave for a few weeks. He seemed glad to be home and just settled down again.

Then one day he told me that he didn't really have a leave. He was AWOL. I didn't know what to say. I told my mother and father, and they didn't say much either. After a while, when nothing else happened, we just sort of forgot about it. We were happy Arnie was home. He's a great guy, always kidding around. But we were scared for him really. I could tell he was scared too, although he tried not to show it. He even got a job in a dry cleaners.

Then at supper that night, with all of us there around the dinner table, we heard a knock on the door. Not a loud knock. It sounded like the lady downstairs when she wants to borrow something. When my sister opened the door, two men in brown suits pushed her into the room saying "FBI." They showed their badges and walked right over to the table.

They looked at Arnie and said, "Your name Arnold Jones?" He said, "We're just having supper, can't you wait?" One of the men interrupted him and said, "Come along." He took Arnie by the elbow, almost picked him out of his chair, and pushed him ahead of the two of them out the door. My father shouted, "Hey, wait a minute," and got up, but they were out before we knew it. There was nothing else we could do.

We got a letter from Arnie a few days later saying that they put him in jail. He said he wished he was home. When he gets out of jail, he said, they're going to send him overseas. He didn't know where. □

A FAMILY STORY

Tell a family story. A *family story* is one that a member of your family tells when everyone gets together for holiday dinners, parties, picnics, or other celebrations. It is the story Aunt Joan tells about how Uncle Fred stripped the gears on the old Ford during their honeymoon. The story Grandma tells about meeting Grandpa on their first day in America. Your sister's story about how Gavin sat on the Thanksgiving turkey. Uncle Fred's story about the barn burning down.

Tell your family story with as much detail as you can remember. But keep in mind that *your* audience is not your family. It is a class full of strangers. You may have to explain to them as you go along why things happened as they did, the conditions people were living in or working under when the event occurred, the personal peculiarities of the people involved, and some of your family or ethnic traditions that are related to the story.

Begin by describing the occasion when the story is usually told, and who usually tells it. Tell the whole story as people tell it in your family. Then explain how you feel about it.

When you have finished telling your family story skip to exercise 4 to discover issues based on your family story and formulate a generalization you can use in writing an essay.

☐ EXAMPLE FAMILY STORY ───────────────────────────

I Like Ike

My father only gets to see his favorite cousin, Jack, once a year on the Fourth of July. That's when our whole family gets together— all my aunts and uncles and my cousins and my mother's cousins and my father's cousins—everybody turns up at somebody's house, usually ours, and we have a barbecue.

My father looks forward a lot to seeing Jack. One reason he likes him is that they are exactly the same age. They both voted for the first time when President Eisenhower first ran for president. They liked Ike and they both voted for him. Back in those days, Dad says, some people thought Eisenhower was a great president. But some others thought he wasn't so good and not even very smart.

So whenever my father and Jack get together they tell old Eisenhower jokes. Dad's favorite Eisenhower joke starts, "Did you know that President Eisenhower was a literary man?" Whenever he starts with that my mother says, "Oh, no, not again," and laughs. Then she gets up and goes into the kitchen. But of course my father keeps on telling the story, because Jack always laughs at it. He's the only one who ever does laugh at it besides my Dad.

The story goes this way. "Did you know that Eisenhower was a literary man? Yes, he was. It's a fact. He read all the time. In fact, he read every night when he went to bed until his lips got tired."

Frankly, I think it's a dumb story, but you ought to hear Dad and Jack laugh when my father tells it. Sometimes I go out to the kitchen to get away from them, and then I catch my mother laughing too. But I never think she's laughing at the story. I think she's laughing at my father and Jack. She thinks *they're* funny. I think they're funny too, so I laugh with her.

But, you know, I don't think either of us are making fun of Dad and Jack. I think when we laugh at them telling their old stories we feel very fond of them. In fact, I don't think the Fourth of July would be quite the same, or quite as nice, if they didn't tell their old stories and my mother didn't leave the table and go out in the kitchen and laugh. I'd miss it a lot if that didn't happen. □

ACCOUNTING FOR CHANGE

Write a story about some aspect of your life that has changed quite a bit during the past year. Describe yourself as you were. Describe yourself as you see yourself now. Then try to describe how you think the change came about.

The sort of change in your life that you are likely to find most valuable to write about might include changes in things that interest you, changes in things you do, changes in things you like or don't like, changes in the way you feel about who you are, changes in your relationships with people, or changes in your ideas about what you want to do with your life.

☐ EXAMPLE ACCOUNTING FOR CHANGE ──────────

How I Got to College

Most of my school years were spent during an era when society, including my family, felt a college education was necessary for a prosperous future. The trend was for everyone, men and women, to attend college. But my father maintained society's older values regarding women. He believed that a woman's place was in the home, and since a woman would ultimately become a housewife despite a college education, it was not necessary for her to obtain one. A man had to become a breadwinner, so my father believed an education was integral to a man's future. The quality of that future depended on a college degree.

I internalized these values as my own, and I directed my life toward marriage and that ultimate role of housewife. During my junior year in high school I took courses geared for future homemakers. They included Home Economics and Clothing and Foods. In my senior year I took Advanced Clothing and Foods.

All this time, while I was preparing to become a housewife, my three brothers got college degrees. Then my brothers married teachers. All these degrees constantly reminded me that I lacked one of my own. As a result, I always felt inadequate—stupid, really—when I was surrounded by all the professionals in my family. When I hung my husband's sheepskins on the wall, I realized that I was the only member of the entire family who didn't have a degree, the only one who "didn't know anything."

Finally, thirteen years after I graduated from high school, I applied for admission to college. My acceptance had an immediately positive effect on my self-confidence. And attending college has continued this positive effect. ☐

(See "Going Back to School," by Kathleen Wilson, p. 323.)

COLLABORATIVE LEARNING

Work in a group of five to seven people. Have one person record the views expressed in the group and the consensus that the group arrives at collaboratively. Try to arrive at answers most people in the group can live with. Make sure the recorder makes note of any differences of opinion. Finally, review the recorder's notes. They should accurately state what the group has decided, and include differences of opinion and dissent. When you have finished the task, the recorder will report the results of the group's discussion to the rest of the class.

Task 1 Personal Experience Story: Practice Analysis

Have one person in the group (not the recorder) read aloud to the others in the group "How I Got to College" (p. 20). Then, working together, answer the following questions:

1. **What did the story mean to you** when you heard it for the first time? Explain in a sentence or two.

2. Now have someone read the story aloud again. Then, working collaboratively,
   a. **List the characters** in the story and describe the relationships among them. What does each relationship look like from the point of view of each character?
   b. **List the incidents** in the story. What does each incident look like from the point of view of each character?
   c. **List the settings** (the places) in which the incidents occur, and explain their significance to the story.
   d. **List the key words** (the most important words, or repeated words) used in the story. What do they tell us about the most important characters in the story, about what happens, and about how the events affect people's attitudes or feelings?

3. **Does the story seem complete?** Does the narrator seem to be leaving anything out that you want to know more about?

4. Focus on the person who is telling the story—the narrator.
   a. **How does the narrator seem to feel about the experience now?** How can you tell? How does the narrator's attitude differ from the way he or she seems to have felt about the experience when it occurred? How can you tell?
   b. If there is a difference between the narrator's present and past feelings about the experience, what does it mean to you personally that people's feelings about something that happens to them can change?

5. Reread what you wrote in answer to question 1 (what the story meant to you when you first heard it or read it). **What does the story mean to you now, after reading it more carefully and answering these questions?** What do you see in the story now that you didn't see before?

6. Review your answers to questions 1 through 5. Based on these answers **decide what you think the narrator feels is the most important aspect of the story.**

Task 2   *Personal Experience Story: Exchange and Analysis*

Exchange one of the stories you wrote for exercise 1 with another member of the class. Answer the preceding questions 1 through 6 about your partner's story.

When you get to question 6, this analysis of a real experience may produce some results that go quite a bit beyond those of the practice analysis. You may discover that your partner's understanding of your story differs from your own understanding of it, and that your understanding of your partner's story differs from his or hers. What happens to you may not mean the same thing to other people or be as important to them as it is to you. The reason for these differences is that people have different experiences and belong to different ethnic and cultural discourse communities—those groups of people we agree with and trust. As a result, they have different values and expectations.

These differences can mean that you may find out something new about your story and what it's about. That is, you may learn something new about yourself.

The differences between the way you understand your story and the way other people understand it can also mean, however, that in order to share with other people what your personal experiences mean to you, you have to find ways of talking about those experiences and explaining them that other people will understand.

When you and your partner tell each other what you see in each other's personal experience stories, you will find some aspects of your experience that are sharable and some that are not. You will begin to discover that you have had some experiences in common or that there are aspects of your partner's experience that are similar or related to your own.

On the basis of these common, similar, or related aspects of your experience, you will eventually be able to formulate the sort of generalization explained in exercise 4, a generalization that you can turn into the proposition of an essay. You will find points along the boundaries of the communities that the two of you belong to where it is possible to translate from the language your partner speaks to the one you speak, and vice versa. (For the dangers inherent in generalization, see Assumptions, p. 132.)

▷ EXERCISE 2   FREE WRITING (BRAINSTORMING)

This is an exercise in letting your mind run wild. It can be useful any time you want to find out what you're thinking. Sit down with plenty of paper and several well-sharpened pencils or a pen you can be sure won't run out of ink. Then let your mind go.

Begin by remembering what happened earlier today or during the past week—what you read, what you did, where you went, what other people said and what you said yourself. As you recollect, begin making lists. Don't try to make coherent sentences or paragraphs. Don't try to make sense. Write words and phrases, just as they come to you. Let your mind go as fast as it wants, where it wants. Keep writing things down in lists; keep up with your mind as best you can.

Write *everything* down, even if it seems silly or offensive or repetitious. Just scribble away.

Try doing this several times, perhaps at different times of day and in different places, until you get the knack of it and find the conditions that suit you best for doing this kind of work. If you draw a blank sometimes, don't force yourself. Relax. Come back to it later and try again.

When you have collected several pages of material, read them over all at once. Try to make some sense out of what you have written. Compare lists. Group words and phrases that appear in them. See where your mind went when you were not consciously controlling it. See what the material reveals about what your interests and ideas are. You may find some interests and ideas that you did not know you had.

Finally, write a short paragraph saying how your free writing turned out and the topics that came up in it. You might also say what you learned, if anything, about yourself.

COLLABORATIVE LEARNING

Brainstorming or free writing is an unfamiliar activity to many people. It may help to introduce yourself to free writing collaboratively. A group of writers can learn a lot about it in a single pleasant, if chaotic, hour.

Task   Collaborative Brainstorming

Have someone start the hour off by writing a single word on the blackboard or at the head of a sheet of paper. It should be a concrete word (satellite, dog, rifle, street) or an abstraction with powerful associations (money, fear).

From then on the rule is that everybody tosses in words and phrases that they associate with the original word or with any word that has been added to it by association. Try to keep your contributions concrete, but if you have to choose between abstractions and stopping the flow of association, by all means include the abstractions. The recorder—the person writing down words and phrases—may need a helper as people begin to catch on and the pace picks up. Everything should be written down as quickly as possible and totally at random.

After ten minutes or so, stop. Working together, classify into sets the words and phrases that you have collected. Many groupings will be possible and some will overlap. You can rearrange and add to the material as time permits.

Use the last fifteen minutes or so of the hour to begin making connections and drawing relationships among the sets of words. These connections and relationships can lead to ideas that you haven't thought of before, some of which may be a long way from the word you started off with.

The material you produce in this group is not likely to be very coherent. The incoherence results from the fact that group members have had different experiences, many belong to different communities, and everyone knows different things and talks about things differently. Writers have to develop their ideas in order to get through to people who differ from themselves.

▷ EXERCISE 3   DRAWING ON WHAT YOU HAVE LEARNED

One excellent source of topics for essays in a writing course is what you have learned in other courses, what you have learned in educational organizations that you belong to (such as scouting, 4-H, museum programs, science clubs, and so on), what you have learned at work, and what you have been reading. Some of the best sources of topics are introductory courses in subjects such as psychology, history, chemistry, sociology, anthropology, biology, music, mathematics, and art. Interesting material for essays can also be found in specialized courses such as forestry, engineering, business management, public administration, home economics, philosophy, nursing, and computer science.

Another excellent source of topics is an essay assigned to you to read in your writing course or some other course. Here the range of possible topics is if anything even greater than what you have learned in other courses. You can read any of the professionally written essays included in this book, you can read one in any anthology of essays, or you can read some student-written example essays in the Anthology of Student Essays, p. 319.

This invention exercise may be so fruitful and instructive that you can return to it more than once, if you like, drawing on several courses you have taken and analyzing several essays to develop topics for writing position papers.

When you are just starting out generating ideas and material, don't worry about whether someone else will understand you. Just explain what you know to yourself, in a way that satisfies you, in any order and in whatever language that comes most easily to you. Eventually, when you write an essay about something you have learned from another course or from what you have read, you will have to translate that specialized language into clearer, more familiar language, so that people who may not know what you know (other students and your writing teacher perhaps) can understand you.

RECALLING SOMETHING YOU HAVE LEARNED

Pick a course that you have taken or some other learning experience you have had. Write down everything you can remember learning. At this stage you can also say why you think it was a good thing to learn and why other people should learn it. But stress *what* you learned about: what caused the American Revolution, seven ways to stop erosion, how to repair a carburetor, the functions of DNA, why Hamlet puts off revenging his father's murder.

Second, read through this preliminary material and separate your statements about the subject matter itself from your remarks about the value of learning it. Put aside for now what you said about how valuable it was to learn the subject and why other people should learn it. You can use that later to introduce the essay you write that explains what you learned.

You have now isolated the part of your preliminary material that has to do with the subject itself. Exercise 4 will show you some ways to develop issues based on this method of exploring what you have learned and to formulate generalizations you can use to write an essay.

☐ EXAMPLE RECALLING SOMETHING YOU HAVE LEARNED

What I Learned in Film 1

Last semester I took Film 1: Basic Filmmaking. It was a terrific course. Everyone should take it because everyone likes to take pictures of their family and show them to their friends. Film 1 shows you how to do that on film, not just videotape. The advantage of film is that you can edit what you've taken and make it into a movie. The result of editing is that you get a real story, not just a string of miscellaneous shots of Junior jumping on the dog and Lucy falling over in the wading pool.

Film 1 taught me how to be a real amateur filmmaker. I learned how to write a treatment and sketch a storyboard. I learned how to plan out a movie with these two devices too, so that I wouldn't waste time and film. I learned the difference between long shots and close-ups and pans, and I actually had a chance to make a short movie using one of the school's super-8 cameras, use my own treatment and storyboard, and take different kinds of shots.

I guess it was learning how to plan making a movie with a storyboard and shooting script that was the most exciting part of the course for me. The teacher told us that, although we could use one of the school's cameras, we had to buy our own film. When she told us that, and told us how much film *cost*, she also said that since we were spending our money, we should try to figure out how to make our movie using the least amount of film.

Then everybody got scared. Nobody in the class knew how to plan like that. So then she explained how movies are made efficiently by shooting several scenes at one time that take place in the same location, whether or not they will occur in sequence in the movie. To do that they write a shooting script. Then they edit the film, splicing the scenes in where they belong.

So we all wrote shooting scripts, and I can tell you that writing mine saved me lots of money on film. And it also saved me lots of time when I shot the movie. □

Based on this free-written recollection of what he had learned in his film course, this student wrote the following essay:

□ EXAMPLE ESSAY ———————————————————————

The Role of Planning in Making Films

Greg Suarez

Making home movies on TV camcorders showing family members playing ball, celebrating birthdays, or having picnics is a popular hobby in the United States. All anyone has to do is aim the camera at what is happening and push the button. The story tells itself. But a small number of these amateurs shoot movies that tell a more complex story or that convey information in a more complex way. To do this, many of them still work with film. They use super-8 movie cameras and cut and splice their footage on inexpensive home-editing machines. To these die-hard filmmakers, filmmaking is more than just a hobby. It is an art medium and a medium of communication. It is not just something they enjoy doing. It is something they enjoy doing well. And it is a complicated process that requires several steps in order to produce the kind of film they aim for. The most important of these steps is planning.

There are two reasons why planning is essential to making good super-8 films. The first reason is that planning ensures that each shot (each segment of film recorded in one continuous run of the camera) and each sequence of shots will have the desired effect on viewers. Drawing up a storyboard ensures this. A storyboard consists of a rough sketch for each shot. Each sketch indicates the camera angle of the shot (high, low, eye level), camera distance (close-up, medium, long shot), and camera motion (pan, tracking, stationary). Each sketch also estimates how long each shot will last. The result—the storyboard—is an ordered collection of filming instructions that represents consecutive shots of the film as they will appear to the viewer.

The second reason planning is essential to making good films is that it ensures that the actual filming of the movie will be as uncomplicated and efficient as possible. Filming is governed by a shooting script. To write a shooting script, the filmmaker has to figure out the order in which to film the shots. A movie is seldom filmed in the order we see it in the final version. With most films it is not convenient to film the shots in the order they run in the story. Consider, for example, a film about a runner that begins at the beginning of the race, cuts to a scene with his family at home before the race, and ends with the finish of the race. It would be expensive and inefficient to shoot the film in this order. The sensible way to shoot the film would be to shoot the beginning and the end of the race all at once, film the scene at home, and then cut the race scene in two and splice the home scene between the two halves. A shooting script would tell the director and camera to do just that. □

DETAILED DESCRIPTIVE OUTLINE

PROPOSITION	Planning is essential to making a good film.
PLAN	Develop two reasons supporting the proposition.
PARAGRAPH 1	*says:* Many Americans make home movies on camcorders, but a few make more serious, complex films using super-8 film and equipment.
	does: Introduces the proposition by identifying an activity and the group of people who engage in it. Distinguishes between two subcategories in this

group according to their attitude toward the activity and the way they do it.

PARAGRAPH 2   *says:* Planning ensures the effect of the film on viewers. Writing a storyboard is the main technique in planning this effect.

does: Supports the proposition by subdividing it into two techniques. Identifies one technique. Describes the device used in the technique and lists four ways that device is used. States the value of the end result.

PARAGRAPH 3   *says:* Planning also ensures that shooting the film will be done efficiently. Writing a shooting script is the main technique in gaining efficiency.

does: Supports the proposition by identifying a second technique. Describes the device used in the technique. Explains how the device is used with an example that contrasts two ways of accomplishing a goal and shows how one way is more effective than the other.

ANALYZING SOMETHING YOU HAVE READ

First Step

In developing a topic from something you have read you have to become more familiar with it than you can be when you have read it only once. To become more familiar with something you have read, reread it and then analyze it by writing a basic descriptive outline of it.

First, number the paragraphs of the assigned essay lightly in pencil.

Then, working on your own, write a descriptive outline of the essay. If the essay is longer than five or six pages, treat clusters of related paragraphs as units. Your descriptive outline will explain how each cluster of paragraphs fits into the essay as a whole.

In writing your descriptive outline, use the following guide:

1. Write out the sentence in the essay that you think states the essay's position or main point most succinctly, or write the main point of the essay in your own words.

If you are not sure at first what the essay's main point is, write down two or three possibilities and continue with the descriptive outline. When you have finished writing your descriptive outline, decide which of your possible propositions now seems correct.

2. Describe the essay's introduction. Where does the introductory part of the essay end? Why do you think it ends there? How many paragraphs are in it?

Write the sentence in the introduction that you think states the introduction's main point most succinctly, or write what you think the introduction's main point is in your own words. Consider that sentence as being what the introduction *says*. (There is more about what an essay *says* on p. 154.)

3. Describe the essay's ending. Where does the essay begin to end? Why do you think the ending begins there? How many paragraphs are in the ending?

Write out the sentence in the ending that you think states the ending's main point most succinctly, or write what you think the ending's main point is in your own words. Think of that sentence as expressing what the ending *says*.

4. Describe the middle of the essay—how the essay explores, explains, or defends its position or main point. Begin by mapping the middle of the essay. First, subdivide it into parts, or chunks that seem to hang together. Then write out the sentence in each subdivision that states its main point most succinctly, or in your own words write what you think the main point of each subdivision is. Consider that sentence as being what you think each subdivision of the essay *says*.

5. Now describe the essay's overall plan. The essay's overall plan is what the essay *does* as a whole to explore, explain, or defend its position or main point. (There is more about what an essay *does* on p. 158.)

6. Based on this rereading and analysis of the essay, revise your initial statement of the essay's proposition.

COLLABORATIVE LEARNING

In groups of three, confer with other students who have written a descriptive outline of the same essay. Compare the descriptive outlines each of you have written, marking where they differ. Discuss why each of you described the essay in different ways. Then write a single descriptive outline that you can agree on and that represents your combined efforts.

Second Step

Having familiarized yourself with the essay in this way, to develop a topic from something you have read, treat what you have read as something you have learned.

Put the essay and your descriptive outline of it away. On another sheet, **list everything you can remember learning for the first time in reading that essay.** Add to the list everything in the essay that reminded you of something you already knew.

This is the material that you will use in exercise 4 to develop issues based on reading the essay and to formulate a generalization that you can use in writing an essay. That essay will be a position paper based on the essay you read. In it you can oppose or take issue with the essay. You can agree with or support the essay. Or you can use the essay as a point of departure or point of reference to develop a related idea of your own. (This exercise is similar to the collaborative learning task called Practice Descriptive Outline: Long Essays, p. 168. See also Part Three: Constructive Reading, p. 147.)

COLLABORATIVE LEARNING

No one knows how we get ideas. We know less about creativity than about any other aspect of the human mind. But we do know that conversation helps. Talking a topic over with sympathetic, like-minded peers can often lead to new and interesting thoughts. This probably happens because thought uses language that we learn by internalizing conversations we have with each other.

Other people don't get an idea for us when we talk a topic over with them. But we have all heard ourselves say when we're talking with someone, "Hey, that gives me an idea." Talking with other people can help us construct or assemble new ideas. So in the process of working up a topic for an essay, you can bring fellow students, friends, relatives, and teachers into the process. You can use them as sounding boards for ideas, as resources for information, and as prods that push you to explore, explain, and defend your ideas.

Task   Topic Interviews

Working in a group of three, tell each other what you think you are going to write about (your topic) and what you think you are going to say about your topic (your position).

Then, ask each other two questions:

"What do you want to know about my topic?" and

"What do you know about my topic that I can use in my essay?"

Your partners in this topic interview don't have to know anything about the subject that you expect to write about. That's your job. Their job is to help you recognize that you really do know something and that you really can explain it to other people.

In fact, it sometimes helps if your partners play dumb and ask obvious questions in order to draw you out. They can sometimes help you in this way to realize what you have to say and to help you put it into words that other people can understand.

▷ EXERCISE 4   QUESTIONING AND GENERALIZING

Exercises 1, 2, and 3 ask you to explore some of your private feelings, memories, and experiences (including learning experiences), and to express them in a loose, personal way without caring whether anyone will understand you or not. This is a first step in writing. Taking two more steps will help you understand yourself even better and also make your thoughts available to other people. These two steps are to discover issues implied in your experience and to draft generalizations that address those issues.

An *issue* is a *sharable concern*, a topic that people talk, read, and write about. Issues grow out of concrete experience and connect several similar or related experiences. You can state an issue in two ways. You can state it as a *noun phrase* (such as "water pollution" or "the relationship between governmental agencies and people's private lives") that identifies or labels the issue. Then you can restate it as a *question* that expresses relationships implied in the noun phrase (such as "What are we doing to pollute the oceans?", "How polluted are the oceans today, anyway?", "What can we do to keep the oceans clean?", or "How can people protect themselves from interference by governmental agencies?").

SOME WAYS TO QUESTION AND GENERALIZE

Suppose you are the manager of a store. Three people who work for you begin coming to work late three or four times a week. The similar or related concrete experiences that the issues grow out of are those late arrivals. It is easy to see what some of the issues are. **Noun phrase:** punctuality. **Questions:** Why have several people at one time been late to this job instead of just one at a time? Can this store succeed without punctual personnel? Does the need to be punctual cause employees disabling emotional stress?

Suppose then you find out that the first question may have a factual answer: All three people who are frequently late take the same bus to work, and recently the bus hasn't been running on time. This fact answers the question. But the factual answer about the bus not running on time leads to new issues. **Noun phrase:** public transportation. **Questions:** What can be done to make the buses run on time? What kind of service should bus companies provide? Should public transportation be a business or a government service? And so on.

Here it is probably worth noticing that most factual answers don't generate issues directly. Questions such as the following can be answered with numbers: How many tons of PCB enter the Atlantic Ocean annually through the Hudson River? At what rate does silt accumulate at the mouth of the Mississippi? How many barrels of crude oil are spilled annually on the high seas? But even questions with factual answers can lead to more questions (What are the sources of this information? How reliable is it? Who gathered it? Where does all that PCB come from? How many tons of PCB can the oceans absorb before human beings are affected?).

Here's another example. Suppose you remembered the time when you were very little and an older child cheated you out of a dime you were saving to buy something you wanted very much. That experience is just a private memory. But the issues implied in it may be of interest to many people. Everyone was once a child, vulnerable to the wiles of older children. As children, many people have had experiences similar to yours. Almost everyone takes care of children or deals with them in some way at some time, as a parent, a teacher, a shopkeeper, a camp counselor, a social worker. So as adults we may be faced with a similar situation occurring among the children we meet. And anyone, child or adult, may be taken in sometimes by an unscrupulous person who happens to be stronger, shrewder, or more experienced.

Although your own private experience is inevitably different from other people's experience, it also coincides with other people's experience at many points. At each of these points issues arise that are of direct interest to many people. Some of these issues are about relationships among small children. **Question:** What makes children selfish and cruel? Other issues concern relationships between adults and children. **Question:** How much should adults interfere in relations among small children? Still other issues concern socializing young children. **Question:** When should adults allow children to learn by experience, and when should adults protect children against injury and exploitation? There are also issues such as the nature of cheating, the seriousness of various forms of cheating, how cheating should be punished in children and adults, and so on.

Each of these issues can be turned into several generalizations by answering the questions they generate. A *generalization* is an observation or judgment that says something about more than one person, object, or experience. It says something about many similar people, objects, or experiences. A generalization is always a complete sentence.

For example, the issues implied in your experiences dealing with people coming in late for work lead to several possible generalizations.

ISSUE	GENERALIZATIONS

Punctuality

Why have several people at one time been late to this job?

Can this store succeed without punctual personnel?

Does the need to be punctual cause employees disabling emotional stress?

Service on Sluggard Bus Lines has gotten a lot worse.

Driving conditions on Route 7 are awful.

Most punctual people are successful.

Punctuality has nothing to do with success in business.

Employees' worries about being punctual make their sales decline.

Customers are willing to wait for cheerful, efficient service.

ISSUE	GENERALIZATIONS

Public Transportation

What kind of service should bus companies provide?

Bus companies should concern themselves with their customers' needs, not their own.

Should public transportation be a business or a government program?

All public transportation should be run by the government.

What other aspects of people's lives are affected by a lack of public transportation?

If the government ran public transportation, nobody would get anywhere on time.

Are some groups of people more affected by a lack of public transportation than others?

Businesses should run transportation services for their employees.

Can the government run an adequate transportation system?

What alternatives are there to public transportation?

The issues that arose out of your experience as a child also yield dozens of generalizations.

Children are cruel sometimes because they are selfish.

Children are sometimes cruel when they become afraid.

Children are cruel because they cannot conceive of the feelings (or the rights) of others.

Parents should let children learn by hard knocks.

An adult who stands by and watches a child get cheated without intervening is committing a crime.

Children who get away with cheating are on their way to becoming adult criminals.

Children who allow themselves to be cheated by another child are on their way to becoming adult criminals.

Trying to get away with something is only human.

And so on. You can probably think of many more.

Each of these generalizations may be stated in several different ways. They may be stated in clear, simple, concrete language, as they are expressed here, or they may be stated in language that is more vague, verbose, or abstract. For example, the clear generalization, "Children are cruel sometimes because they are selfish," may also be expressed in an unnecessarily complex way like this:

Young human progeny occasionally evidence lack of concern for the rights and feelings of peer group members because of a tendency to exclusivity and acquisitiveness.

And the sentence "Trying to get away with something is only human" may be expressed in a similarly verbose way:

The urge to discover means by which to avoid penalties for increasing one's own advantage at the expense of others is a fundamental characteristic found in all human beings.

In each case, the simpler way of expressing the idea is more precise and easier to understand. Since the purpose of drawing generalizations from personal experience is to share that experience with other people, always try to express yourself in the simplest, clearest, most precise way possible.

Another reason for stating a generalization succinctly and clearly is to preserve the power and human value that comes from intensely personal experience. To express an idea in simple language does not make it a simple-minded idea. Simple language just makes it easier for you to know what you mean and communicate it exactly. It helps you make up your mind and helps readers understand you. (There is more about writing clearly in Style, p. 137, and about issues in Contexts of Issues, Shareable Concerns, p. 197.)

WHAT TO DO

The purpose of exercise 4 is to discover some of the issues implied in the material that you developed for exercise 1, 2, or 3, and to formulate some generalizations that address these issues. These generalizations can then become propositions (what some people call thesis statements) for essays assigned in exercise 5 to 11. They state the position you are taking in the essay. So in preparing to write an essay there are three steps you can take.

First Step: Make a List

Make a list of issues that interest you. Read the work you did for exercise 1, 2, or 3. Think about what that material taken together says about you, your opinions, your beliefs, your interests, and your relationship to other people and the world you live in. Look for things about yourself that you didn't know before, and don't be surprised if you find some.

Then, list as many issues as you can think of based on the material in each exercise.

Some of the issues you draw from exercise 1 (personal experience) may be about the story you told in your reminiscence, family story, or account of change. Some of the issues may have to do with the way you or other people acted or what they may have felt or thought. Some issues may have to do with the choices people made or the situation people found themselves in. You may also feel that there are some issues in exercise 1 that are relevant to you as a writer.

Here are some examples.

Examples of issues drawn from personal experience. You might draw several issues from the example account of change in a person's attitude toward going to college, p. 20. How does the narrator's father feel about her? How do her brothers feel about her? How does the narrator feel about herself? How are each of these people likely to feel about the kind of change she underwent?

The example might generate the following issues, among others:

NOUN PHRASES

the value of a college education

changes in family attitudes toward women

relations between brothers and sisters

relations between fathers and daughters

roles of men and women at home

the difference between stupidity and ignorance

QUESTIONS

Why should women go to college?

Why shouldn't high schools teach everyone, boys and girls, about clothing and food?

Why should high schools bother to teach anyone, boys or girls, about clothing and food?

What is there about going to college that tends to make people feel better about themselves?

Examples of issues drawn from free writing or brainstorming. The issues you might draw from exercise 2, Free Writing (Brainstorming), p. 22, could be suggested by any number of words and phrases, and any combination of words and phrases, that appear on your lists. What did you find out about yourself and your interests from doing this exercise? What issues are implied in combining lists or contrasting them? What issues are implied by individual objects, places, people, or actions mentioned in your lists? You could also find some issues if you thought about the activity of brainstorming itself—how it affected you, why it worked or did not work in your case, and so on.

Examples of issues drawn from explaining something you have learned. The issues you draw from exercise 3 (explaining something you have learned) might be about the nature of what you learned (What is a benzene ring? What was the main cause of the American Revolution? What is erosion?). Other issues may have to do with a process (How is methyl alcohol synthesized? What were the immediate effects of the Boston Tea Party? How do various techniques to stop erosion work?). Still others may concern ways of applying or generalizing a key object, idea, or event (How can gasohol be made efficiently enough for use in automobiles? Was the Boston Tea Party an act of terrorism? Which methods for limiting erosion have worked best along the California coastline?).

The explanation of something a person had learned about taking home movies (What I Learned in Film 1, p. 25) might generate the following issues, among others:

NOUN PHRASES

> film versus videotape
>
> making films efficiently
>
> making films cheaply

QUESTIONS

> What do a treatment, a storyboard, and a shooting script have to do with making a movie?
>
> What are long shots, close-ups, and pans?
>
> Why do you edit film?
>
> How do you edit film?

Second Step: Choose and Restate

After you have listed all the issues you can think of that are suggested by one of these invention exercises, choose several issues, restate them as questions if they are stated as noun phrases, and write two or three answers (generalizations) for each question.

Don't feel that you have to agree with every generalization you write. Remember that what you are doing here is trying to discover possibilities. You are not committing yourself to anything you say at this point. For the fun of it, you might try including some generalizations that you absolutely do not agree with. Some of these could negate each other. Others could oppose each other. For example, to *negate* the generalization "It's a nice day out," you would say "It's not a nice day out." To *oppose* the generalization "It's a nice day out," you would say "It's raining hard," or "It's snowing," or "We're having a dust storm."

Generalizations that negate and oppose

> **Issue stated as a noun phrase:** Punctuality
>
> **Issue stated as a question:** What good is being punctual?
>
> **Generalization:** Most punctual people are successful.
>
> **Negation:** Most punctual people are not successful.
>
> **Opposing generalization:** Punctuality has nothing to do with success.
>
> **Issue stated as a noun phrase:** Well-trained service personnel

Issue stated as a question: Why do businesses need well-trained service personnel?

Generalization: Customers have a right to skilled service.

Negation: Customers do not have a right to skilled service.

Opposing generalization: Skilled service is worth waiting for.

Issue stated as a noun phrase: Children's cruelty

Issue stated as a question: Why are children cruel?

Generalization: Children are cruel because they are selfish.

Negation: Children are not cruel because they are selfish.

Opposing generalization: Children are cruel because they cannot yet imagine other people's feelings and needs.

Ask yourself which of these generalizations you could explore, explain, or defend in a short position paper. A position paper (such as those assigned in exercises 5 through 9) does not set out to prove a statement. It sets out to explore its possibilities. It sets out to find out how true, convincing, or useful the generalization might be in a given situation or under given conditions and to persuade people that the position taken is worth considering.

Third Step: Choose and Discard

Finally, choose one of the generalizations to use as the proposition of the position paper you are getting ready to write. Notice when you do this exercise that drawing generalizations from exercise 1, 2, or 3 leaves behind a great deal of concrete material—details of the experience, names, places, words and phrases, things people said, particular characteristics of people, things, and events. You will be able to use some of these generalizations as the propositions of position papers.

COLLABORATIVE LEARNING

Work in groups of three, taking turns stating the issue to be discussed.

Task   Issues and Generalizations

State an issue in question form. Then ask your partners to write out two or three possible answers to that question in the form of generalizations.

Finally, decide as a group whether or not each generalization could be explored, explained, or defended in a short position paper. What would you have to know about the topic in order to do that? How do you think you might go about learning what you would need to know in order to do it? Could the topic be explored, explained, or defended in a short position paper? What would you have to know about the topic in order to do that? How do you think you might go about learning what you would need to know in order to do it?

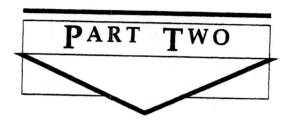

Writing Position Papers

The purpose of Part One was to help you learn how to make your own experiences accessible and useful to other people by drawing issues from them and stating those issues in clear, well-expressed generalizations. In Part Two each exercise asks you to choose one of those generalizations (or make up another one), commit yourself to it for the time being, and develop it in a position paper. A *position paper* explains what your own position on the topic is at the moment: what you think about it, what you know and can explain about it, what your views on it are, and why.

The purpose of a position paper is to explore your position in a well-developed, well-planned way and convince other people that your position is worth considering. Its purpose is to begin a conversation or to enter a conversation that's already going on. Its purpose is not to end conversation by proving your point. It is to get other people to join you in thinking about a topic you are interested in and about a position you have taken on it. The response you want from your readers isn't "By George, you're right." The response you want is "Gee, I never thought of it that way. I'll have to give that some thought."

Writing a good position paper begins with committing yourself tentatively, for the time being, to a generalization—maybe one of the generalizations you worked out in exercises 1 through 4. When you commit yourself for the time being to a generalization, you turn it into a proposition. A *proposition* is the most important sentence in a position paper. It succinctly states the position you are taking. It says in a nutshell what the whole essay says.

Once you have stated your position, the next step is to develop it. **You develop your position by exploring, explaining, or defending it.** To help you learn a simple, commonly used way to develop almost any position on almost any topic, exercises 5 through 9 ask you to practice the same basic form: an introduction and two paragraphs of exploration, explanation, or defense. But they also show you how to vary the way you explore, explain, or defend your position within that form. Each exercise offers you a different template or pattern to use as a guide in choosing reasons to support your position, in arranging them effectively, and in relating or linking them to each other and to the essay's proposition sentence.

That is, one thing essay exercises 5 through 9 have in common is that each one introduces you to one kind of *explanatory subordination,* one way of subordinating one part of an exploration, explanation, or defense to other parts. The reason for learning these different kinds of explanatory subordination is that, in the long run, you will be able to choose among several options whenever you set out to think through and develop a position you are taking. They give you a repertoire of organizational types that frees you to support different positions in different ways, or in some cases, to support the same position in different ways under different circumstances.

When you choose among templates or patterns of explanatory subordination, you are deciding what you have to say and how much you have to say. For example, if you think you have *two* good reasons in support of your position, you would choose the template introduced in exercise 5. If you think you have *several* pretty good reasons, some better than others, you would use Nestorian Order (exercise 6). If you think there may be some *disagreement* about the position you are taking, you would choose one of the templates that takes disagreement into consideration explicitly: a straw man argument or a concession (exercises 7 through 9). When you write longer essays, you may find use for several of these kinds of explanatory subordination in different sections of the essay. (There is more about writing long essays in Length: Term Papers and Other Long Writing Assignments, p. 231 and Practice Descriptive Outline: Long Essays, p. 168)

The three-paragraph form these essay assignments require is not the only form to write an essay in. But it is a good one. And it can teach you how to construct reasons that effectively synthesize and subordinate concrete experiences so as to give them new significance, a significance that affects other people as well as yourself. (See Reasons, p. 96.) When you can write easily in this form, you will be able to write many different kinds of essays with confidence—not just position papers, but also examination essays, term papers, and reports. Eventually you will be able to make up your own ways to vary the basic form, explore other common forms, and even invent forms that are entirely new.

But for now, please stick to this one form.

Each of the five essays should be about five hundred words. You don't have to count words. Anywhere between 480 and 520 will do just fine.

Make an estimate. The average will be about two pages typed, double-spaced.

Write each five-hundred word paper in three paragraphs: one paragraph to introduce the proposition and two paragraphs to defend it, with transitional generalizations at the beginning of paragraphs 2 and 3 tying each paragraph to what went before. Don't write a "conclusion" for any of these first five essays. Don't even write a "concluding sentence." When you get through defending the proposition, stop. That may hurt at first, but let it hurt. Resist the urge to "conclude." (See "But Why Can't I Write a 'Conclusion'?", p. 131.)

Every essay you write from now on should take a position. State your position as a proposition in the last sentence of the first paragraph. Explore, explain, or defend it in paragraphs 2 and 3.

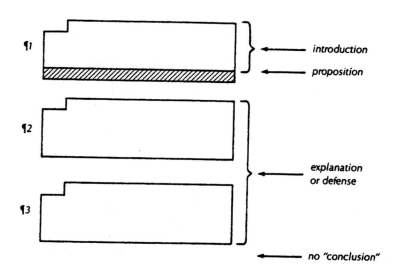

Notice that these essay exercises do not ask you to write from the top down. They ask you to write from the inside out. Your finished essays will begin at the top with an introduction. But do not begin writing the essay where the essay will begin when you are finished with it—don't begin writing by trying to write an introduction. Warm up for a while at first if you like, writing whatever comes into your head. But when you finally get down to business, begin as far inside as you can go, at the very core of the essay, by writing a proposition. Next, continue working on the "insides" by exploring, explaining, or defending the proposition.

Then go back to the top and write a paragraph introducing the proposition. Your introductory paragraph is the essay's "outsides"—its wrappings.

When you have written your essay in that order, you will have written it from the inside out. (There is more about writing introductions beginning on p. 81, and in Part Four: Reaching Out to Members of Other Communities, p. 189.)

▷ EXERCISE 5   TWO REASONS

Exercise 5 is a five-hundred word position paper in three paragraphs: an introductory paragraph ending with a proposition, and two paragraphs of exploration, explanation, or defense. Each paragraph develops a single reason that supports or explains the proposition. Don't write a conclusion. But write a descriptive outline that explains what the essay *does* and *says*.

Write the essay from the inside out. Approach it this way:

THINK OF A TOPIC

Draw upon some of the material you developed in the invention exercises 1 through 4, or develop a topic in your own way, on your own. Write about anything, as long as it means something to you and is something you feel you can take a position on and make interesting to other people. (For topics based on personal experience, see Exercise 1. Mining the Past, p. 16. For topics based on a reading assignment, see Analyzing Something You Have Read, p. 28, or Recalling Something You Have Learned, p. 25.)

In most cases it is entirely up to you what to write about, although there are some limits. One limit is an external one. You may sometimes find that it will save time if your class or your teacher defines a general area of choice, such as entertainment, politics, family, or something you learned in another course, or if your teacher gives you a reading assignment and asks you to base your essay on what you read. Then you are not likely to feel quite so totally at sea trying to find a topic to write on. Or the class may agree that you will write on a topic that everyone in the class knows something about, so that you will be able to discuss the substance as well as the form of your essays. (See Essay Exchange and Descriptive, Evaluative, and Substantive Peer Review, p. 185.)

Another limit is more personal. You may find that you write better on some topics than on others. For example, experience suggests that it is hard to learn much about writing when you try to explore topics that trouble you emotionally or topics that do not engage you at all. When you write on topics that trouble you, you may become so involved in the topic that you find it hard to pay attention to craftsmanship: the *way* you are writing the essay. When you write on topics that don't engage you at all, you are likely to be too bored to produce a readable essay. It's almost impossible to interest someone else in a position that doesn't interest you.

But within these very broad limits, you are free to choose your own topic, decide the position you want to take on that topic, and explore, explain, and defend your position in a way that will convince your readers to take it seriously and give it some thought. If you find that you cannot explain or defend your position, at least you have learned that. So you can change your position, or you can give it up and take a position on another topic entirely.

Be a little adventurous in picking topics. Take some risks. Avoid the Groucho Marx effect. The story goes that when Groucho was invited to join a club, he turned it down, because he didn't want to belong to any club that would have him as a member. As a writer you may sometimes feel that way too. You may feel that you don't want to write on a topic that interests you because, if it interests you, it must inevitably be uninteresting to other people. That simply isn't true. Your friends at least will be interested in what you're interested in just because you are interested in it. And later in this book you will find out how to interest people other than your close friends. (See Speaking Other People's Language, p. 191.)

In another version of the same attitude, you may feel that everybody must already know about anything that you happen to know. What's the point of telling them? That's not true either. You know a lot that other people don't know and would be fascinated to discover. You just don't know yet that you know it, or else you just don't know yet that they don't. Not only is it not true that everyone already knows what you know, but one of the biggest problems you are likely to have in writing is that people do not know enough about what you know to follow what you have to say about it. Then the question is, how much background do you have to give your readers, and what should you explain so that they'll be able to follow?

Overcoming these feelings of self-deprecation can be the most important step you take toward becoming a good writer. It may be the first and most important step you take toward beginning new conversations and joining conversations already in progress.

Suppose, for example, you happen to be very interested in transportation, in particular the future of automobiles and highway systems. Boring, right? Who cares, right?

Maybe. But there is a lot to write about on that topic. You could write about safety, for instance. More people are killed every year on American highways than in airplane crashes. That's pretty interesting. The Federal Interstate Highway System is pothole city. I bet you know a lot of people who hate the national 65 m.p.h. speed limit. And maybe you even know one or two who ignore it. You could also write about bridge design and repair or energy conservation. Cars and transportation are *your* interests. Choose a topic you would most like to write about and choose a position you would like to take on that topic.

THINK OF A TENTATIVE PROPOSITION

Write a generalization on the topic (see Exercise 4   Questioning and Generalizing, p. 31). Pick an aspect of the topic that interests you most and relates to your own experience in some way. You might write down several generalizations and then pick the one that you like the best and that you think you have the most to say about. Make a tentative commitment to it for the time being. That generalization, until you decide to change it, will be the proposition of your essay.

Suppose you decide to write about the future of cars as a means of transportation. What can you say about that? What position could you take? You might say, "Cars are obsolete." Or, "In ten years there will not be a quarter of the cars on the road that there are on the road today." Or maybe you could take the other side: "Cars are here to stay because we can't get along without them." You could make any of these into a strong proposition. (See Propositions, p. 85.)

THINK OF WAYS TO EXPLORE, EXPLAIN, OR DEFEND YOUR POSITION

As you think about what position to take, also think over what you could say to defend or explain your position. Draw as much as you can on immediate personal experience. Reading is of course one kind of immediate personal experience, so one source of things to say to defend your position might be something you have read. For these exercises it is important to stay as personally involved as possible in what you are writing. If you like, you can reuse some of the material you produced in exercises 1 through 4.

The essays you write for this first set of exercises are not research essays. But if you need more material to develop your explanation than you have at hand, you can draw upon popular and easily accessible material: TV, newspapers, news magazines, and so on. If you do use information from one of these sources, be sure you indicate in your essay what that source was. For example, say something like, "*Time* magazine reported last week that . . ." or "The president said in his last news conference that . . . ," and so on.

WRITE A TENTATIVE PROPOSITION AND EXPLORE, EXPLAIN, OR DEFEND IT IN THE FORM THE ASSIGNMENT REQUIRES

Now begin writing. Write your tentative proposition (the position you are taking in the essay) in a single sentence. Beneath it, write an explanation or defense of the proposition in two paragraphs. For exercise 5, put one supporting reason in each paragraph, and develop each reason separately.

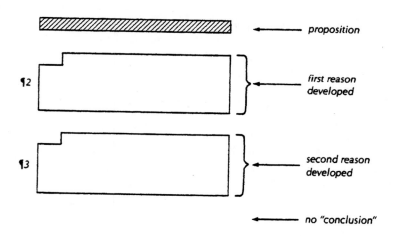

Let's say you decided to defend the following proposition: "Cars may be on the way out as our major means of transportation." And you decided that the two best reasons for thinking that cars may be becoming obsolete are that (1) our oil supply is going to diminish so much in the next hundred years that we will not be able to afford to waste it by burning gasoline to get around, and (2) people want to get places faster than cars can possibly take them.

In that case, you would **develop one of these reasons in paragraph 2** by saying how much oil scientists estimate is left on earth, and by matching that figure with the equivalent amount of crude oil automobiles burn up as gasoline every day. In the long run, you might say, whether the supply lasts one hundred years or one thousand years does not matter much. As the supply diminishes it can never be replaced. Its price will rise so high that no one will be able to afford it. You might also refer to the inefficiency of internal combustion engines: how they waste more oil than they turn into power.

Then, you would **develop the other reason in paragraph 3** by calling on your own experiences traveling and the experiences of your family or friends. Some statistics might be useful here, but you can certainly get along without them. Instead, you could tell an anecdote about, say, somebody you know who used to drive from Chicago to Omaha every week on business. Now, you say, he can't be bothered. Last year he hooked up his Omaha office by modem to his computer in Chicago, bought a fax machine, and needs to go to Omaha only once a month. And he flies there in a quarter of the time it used to take him to drive. (See Paragraph Development, p. 111, and Reasons, p. 96.)

In writing these two paragraphs of explanation, remember that your proposition is not sacred just because you committed yourself to it for the time being and wrote it down. It's tentative. It is the position you have taken in order to explore it and see what sense you can make of it. As you write and think further about the idea, you may want to change your mind. If you do change your mind, change the proposition. The only thing to make sure of is that when you have finished the essay, the explanation and the proposition match. Adjust one or the other of them until they do. (See Propositions, p. 85.)

When you have finished defending the proposition at the end of paragraph 3, stop. Resist the urge to write a "conclusion." (See "But Why Can't I Write a 'Conclusion'?", p. 131.)

WRITE AN INTRODUCTION

Now think about what you could say to introduce readers to the position you have taken. Try to put yourself in your readers' position for a moment. Assume at first that they are not much interested in what you are writing about. What could you say that might catch their interest?

For starters, you could try to show them that they really are interested, whether they know it or not. In the essay about cars, for example, you could say that there are more cars on the road today than ever before, and yet there are signs that the public is not entirely happy with that situation. You could bring in air pollution, government investigation of car safety, and recent experience with high-speed trains. That could lead you to speculate that travel by car may have reached a high-water mark, and that the future trend will be for people to use cars as we know them less rather than more. Indeed, you could say, it looks like cars may be on the way out. And there you would be, back to your proposition. (See Introductions, p. 81, and Part Four: Reaching Out to Members of Other Communities, p. 189.)

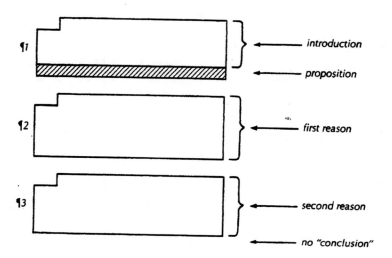

CHECK THE PARAGRAPH TRANSITIONS

Paragraphs in an essay do not stand alone. They are related to each other and they are related especially to the proposition of the essay. One of a writer's most important jobs is to show these relationships very clearly so that the reader will always know what the writer is up to. Writers have to very clearly lead, so that readers can very easily follow.

The first major transition in an essay is between the introduction and the proposition at the end of the first paragraph. You have to make sure that the reader understands just how the introduction is related to the proposition that it introduces.

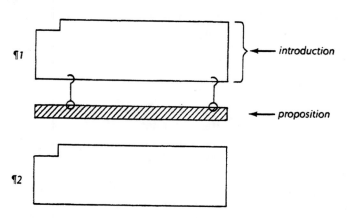

end of ¶1
transition
proposition

. . . the trend will be for people to use cars as we know them less rather than more. In fact, it looks as if cars may be on the way out as our major means of transportation.

The second major transition in an essay is between paragraph 1 and paragraph 2. Usually writers show the relationship of each paragraph to other paragraphs and to the proposition at the beginning of each paragraph. That is, the transition to paragraph 2 should occur in the first sentence of paragraph 2, not in the last sentence of paragraph 1. And the transition to paragraph 3 should occur in the first sentence of paragraph 3. Transitions reach back, not forward.

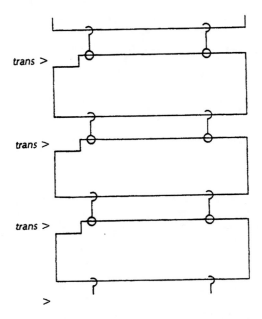

end of ¶1
proposition

¶2 transition

. . . the trend will be for people to use cars as we know them less rather than more. In fact, it looks as if cars may be on the way out as our major means of transportation.
    And it is high time they were. The world oil supply, which cars depend on for fuel, has been diminishing at the rate of. . . .

The first sentence of paragraph 2 is the transition sentence. The words *and* and *they* in that sentence connect the first element of the explanation or defense with the last sentence in paragraph 1. The last sentence in paragraph 1 is the proposition. It expresses the central idea of the whole essay.

Because the proposition is nearby, the transition sentence for paragraph 2 is relatively easy to write. The third major transition in an essay, the transition to paragraph 3, is a little harder. It has two jobs to do, not just one. It has to connect the second element of the explanation or defense with two parts of the essay. It connects paragraph 3 with the end of paragraph 2. It also connects paragraph 3 with the proposition.

But the proposition is way back at the end of paragraph 1.

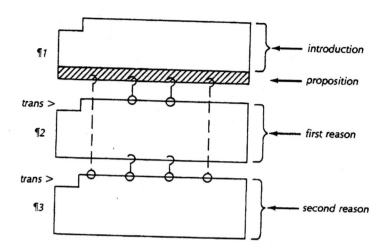

end of ¶1 proposition	. . . the trend will be for people to use cars as we know them less rather than more. In fact, it looks as if cars may be on the way out as our major means of transportation.

end of ¶1
proposition

¶2 transition

last sentence in
¶2

¶3 transition
to proposition,
to ¶2
third reason

    . . . the trend will be for people to use cars as we know them less rather than more. In fact, it looks as if cars may be on the way out as our major means of transportation.
    And it is high time they were. The world oil supply, which cars depend on for fuel, has been diminishing at the rate of. . . . But we travel these super routes at speeds that threaten our lives no matter how safely our cars may be built.
    *Cars will become less important in the future <u>not only be-
cause they waste fuel and are dangerous</u>,* but also because they waste time and human energy. The man I worked for last summer used to drive from Chicago to Omaha on business once a week. It would take him on the average. . . .

Notice, finally, that a transition sentence at the beginning of a paragraph is usually also the topic sentence of the paragraph. That is, a paragraph transition sentence is usually a transitional generalization. A *transitional generalization* does two things. It states succinctly what the paragraph goes on to explain. *And* it shows how the paragraph is related to the proposition of the essay. (See Reasons, p. 96, and Unity and Coherence, p. 116.)

Write a Descriptive Outline and Revise

You have now written the first draft of your essay. **Before you revise it, write a descriptive outline of the essay** as it stands. Writing descriptive outlines is a way of learning to read constructively. One purpose of writing a descriptive outline is to make both writing and learning to write more actively collaborative. In writing descriptive outlines and conferring about them, you learn the language that readers and writers use when they talk constructively with each other about reading and writing. (There is more about constructive reading and about writing descriptive outlines in Part Three: Constructive Reading, p. 147.)

Set your descriptive outline up in this way:

PROPOSITION

PLAN

PARAGRAPH 1   *says:*

does:

PARAGRAPH 2   *says:*

does:

PARAGRAPH 3   *says:*

does:

For the **proposition,** write the proposition sentence as it appears in your essay, the last sentence in the first paragraph. For the **plan,** say how the parts of the essay are arranged. In exercise 5, your plan is to explore, explain, or defend two reasons supporting the proposition.

For **what each paragraph *says,*** write a one-sentence paraphrase or summary of the paragraph; put the paragraph in a nutshell. (See What an Essay *Says,* p. 154.)

Up to this point, a descriptive outline differs little from a conventional sentence outline. What distinguishes descriptive outlines is the second item in the description of each paragraph, **what each paragraph *does.*** What a paragraph *does* is not what it *says.* It is not the point the paragraph makes or its message. When you say what a paragraph *does* you explain

- how the paragraph is related to the essay's proposition,
- how the paragraph is related to preceding paragraphs,
- the function the paragraph serves in the essay, and
- the way the paragraph is organized internally to perform that function.

The idea that every paragraph *does* something in an essay can be difficult to grasp. But to become a good writer, you have to understand this important concept. Every part of an essay serves a function in the essay as a whole, just as every part of a sailboat, an airplane, or the human body serves a function in the sailboat, airplane, or body as a whole. Sails and motors propel boats and planes. Rudders steer them. The heart pumps blood. Nails protect the ends of our fingers. And paragraphs explore, explain, or defend the proposition or main point of an essay. These functions are the "work" that each part does. Each part is designed and constructed to do that work effectively.

Paragraphs can of course do many things and serve many functions. For example, they can argue logically, analyze, and explain. They can list or catalogue objects, events, scenes, witnesses, problems, and so on. They can tell stories. They can describe things, people, places, or processes. They can show the logical relations among the parts of an argument.

But no paragraph does any of these things for its own sake. Every paragraph serves some purpose in the essay as a whole. Paragraphs analyze, describe, argue, and so on, in order to help explore, explain, or defend the main point of the essay, the position expressed in the essay's proposition. When you explain in a descriptive outline what a paragraph *does*, you are explaining how it is organized in order to explore, explain, or defend the proposition. So, **a basic *does* statement has two parts:**

1. it *names* the work that the paragraph does relative to the proposition, and
2. it *explains* how the paragraph does that work.

For the essay on cars, for example, a basic descriptive outline might look something like this:

PROPOSITION   Cars may be on the way out as our major means of transportation.

PLAN   Support the proposition with two reasons.

PARAGRAPH 1   *says:* Use of cars is at a peak, but there are signs of change.

does: Introduces the proposition by describing the present situation.

PARAGRAPH 2   *says:* Our oil supply is diminishing, a loss made worse by the way cars waste gas.

does: Develops the first reason by citing comparative statistics.

PARAGRAPH 3   *says:* Cars waste time and human energy.

does: Develops the second reason by telling an anecdote.

Notice that the *does* statements in this descriptive outline do not mention the content of the paragraph. They say nothing about cars. All reference to the essay's content, cars, is saved for the *says* statements.

Does statements only explain paragraph organization and development. A *does* statement such as "introduces the proposition by discussing how car use may be changing" would be incorrect because it both describes form and paraphrases content.

The example is a *basic* descriptive outline because its *does* statements explain the paragraph's relation to the proposition and only very succinctly explain how the paragraph works. A more *detailed* descriptive outline would explain further, for example, how the statistics cited in paragraph 2 are organized, classified, and compared (in summaries, in tables, in lists, or whatever), how the examples are related to the rest of the paragraph, and so on. (There is an example of a basic descriptive outline and a detailed descriptive outline written for the same essay on p. 77 [exercise 9]. Also, see What an Essay *Does*, p. 158, and Getting Ready to Write a Detailed *Does* Statement, p. 165.)

By writing a descriptive outline that explains the function and organization of every paragraph, you will learn exactly what is going on in the essay. This is the long-range reason for writing a descriptive outline: to gain some objectivity on your writing. A descriptive outline written after you have written a first draft of the essay, but before you write out the final draft, gives you a way to check how well the essay is organized.

After you write a descriptive outline, reread the essay and compare each paragraph with what you say it *says* and *does* in the descriptive outline. Do they match? If they do, write out the final draft of the essay. If they don't match, change the outline to match the essay or change the essay to match the outline. It makes no difference which, as long as in the end the descriptive outline accurately describes the final draft of the essay. *Accurately* means that the descriptive outline describes what is really going on in the paper, not what you think should be going on or what you want to be going on.

You should write an accurate descriptive outline for every essay exercise you write for this book. Remember, write your descriptive outline between drafts, not before you begin writing the essay or after you have finished writing the final draft. Correct the outline as you revise the essay. **Use your descriptive outline as a tool for rewriting.**

READ THE ESSAY ALOUD AND POLISH IT

The last thing to do before you copy or type the final draft of your essay is to read the whole thing aloud to yourself.

Listen to what you have said and how you have said it. Make what you have written sound as much as you can like standard written English. If it doesn't, change it. If it sounds as if you have tried to make it seem grand or impressive, change it. Try to make your writing sound clear, so that someone you know could easily understand what you mean. (See Style, p. 137.)

Reading your essay to yourself is also practice for reading it aloud to your fellow writers. One purpose of reading aloud to each other in class is to make both writing and learning to write more actively collaborative. Read slowly and clearly, and after paragraph 1 announce the number of each paragraph before you begin to read it ("Paragraph 2 . . . ," "Paragraph 3 . . ."). Ask your listeners to restate in their own words the position they think you are taking in the essay. Compare what they say with what you want your position to be. Consider revising the way you state your position (the essay's proposition) if your listeners haven't gotten the main point you intended to make. Then ask them what else they think you could do to improve the essay. (There is more about reading aloud in Part Three: Constructive Reading, p. 147.)

Make a Final Copy

The last thing to do in writing an essay is to copy or type it neatly, double-spaced. Give it a title. Leave ample margins at the top, bottom, and sides of each sheet. Check your spelling and punctuate correctly. Try not to leave blotches or smudges on the essay. In general, prepare the copy so that the reader will be favorably disposed to reading it. (See the section on preparing a manuscript in a standard writing handbook.)

Collaborative Learning

Task 1   Reading Aloud

Read your essay aloud to the other students in the class.

To prepare, read your essay aloud at home to yourself or to a friend or a member of your family.

Read slowly and clearly so that the people listening can understand what you are saying. Read the title first. Then, as you go along, announce the number of each paragraph following paragraph 1.

Task 2   Essay Exchange and Peer Conference

Exchange essays with another writer in the class, but keep the descriptive outline that you wrote of your own essay.

Write a descriptive outline of your partner's essay.

In the next class, confer with your partner. Examine the two descriptive outlines of your essay, your own and your partner's. Underline where they differ. Try to discover why the two of you described the same essay in different ways. Discuss how to make both descriptions more thorough and accurate. But at this stage please do not try to evaluate each other's essays.

At the end of your descriptive outline, write a note explaining how the conference went from your point of view. If you think now that you would like to make some changes in your essay, in the descriptive outline you wrote of it, or in both, say so in your note and explain. (There is an example of essay exchange and peer review in Example Descriptive and Evaluative Peer Review, p. 177.)

☐ EXAMPLE ESSAY ───────────────────────────

To Number or Not to Number

Barbara Pleener Sackrowitz

Modern advances in technology and science have increased the amount that students have to learn. In order to help students learn all they have to learn, society has had to revise its educational programs and its teaching methods. Society has also had to raise standards in the schools in order to ensure the highest degree of scholastic excellence. Unfortunately, this effort has led to competition for grades among students, rather than a desire to perfect skills. One result of this competition is that the alphabetical grading system has become more important than any subject taught, and is therefore undermining the educational system rather than improving it. One solution to this problem is to do away with grades entirely. Many people feel that this solution would be impractical. Another is to make the grading system reflect more accurately the differences in quality among student work. To make grading more fair in this respect, the alphabetical grading system should be replaced by a number system.

The alphabetical grading system, consisting of grades A, B, C, D, and F, is by no means a subtle or fair way to represent the quality of students' work. At best it is a rough guideline. Teachers must translate fine distinctions into awkward blocks of evaluation. Plenty of personal bias is involved in evaluating student work in the first place. Add to that the need to make alphabetical equivalents, and evaluation becomes impossibly biased. To one teacher a grade of 79 is a low B, but to another it is a high C. The result is that grading becomes a serious point of contention between student and teacher. Assigning a numerical grade to begin with does not pose this problem. If students get a 79, that is their mark. No adjustment or interpretation is possible. Teachers are saved from an onslaught of student protests, and from the additional agony of trying to be fair to students through a system that is inherently unfair. And students are not likely to want to contest the fairness of their grades, since they will feel that the grades they have received represent accurately their teachers' estimate of their work.

Because of its greater accuracy, the numerical grading system also gives a more reliable account of a student's potential. If alphabetical grades do not give a clear picture of what students have achieved in the past, how can they possibly give an idea of what they are likely to achieve in the future? The main reason for this lack of clarity is that grades are computerized. Besides teacher bias, there is computer bias. Students who get Cs for a near-80 average wind up looking just like students who barely made 70. But can one honestly say that these students have the same potential? Obviously some students could do 10 percent better than others, yet the computer inevitably ignores this significant difference. The graduate schools or businesses that the student applies to are not aware of the discrepancy. So not only do student and teacher lose, but society as a whole loses as well. □

BASIC DESCRIPTIVE OUTLINE

PROPOSITION   To make grading fair, the alphabetical grading system should be replaced by a number system.

PLAN   Develop two reasons supporting the proposition.

PARAGRAPH 1   *says:* Grading has become competitive, but doing away with grades is impractical; a middle ground is to make grading more accurate and fair.

does: Introduces the proposition by explaining the problem.

PARAGRAPH 2   *says:* Numerical grading is fairer to students and less agonizing for teachers.

does: Develops the first reason by comparing two systems.

PARAGRAPH 3   *says:* Numerical grading represents students' career potential more accurately.

does: Develops the second reason by speculating about long-run effects.

☐ EXAMPLE ESSAY ─────────────────────────

Haiti: The Need to Unite
Annemarie Edwards

The early leaders of Haiti wanted their country to be free, humane, and peaceful. But from its inception, Haiti's politics have been violent, its wealth has been unfairly distributed, and living conditions for most Haitians have been poor. Three major issues underlie the country's problems. One is the question of color. Distinctions between blacks and mulattoes arose during slavery and have always been a source of conflict. The second issue is economic. Haiti's economy is dependent on agriculture. Most peasants own the land they work, but they lack the knowledge and equipment to use their land productively. And foreigners doing business in Haiti spend most of their income overseas, limiting reinvestment in the country and keeping unemployment high. The third issue is education. Most Haitians are illiterate and few speak the official language, French. Instead, most speak creole, a dialect of French. David Nicholls's *From Dessalines to Duvalier: Race, Color, and National Independence in Haiti* shows that these problems, which have always been a part of Haitian life, can be solved, but all of the possible solutions require Haitians to unite. It is clear that unity of purpose has been rare in Haitian history. Yet it is also clear that Haitians can unite effectively.

For one thing, history shows that Haitians have united at crucial times in the past when their freedom and independence were threatened by external force. In 1802, blacks and mulattoes put aside the question of color and stopped fighting each other long enough to crush the French, who intended to enslave both groups. They united again after the invasion of Haiti by the United States in 1915. This intervention was brought on by civil unrest throughout the country. The peasants and members of the elite worked to rid their country of foreigners. The peasants, armed with machetes, attacked American military personnel. The elites attacked the Americans in local journals and refused to work with them. Together, they made the economic situation that created the unrest in the first place even worse, making it clear to the Americans that their presence was unwanted. The Haitians' attacks, although they did not drive the Americans away, made them realize that they were doing more harm than good.

Haitians have also demonstrated their ability to work together outside their country. In fact, ironically, Haitians abroad have united in ways that they have been unable to do, or have refused to do, at home. Haitian-Americans are among the most unified of all Caribbean-Americans. They have created publications such as *Haiti Progress* and *Haiti Insight*. They have established organizations, such as the Haitian American Alliance, that help Haitian-Americans cope with situations arising from mass migration such as employment, language acquisition, and family disruption. They have taken advantage of public education in the United States, reducing illiteracy. Although most Haitian-Americans continue to speak creole with each other, increasingly adults and of course children born in the United States speak, read, and write English. Haitian-Americans are also a fast growing economic force. Whereas in Haiti itself Haitians have rarely reinvested in their own people, in the United States reinvestment is common. As a result, unemployment among Haitian-Americans is very low. In New York City, for example, Haitian-Americans have established themselves in the dry-cleaning and catering businesses by helping new arrivals accumulate the capital they need in order to buy going concerns or build entirely new business establishments. ◻

WORK CITED

Nicholls, David. *From Dessalines to Duvalier: Race, Color, and National Independence in Haiti.* Cambridge: Cambridge Univ. Press, 1979.

▷ EXERCISE 6   NESTORIAN ORDER

Exercise 6 is also a five-hundred word position paper in three paragraphs: an introductory paragraph ending with a proposition and two paragraphs of exploration, explanation, or defense. Each paragraph develops a single reason that supports or explains the proposition. Don't write a "conclusion." But write a descriptive outline that explains what an essay *does* and *says*.

In these respects, exercise 6 is just like exercise 5. In another important respect, though, exercise 6 differs a good deal from exercise 5.

Begin your work by thinking of a topic. You might reread the material that you generated in exercises 1 through 4 to see what new ideas it may suggest. Or you might do one of those invention exercises again, in your head or on paper, in order to generate new material and new ideas. Once you have a tentative topic, decide what position you want to take on it—that is, decide on a proposition. (For a topic based on personal experience, see Exercise 1   Mining the Past, p. 16. For a topic based on a reading assignment, see Analyzing Something You Have Read, p. 28 and Recalling Something You Have Learned, p. 25.)

Then, instead of giving two reasons to support your position as you did for exercise 5, think of several reasons and develop them according to Nestorian order. In Nestorian order (named after the character Nestor in the *Iliad*), you **create a climax by putting the best reason last.** The *best reason* is the strongest or most effective explanation or defense, the one that explores the position you are taking most deeply, or the one you can develop most fully and convincingly. **Put the second best reason first. Arrange the rest in between.**

For this exercise, present your arguments this way: Begin paragraph 2 with the second best reason and finish the paragraph with minor reasons. Develop the strongest argument, the major reason, in paragraph 3.

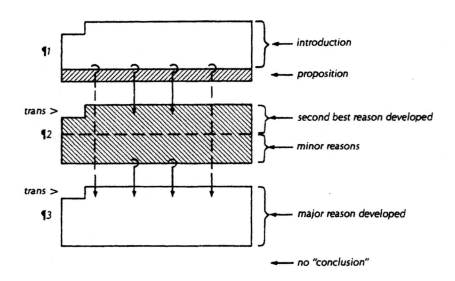

Notice that this exercise adds a new difficulty. Paragraphs 1 and 3 are formally the same as they are in exercise 5, but paragraph 2 is different. It presents a new problem in coherence. You have to make paragraph 2 coherent, despite the fact that you are giving several reasons in it, not just one. You have to avoid just giving a list. You have to show that there is a relationship among the parts of the paragraph. That is, **you have to create coherence among the parts of this paragraph** just as you have to create coherence between paragraphs.

You can make it easier to gain coherence in paragraph 2 by arranging the minor reasons in a sequence that will make them easy to connect. Then you can find ways to relate them so that they will not seem to the reader to be just dumped in. (See Unity and Coherence, p. 116.)

Read through the procedure outlined in exercise 5. Follow it again. Remember, the difference this time is that you have to settle on a proposition that you can defend in paragraphs organized as this essay exercise requires: several reasons, not just two. To find a topic for this exercise, think about things that interest you for a lot of different reasons, think about things you like to do for a lot of different reasons, or think about things you think people should do for a lot of different reasons.

For example, the essay supporting the proposition on cars (Exercise 5, p. 44) develops two reasons. But suppose you had in mind more than two reasons—say, five. Then you could write the essay in Nestorian order. To do that, in paragraph 2 you would shorten the first reason, giving the statistics on oil depletion more briefly, and then give several minor reasons in support of the proposition. Those reasons might be the air pollution caused by cars, lack of safety at high speeds, and discomfort driving on long, straight superhighways.

You might create coherence in paragraph 2 in the following way:

end of ¶1 *proposition*	. . . the trend will be for people to use cars as we know them less rather than more. In fact, it looks as if cars may be on the way out as our major means of transportation.
¶2 transition *second best* *reason*	And it is high time they were. The world oil supply, which cars depend on for fuel, has been diminishing at the rate of millions of barrels a year. Some geologists estimate that at the present rate of increase in use of oil, we will have drained off almost all the earth's oil by the year 2000. The worst of this
transition	situation is that because of the poor efficiency of the internal combustion engine, most of that oil won't even produce useful
first minor *reason*	energy. Most of it will pass off in exhaust from car motors. This exhaust is still another reason cars may disappear, that is, because they pollute the air. Eighty percent of Los Angeles's pollution comes from cars, and the worst of it cannot be
transition	trapped by any known exhaust cleansing device. And the new superhighways throughout the whole country do more than
second minor *reason*	choke our lungs. Their monotony stultifies our minds with boredom when we drive on them. Gone are the days of pleas-
transition	ant drives over the bridge and into the woods to grandmother's house. Today it's through the mountain and around the city.
third minor *reason*	But we travel these super routes at speeds that threaten our lives no matter how safely our cars may be built.
¶3 transition	Cars will become less important in the future not only because they waste fuel and are dangerous, but also because
major reason	they waste time and human energy. The man I worked for last summer used to drive every week from Chicago to Omaha. . . .

Remember:

- Think of a subject.
- Think of a tentative proposition.
- Think of ways to explore, explain, or defend your position.
- Write the proposition and explore, explain, or defend it in the form required by the assignment.
- Write an introduction.
- Check the transitions.
- Write a descriptive outline and revise.
- Read the paper aloud and polish it.
- Make the final copy.

COLLABORATIVE LEARNING

Task 1   Reading Aloud

Follow the instructions for reading aloud on p. 55.

Task 2   Essay Exchange and Peer Conference

Follow the instructions for essay exchange and peer conference on p. 55.

☐ EXAMPLE ESSAY ——————————————————

The Sea Gull: A Great Play Makes a Bad Movie

Dana Wenger Morris

I was excited to read that a movie had been made of Chekhov's *The Sea Gull. The Sea Gull* seems very contemporary, even though it was written over ninety years ago. It is what teachers would call a perfect example of "universality." Two very "now" terms, isolation and alienation, although not used in the play, describe the situation of all the characters. The play begins with talk that exposes the narrowness of contemporary theater and dramatic arts. Before the play is over, talk between the major characters pries open their inner lives. That the play dramatizes these many levels of human experience makes it great. But though *The Sea Gull* is a great play, it makes a disappointing movie.

The fault is not all the play's. Sidney Lumet, the movie's director, fails in several respects. His greatest mistake is in casting. Although the cast includes fine actors and actresses, it is all wrong for the play. One of the problems is that many of the performers are so well-known that it is hard to picture them in the roles Lumet casts them in. Vanessa Redgrave seems out of place and unconvincing as Nina, a young, naive, and stagestruck country girl. Simone Signoret plays Arkadina, the aging actress who will not believe she is getting old. Arkadina arouses mixed feelings when we read the play, among them sympathy, but Signoret's film portrayal leaves us with only ill feeling. Lumet also interfered with the author's intention in directing the movie. The visual quality of movies has to be used very subtly in filming an understated play like *The Sea Gull*. Yet Lumet exaggerates with visual effects. By showing the dead body of Konstantin, who everybody knows has shot himself, the effect of the moment is lost. Between the third and fourth acts two years pass, but in the movie, the characters seem to have aged ten years. And the dialogue of the play, which gets philosophical quite often, seems unreal on the screen. On stage, the lines are believable because the human relations involved seem natural. Close-ups of people talking isolate characters and destroy the effect of the scene as a whole.

Probably the best explanation for the failure of the picture is that Chekhov is a playwright who uses little action, the very stuff that movies are made of. The stage does not allow much movement, but a film demands it. Movies also tend to shift scenes rapidly, in order to show different people doing different things. Chekhov, of course, does not allow for these shifts of scene. The play has four acts. Each act takes place in the same place. The scenery remains the same. The actors enter and exit. Finally movies have their own ways of showing change and passage of time. All a playwright has to do is announce passage of time in the program, but the same device used in movies is absurd. The most ludicrous moment in the movie version of *The Sea Gull* comes between the third and fourth acts when the words "Two Years Later" appear on the screen. At this point the viewer cannot help but be convinced that this play belongs where it was born, on the stage. □

BASIC DESCRIPTIVE OUTLINE

PROPOSITION   *The Sea Gull* is a great play but it makes a disappointing movie.

PLAN	State a proposition and develop six reasons supporting it, arranged in Nestorian order.
PARAGRAPH 1	*says:* The theme of *The Sea Gull* is very contemporary.
	does: Introduces the proposition by telling why the play is great.
PARAGRAPH 2	*says:* It is the director's fault that the movie is miscast, unsubtle, technically poor, and reproduces the philosophical dialogue badly.
	does: States five reasons for the movie's failure.
PARAGRAPH 3	*says: The Sea Gull* is a play without much action.
	does: States the main reason for the movie's failure.

☐ EXAMPLE ESSAY ――――――――――――――――――――

Euthanasia: A Violation of Human Life

Karen Dickman Friedman

Over the years, medical science has progressed until it has provided us with cures for many diseases that were once considered terminal. Polio is gone. Small pox is gone. Tuberculosis has become less of a threat. Yet we are still left with many incurable diseases, and our modern age has provided us with a whole slew of new diseases yet to be explored: new viruses, new cancers, and, of course, AIDS. As a result, the issue of euthanasia is still with us as well. Euthanasia is defined in the clean, clinical way typical of the medical profession as "the mode or act of inducing death painlessly or as a relief from pain." More commonly, we know it as "mercy killing." Ending a person's pain seems on the face of it such a kind and humane thing to do, for the benefit of the victims of pain and for the benefit of their loved ones watching them suffer. But it is not what it seems. Euthanasia, a violation of human life, cannot be justified.

   One of the most serious problems involved in the practice of euthanasia is the difficulty of determining the validity of a person's request to die. When terminally ill but mentally competent patients choose to die, do they do so because they are depressed, and might later change their mind? Or do they choose this course because they believe that the relatives who care for them can no longer afford that care either emotionally or financially? Are the people closest to dying patients subtly coaching them, perhaps without being aware of it, to exercise the right to die by choice? Or is the request truly genuine: the patients who ask for relief really are in intolerable pain, really want to die, and are giving their rational and thoroughly considered consent? Another serious problem is the possibility that a cure for the patient's illness may soon be found. In 1921, a man diagnosed with diabetes was told that there was no hope. For two years he fought a losing battle against the disease. Then, in 1923, insulin became widely available. The man survived. Besides the last minute discovery of a cure, there are also many incidents of the remission of disease, including cancer, for no apparent reason. Prognosis is fallible. We know for certain that only death is irreversible. Where there's life, there's hope.

To many people, the most persuasive argument against euthanasia, though, is religious. One deeply rooted religious objection is that to choose death is to play God. It is God's prerogative to determine the end of life, not man's. Religious people believe, furthermore, that the proper attitude towards life is awe and reverence. Tampering with life or ending it prematurely is a profanation of the sacred. There are also those who believe that suffering is part of the divine plan for the good of man, and therefore we must accept it. They look at suffering before death from a spiritual point of view, as a time of absolution. People who suffer undergo punishment in this world instead of the world to come. Even secularized, this spiritual argument is significant. As a famous British lawyer once said with regard to euthanasia, "the final stage of an incurable illness ... can be a vital part of a person's life, reconciling him to life and to death and giving him interior peace." □

▷ EXERCISE 7   STRAW MAN

Exercises 7 and 8 are designed to give you further practice in paragraph development.

Begin once again by exploring issues raised by your own experience, as in exercises 1 through 4. But this time look for a controversial topic, one about which you think other people's opinions may differ a great deal from your own. In this exercise, you will set up one of those opposing opinions as a straw man and knock it down.

The assignment asks for a five-hundred word position paper in three paragraphs: an introductory paragraph ending with a proposition and two paragraphs of exploration, explanation, or defense. Each paragraph develops a single reason that supports or explains the proposition. Don't write a "conclusion." But write a descriptive outline that explains what the essay *does* and *says*. Write the essay from the inside out.

The difference between this exercise and exercises 5 and 6 lies in the way you defend the proposition in paragraphs 2 and 3. In exercises 5 and 6 you argued positively. You presented the best reasons you could to explore, explain, or defend your proposition. Here you argue negatively. You acknowledge that yours is not the only possible position to take on the issue, and you oppose those who think differently. This means that in paragraph 2 you will give reasons *against* the position you take in the proposition. Set out in paragraph 2 to show that the position you have taken is wrong. Then in paragraph 3 support the proposition by refuting the argument against it made in paragraph 2.

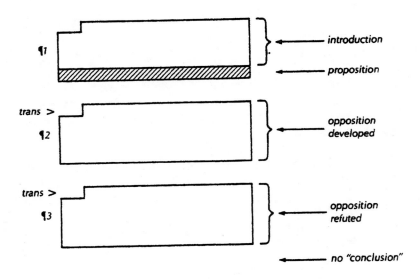

The transition sentence at the beginning of paragraph 2 should indicate clearly that the position you take in that paragraph is not your own but someone else's—someone who would disagree with your proposition. At the beginning of paragraph 2 you can say something like the following:

There are two schools of thought on this issue. One says . . .

Some people take exactly the opposite position. They say . . .

That, in any case, is what Democrats would say. Republicans, on the other hand, would object strenuously . . .

The lumber industry opposes this environmental position as being extreme . . .

In contrast, the National League resisted the temptation to use designated hitters on grounds that . . .

The transition sentence at the beginning of paragraph 3, then, should indicate clearly that you are now going to support the proposition directly by refuting the position taken in paragraph 2. At the beginning of paragraph 3 you can say something like the following:

The other school of thought finds all of these arguments untenable. It says . . .

But that position is obviously illogical . . .

Throughout the campaign, the Democrats have refuted these arguments, saying . . .

Naturally the environmentalists regard every one of these arguments offered by the lumber industry as biased in favor of business interests . . .

The American League says that all these reasons against using designated hitters are old-fashioned in the age of television . . .

Review the assignment for exercise 5 again before you begin. Go about writing this essay as you went about writing that one. By now you should be getting in the habit of approaching an essay in the following way:

- Think of a topic.
- Think of a tentative proposition.
- Think of ways to explore, explain, or defend your position.
- Explore, explain, or defend the proposition in the form required by the assignment.
- Write an introduction.
- Check the transitions.
- Write a descriptive outline and revise the essay.
- Read the paper aloud and polish it.
- Make a final copy.

COLLABORATIVE LEARNING

Task 1 Reading Aloud

Follow the instructions for reading aloud on p. 55.

Task 2 *Essay Exchange and Peer Conference*

Follow the instructions for essay exchange and peer conference on p. 55.

☐ EXAMPLE ESSAY ————————————————————

Keep NASA Going

Eric Raps

"Man has always gone where he has been able to go," said astronaut Michael Collins after successfully completing his moon mission. Many people share this belief. People should go to the moon, and beyond, because now for the first time in history we can go. We can at last satisfy our curiosity about bodies in space other than Earth. Without NASA, the United States space program, we would never have been able to explore this new frontier. Our moon landing was truly the climax of modern science and technology, and yet space exploration is only just beginning. We must keep NASA going, but not just to satisfy our pride and curiosity. NASA is important for the welfare of us all.

Not everyone agrees with this point of view. Ever since the space program began, it has been criticized as humanly irrelevant. Some people have called a moon shot nothing but a big toy for grownups. Others have called the space program an example of American middle-class conspicuous consumption in a category with oversized cars, water skiing, and snowmobiles. Worst of all, some say, not only has the space program accomplished nothing of value, it has wasted money that should have been spent on overdue social programs. According to this view, our cities, our national parks, our educational and health programs, our legal systems, have all been deprived of funds they need to modernize and serve people properly. People who take this position are fond of quoting figures that show how many hospitals, school lunches, playgrounds, drug addiction centers, or reforestation plans could be financed with the money spent on one moon shot.

What these people fail to understand is that space projects are exactly the sort of activity human beings should be spending their money on to advance knowledge and technology, so that the many human problems we have can get solved. The amount of money spent on a moon shot is trivial compared with the amount of money the United States spends in even a few months on warfare and defense weapons. And that money really does go down the drain, because war is unproductive, weapons are continually becoming obsolete, and killing people is, to say the least, a corrupt and self-defeating activity. In contrast, what space exploration does is help improve the conception human beings have of themselves. It creates a belief among people all over Earth that the world is small, vulnerable, and absolutely unique. As a result people will become impatient with poor living conditions and a polluted environment. In short space exploration has the effect of centering our attention on the quality of human life. It contributes to man's understanding of the human condition, of the interdependence of all people, and therefore of the need, to put it in very simple terms, to be better housekeepers here on Earth and to take better care of each other. ☐

BASIC DESCRIPTIVE OUTLINE

PROPOSITION	NASA is important for the welfare of us all.
PLAN	Oppose the proposition, and then refute the opposition.
PARAGRAPH 1	*says:* Space exploration satisfies our curiosity and pride.
	does: Introduces the proposition by quoting an authority and discussing the quotation.
PARAGRAPH 2	*says:* Space exploration is wasteful.
	does: Opposes the proposition with one argument.
PARAGRAPH 3	*says:* Space exploration changes our awareness of ourselves and what life is about.
	does: Refutes the opposition by showing that it is narrow-minded.

(The difference between basic and detailed descriptive outlines is explained in Part Three: Constructive Reading. See also the example basic and detailed descriptive outlines written for the same essay on pp. 77–78.)

▷ EXERCISE 8   STRAW MAN AND ONE REASON

This assignment, like the last one, asks for a five-hundred word position paper in three paragraphs: an introductory paragraph ending with a proposition and two paragraphs of exploration, explanation, or defense.

Each paragraph develops a single reason that supports or explains the proposition. Don't write a "conclusion." But write a descriptive outline that explains what the essay *does* and *says*. Write the essay from the inside out.

What distinguishes this exercise is that it combines two types of exploration, explanation, or defense, the one used in exercise 5 and the one used in exercise 7. You recognize here, as you did in exercise 7, that there are other positions that can be taken on the issue, but you refute them. Then, as you did in exercise 5, you argue in favor of your own position.

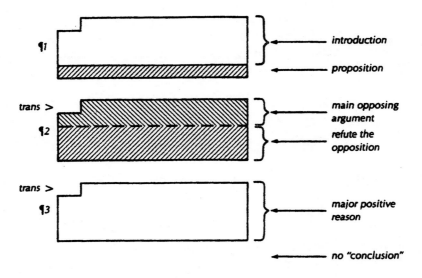

In this essay begin paragraph 2 as you began paragraph 2 in exercise 7, with an argument that opposes the position you have taken in the proposition. **In the rest of paragraph 2 refute that opposition.** Then in paragraph 3 develop a positive reason in support of your position, just as you did in paragraphs 2 and 3 of exercise 5.

The transition sentence at the beginning of paragraph 2 should make clear that the position taken in that paragraph is an opposing position, not your own. Later in the paragraph include a transition sentence or phrase that indicates that what follows supports your position by refuting the opposing position. That is, paragraph 2 in this exercise does in a single paragraph (paragraph 2) what you did in paragraphs 2 and 3 together in exercise 7.

The transition to paragraph 3 should indicate that this paragraph supports your position in a different, more positive way. You can say something like the following:

But this conflict misses the point. The real reason that . . .

The most logical argument is clearly that . . .

Whatever the two national parties say on this issue, most voters today seem to have it pretty much figured out for themselves. The position most people seem to take is . . .

Reasonable people are likely to take the environmentalist position today, however, because . . .

Since the two leagues have now gone their own way on the issue of the designated hitter, the fans have gotten the best of the deal because . . .

Begin once again by thinking over your own experience and what you have learned in other courses in order to find an issue that you can see has two sides (even though you may agree with only one of them).

Write a descriptive outline and use it to help you revise.

COLLABORATIVE LEARNING

Task 1   Reading Aloud

Follow the instructions for reading aloud on p. 55.

Task 2   Essay Exchange and Peer Conference

Follow the instructions for essay exchange and peer conference on p. 55.

☐ EXAMPLE ESSAY ————————————————

A Flood of Debate

Jay Blickstein

Curt Flood was one of baseball's finest outfielders. Or at least he was until the 1970 baseball season. That year, Flood was traded from the Saint Louis Cardinals to the Philadelphia Phillies. Rather than be separated from his home and business interests in Saint Louis, Flood sat out the entire season and legally challenged one of the pillars of baseball's establishment: the so-called "reserve clause." The clause, which bound a player to a team until the team chose to release him, was used by the Cardinal management to justify Flood's trade. Flood argued, however, that the reserve clause was a form of "involuntary servitude," and reduced baseball players to slaves, to be bought and sold at a team's discretion. I could not agree with him more. Baseball's reserve clause had to be abolished.

The management of almost every big-league team defended the validity of the reserve clause. They claimed that it kept ballplayers on the teams that had spent so much time and money developing their talent. The clause also prevented a bidding war between teams for big-league talent and lent order and stability to the game. But these arguments lose all validity when the reserve clause is considered from the player's viewpoint. Even though a team spends time and money developing a ballplayer's talent, he amply repays the team by drawing in the huge crowds that come to see him in action. Certainly the big-league teams can agree among themselves to prevent a bidding war, even without the reserve clause. The baseball establishment's claim that a reserve clause gives the game order and stability is disproved by such incidents as the 1919 "Black Sox" scandal, in which eight players were expelled from baseball for accepting payoffs from gamblers. The reason for the players' actions: woefully inadequate salaries, thanks to the reserve clause.

But baseball's reserve clause had to be abolished for a much more important reason—the way it affected ballplayers as human beings. When a player signed a major-league contract, he was in effect signing away his soul and was reduced to being bought or sold at a club owner's whim. Often, a ballplayer was sent against his will to a city far away from home, family, and friends. A player also could be kept in a city he did not like, and with a team he did not want to play for. Consequently, the player suffered and his performance on the field suffered as well. The team lost, baseball lost, and so did the fans. □

BASIC DESCRIPTIVE OUTLINE

PROPOSITION   Baseball's reserve clause had to be abolished.

PLAN   To oppose the proposition, refute the opposition, and develop one positive reason in support of the proposition.

PARAGRAPH 1   *says:* Because he was traded against his will, Curt Flood began a court fight against the reserve clause.

does: Introduces the proposition by telling the story of one man's struggle against an oppressive rule.

PARAGRAPH 2   *says:* Baseball's establishment had its reasons for supporting the reserve clause, but they lose their validity when considered from the player's view-point.

does: Opposes the proposition and then refutes the opposition.

PARAGRAPH 3   *says:* The reserve clause had to be abolished because it adversely affected ballplayers as human beings.

does: Develops a major positive reason in support of the proposition.

(The difference between basic and detailed descriptive outlines is explained in Part Three: Constructive Reading. See also the example basic and detailed descriptive outlines written for the same essay on pp. 77–78.)

▷ EXERCISE 9   CONCESSION

This is the last assignment in Part Two, offering you the last in the series of templates or patterns to use as a guide for choosing reasons to support your position, for arranging reasons in an effective sequence of explanatory subordination, and for relating or linking reasons to each other and to the essay's proposition. Like the rest, it is a five-hundred word, three-paragraph position paper with a descriptive outline and no "conclusion."

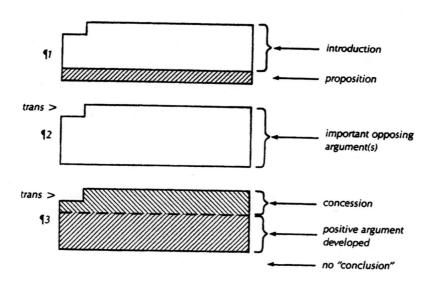

The diagram indicates that this paper is like exercises 7 and 8. You present an important argument against the position you have taken in your proposition. But in this exercise, instead of refuting this opposing view, at the beginning of paragraph 3 you **concede the validity of the opposing view.** Then you offer your own defense of the proposition in spite of this concession, and explain that your position is also valid, and is, you believe, the stronger of the two.

This is a more tactful and practical explanation or defense than the one used in exercises 7 and 8. In those exercises you acknowledged that other points of view exist, but you treated the people who hold those views rather badly. You implied or stated flatly that they were wrong, and you showed why. For writing practice, that was acceptable. The purpose was to learn to discover the opposing views and find out in what way those views were vulnerable. But simply to refute other people's views abruptly is obviously not the best way to change their minds, not to mention remaining friends with them.

A more tactful and therefore more friendly and politic approach is to acknowledge that there might be something to another person's position. So in this exercise you show that you do realize that many issues may be approached and resolved in two (or more) reasonable ways. In most of our everyday affairs, you imply, other people's opinions are often just as sensible and legitimate—from their point of view—as your own. In this essay you take this fact into consideration, even as you strive to make those who may oppose you willing to consider your opinions and judgments.

As in exercise 8, the transition at the beginning of paragraph 2 in this essay should make clear whose argument you are giving: someone else's, not your own. You should then develop and explain that opposing view thoroughly and fairly. In a concession essay it is important not to misrepresent or understate the opposition's case. The reason for this is that in the transition to paragraph 3 you will be conceding that the alternative position you have just outlined is neither unreasonable nor irresponsible. You are taking it seriously. Nevertheless, your transition continues, there is more to be said in favor of the position you have taken in the proposition of this essay. This is the position that the rest of paragraph 3 supports.

To find a topic for this exercise, think carefully about your own interests, and especially about why and how your interests seem to conflict with the interests of other people whom you respect.

Don't forget to write a descriptive outline and use it to improve your essay.

Collaborative Learning

Task 1   Reading Aloud

Follow the instructions for reading aloud on p. 55.

Task 2   *Essay Exchange and Peer Conference*

This collaborative learning exercise takes a step beyond those offered in exercises 5 through 8. It asks you to evaluate your classmate's essay after you write a descriptive outline of it.

Exchange essays with another writer in the class, but keep the descriptive outline that you wrote of your own essay.

Write a descriptive outline of your partner's essay.

Then **write an evaluation of your partner's essay**, following the instructions for peer evaluation in Part Three: Constructive Reading and the Example Descriptive and Evaluative Peer Review, p. 177.

In the next class, confer with your partner. First, examine the two descriptive outlines of your essay, your own and your partner's. Underline where they differ. Try to discover why the two of you described the same essay in different ways. Discuss how to make both descriptions more thorough and accurate.

Then read your evaluation of each other's essay aloud to each other. Help each other plan a revision that will improve the essays in every way you can. As a reader, help the writer know what you think the essay needs to help you understand it. As a writer, ask your reader to help you improve parts of the essay that you are still not satisfied with.

Write a note at the end of your descriptive outline explaining how the conference went from your point of view. If you think now that you would like to make some changes in your essay, in the descriptive outline you wrote of it, or in both, say so in your note and explain.

Revise the essay if you think it needs it.

☐ EXAMPLE ESSAY ――――――――――――――――――――――

Project Head Start

Lucille Tornatore Orlando

No project for disadvantaged children has received the public attention given to Head Start. Project Head Start is a program for preschool children that was developed and funded by the Office of Economic Opportunity. It was created with the idea of helping young children overcome the deficiencies of their early environment. Children were to come from the ghetto areas of cities, rural areas, Indian reservations, and Eskimo villages. The program was conceived in November 1964, and it began in June 1965. While it was being planned, the project was referred to as the Kiddie Corps. It was expected at that time that fifty to one-hundred-thousand children would be involved in the eight-week summer program. By late February 1965, the response was so great that the estimated enrollment was raised to between five and six hundred thousand. The project also eventually involved a hundred-thousand adults: parents, teachers, physicians, psychologists, and social workers. Experts from every branch of social studies, medicine, and education teamed up to give culturally deprived children a better chance at learning. The philosophy of the program came from the belief of those who initiated it that disadvantaged children need not fail in school or in life. In pursuing this goal, Project Head Start has become a necessary part of our present-day system of education.

Despite its promise, Head Start still meets with a great deal of resistance. Many local school boards and teachers complain that they sometimes do not get the money the government promised for supplies and salaries. The general public complains that disorganization in the program wastes public funds. Then, although the idea of the program generates much enthusiasm, in some places parents at first refuse to help. This is a great handicap, and members of the program struggle valiantly to overcome it. Parents simply have to help if Head Start is going to work. If children leave their preschool center only to return home to a suspicious and uninterested family, much of the progress they have made is lost. One of the things parents object to most is the age of many Head Start teachers. Some parents and community leaders feel that youthful teachers mean inexperienced teachers. Parents also complain that the grouping in classrooms is too homogeneous, an inevitable effect since the program was of course developed specifically for poor people. And finally, cynical observers note that once Head Start children enter primary school the gains they register during the preschool period tend to disappear.

Much of this criticism of Head Start is fair, factual, and substantial. Some of it is unanswerable. Like any government sponsored program, Project Head Start has had its pitfalls and imperfections. Its gains, however, have outweighed its shortcomings. The project recognizes, for example, that many American children are deprived in many ways, and that the lack of intellectual stimulation is only one of these ways. This is the main reason for its success. The program provides health services, information for parents, food for undernourished children, and means for organizing communities. Nevertheless, teaching children is its main aim. Something that helps Head Start do this job is its teacher-pupil ratio, which in general is one to thirteen. Young, fresh, innovative teachers can capitalize on the opportunity that small classes provide. Activities include art, stories, science activities, creative play, and visits to museums, parks, and landmarks. The teachers' youth also has a tendency to enhance the communication between them and their pupils. And once the initial misunderstanding and antagonism between parents and teacher are overcome, Head Start provides room for parent involvement in education. In some instances it also provides jobs for those who are unskilled but who are eager to work to help their own people. Parents serve on committees and become teacher's aides, storytellers, cooks, carpenters, and secretaries. But the biggest sign of success is the response of the children themselves. Many things middle-class children take for granted, Head Start children experience for the first time. There have been some dramatic instances of children who have never seen themselves in a mirror before or used a telephone. But for nearly all children there was a first in painting, using crayons, visiting a zoo, a supermarket, and a fire station. And to a child, these things are more than education. They are life itself. □

BASIC DESCRIPTIVE OUTLINE

PROPOSITION In pursuing this goal, Project Head Start has become a necessary part of our present-day system of education.

PLAN Raise arguments opposing the proposition, and then, conceding the validity of some of these arguments, offer reasons in defense of the proposition.

PARAGRAPH 1 *says:* Project Head Start began in 1964 to give culturally deprived children a better chance to learn.

does: Introduces the proposition by describing a public program.

PARAGRAPH 2 *says:* Head Start has met with a great deal of resistance.

does: Gives the arguments against the program and points out its failures.

PARAGRAPH 3 *says:* The achievements of Head Start in helping children learn outweigh its shortcomings.

does: Concedes the validity of some criticism, and then argues in favor of the proposition.

DETAILED DESCRIPTIVE OUTLINE

PROPOSITION In pursuing this goal, Project Head Start has become a necessary part of our present-day system of education.

PLAN   Raise arguments opposing the proposition, and then, conceding the validity of some of these arguments, offer reasons in defense of the proposition.

PARAGRAPH 1   *says:* Project Head Start began in 1964 to give culturally deprived children a better chance to learn.

does: Introduces the proposition by describing a government program. Sentences 1 through 4 state its goal and give a general description. Sentences 5 through 8 trace its early history. Sentences 6 through 8 state expectations and outcome. Sentences 9 through 10 describe the program's human resources. Sentence 11 restates its goal as a general principle.

PARAGRAPH 2   *says:* Head Start has met with a great deal of resistance.

does: Gives the arguments against the program and points out its failures. Sentence 1 makes a transition by introducing arguments against the proposition. Sentences 2 through 10 classify criticism of the program by source. This section has two parts. Sentences 2 through 3 describe criticism from two sources. Sentences 4 through 10 detail criticism from a major source and are subdivided still further: sentences 4 through 7, criticism by passive resistance and its effects; sentences 8 through 10, complaints. Sentence 11 describes evidence of failure.

PARAGRAPH 3   *says:* The achievements of Head Start in helping children learn outweigh its shortcomings.

does: Concedes the validity of some criticism, and then argues in favor of the proposition. Sentences 1 through 3 concede the limitations as explained in paragraph 2. Sentence 4 is a transition that reevaluates the opposition. Sentences 5 through 8 define the program's rationale as a list of goals. Sentences 9 through 21 analyze its success in achieving these goals. Sentences 9 through 12 define one cause of success. Sentences 13 through 15 define a second. Sentences 16 through 21 describe a sign of success, giving striking details in sentences 18 through 21 and showing why this particular supporting point is so important.

(The difference between basic and detailed descriptive outlines is explained in Part Three: Constructive Reading, p. 147)

☐ EXAMPLE ESSAY ─────────────────────────────────

The Blessings of Urbanization

Annette Brill

I have always enjoyed living in a big city. There is a constant feeling of activity, movement, hustle and bustle. There is a sense of things happening: theaters and music halls, brightly lit streets, busy crowds. At lunch hour, when I walk down the streets of the city I live in, it seems to me that I can feel the pulse of the city in my veins. People walk faster in the city, talk faster in the city, and always seem to have someplace to go and something to do. I take these blessings of city living so much for granted that it's hard for me to imagine what life must have been like before big cities existed. And all the really big cities that I know simply didn't exist two hundred years ago. Most of them became what they are today during the rapid urbanization of the nineteenth-century Industrial Revolution. In those days, urbanization was a symbol of progress and optimism. It meant that, for the most part, the world was getting better and better for more and more people every day. And urbanization still means that today.

Of course there are many people who hate city life and will do anything to get out of town into the country. They think that urbanization was a disaster. And they are right about the beginning of urbanization. Throughout the middle of the nineteenth century there was not room enough for everyone who wanted to live in cities. Cities became overcrowded. Developers built long rows of the smallest possible buildings, stuffed with the smallest possible apartments, crammed onto the smallest possible lots. These buildings lacked sun and fresh air, they had no backyards or front yards, and only an alley separated one row of houses from the next. Living conditions were unsanitary and unhealthy, with open drains and sewers running down the middle of the streets. Water became contaminated. People died of diseases that spread like wildfire. People could only accept these life-threatening, overcrowded conditions fatalistically.

People who condemn these horrible conditions are right to do so. No human being should be expected to live in them, including the millions still forced to do so. And yet, for all its limitations, in the long run urbanization has had more positive effects on modern life than negative ones. Many of these benefits are so familiar today that it is easy to forget that not long ago they were novelties. Two of them are fresh running water and sanitary plumbing. Lack of drinkable water and the difficulty of disposing of human waste in big cities finally forced reformers to realize that many of the diseases that regularly wiped out urban populations could be overcome by piping clean water in and piping out the waste. These simple changes in the way people thought about disease were related to some much more sophisticated changes. Belief in the theory that diseases are caused by germs and the effort to improve hospital hygiene also arose at about the same time in urban settings to meet urban needs. Soon mortality rates began to decline. On the average people actually began living longer in cities than in the country. Longer, healthier life meant more need for greater mobility within cities and between them. Horse-drawn vehicles added to the urban filth, but electrified streetcars and trains turned out to be fast, comfortable, and convenient. Today, not even people who love the country could get along without such improvements in health and mobility as these, designed originally to make life in big, modern cities safe, lively, and satisfying. □

NOTES FOR PART TWO

CRITICAL ISSUES IN WRITING POSITION PAPERS

TOPICS

This course limits the form you write in by asking you to write five-hundred word essays in three paragraphs and to arrange their formal elements in predictable ways: proposition, transitions, and reasons. This formal limitation, assuring your readers that they will always know where to find those formal elements, frees them to concentrate on what you have to say.

The course compensates for these formal limitations by giving you freedom to write on any topic you choose. As Part One says, all that limits the range of topics that you can write about in this course are your opinions, your feelings, and your experience, including your experience as a reader.

But the freedom the course gives you as a writer to write on any topic limits your freedom as a reader. If *you* can write about almost anything you want to write about, your classmates can too. So all of you have to be willing to read about anything any one of you decides to write about.

To put it another way, just as the course asks you to try writing on some topics that may be new and unfamiliar to you, it also asks you as a reader to be receptive to some new and unfamiliar topics and some opinions that you don't necessarily agree with. Moreover, the course asks you to be a constructive reader. That is, it asks you to learn how to help your fellow students write effectively on topics that may be familiar to them but unfamiliar to you and maybe even help them explain opinions that you do not agree with.

The course asks you to learn to work with your fellow students on unfamiliar topics and opinions not only to help others but to help yourself. Helping other students work on unfamiliar topics and ideas may help you learn how to understand and come to terms with topics that are new, strange, complex, maybe even troubling. But it may turn out that you will someday find some of these very topics and ideas interesting and rewarding yourself. (See Collaborative Learning Task: Topic Interviews, p. 30.)

INTRODUCTIONS

When you read a finished essay, the first thing you read is the introduction. But an introduction is not usually the first thing that writers write. The purpose of this note on introductions is to help you begin thinking about writing introductions in a way that may differ quite a bit from the way you are in the habit of thinking about writing them.

WARMING UP

Like most writers, when you first sit down to write you usually have to warm up. You have to write something that will get you into the topic, get your mind working, and get your words flowing. Some writers may take a sentence or two to warm up, others may take several paragraphs, some may take several pages. Invention exercises, such as free writing, brainstorming, and other exercises found in Part One can also be used to warm up for writing.

But the writing you do to warm up seldom makes a good introduction to an essay. Although you may eventually include some warm-up material in your introduction, that material usually needs a good deal of cutting and revision. A lot of it may never get into the finished essay at all. But it has served its purpose if it has helped you discover a tentative position that you want to explore, explain, or defend in the essay you are setting out to write.

In contrast, an essay's introduction is not what *you* needed to warm up to a topic. An introduction is what *readers* will need to warm up to a topic. Warm ups begin wherever you need to begin. Introductions begin wherever you think your readers need to begin. An introduction is calculated to lead readers to the proposition of an essay. You can't lead people when you don't know where you're going yourself. So you can't introduce readers to what you're saying until you know what you're saying yourself. You can't introduce readers to a proposition before you've written it, and maybe not until you have explored, explained, and defended it.

WRITING AN INTRODUCTION

That's why this book teaches you to write essays from the inside out. It asks you to think of an introduction not as the first thing to write in an essay but rather the third thing. After you warm up, **the first thing to write is a tentative proposition.** A *tentative proposition* states the position that you think you will take in the essay. **The second thing to write are some paragraphs that explore, explain, or defend the proposition. Then, the third thing to write is an introduction.**

Once you understand this principle of writing from the inside out you will find it fairly easy to write good introductions. The main purpose of an introduction is to make contact with your readers by providing them with a context of issues that they will recognize. What you are trying to do is help readers see how the position you are taking in the essay is related to their own experiences, what they are interested in, or what they already know.

To do that, you have to acknowledge that most readers have other things on their minds than you have on yours. They are likely to use language that is somewhat different from the language that you are using in the essay. They are interested in ideas, issues, and events that are not quite the same as the ones you want them to turn their attention to by reading your essay.

Your task in the introduction is to make your readers feel willing to put aside their own interests and concerns for a moment and consider your interests and concerns, or put aside their normal way of understanding something for a moment and consider your way of understanding it. To do that, you have to talk about ideas, issues, or events in the introduction that your readers are likely to be familiar with and find language that your readers will respond to.

So to write an effective introduction, you have to find points where your position is related to the experience, interests, or knowledge of your readers. You have to prepare them to care about the topic and to be receptive to your position by appealing to their normal, everyday way of thinking about things, what they are likely to know, how they are likely to be feeling, or their general sympathy for their fellow human beings. In an introduction you may also want to appeal to your readers' sense of sound reasoning by making your assumptions explicit, by stating the facts that lie behind the position you are taking in the essay, or by defining important terms. The best introductions assume that the reader is thinking, "Why should I bother to read this? What's in it for me? How does it affect my life? How is it related to what I already know or what interests me?"

Another way to define introductions is to say that they set the scene for the position you are taking in the essay. You may want to take this definition literally. Tell a story or write a description that vividly establishes the situation or problem that the proposition addresses. You may already have written some material of this sort if you wrote personal or family stories for exercise 1. Because these stories are likely to be lively and distinctive, they may become an important part of a lively and distinctive introduction. (There is more about contexts of issues in Assumptions, p. 132, and in Contexts of Issues, Shareable Concerns, p. 197.)

Suppose, for example, that we set out to write an introductory paragraph for the essay about cars that we used as an example in exercise 5 (p. 44). First, we could describe a current situation that everyone would recognize (there are cars everywhere). Then we could point out something wrong with that situation (some people complain about cars). Finally, we could suggest what the solution to the problem might turn out to be (people may find other means of transportation). This solution then would lead to the position we took in the paper: Cars may be on the way out.

the current situation

Cars seem to be everywhere today. We find them in the desert and the mountains, the forests and the plains. They jam the city streets. They flow like rivers along our superhighways. There are more cars on the road today than ever before. Yet,

a problem

there are signs that people are not entirely happy with this situation. We complain about air pollution and high accident rates. We worry when we read the news that even though domestic cars have improved a great deal in recent years, still another manufacturer has had to recall thousands of cars because the brakes are defective or the gas line leaks. More and more people are traveling by plane and train. Bicycles are increasingly popular in many cities and towns. Some two-car families are selling their second car because they simply can't afford the cost of insurance and upkeep. Of course, it is hard to imagine how we could get along without cars entirely. But it is certainly reasonable to speculate that, as people choose

transition to proposition

other ways of getting around, travel by car may have reached its high-water mark and begun to recede. It seems fantastic and unlikely, yet it is now possible to say that in the future the trend will be for people to use cars as we know them less *proposition* rather than more. In fact, it looks as if cars may be on the way out as our major means of transportation.

¶2 *transition*   And it is high time they were. The world oil supply, which cars depend on for fuel, has been diminishing at the rate of . . .

Some Types of Introductions

It is impossible to list all the types of introductions that can prepare readers to consider what you have to say and encourage them to read your essay with interest. Here are a few to consider:

- **Explain the assumptions you are making** in a way that shows that your readers probably make them too or could easily agree with them. (See Assumptions, p. 132, and paragraph 1 of "Family and School," p. 319.)
- **Define key terms you will be using** in language that your readers are likely to be familiar with. (See paragraph 1 of "The Pluralist Model of Power and Modern Society," p. 332.)
- **Tell an amusing or striking story or an anecdote** that will make your readers interested in your topic. (See paragraph 1 of "Going Back to School," p. 323.)
- **Give some historical background** that shows how the problem you are addressing got started. (See paragraph 1 of "Project Head Start", p. 75.)
- **Describe the problem** that you will be suggesting a solution to. (See paragraph 1 of "Kingsgate High School," p. 240.)
- **Describe a place, object, person, or event** relevant to your topic. (See paragraph 1 of "What Should Patients Be Told?", p. 220.)
- **Quote an authority** whom your readers are likely to respect and explain the relevance of the quotation. (See the beginning of "Substitutes for Violence," p. 367.)
- **Summarize** the main points of something you have read and will be drawing on in exploring, explaining, or defending the position you are taking in the essay. (See paragraph 1 of "Aspects of Political Crime," p. 263.)
- **Describe an existing situation** that you think people would (or should) like to change. (See "Euthanasia: A Violation of Human Life," p. 64, and "The Benefits of a Writing Community," p. 325.)

(There is more about introductions in Part Four: Reaching Out to Members of Other Communities, p. 189.)

COLLABORATIVE LEARNING

Follow the instructions for working in consensus groups on p. 20.

Task Descriptive Outline of an Introduction

Choose two or more example essays in this book that do not have a descriptive outline attached and read the first paragraph of each one aloud.

Draft a detailed descriptive outline of each introductory paragraph. The outline should explain how the paragraph introduces the proposition in each case. Be sure to explain how the paragraph makes a transition between the introductory material and the proposition.

Then classify the introductions by type. What sort of introduction is each one? Are they all different? Or do some of them do the same sort of thing in a somewhat different way?

PROPOSITIONS

Suppose you were told after you had just finished writing an essay, "Don't hand that essay in. Tear it up. Save only one sentence—the sentence that states most succinctly the position you are taking in the paper. Throw the rest away."

That would be a cruel thing to do to any writer, and it is not likely to happen to you. But if it did, the one sentence you should want to save would be your essay's proposition sentence, the sentence that states your position. In all of the essay exercises assigned in this book, that sentence would be the last sentence in the first paragraph.

The proposition of an essay is important because it states the point of the essay. A proposition, or position sentence, is a generalization that you can explore, explain, or defend. It is also a sentence that someone else could agree with, challenge, deny, or oppose. *Proposition:* "Cars may be on the way out." *Response:* "Hey, wait a minute, no they're not! What makes you think so?" or "I'm not so sure. Look at it this way." or "Gee, you know, I think you may be on to something there. Just the other day driving home I began to think. . . ."

A proposition is a statement that you explore, explain, or defend in a way that will lead readers to think it is convincing, worth considering, or persuasive enough to refute. A proposition states your opinion. In writing an essay that explores, explains, or defends that opinion, you turn your opinion into a proposal or a position, your feelings into ideas, your hunches into judgments worthy of the reader's consideration. To be judgmental does not have to carry a negative connotation. You make judgments all the time, whenever you decide which color shirt to buy, what to have for lunch, which movie to recommend to a friend. A judgment is a decision. It is what, for the moment, you want to say.

The proposition is therefore the essay's most important sentence. Your introduction prepares readers to consider the proposition. The defense explores, explains, or defends the proposition. Transitions relate paragraphs to the proposition and to each other. The proposition is the key to every transition you write, since every part of your essay has to refer to it in one way or another.

Because the proposition is so important to an essay, you should concentrate on writing short, clear, simple propositions. A proposition should not have more operative words, and should not establish more relationships between those operative words than you can explore, explain, or defend adequately in the length of essay you are going to write. *Operative words* are the words that do the work in a sentence. They are the words that carry the most weight and require the most explanation. For example, in the sentence "Operative words are the words that do the work in a sentence," the words that need explanation are *operative words, work,* and *sentence.* The verb phrase *do the work* establishes a relationship that needs explanation between two of those operative words.

That is another way to think about the proposition of an essay. It creates the most important relationships in the essay: between the introduction and the rest of the essay, among the paragraphs of the essay, and among the essay's operative words.

Consider the following examples. Most of these sentences, if you used them as a proposition, would probably be limited enough to explore, explain, or defend in a five-hundred word, three-paragraph position paper in *Short Course* form.

> Cars may be on the way out.
>
> This school should replace the alphabetical grading system with a pass—no credit system.
>
> Although Caesear dies in the first scene of Act III, his character dominates the whole play.
>
> The city is an excellent place to bring up a family.
>
> A farm is an excellent place to bring up a family.
>
> The suburbs are a terrible place to bring up a family.
>
> Children are cruel sometimes because they are selfish.
>
> Peacekeeping, as the UN practices it, is doomed to failure.
>
> We can solve the smog problem by keeping cars out of our cities.

UNCLEAR PROPOSITIONS

These sentences are short, clear, and simple. They are also relatively limited in scope. That is, their operative words cars

alphabetical grading system

bringing up a family

the smog problem

are relatively easy to define. The relationships between the operative words in each sentence are expressed by the following verbs or verb phrases:

may be on the way out

replace

dominates

bring up

doomed

keeping out

These too are relatively easy to explain and specify.

But sentence length alone may be deceptive. Some short sentences express ideas that are too broad to serve as the proposition of a short essay. Some operative words refer to too many different kinds of things or to things that are too hard to define, or the relationships they express among these words are too vague or complex. The following sentence is an example:

People should think primarily of themselves in trying to adjust to society.

This sentence would be very hard to defend adequately in a short essay. The key words, *people* and *society*, are all-encompassing. The sentence distinguishes neither which people the writer is talking about nor which society. It states neither the time nor the place in which these people and their society exist. The word *primarily* is ambiguous. Does it mean first in time or first in priority? The principal action referred to in the phrase *trying to adjust to society* has for many years been the subject of complex and inconclusive debate among professionals in the fields of psychology, sociology, anthropology, and political science. It would be impossible to define briefly the main verb in the phrase *think of themselves*. And the word *should* makes it unclear whether the writer is merely asserting a prejudice or is implying instead some tested method or proven way of life.

It is easy to sympathize with writers who try to explore, explain, or defend such a proposition. They want to say something important. That is an understandable motive. Furthermore, writers may be afraid that if they take a position that is limited or simple, readers will think that they have limited or simple minds.

But simple positions do not necessarily represent simple minds. $E = mc^2$ is after all a statement that is simply expressed. So is "All men are created equal." But neither the author of the first (Albert Einstein) nor the author of the second (Thomas Jefferson) had a simple mind. As you become more experienced as a writer, you will understand that in most cases the best way to say something important is to say it as briefly, clearly, and simply as you can.

In any case, that rule applies to the essays in this book. You cannot solve the problems of the world in five hundred words. So for these essays, take a position that you can develop thoroughly in the limits of time and space set by the assignment. (There is more about making succinct and readable sentences in Style, p. 137, and in Paragraph Development, p. 111.)

HOW TO TEST A PROPOSITION

One way to tell if a proposition is limited enough for the time and space you have at your disposal is to **look for the operative words in it and the central relationship among those words** expressed by the main verb of the sentence.

Suppose, for example, that you were trying to decide whether or not to use the following sentence as a proposition:

Although Caesar dies in the first scene of Act III, his character dominates the whole play.

This sentence is about Shakespeare's play *Julius Caesar*. At sixteen words, it is a fairly long sentence. It is almost twice as long as several other examples listed previously. The question is, is it too long and complicated to use as the proposition of an essay?

You can answer this question by taking the sentence apart. It has two sections, a subordinate clause

Although Caesar dies in the first scene of Act III

and a main clause.

his character dominates the whole play.

For the purposes of the short essay you have been assigned to write (five hundred words, three paragraphs), the subordinate clause (Caesar dies in the first scene of Act III) doesn't count. It states one of the sentence's basic assumptions. You could establish that assumption by telling the story that the play dramatizes in your essay's introductory paragraph.

So the sentence is actually a lot shorter than it seems. Its working, or operative, part is the second half of the sentence, the main clause, six words long:

[Caesar's] character dominates the whole play.

That would be the real proposition of the essay you would write, the position you would be taking. The operative words in it are the subject of the sentence, *character*, and the verb, *dominates*. Your main task in exploring, explaining, or defending this sentence would be to define and explain the word *character* and define and explain the word *dominates*.

That seems like a reasonable thing to try to do in a short essay. But before you decide finally, you should take a closer look at those two operative words to see what issues arise when you try to define them.

The subject of the sentence, *character*, raises a number of general issues, such as what human character is and how it is dramatized in a play. The word also raises some issues that are specific to this particular play: What is the nature of Caesar's character in the play? What evidence is there in the play for deciding that his character is of one sort rather than another, and how are we to interpret that evidence? What limits our understanding of Caesar's character in this play? How could we overcome these limits?

The main verb in the sentence, *dominates*, also raises several issues, both general and specific. Two general issues that the verb raises are how characters may be said to "dominate" any literary work, and whether dominating other characters in the work physically or psychologically (or politically) is one of these ways. Issues specific to this play are related to these general issues: How exactly does Caesar dominate this play? Does he do so only by dominating other characters? If so, in what way does he dominate them? Is it psychologically, or physically, or politically? And finally, how does Caesar dominate parts of the play in which he does not appear, especially the scenes that occur after his death?

Several other words are also operative in this sentence, but they are less important than the subject and verb. These words set the conditions within which the operative words you have already looked at have significance. The name *Caesar* may raise a question about the differences between the historical figure and the character in Shakespeare's play. The way Caesar *dies* in the play, or rather the way the historical facts surrounding his death are dramatized in the play, may have something to do with your understanding of the way Caesar affects the characters who surround him. And certainly how you understand what happens in the *whole* play has something to do with your understanding of the difference between action that occurs before Caesar dies and action that occurs afterward.

Furthermore, *dominates*, the main verb in the sentence, expresses the main relationship in the sentence. As a result, if you used the sentence as a proposition, the definition and explanation of that word would be a major part of the essay.

But there is still another relationship implied in the sentence that would affect what you said. This is an implied relationship between the main clause ("his character dominates the play") and an unstated opposing view implied by the subordinate clause that introduces the sentence: that it is nonsense to think that a character who disappears from the action halfway through a play could actually dominate the play. This relationship is expressed by the transition word *although*. The sentence is written so that you would be setting out with an obstacle to overcome. Overcoming that obstacle might have to play some part in exploring, explaining, or defending the proposition.

This test of the proposition has brought to light most of the issues raised by the position you think you might take in your essay about *Julius Caesar*. Now it's time to decide whether or not to go ahead with it. Should you use the sentence as the proposition of your essay? Probably yes. The final criterion is not just how many issues a proposition raises, it is how easily you could deal with most of those issues. If you judge that your readers are likely to agree without argument to your assumptions on most of the minor issues, then you can refer to these issues in passing, or not at all. You can safely concentrate on the central issue in the sentence, expressed in the main clause: How come Caesar seems to dominate the whole play?

(There is another example analysis of operative terms in What an Essay *Says*, p. 154. See also Paragraph Development, p. 111, Some Ways to Question and Generalize, p. 31, and Assumptions, p. 132.)

PROPOSITION PITFALLS

Learning to analyze propositions in this way can help you avoid one of the most common pitfalls in writing propositions, namely, trying to say too much. It may also help you avoid some of the other difficulties writers sometimes have in writing a good proposition.

Wordiness

A *wordy* proposition (or any other sentence) is imprecise and vague. Here's an example.

Security has meant varying pursuits and differing goals for diverse periods of history.

This sentence means something like, "Security means different things to different people at different times."

(There is more about making sentences more succinct and readable in Style, p. 137, and in Some Ways to Question and Generalize, p. 31.)

Bifurcation

A *bifurcated* proposition is really two propositions in one:

These proposals are unreasonable and implementing them could make midair collision more frequent.

Each clause in this sentence says something quite different about "these proposals," and each could be explored, explained, and defended in a position paper of its own. To explain why "the proposals are unreasonable," we would have to explore the reasoning that lies behind them. To explain why "implementing the proposals would make midair collisions more frequent," we would have to discuss cause-and-effect relationships.

The sentence could be made into a nonbifurcated proposition by changing *and* to *because:*

These proposals are unreasonable *because* implementation could make midair collision more frequent.

Because indicates a cause-and-effect relationship between the dangers resulting from implementing the proposals and the writer's position that the proposals are unreasonable. The rest of the essay would explain this causal relationship, answering the question, "*Why* could these proposals make midair collision more frequent?"

A bifurcated proposition can limit an essay in three ways. First, it can give away the defense prematurely. It tips your hand, revealing subordinate points in the argument along with the main one. In the following bifurcated proposition:

Solid construction and a wide median make I-45 a very safe road.

the main point is "I-45 is a very safe road." This would be the proposition of a unified essay on this topic. In the unified essay, solid construction and a wide median would be subordinate points that the essay makes in order to support that main point. Part of the descriptive outline for such a unified essay would read something like this:

PROPOSITION   I-45 is a very safe road.

PARAGRAPH 2   *says:* One reason I-45 is safe is that the road surface is very well constructed.

PARAGRAPH 3   *says:* Another reason I-45 is safe is that it has a wide median.

But an essay with the proposition in its bifurcated form, "Solid construction and a wide median make I-45 a very safe road," would reveal these reasons ahead of time. There may of course be times when it is advisable to do just that. For example, if you are just learning how to state a clear position and explore, explain, or defend it, you may find it easier to state the major reasons in the proposition in this way. But you should work toward writing propositions that generalize the argument you are making in the essay without summarizing your argument or stating reasons in support of it. You should not summarize your argument or supporting reasons in the proposition, generally speaking, because readers are likely to lose interest in following you through the rest of the essay. Why read on when the whole argument has been succinctly summarized already?

The second way a bifurcated proposition can limit an essay is by changing its focus. It makes readers shift their attention from the position taken in the proposition to less important issues. The sentence about I-45 is an important statement because the writer has made a judgment (that the road is very safe) and takes responsibility for that judgment by supporting it. If, for example, the writer was a consultant to the Traffic Safety Commission, that expert judgment is what the commission would be paying for. The commission already knows what every commuter who drives along the road knows, that the road surface is unblemished by broken seams and potholes and that the median is wide. The commission doesn't have to pay an expert to find that out. The issue (and what the commission is paying the consultant to decide) is whether or not those two conditions mean that the road is really safe.

Therefore, what the essay says in paragraphs 2 and 3 about the road surface and the wide median is not important in itself. It is important because **it encourages readers to consider carefully the position that the writer has stated in the essay's proposition.** The writer should not let the supporting observations in paragraphs 2 and 3 deflect readers' attention from that most important issue.

The third and most important way a bifurcated proposition can limit an essay is related to the second way: It can limit an essay by disunifying it. Bifurcation tends to produce two two-paragraph essays with the same introduction instead of one three-paragraph essay. In this case, para-

bifurcated proposition

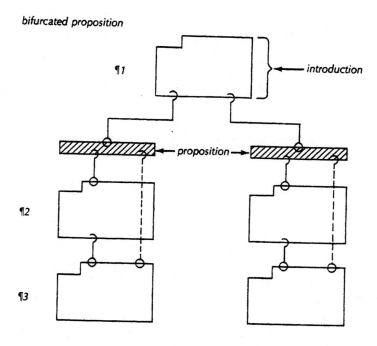

nonbifurcated proposition

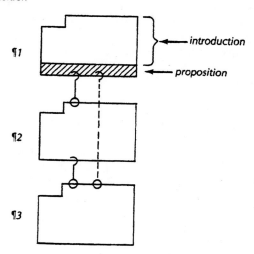

graph 2 defends one-half of the proposition, that the road is well constructed. Then paragraph 3 defends the other half, that the median is wide.

Describing the Argument

The following example describes the argument instead of stating it:

> The purpose of this essay is not to defend the president, but to present an argument for a strong presidency.

This sentence describes the strategy of the paper. It states what the essay *does*, not what it *says*. To make a defensible proposition on this subject, the writer would have to say something like

> What the United States needs now is a strong presidency.

Weak Verbs

The final pitfall to avoid in writing propositions is using weak verbs. Weak verbs understate or misstate the point you want to make. The weakest verb to use in a proposition is one that merely sets up an equation. Take for example the following tentative proposition:

> In Whitman's poetry, the sea is solitude.
> In Whitman's poetry, the sea = solitude.

It's hard to say what this sentence really means. But there are many alternatives to *is* that would make the sentence more precise and easier to explore, explain, or defend. One possibility is

> In Whitman's poetry, the sea *represents* solitude.

Here are some others.

In Whitman's poetry, the sea
{
might represent
usually represents
never represents
in part represents
symbolizes
suggests
negates
deprives the speaker of
challenges
}
solitude.

The reason for taking care in choosing the verb in a proposition sentence is that the verb is almost always an operative word. It establishes the central relationship among the other operative words in the sentence.

In the following example, the word *dog* expresses a concept. So does the word *man*. These concepts have some meaning standing alone. But their meaning increases when you relate them with a verb that is active, vivid, and exact:

The dog bit the man.
The man bit back.
Thereby hangs a tale.

(There is more about effective propositions in Descriptive Outlines, p. 152.)

COLLABORATIVE LEARNING

Follow the instructions for working in consensus groups on p. 20.

Task 1   Testing Propositions

Write out the proposition sentence from several example essays in this book. Then make the following decisions collaboratively:

1. Underline the operative words in each proposition.
2. List the issues raised by the operative words that you have underlined.
3. State the kind of relationship or action each proposition expresses. For example, the sentence "Children are cruel sometimes because they are selfish" expresses a cause-and-effect relationship. The sentence "Cars are on the way out" expresses change or decline. Other kinds of relationships that a proposition can express are change for the better, juxtaposition (one thing next to the other), one thing following another (narration or process), one thing the same as or similar to another (classification or comparison), and so on.
4. Are there any relationships or assumptions implied but unstated in any of the propositions you have tested? (For help on this question, see Assumptions, p. 132.)
5. Read the whole essay that explores, explains, or defends each proposition you have tested. Does the essay address all the issues implied in the proposition? If not, which issues does it leave out? Which does it emphasize? Why do you suppose the writer left out some of the issues implied in the proposition and emphasized others?

6. Are all the propositions you chose to test succinct and readable? What makes them so? Try revising some of these propositions to make them more succinct and readable without changing the position they are taking. (See Assumptions, p. 132.)

Task 2   *Questions That Sentences Raise*

List as many questions as you can that are generated by each of the following sentences:

We could solve the smog problem by keeping cars out of the city.

The purpose of this book is to provide a new method for teaching expository writing.

Ask not what your country can do for you; ask what you can do for your country.

I don't care what you say, I'm leaving.

If the TV doesn't work this time, I'm going to buy a new one.

REASONS

The essay exercises in Parts Two, Four, and Six ask you to give reasons that explore, explain, or defend your position. That is, they ask you to apply the principle of explanatory subordination by making a statement and then subordinating to it other statements, or reasons, that explain it. The example essays throughout this book show that these reasons can be made up of many things: judgments, examples, statistical data, things people have said or written, a law or directive, a way of going about doing something, and so on.

And yet, as this book uses the word, even though it can be many possible things, a reason is clearly one sort of thing. A *reason* is a statement that does not stand alone as the most comprehensive or important statement made in the essay. **A reason is an ingredient in the essay, one that helps readers understand or agree with some other statement that is more comprehensive and important than itself.** A statement is comprehensive when it covers many instances, not just one, and important when we value it highly. The most comprehensive and important statement in any essay is the proposition.

This book calls *reasons* what you construct to support the proposition in a position paper. One way to construct reasons—possibly the easiest way—is to use examples. The purpose of this note is to explain how to develop examples in order to support a proposition in an increasingly effective and complex way.

EXAMPLES AS REASONS

Suppose you are looking for a topic to write an essay on. You remember a talk you had with a friend of yours the other day that went like this:

YOU: You know that long Sixth Street underpass with the curve in it? I almost broke an axle there this morning on a pothole. I bet there's a pothole every fifty feet.
YOUR FRIEND: Do I know it? The lighting in that underpass was so bad last week I almost drove over into the left lane at the turn.

Obviously, you and your friend don't much like the Sixth Street underpass. That feeling is what your similar stories about similar experiences add up to when you tell them to each other in a spontaneous chat like this. You and your friend *synthesize* and make sense of some of your experiences by discovering common attitudes that have similar origins: both of you drive through the underpass to get home; both of you hate it. The considerable interest, utility, value, and personal satisfaction of your talk with your friend derives almost entirely from the common origin of the stories you have told each other and from the commonality that you feel in telling them.

The next day, as you think the conversation over, though, those two stories begin to add up to something else too, and you begin to think that what has happened to you and your friend should matter to other people as well—others who drive through the underpass and maybe even some who have never driven through it.

So you make a decision. You decide that between the potholes and the bad lighting, that underpass is really dangerous. That is, you now *infer* from the similar stories you and your friend have told each other, not the feeling you had yesterday that the two of you have something in common, but the generalization that certain characteristics of the underpass have something in common. This inference changes the way you talk about your experiences in the underpass in an important way and changes the sense you make of them. Before, you talked about the underpass as something the two of you dislike. Now you talk about it as something that's dangerous and, as a result, threatens other people as well as yourselves.

This decision is a crucial step. It opens the way for you to take a position in your essay on the dangers of the Sixth Street underpass that you can explore, explain, or defend with two reasons. Examples are the simplest kind of reason, and you just happen to have two terrific ones that you can use straight out of the can:

The Sixth Street underpass is dangerous.

For example, there is a pothole in the road surface every fifty feet. I almost broke an axle there this morning on a pothole.

And the lighting in the underpass is so bad that in some places you can't see your way. Last week a friend of mine almost swerved over into the left lane at the turn driving through there at night.

These examples fill the main requirement for reasons. Neither one stands alone as the most comprehensive and important thing you want to say, because each one is about only one aspect of the underpass. And synthesized as reasons instead of as personal anecdotes, the examples become ingredients that enhance another statement in the essay that *is* comprehensive and important: that the Sixth Street underpass is dangerous. This statement is comprehensive because danger is usually a product of several factors, not just one. It is important because danger can be a matter of life and death.

The following hook-and-box diagrams show your examples in both of the situations you have now used them in. Diagram 1 shows the examples in relation to your chat with your friend, before you converted them into reasons. We can call this relationship *narrative conversation*. Diagram 2 shows the examples in relation to the inference you drew from them after you converted them. We can call this relationship *reasoning conversation*.

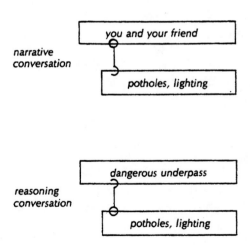

At first glance these diagrams seem to show that the two pairs of elements occupy the same position in a series of events. First, you meet your friend, then you tell the stories. First you state your inference, then you tell the stories. Because they follow in each case, the stories seem dependent on what precedes them: the second occurs because the first occurred. But the diagrams are actually somewhat ambiguous on this point. The hooks connecting the boxes are drawn to suggest that, for its own interest, utility, and value, one of the two elements in each case *reaches out and hooks on to* the other element. This reaching out suggests that one element needs the other element in some nonreciprocal way. That is, whatever its apparent place in the order of events, first or second, leading or following, the element that reaches out and hooks on to the other is subordinate to or dependent upon the element it hooks on to.

So the relationships between the boxes in the diagrams could be spelled out this way:

> *diagram 1:* Narrative conversation *synthesizes stories that people tell each other in order to establish or confirm friendship.*
>
> *diagram 2:* Reasoning conversation *synthesizes stories that people tell each other in order to draw inferences from the stories and then use them to explain or defend those inferences.*

That is, although the two diagrams look very much alike, they are actually quite different. To understand this difference and to understand reasoning conversation better it helps to look more closely at the nature of narrative conversation.

NARRATIVE CONVERSATION: WHAT IT IS, WHAT IT'S FOR

In narrative conversation, as in every kind of conversation, we interpret in language what we believe we have experienced, in order to establish or maintain our membership in communities that are important to us. What distinguishes narrative conversation is that we construct what we believe we have experienced in story form: novels, tales, anecdotes, movies, plays, poems, myths, and so on.

In telling each other these stories, we connect experiences in a chain-like way that is both associative (one thing makes you think of another) and temporal (things happen as time passes, one thing causes another). Sentences in narrative conversation may answer questions raised by the preceding sentence or sentences, whether we say them or someone else does ("And then what happened?" or, "What does that remind you of?"). Or sentences may answer questions that neither person in the conversation seems to have raised before ("It just struck me that . . ."). In short, narrative conversation is driven, sometimes rather mysteriously, by feelings as deep as the intimacy among community members that the conversation establishes or maintains.

What makes narrative conversation lively and intrinsically worth taking part in is that we get to hear people telling some good stories in this easy-to-take, chainlike, sometimes unpredictable way, and we also get to tell some stories ourselves. Experiences interpreted as stories are exactly what give most narrative conversations their interest, utility, value, and satisfaction. That is why the hooks connecting the boxes in diagram 1 reach from the people engaged in dialogue down to the examples, the stories people tell. The diagram suggests that narrative conversation reaches out for what it needs, what it depends on, and what it is subordinate to: people's experiences interpreted and constructed as stories.

Narrative conversation depends on these origins—experiences told as stories and the people who tell them—more than it depends on any product, effect, or result of telling the stories. The possible products, effects, or results of narrative conversation are the ends to which people may put the stories they tell, such as, for example, telling the truth. But anyone who reads novels, goes to the movies, or even watches the evening news knows that telling the truth, whatever lip service people may give it, is not at the top of many storytellers' list of priorities. What is at the very top of every storyteller's list of priorities is making people feel as if they are members of a community based on mutual understanding.

We are all engaged in narrative conversation a good deal of the time. So we all know what narrative conversation usually sounds like. It sounds a bit disjointed, stringy, and unresolved: a lot like the following example paragraph. This paragraph is interesting, sort of fun to read, and maybe even instructive because the experiences that it constructs as stories and links together with the passage of time and by association have a common origin, namely the implied beliefs of the friendly, perceptive, but slightly scatterbrained speaker.

> I really enjoyed Gail's party. It was the best one I went to all year. In fact it was the first party I had gone to since my birthday party last August. That was a terrible party. We were at Ocean Beach that month, and the place was jammed with tourists. There were so many tourists in the stores it was even hard to get through the supermarket to buy hamburger and corn flakes, let alone get what you needed for a party. And the tourists in the stores there are so *rude*. Two summers ago a man carrying a big beach ball ran into me in the supermarket and almost knocked me over. Then he shouted it was all my fault. I got so mad I nearly ran his beach ball over with my shopping basket. I've got a terrible temper. It runs in the family.

The section on Unity and Coherence implies, of course, that there is something wrong with this paragraph. But from the point of view of narrative conversation, there's nothing wrong with it at all. The kind of conversation it represents, the kind of synthesis that produces it, and the kind of sense that it makes can be interesting, delightful, and useful on their own terms. Because narrative conversation is so inherently appealing, it is probably as close to a universal kind of conversation as there is. Almost everyone, almost everywhere, has almost always told stories in order to bring people together and cement commonality. We learn narrative conversation early in life. For most people, its satisfactions and intrinsic merit are sufficient unto themselves.

REASONING CONVERSATION: WHAT IT IS, WHAT IT'S FOR

There are some communities, however—typically, in the Western cultural tradition—that sometimes, in some situations, do something else with narrative conversation than enjoy the sense of commonality it provides. They recycle it by converting it into another kind of conversation, the kind we have called *reasoning conversation*.

Reasoning conversation in almost every case develops out of narrative conversation. We construct it by converting the narrative way of synthesizing experience into another, quite different way of synthesizing experience. Reasoning conversation is neither better nor worse than narrative conversation. It is just different. Both narrative and reasoning conversation are valued highly by some conversational communities and not valued much at all by others. And both are also valued by the same communities at different times, under different conditions, for different purposes.

But the differences between reasoning and narrative conversation mean that some of what is acceptable in one of them isn't always acceptable in the other. For example, although there is nothing at all wrong with the paragraph about Gail's Party from the point of view of narrative conversation, from the point of view of reasoning conversation—taking a position and exploring, explaining, and defending it—there is a lot wrong with it. What's wrong is that the paragraph is coherent but not unified. There are no reasons in it.

Reasoning conversation converts stories that make up narrative conversation by subordinating them all to a single generalization—the proposition of the essay, the position taken in it. In the paragraph about Gail's party, that hasn't happened. The kind of conversation that the paragraph represents is dependent upon and subordinate to experiences told as stories. There are of course inferences drawn from stories in the paragraph ("I've got a terrible temper"), but clearly, stories reign supreme.

In reasoning conversation, the reverse would be the case. Reasoning conversation does not depend on experience interpreted as stories—examples—for its interest, utility, value, and satisfaction. Examples depend on the conversation. Nor does reasoning conversation depend much on the origins of its examples. Reasoning conversation may certainly honor its sources through source evaluation and citation (see Part Five: Research and Research Writing, p. 245), but it is not subordinate to those sources.

What reasoning conversation does depend heavily on and is almost totally subordinate to are the inferences that it converts its examples into. The hooks in diagram 2 are drawn reaching upward to the inference instead of down to the examples because reasoning conversation depends for its interest, utility, value, and satisfaction on its products, the ends to which reasoning conversation puts them—such as, for example, a position paper on the dangers of the Sixth Street underpass.

Reasoning conversation is similar to narrative conversation in at least two ways: in both we construct something new—some kind of story— by reconstructing and interpreting in language what we believe we have experienced, and in both we do that in order to establish or maintain membership in communities that are important to us. Narrative conversation and reasoning conversation differ in the kind of stories we construct and what we do with them. In narrative conversation, we use stories to establish or maintain a sense of personal, immediate, spontaneous emotional contact and intimacy with other members of a conversational community. In reasoning conversation we establish or maintain membership in a conversational community by using stories to develop and support generalizations that we infer from them.

That is what is distinctive about reasoning conversation. In reasoning conversation, the ends to which we put stories that interpret experience matter more than the experience that produced them. In reasoning conversation stories don't reign supreme. The inferences we draw from them reign supreme.

In synthesizing experience in the reasoning way instead of the narrative way there is of course a trade-off. When we convert experience as stories into inferences, we may lose much of the significance of the stories. The significance of stories in narrative conversation is immediately emotional, personal, spontaneous, and intimate, but it is limited in most cases to a very small group—in the case of you and your friend talking about the underpass, it was limited to a group of only two. This loss of emotional, intimate significance is less likely to occur in narrative conversation, but it does happen. For example, in the paragraph about Gail's party, the inference, "I have a terrible temper," suggests a lot less of the speaker's quirky personality than the story the speaker draws it from, "I got so mad I nearly ran his beach ball over with my shopping basket."

But in return for this loss of spontaneity and intimacy in reasoning conversation, we do gain something else. What we gain is another kind of significance, one that is less personal, more studied and mediated, but shareable with a larger, more diverse community of people. Converting personal anecdotes into somewhat impersonal observations gives stories a role to play in another, more comprehensive kind of story, a reasoning story. The reasoning story implied in the position you are taking in your paper about the underpass is something like, "Many hazards add up to danger."

That's the bottom line. That is how reasons are constructed. In diagram 2 you have converted your examples and made the necessary trade-off by recycling your examples about potholes and lighting. That is, you have converted them by using them to illustrate the inference you have drawn: the inference that the underpass is dangerous. Instead of emphasizing where and how you found your examples, as you did when you were chatting with your friend, you emphasize the use you are putting them to.

PUTTING EXAMPLES IN CONTEXT

Converting examples into reasons straight out of the can in this way is the first step in learning explanatory subordination: using reasons to explain inferences. But examples used in this way are simple reasons. You are assuming that, without further explanation, readers will understand the relationship between your examples and the more important statement that you have related them to. So supporting a proposition without explaining that relationship is a weak defense. Most readers will not doubt that there must be some relationship between potholes, bad lighting, and the dangerous underpass. But some readers could probably think of several different kinds of relationships that might pertain. The essay does not yet make clear the particular nature of the relationship that you intend.

The next step is to explain how the examples, or any concrete experiences you use, enhance the position you are taking. By going on to make the nature of the relationship clear, you lengthen the reach of your controlling inference—you make its influence broader and more inclusive. And in that way you also make your inference more complex and informative.

Explaining your examples in this way makes the relationship between the essay's proposition and the examples a little like the relationship between the casserole you were planning to have for supper and the ingredients in it. You've got the mushroom soup, the tuna, the noodles, and the frozen peas, so you've got supper, right? Not by a long shot. If all you did was take the cans of soup and tuna, the box of noodles, and the frozen peas out of the cabinet and the fridge and put them on the table, you'd face a family rebellion. They'd say they can't eat raw ingredients. And they'd be right. There's a lot more to making a casserole than that. You have to open the cans and boxes, use the right amount of each ingredient, combine them in the right way, and put them in the oven long enough to cook, but not long enough to burn.

Whenever you construct reasons to support the position you are taking in an essay, you have to choose, combine, and cook the ingredients up in a similar way. The essay has to synthesize what you know so that it supports your position. Until now, you have assumed that both you and your readers know how your own experience and your friend's led you to the conclusion that the underpass is dangerous. But maybe your readers haven't been through that underpass lately. Maybe some of them have never even been through it at all. Even more important, most of them probably haven't been thinking about the issue for a week or so as you have.

So you have to help them catch up with you. Just as the casserole needs a cook who effectively subordinates mushroom soup, tuna, macaroni, and peas, your position needs a writer to construct and relate reasons so that they effectively synthesize and subordinate your concrete experience. Reasons show readers how you think concrete experience, such as examples or data, is related to your position. They help your readers catch up with the thinking you've been doing on the topic so that they can follow you more easily.

Maybe you haven't quite caught up with your own thinking. Trying to show your readers how you think concrete experience is related to your position may also help you explore and think through your position. What exactly is the relationship between your experience and the inference you have drawn from it?

When your readers see your statement that the underpass is dangerous, some questions are likely to come to mind:

What conditions in the underpass are dangerous?

Why, in your opinion, are those conditions dangerous?

How did those dangerous conditions come about?

The same questions might come to your own mind too, as you explore your thinking further. What would you come up with if you constructed answers to each of those questions? What you would come up with are reasons to support your inference in increasingly effective and complex ways.

Each question would of course have a different answer. That is, each question would subordinate your examples to the proposition in a different way. Each answer would generate a different kind of reason. Each answer would explore a different aspect of your position.

To answer the first question, "What conditions in the underpass are dangerous?", you would explain what is wrong with the underpass.

This kind of reason is closest to using examples straight out of the can. It is still a weak defense.

> The Sixth Street underpass is dangerous.
>
> One reason it's dangerous is that the road surface is riddled with potholes.
>
> Another reason the underpass is dangerous is that it is poorly lit.

But to answer the second question, "Why do you think those conditions are dangerous?", you would have to go beyond evidence of dangerous conditions. You would have to explain what makes those particular conditions dangerous, and that would involve explaining what exactly you mean by *dangerous*. In doing that you would be strengthening your defense.

> The Sixth Street underpass is dangerous.
>
> The underpass is dangerous because everyone who goes through it is forced to drive dangerously. I drive through it twice a day to and from work. I have to zigzag all the way through the underpass in order to avoid dozens of potholes. If I didn't, I'd break an axle. And people who have to drive there at night are in even greater danger. My friend almost swerved into the left lane last week because the underpass is so poorly lit.

You strengthen your defense with this explanation by going beyond the examples themselves to tell your readers more of what you know about the situation in the underpass, how you have been thinking about it, and what your assumptions are (what you mean by *dangerous*). Inserting people's perception of danger between the examples and the proposition places the examples farther away from your inference by synthesizing them under a subheading. It therefore lengthens the reach of your controlling inference, making its influence broader and more inclusive. The paragraph now subordinates potholes and lighting to your position indirectly rather than directly. First, it subordinates potholes and lighting to dangerous driving; then it subordinates dangerous driving to the dangerous underpass.

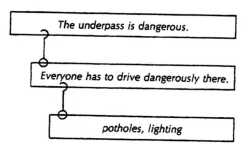

CONSTRUCTING A STRONG DEFENSE

Notice also that when you subordinate examples in this way, under a subheading of the proposition rather than under the proposition directly, that subheading may be the transitional generalization that controls the organization of a single paragraph. There are two kinds of transitional generalizations. One of them is the paragraph 2 kind of transition. It relates a paragraph directly to the essay's proposition, which is at the end of the previous paragraph.

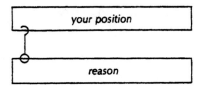

The other is the paragraph 3 kind of transition. It relates the paragraph to the proposition indirectly, around an intervening paragraph (or, in a longer essay, around several intervening paragraphs), and it also relates the paragraph directly to the immediately preceding paragraph.

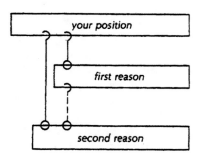

Using these two different kinds of transitional generalizations allows you to subordinate your reasons under more than one heading. Now your examples contribute to only one of these subdivisions (paragraph 2 of your essay) because you have subordinated them to only one sub-inference ("The underpass is dangerous because everyone who goes through it is forced to drive dangerously."). In order to develop a second subdivision (paragraph 3) you will have to make a second supporting subinference from other kinds of experiences you have had, such as, for example, things you have read. And then you will have to use that experience to support that second subinference. Once again, you will be telling your readers more of what you know about the situation in the underpass, how you have been thinking about it, and what your assumptions are.

That is why this book asks you to write three-paragraph essays. They help you learn to synthesize more than one major element, or reason, in your writing. It is important to know how to synthesize more than one reason in support of your position because in order to make your readers willing to consider your position, you have to show them that the inference you have drawn generalizes from more than one experience, more than one example, more than one piece of evidence. Three-paragraph essays make you a smarter writer than you may think you are by requiring you to develop your ideas more fully than you may have been in the habit of developing them, and by requiring you to make connections among your ideas that you might not otherwise have made.

To put it another way, subordinating examples to more than one reason supporting your position helps you go beyond the material you have at hand, the material that may have set you off writing on this topic in the first place. So it helps you explore your position more thoroughly. That's what you would be doing if you answered the second question that might have come to mind about why certain conditions in the underpass are dangerous. In this case, let's say you have noticed that the local newspaper has run some articles lately on the Sixth Street underpass.

The Sixth Street underpass is dangerous.

Everyone knows that the underpass is dangerous because everyone who goes through it is forced to drive dangerously. I drive through it twice a day to and from work. I have to zigzag all the way in order to avoid dozens of potholes. If I didn't, I'd break an axle. And people who have to drive there at night are in even greater danger. My friend almost swerved into the left lane last week because the underpass is so poorly lit.

An article in the newspaper last week confirmed this danger by listing its effects. The article said that in the past two years one fatal accident and three near-fatalities have occurred in the Sixth Street underpass. Wreckers have to pull cars out of there on the average of two or three a month.

As strong as this defense is, however, it is possible to make it still stronger. That is, it is possible to tell your readers more of what you know about the situation in the underpass, how you have been thinking about it, and what your assumptions are. One way to construct an even stronger defense of your position would be to answer the third question

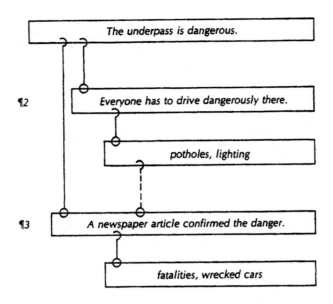

that might have come to mind, "How did those dangerous conditions come about?" In this case, you would explore your position more thoroughly still by including other relevant elements and in that way place your examples still further away from the controlling inference, the position you are taking in the essay as a whole.

The Sixth Street Underpass Is Dangerous.

One reason the underpass is dangerous is that the city's Thoroughfare Commission, which is responsible for maintaining the underpass, has been in a state of political turmoil for the past five years. As a result of this poor leadership, the commission's staff has failed to carry out many of its responsibilities. One of these responsibilities is to keep the city's roads, bridges, and underpasses in good repair. Clearly this has not happened in the case of the Sixth Street underpass, where the road surface is riddled with potholes and most of the overhead lights are burned out or broken.

Another reason that the underpass is dangerous is that the state has been holding up funds to repair it until the Thoroughfare Commission turns in its biannual report on the accidents that have occurred there. Last week an article in the newspaper did the job for them. It said that in the past two years one fatal accident and three near-fatalities have occurred in the Sixth Street underpass. Wreckers have to pull cars out of there on the average of two or three a month. As a result of that article, the governor says that the state will appropriate new funds to pay for repairs and will watch carefully to see that the commission uses the money wisely.

Although the examples are now a lot further away from the controlling influence of your inference, you have increased their value to the essay

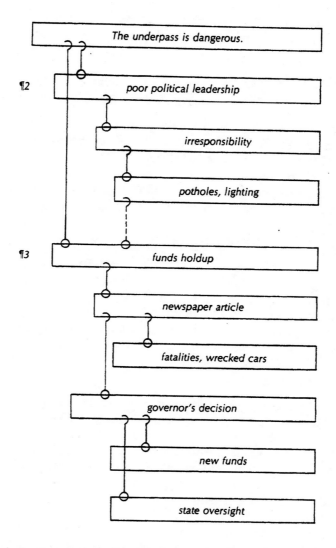

as a whole by increasing the significance of the context in which you have placed them. In that way you have lengthened the reach of your controlling inference, the essay's proposition, a great deal, making its influence still broader and more inclusive. You have increased the leverage, the weight, that your examples can bear.

When you began, engaged in narrative conversation with your friend, your examples were experiences that annoyed two people. Now they are experiences that represent the similar experiences of lots of people and that help indict an irresponsible government agency. You now know a lot more now than you did before about the position you took, and you have explained what you know a lot more thoroughly and convincingly to your readers. The strong defense you have constructed is likely to lead readers to take your position a lot more seriously.

COLLABORATIVE LEARNING

Task 1   *A Hook-and-Box Diagram of a Descriptive Outline*

Working in a group of two or three, diagram with hooks and boxes the *does* sections of the descriptive outline of "What Should Patients Be Told?" (p. 220) or "Going Back to School" (p. 323). Use the hook-and-box diagram on p. 109 as a model.

Join another group of two or three and compare the diagrams drawn by the two groups. Account for the differences in the diagrams.

Task 2   *A Hook-and-Box Diagram of an Essay*

Working in a group of two or three, diagram with hooks and boxes "McKay, Trepp, Inc.," p. 242, or "Stock Options," p. 327, or some other example essay that your group would like to work on. Use the hook-and-box diagram on p. 109 as a model.

Join another group of two or three and compare the diagrams drawn by the two groups. Account for the differences in the diagrams.

Task 3   *Constructing Reasons*

Working in a group of two or three, decide first on a movie that all of you have seen recently and liked (or particularly disliked), an episode of a TV show you have all seen and liked (or disliked), or an exciting ball game or other public event that you all watched. Or you could choose instead a problem that you have in common, a teacher or course you are taking, a place you like to go, an improvement or repair you think should be made, a person you like or dislike, or a task you like or dislike doing.

Working independently, each one write a few sentences that tell a story illustrating what is appealing, repulsive, interesting, or difficult about the subject you have chosen.

Read your stories to each other and then, working together, write a single short sentence that seems to synthesize your common experience. That is, take a position on the subject that you can all agree on and that you think your stories illustrate.

Then, working together,

1. Use your stories as examples to construct a weak defense of that position in which each example constitutes a paragraph (see pp. 97–98).

2. Decide on some subordinate generalizations or subinferences that would support the position; then write a paragraph that explores, explains, or defends your position using your examples indirectly by relating them to the proposition through the subordinate generalizations you have chosen (see pp. 103–105).

3. Write a second paragraph that strengthens your argument by referring to other aspects of the subject, and write another subordinate generalization expressing that synthesis (see pp. 106–110).

PARAGRAPH DEVELOPMENT

Some writers have trouble developing their ideas. They tend to write a series of related propositions without explaining or illustrating them or without exploring the implications of the operative words. For example, suppose a writer drafted an essay that looked something like this:

¶1   The smog in this city is terrible. We could solve the smog problem by keeping cars out of the city.

¶2   For one thing, cars produce all the worst kinds of air pollution.

¶3   Another reason is that cars produce a greater volume of pollutants than any other source.

This essay fits the form required by exercise 5. In fact, the writer shows that he has learned most of the principles that exercise 5 has to teach. The essay introduces a defensible proposition, states it succinctly and readably, and explains it, making appropriate transitions among the parts of the explanation.

But the essay is far from five hundred words long. Obviously it needs development. Every paragraph lacks development. The essay assumes that every reader will know which city the writer is talking about. In fact, it seems to assume that every reader lives in the city that the author of the essay lives in. It assumes that every reader would agree without further explanation that there is no other source of smog in that city.

HOW TO DEVELOP A PARAGRAPH

To *develop an essay* means to explain these assumptions rather than assume that every reader knows what you know and assumes what you assume. You can learn paragraph development by analyzing the sentences you write according to the following principle:

Every sentence raises questions in readers' minds.

To develop a sentence, find the questions it raises and answer them.

Some of the questions that any sentence may raise in readers' minds are "What do you mean by that?", "Why?", "How come?", "Who says?", and "So what?"

Take yourself, for example. When you first read the sentence "Every sentence raises questions in readers' minds," you may have wondered, "What does that mean?", "What kinds of questions does every sentence raise?", and "So what? What should I do about it?" To develop that sentence I had to imagine these questions, and then I had to answer them. You have to do that as a writer, too. In order to develop your paragraphs, you have to try to imagine the questions that the sentences you write may raise in your readers' minds and then answer them.

In the example essay about smog, the first sentence, "The smog in this city is terrible," raises at least the following questions:

What is smog?

Where does the word *smog* come from?

How can you tell that we have smog in this city?

Which city?

Is this the only city that has smog?

If so, why?

If not, why not?

What makes smog so terrible?

The essay's first paragraph, its introduction, could be developed by answering some of these questions. It could answer them directly by explaining or defining the operative word, *smog.* Or it could answer them indirectly, by describing a scene or telling a story. (There is more about writing introductions in Introductions, p. 81, and in What an Introduction Does, p. 201.)

The second sentence in the undeveloped example essay, "We could solve the smog problem by keeping cars out of the city," is the essay's proposition. The proposition is developed in paragraphs 2 and 3. (There is more about what makes a good proposition and how to develop one in Propositions, p. 85.)

To develop paragraph 2, we repeat what we did to develop paragraph 1. We try to imagine the questions that the sentence that now constitutes paragraph 2, "For one thing, cars produce all the worst kinds of air pollution," might raise in readers' minds. It looks as if that sentence might raise these questions:

What are the worst kinds of air pollution?

What makes them so bad?

How do we know cars produce all the worst kinds?

And the fourth sentence, which now constitutes paragraph 3, "Another reason is that cars produce a greater volume of pollutants than any other source," is likely to raise the following questions in readers' minds:

How do you measure the volume of air pollution?

How can cars, which are relatively small machines (compared to trucks and power generators), produce so much pollution?

How much pollution do other sources produce, and what kind?

If we were going to develop paragraphs 2 and 3 of this essay, we would have to answer some or all of these questions by explaining operative words, by logical argument, by reference to authoritative sources, or, as in the first paragraph, by description or narration.

READING WELL-DEVELOPED PARAGRAPHS

Understanding paragraph development in this way can help you write better. It can also help you read more constructively. If you are aware that every sentence has operative words and that every sentence raises questions in the reader's mind, you can look ahead as you read to what is coming. You can anticipate what is likely to follow (or what should follow) in whatever you are reading simply by asking yourself what questions each sentence raises in your mind. You will also be able to keep track of what's going on in whatever you read, because you will be aware of how writers organize (or should organize) paragraphs, and how writers relate paragraphs (or should relate them) to the main point of an essay.

For example, let's read the third paragraph of Frederic Garsson's essay, "Family and School," p. 319:

Another way families can give their children emotional support in college is through rituals, acts performed on a regular basis that a person can depend on to occur. Rituals tend to put order into a person's life and provide a sense of self-assurance and security. A common ritual is Sunday dinner. No matter what the children in the family are doing, even studying for exams, family rules may require them to eat dinner with the family. In this case the whole family can anticipate this one time of the week, knowing that no matter what, they will be together. It is an event that the whole family, and most important, the children, can rely on and find comfort in. My family first learned about this use of Sunday dinner as a family ritual through a friend of mine. On several occasions, he turned down an invitation to have dinner at my house, explaining to my parents that his father insisted that his whole family eat dinner together on Sunday evenings. My parents thought that this mandatory attendance at Sunday dinner was something that would work well at our house too. At the time I did not understand the psychology behind the plan. But now I think I do. Furthermore, I feel that it has succeeded in achieving its desired effect. It gave my sister and myself a feeling of security that we not only experience every Sunday, but that we also carry with us into the world beyond our family.

In reading this paragraph, to make use of the principle that every sentence raises questions in the reader's mind, we would ask ourselves as we read what questions each sentence raises in our mind, and then look to see how those questions are answered, or if they're answered.

The first sentence in the paragraph, which is likely to be the most important sentence in the paragraph, generates several questions based mainly on the sentence's operative words, *families, emotional support,* and *rituals.* The sentence itself answers one question it raises, "What are rituals?" They are "acts performed on a regular basis that a person can depend on to occur."

Here are some of the other questions that the sentence raises.

What do family rituals do for people?

Can you give me an example of a family ritual?

What happens in one?

What does that particular ritual do for people?

How did you find out about family rituals?

The paragraph answers all these questions:

What are rituals?
Rituals are acts performed on a regular basis that a person can depend on to occur.

What do family rituals do for people?
Rituals tend to put order into a person's life and provide a sense of self-assurance and security.

Can you give me an example of a family ritual?
A common ritual is Sunday dinner.

What happens in a family ritual?
No matter what the children in the family are doing, even studying

for exams, family rules may require them to eat dinner with the family. In this case the whole family can anticipate this one time of the week, knowing that no matter what, they will be together.

What does it do for people?

It is an event that the whole family, and most important, the children, can rely on and find comfort in. . . . It gave my sister and myself a feeling of security that we not only experience every Sunday, but that we also carry with us into the world beyond our family.

How did you find out about family rituals?

My family first learned about this use of Sunday dinner as a family ritual through a friend of mine. On several occasions, he turned down an invitation to have dinner at my house, explaining to my parents that his father insisted that his whole family eat dinner together on Sunday evenings. My parents thought that this mandatory attendance at Sunday dinner was something that would work well at our house too.

The first sentence in the paragraph raises some other questions too, of course, questions such as

What is emotional support?

Why do people in college need it?

What are some other ways that families can support their children in college?

The paragraph we have read does not answer these questions. But other paragraphs in the essay do answer them. Take a look at the whole essay "Family and School," on p. 319. The first paragraph explains why college students (in particular, commuting students) need emotional support. It says that they tend to feel insecure because they find it hard at first to replace their high school friends, and because in college they have more freedom than they're used to. The second paragraph explains some of the other ways that families can provide emotional support for their children in college. It says that families can be sympathetic people to talk to and they can reassure their children that everything will work out.

But the essay never does explicitly define *emotional support*. Instead, it gives an example of it: a family ritual that helps people "put order into their lives and provide a sense of self-assurance and security."

(There is more about paragraph development in Introductions, p. 81, Propositions, p. 85, Reasons, p. 96, Descriptive Outlines, p. 152, Unity and Coherence, p. 116, and Assumptions, p. 132. Essay exercises 7 and

8 can help you learn to develop paragraphs, because they ask you to discover opposing arguments and refute them. Invention exercises 1 through 4 can help you discover what you have to say and help you produce material that you can use to develop paragraphs. There is more about reading constructively in Part Three: Constructive Reading.

COLLABORATIVE LEARNING

Follow the instructions for working in consensus groups on p. 20.

Task 1   Developing a Paragraph (Developing Operative Words)

Identify the operative words in the following sentences. Then explain what you think a writer would have to say to develop each of them fully.

> This school should revise its grading system.
>
> Project Head Start has become a necessary part of our present-day system of education.
>
> Yet it is also clear that Haitians can unite effectively.
>
> Our investigation has shown that although some personnel problems exist, a complicated mix of internal and external factors was the main cause of the slowdown.
>
> By being so long in the lowest form, I gained an immense advantage over the cleverer boys.

Task 2   Reading a Well-Developed Essay

Choose a sample essay in this book and write out the proposition sentence and the first sentence of paragraph 2 and paragraph 3.

Mark the operative words in each sentence.

List the questions that you think the sentences generate.

Which of these questions do paragraphs 2 and 3 of the essay answer? How do they answer them?

That is, what does the essay *say* and *do* to answer the questions? (See What an Essay *Says*, p. 154, and What an Essay *Does*, p. 158.)

UNITY AND COHERENCE

Unity and coherence refer to the structure of an essay. *Unity* means one-ness. *Coherence* means stick-togetherness. Good essays need both. If your essay lacks coherence, its parts don't stick together. Readers won't be able to follow you. That is, they'll miss the point you want to make, the position you're taking. If an essay lacks unity, your readers won't get any point at all, because the essay hasn't a point for them to get, or maybe it has too many points, all of them undeveloped.

Unity and coherence do not come easily. Nobody's mind works naturally with the kind of unity and coherence that a well-planned, well-developed essay requires. That kind of unity and coherence is a convention—an agreement among readers and writers about how they expect writing normally to be organized. To achieve unity and coherence of that kind, most of us have to work consciously to shape the parts of an essay and make them fit together, just as a cabinetmaker shapes the parts of a table or chair so that they fit together. To gain unity you have to work consciously to focus the essay on one topic alone. And to gain coherence you have to work consciously to make sure that all the parts of the essay are explicitly related to one another.

The key to both is the essay's proposition. Anything that contributes to exploring, explaining, or defending the proposition is relevant to the essay and therefore helps gain unity. Anything that does not contribute to exploring, explaining, or defending the proposition is not relevant to the essay, disunifies it, and therefore does not belong to it. To unify an essay, include only what is related to the proposition. Cut out everything that isn't related to the proposition. If you like, save what you cut out for another essay.

The proposition not only creates unity, it also helps create coherence. For unity, it is enough that everything in an essay is relevant to the essay's proposition. For coherence, relevance is not enough. For coherence, the essay has to make clear how everything is relevant to the proposition. Throughout the essay, readers should be able to say what the relationship of what they are reading is to the proposition. An essay should make explicit the relationships both among the parts of the essay and between the parts and the whole. These relationships are important because they construct the idea of the essay. An *idea* is not an isolated concept or a loose collection of facts. An idea is an explicit relationship between facts and concepts. In this sense, then, an incoherent essay simply has no idea in it.

COHERENCE BETWEEN PARAGRAPHS

Writing a transitional generalization or transition sentence at the beginning of every paragraph is one way to create coherence in an essay. Transition sentences relate the paragraph to preceding paragraphs and to the proposition. They guide readers so that they will be able to follow the writer's thought. They are necessary at the beginning of every paragraph, because at the end of every paragraph readers reach a corner. Having gotten to that corner, their minds are willing to go in any number of directions. As the writer, at just that point you have to take readers by the hand and lead them in the direction you want them to go. That is the purpose of transition sentences: to reach back to something the writer has already said and at the same time point ahead to what you are about to say next.

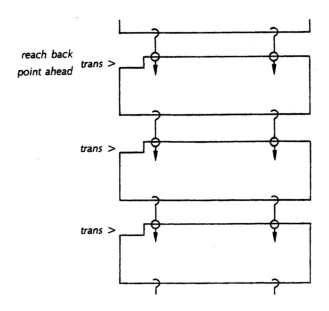

reach back
point ahead   *trans >*

trans >

trans >

If you do not reach back and guide readers in this way, they won't understand. They won't follow. They'll get lost. (There is more about transitional generalizations in Constructing a Strong Defense, p. 106.)

UNITY AND COHERENCE WITHIN PARAGRAPHS

Readers can get lost within paragraphs as well as between them. Just as the end of every paragraph is a corner, the end of every sentence is a corner too. At the end of every sentence, you have to take the lead and direct your readers' attention where you want it to go. If you don't lead, readers won't follow. The paragraph will lose coherence and won't make sense.

There is another way to describe unity and coherence within paragraphs. It uses the principle explained in the section on developing paragraphs:

Every sentence raises questions in the reader's mind.

To develop a sentence, find the questions it raises and answer them.

A paragraph is *unified* when all its sentences answer questions raised by the paragraph's first sentence and when none of its sentences answer questions that are not raised by the paragraph's first sentence. And a paragraph is *coherent* when every sentence answers a question raised by the sentence (or sentences) that precede it. This paragraph, for example (the paragraph you are reading), is unified because the sentences that begin "A· paragraph is unified . . ." and "And a paragraph is coherent . . ." answer the question raised by the paragraph's first sentence, "There is another way to describe unity and coherence within paragraphs" (*What* is another way to describe unity and coherence?). The second half of the paragraph (beginning "This paragraph, for example . . .") also helps answer that question by giving concrete examples.

The paragraph you have just read is also coherent. Each sentence in it answers a question raised by a sentence that precedes it. The paragraph begins with a sentence that raises the question: What is another way to describe unity and coherence? The second and third sentences in the paragraph answer that question with generalizations ("A paragraph is unified when . . ."; "And a paragraph is coherent when . . ."). These sentences in turn raise the question that every generalization raises: Can you give me an example? The last two sentences in the paragraph answer that question by giving examples drawn from the paragraph itself.

EXAMPLES OF DISUNITY AND INCOHERENCE

The following paragraph is *disunified*. Even though everything in it pertains in some way to the writer's trip home, nothing in it answers the question raised by the first sentence: Why was your trip home a disaster? The paragraph is also *incoherent*. No sentence in it answers a question raised by the sentence or sentences that precede it.

> [1]My trip home was a complete disaster. [2]The weather was fine all the way. [3]It took me eleven hours to drive a little over a hundred miles. [4]And I have never seen such beautiful fall foliage as I saw that day along the road. [5]The sky was clear until almost three in the afternoon, with the sun shining brightly. [6]Once I saw two rabbits playing in a field beside the road, chasing each other through the grass back and forth across a stream that ran along the edge of some woods. [7]The bright sun brought out the color in the leaves so that I could distinguish a dozen shades of red and orange. [8]You can't spend all that time traveling without noticing a lot of scenery as you go along.

If you were rewriting this paragraph, you would have to decide first of all what exactly you want to say most. Is the point really that the trip was a disaster, or is the point that the trip was fun even though it took so long? If you decided that you really do want to say how awful the trip was, you would have to discard most of the paragraph as it is now written and save that material for another paragraph in the same essay or put it aside for another essay altogether. In its place, you would write some new material that really does answer the question raised by the first sentence.

> [1]My trip home was a complete disaster.
> *Why was it so bad?*

If this was the question you decided to answer, you might keep the third sentence.

> [3]It took me eleven hours to drive a little over a hundred miles.

You would then develop that sentence by describing all the things that slowed you down: a flat tire, a bridge washed out, the muffler that fell off at seventy miles an hour and then the ticket you got for speeding and not having a muffler, two ten-mile traffic jams, dropping your only quarter under the car in the toll booth correct-change line, and a spontaneous nosebleed.

If you decided instead that what you wanted to say was that in spite of the long, slow drive you had a pretty good time, then you could keep most of what is in the paragraph now. But you would have to change the first sentence so that it raises a question that the rest of the paragraph answers. And you would have to rearrange some of the sentences that follow:

> [1]My trip home wasn't a complete disaster.
> *What went wrong and what made up for it?*
> [3]Of course, it did take me eleven hours to drive a little over a hundred miles. [2]But the weather was fine all the way.

So far, you would have answered in general terms the question raised by the first sentence. Now you would have to develop that answer. To do that, you would have three alternatives. You could give details of what was good about the trip, you could give details about what was bad about it, or both. The most economical choice would be to make better use of the sentences you have already written that explain what was good about the trip.

But those sentences are not coherent as they stand. They're out of order. To make them cohere, you would have to rearrange them by asking, at the end of each sentence, "What should follow here?" The result might look something like this (the superscript numbers refer to the order of the sentences in the first version):

[1]My trip home wasn't a complete disaster. [2]The weather was fine all the way. [5]The sky was clear until almost three in the afternoon, with the sun shining brightly. [8]And you can't spend all that time traveling without noticing a lot of scenery as you go along. [4]I have never seen such beautiful fall foliage as I saw that day along the road. [7]The bright sun brought out the color in the leaves so that I could distinguish a dozen shades of red and orange. [6]Once I saw two rabbits playing in a field beside the road, chasing each other through the grass back and forth across a stream that ran along the edge of some woods.

In rearranging these sentences, you would of course have to change the direction signals at the beginning of some of them. For example, sentence 4 would lose its introductory *And*, because it doesn't need it any more. But sentence 8 would get a new introductory *And*, because it now introduces the third item in a series (fine weather, clear sky, time spent traveling).

The following example is coherent because every sentence answers some question raised by the sentence that precedes it. But the paragraph is disunified because nothing after the third sentence has anything to do with the topic announced in the first sentence.

[1]I really enjoyed Gail's party. [2]It was the best one I went to all year. [3]In fact it was the first party I had gone to since my birthday party last August. [4]That was a terrible party. [5]We were at Ocean Beach that month, and the place was jammed with tourists. [6]There were so many tourists in the stores it was even hard to get through the supermarket to buy hamburger and corn flakes, let alone get what you needed for a party. [7]And the tourists in the stores there are so *rude*. [8]Two summers ago a man carrying a big beach ball ran into me in the supermarket and almost knocked me over. [9]Then he shouted it was all my fault. [10]I got so mad I nearly ran his beach ball over with my shopping basket. [11]I've got a terrible temper. [12]It runs in the family.

Readers can follow this paragraph's chain of association fairly easily, mostly because the paragraph repeats several key words (*I, we, party, tourists*) throughout. These words give it coherence. But the paragraph begins with a party and ends with a peculiarity of family temperament. In between, it wends its way amusingly through an anecdote about an argument in a supermarket. But when we get to the end of the paragraph, we don't know quite how we got there. And we don't know any more about what happened at Gail's party than we did when we began.

In short, the paragraph is coherent but disunified because every sentence answers a question raised by a sentence that precedes it, but after sentence 3, none of the questions that the paragraph answers are related to the first sentence in the paragraph. Just conceivably the second, third, and fourth sentences could be said to answer questions raised by the first sentence, but only if you stretch the point, since the fourth sentence qualifies the answer given by the third.

> [1]I really enjoyed Gail's party.
>
> *Why did you enjoy it?*
>
> [2]It was the best one I went to all year. [3]In fact it was the first party I had gone to since my birthday party last August. [4]That was a terrible party.

But sentence 4 also represents an important corner in the paragraph. At this point, if you were rewriting this paragraph you would have to take a firm hand in order to lead readers where you want them to go. To do that, you would have to choose between the two questions that sentence 4 raises. One of these questions "remembers" the sentence's context: the three sentences preceding it that refer to Gail's party.

> [1]I really enjoyed Gail's party.[2]It was the best one I went to all year. [3]In fact it was the first party I had gone to since my birthday party last August. [4]That was a terrible party.
>
> *What made your birthday party worse than Gail's party?*

The second question raised by sentence 4 "forgets" the sentence's context, the preceding sentences about Gail's party. Instead, it treats the sentence as if it stood alone. That is, it treats sentence 4 as if it were itself the main point of the paragraph.

> [4]That was a terrible party.
>
> *Why was your birthday party such a terrible party?*

To make the paragraph unified, you would have to answer the first of these two alternative questions, the one that remembers why the birthday party came up at all (because it contrasted so unfavorably in the writer's mind with Gail's party) and *also* remembers the direction that the first sentence in the paragraph seemed to be going (to tell us why Gail's party was so great). As it was originally written, the paragraph chooses instead to answer the second alternative question, the one that forgets its context. So it leads readers way off the track.

We can analyze any paragraph to discover whether it is unified and coherent by discovering the questions generated by each sentence in it. If the paragraph is unified, discounting allowable assumptions, it will answer only the questions raised by the first sentence, or first few sentences, in the paragraph (see Assumptions, p. 132). If the paragraph is coherent, every sentence will also answer questions raised by preceding sentences that are also relevant to the first sentence or first few sentences in the paragraph.

To put it another way, when you set out to discover the questions raised by sentences in a paragraph, you are really looking for the *expectations* that those sentences imply. We ask each sentence: **What does this sentence make me *expect* the paragraph will say next and then say later on?** Then we look to see if the paragraph fulfills our expectations. If you anticipate the questions that your sentences are likely to raise in the reader's mind and answer them, then you will probably satisfy the reader's expectations. As your skill as a writer increases, you will not only be able to answer the questions that your sentences raise, but you will be able to do so in ways that truly inform, enlighten, surprise, or entertain your readers.

ORGANIZING FOR COHERENCE

Even if a paragraph answers all the questions its initial sentences raise (and does not answer any questions that they do not raise), it will be coherent only if its sentences proceed in a fairly clear and simple overall order or sequence. Essay exercises 5 through 9 will help you learn a few basic ways to organize paragraphs so that they will follow each other in an orderly sequence. You can, and should, use these same organizational forms within paragraphs as well.

For example, essay exercise 6, Nestorian Order, p. 59, asks you to put several less important reasons in paragraph 2, and put the single most important reason in paragraph 3. You can also use this climactic order within a single paragraph. Nestorian order is an appropriate organization to use whenever you have to arrange a list containing a number of items—evidence, reasons, proposals, books, rivers, string quartets, whatever. Put an important item first, collect less important things next, and save the best for last.

Here are some more ways to organize material that you can use for relating the parts of a paragraph:

- **enumeration** (first, second, third)
- **spatial relation** (left to right, top to bottom, here to there, from the inside out)
- **time** (Then . . . now; at 5:30 . . . and then at 7:15; two summers ago . . . last August . . . today)
- **association** (bird, wing, feather, down, pillow, sleep)
- **logical sequences**
  deductive (from the general to the particular: from carnivores to

mammals to dogs to Spaniels to Rex. Novels . . . Conrad's novels . . . *Lord Jim*)

inductive (from the particular to the general: there are ten dogs in
every room of that building . . . so it must be a dog pound)

progressive (a series of rhetorical syllogisms—or, more correctly,
incremental associations that sound logical but may or may not
be: today is Wednesday; I go to work on Wednesday; I hate
work because what I do at work bores me; so on Wednesdays
I'm always bored; that's why I feel so bad today)

dialectical (a series of questions and answers in which every answer
generates the next question)

- **structure**

    simple climax (he carries tens, twenties, even hundred-dollar bills
    in his pocket all the time)

    Nestorian (a cross between simple climax and simple enumerative;
    see essay exercise 6, p. 59)

- **parallel syntax** (with dogs on the porch, mice in the cellar, and cats
  in the boys' room, this place is a zoo)

- **hypothetical** (if one thing, then another: if the TV doesn't work this
  time, I'm going to buy a new one; if both Keats and Byron are
  romantic poets, then *romantic* does not mean what most of us think
  it means)

DIRECTION SIGNALS: TRANSITIONAL WORDS AND PHRASES

If the ends of sentences and paragraphs are corners where you have to
direct your readers' attention, one of the best ways to do that is with
direction signals, both at the beginning of every paragraph and at crucial
points within them. Direction signals help readers remember the context
of what they are reading—what has gone before. We include these
direction signals in an essay for the same reason that we signal left or
right when we drive a car, so that other people will know which way
we are turning.

You may sometimes be tempted to leave direction signals out of your
writing because you feel that you would be insulting the reader's intelligence with them. They're too obvious. This is misguided humility.
What is obvious to you may not be obvious to your readers. Even the
best professional writers feel lucky if they can get 50 percent of what
they have to say across to their readers. It is part of your job as a writer
to command the reader's attention and keep it.

Often you can keep your reader's attention with the simplest kinds
of transitions. In climactic or Nestorian order (exercise 6), for example,
the transitional phrases are almost automatic: "One reason is. . . . There
are also several other reasons. . . . But the most important reason is. . . ."

The main kinds of transition among sentences within a paragraph are

- **conjunctions** (*and, but, however, therefore,* etc.)
- **referential pronouns** (*this, these, it, she, he,* etc.)
- **key words repeated**
- **parallel constructions**

In the following paragraph from *My Early Life,* Winston Churchill uses all these. He connects the sentences to each other with conjunctions such as *however, but,* and *thus;* with referential pronouns such as *they* and *it;* with key words, such as *English, I,* and *he* repeated throughout the paragraph; and with parallel construction ("Each had its color and its bracket. It was a kind of drill. We did it almost daily." "Latin as an honor, and Greek as a treat.").

I continued in **this** unpretentious situation for nearly a year. **However,** by being so long in the lowest form I gained an immense advantage over the cleverer boys. **They** all went on to learn **Latin** and **Greek** and splendid things like that. But I was taught **English. We** were considered such dunces that **we** could learn only **English. Mr. Somervell**—a most delightful man, to whom my debt is great—was charged with the duty of teaching the **stupidest boys** the most disregarded thing—namely, to write mere **English. He** knew how to do **it. He taught it** as no one else has ever **taught it.** Not only did **we** learn **English** parsing thoroughly, but **we** also practiced continually **English** analysis. **Mr. Somervell** had a system of **his** own. **He** took a fairly long sentence and broke it up into its components by means of black, red, blue, and green inks. Subject, verb, object: Relative Clauses, Conditional Clauses, Conjunctive and Disjunctive Clauses! **Each** had its color and its bracket. **It** was a kind of drill. **We** did **it** almost daily. As I remained in the Third Form (B) three times as long as anyone else, I had three times as much of **it. I** learned **it** thoroughly. Thus I got into my bones the essential structure of the ordinary British **sentence**—which is a noble thing. **And** when in after years **my schoolfellows** who had won prizes and distinction for writing such beautiful **Latin** poetry and pithy **Greek** epigrams had to come down again to common **English,** to earn their living or make their way, I did not feel **myself** at any disadvantage. Naturally I am biased in favor of boys learning **English.** I would make them all learn **English,** and then I would let the clever ones learn **Latin** as an honor, and **Greek** as a treat. But the only thing I would whip them for is not knowing **English.** I would whip them hard for **that.**

This conscious transitional process that joins sentences within paragraphs and paragraphs within essays strengthens your work and makes your essays capable of standing up of their own accord. It's good carpentry.

TESTING FOR UNITY AND COHERENCE

One way to check to see if an essay is unified is to write a detailed descriptive outline of it and then compare the *says* statements for paragraphs 2 and 3 with the proposition given in the essay. *Says* statements should paraphrase in a single sentence the main point of each paragraph. Check them by looking to see if they support the proposition as written. If they do, and you have paraphrased the paragraphs accurately, then the essay is probably unified.

One way to check to see if an essay is coherent is to write a descriptive outline and then compare the *does* statements for paragraphs 2 and 3 with the essay's overall plan. Check them by looking to see if paragraphs 2 and 3 do what the plan says they should be doing. There is more about writing descriptive outlines in Part Three: Constructive Reading.

Another way to check for coherence is to reread the transition sentences of paragraphs 2 and 3 and compare them with the essay's proposition. Does each transition sentence deal explicitly with one or more of the proposition's operative words? If so, then go on to reread the whole paragraph. Do all the sentences in each paragraph deal with the generalization made in the transition sentence? If the essay passes both of these tests, it is probably coherent.

COLLABORATIVE LEARNING

Follow the instructions for working in consensus groups on p. 20.

Task 1   Testing for Unity

Someone in the group read the following passage aloud. Then answer the questions and follow the instructions collaboratively.

[1]Writing on a computer isn't like writing on a typewriter. [2]The typewriter I worked on for years is an old upright standard Underwood that must weigh fifty pounds. [3]When a burglar broke into my home fifteen years ago, he stole my TV, but he didn't steal my typewriter. [4]I don't think he could lift it, much less carry it out of the house. [5]It is taking me almost as long to learn to work on my computer as it took me to learn to type in the first place. [6]I feel forever confused by RAM, DOC, and DOS. [7]That bewildering array of F keys makes me nervous. [8]To do word processing, even though I can already type, I've had to learn a lot. [9]When the monitor says "Bad command," I feel like a puppy that's made a mess on the carpet. [10]I want to whine and creep off into a corner with my tail between my legs. [11]But today my old typewriter is an antique gathering dust in a closet. [12]My brand new computer weighs a lot more than fifty pounds, and it takes up a lot more space than my old typewriter.

1. What question does the first sentence in the paragraph generate?
2. How is the question answered?
3. What question does most of the paragraph seem to be answering?
4. Is there a sentence anywhere in the paragraph that seems to imply that question?
5. Which sentences seem out of order?
6. Rewrite the paragraph. Begin your revision with the first sentence as given, but rearrange the rest of the sentences, adding or deleting material to make the paragraph more unified and coherent.

Task 2   *Testing for Unity and Coherence*

Someone read the following passage aloud. Then answer the questions and follow the instructions collaboratively.

>[1]There are two reasons I like thunderstorms. [2]One of them is that I just like strange things. [3]I have strange tastes in just about everything. [4]Not that I'd eat chocolate-covered ants. [5]But I know someone who'll even do that. [6]He spent three years in Africa where they have ants like you wouldn't believe. [7]Once he got caught in the path of some army ants and they began to crawl up his legs, so he had to be broomed down or the ants would have eaten *him*. [8]People who live in that part of Africa have to be on guard against that sort of thing all the time. [9]The heat gets to you there too. [10]That's one thing I can't stand. [11]Last summer the sidewalk in front of our house was so hot I bet my buddy I could fry an egg on it and, you know what, I did. [12]Not that I wanted to eat the egg after I fried it. [13]Dirt bothers me a lot. [14]I spend a lot of time cleaning house.

1. What question does the first sentence in this paragraph generate? Does the second sentence help answer that question?
2. List by number all the sentences in the paragraph that *do not* answer a question raised by the sentence that precedes it. (That is, does sentence 3 answer a question raised by sentence 2? Does sentence 4 answer a question raised by sentence 3?
3. Write a general principle of paragraph coherence based on this analysis.
4. Write a question that most of the paragraph seems to be answering.
5. Is there a sentence anywhere in the paragraph that seems to raise that question?
6. List by number all the sentences in the paragraph that help answer the question that the first sentence generates.
7. Write a general principle based on this analysis that distinguishes between paragraph unity and paragraph coherence.

8. If a friend of yours wrote this paragraph in an essay and asked you to help her with it, what would you tell her is well done? What suggestions would you give her to improve the paragraph?

Task 3 *Direction Signals*

Someone in the group read aloud the following paragraph from John Fischer's "Substitutes for Violence." Then answer the questions and follow the instructions collaboratively.

[1]As civilization began to dawn, fighting became more organized—a community enterprise rather than a family one. [2]In addition to their daily skirmishes with wolves, cattle thieves, and passing strangers, the able-bodied men of the village (or polis, kingdom, or pueblo) normally banded together at least once a year for a joint killing venture. [3]The covenient time for settled farming people was early fall, after the harvest was in; then they had both enough leisure and enough surplus food to mount an expedition. [4]So it was about September when the Assyrians swept down like a wolf on the fold, when Gideon smote the Philistines, when Vikings ravaged the Kentish coast, when the Greeks shoved off for Troy, when the Dorians swept into the Argive plain, irresistibly armed with that first mass weapon, the iron sword. [5](Because iron ore was much more plentiful than copper, it could be used—once the secret of smelting was learned—to equip every man in the ranks. [6]The victims of the Dorians, still lingering in the Bronze Age, normally armed only their officers with metal blades; the rest carried flint-tipped spears and arrows.) [7]Tribes in the preagricultural stage sometimes found other seasons more suitable for rapine. [8]The War Moon of the Great Plains Indians, for example, came in May—since the spring grass was then just high enough to graze the horses of a raiding party, and the full moon made it easy to travel fast at night. [9]Regardless of timing, however, warfare was for centuries the main social enterprise, absorbing virtually all of the community's surplus time, energy, and resources. [10]"History," as William James put it, "is a bath of blood . . . war for war's sake, all the citizens being warriors . . . [11]To hunt a neighboring tribe, kill the males, loot the village, and possess the females was the most profitable, as well as the most exciting, way of living."

1. Map the paragraph (mapping is explained in Getting Ready to Write a Detailed *Does* Statement, p. 165).
2. Mark the words and phrases in each sentence that refer backward to something said in an earlier sentence and those that refer ahead to something said later. Draw an arrow under each of these words showing the direction of their connection, backward or forward.
3. List the types of transitional elements that occur in the paragraph.

Task 4 Paragraph Organization Game

The following sentences are the scrambled second paragraph of an essay. The essay's proposition is "Reform must take place within the reservation system."

Read the sentences aloud in the order that they appear here. Then number them in an order that seems to make the paragraph coherent. Read them aloud again in that order to check your results.

1. _____ a. They offered $24 in glass beads to take it off the hands of the white man.

2. _____ b. They want government's role reduced to hired experts living outside the reservation and some financial aid—
3. _____ not total control.

       c. In a dramatic demonstration of this dissatisfaction, four-
4. _____ teen Indian college students invaded Alcatraz, claiming ownership "by right of discovery."

5. _____ d. In 1961, they published the *Declaration of Indian Purpose*, advocating the development of their own program and
6. _____ asking for assistance from a local decentralized staff.

       e. In addition, they formed the "Bureau of Caucasian
7. _____ Affairs," the counterpart of the white Bureau of Indian Affairs.

8. _____ f. The Indians themselves do not favor ending the system, although they are greatly dissatisfied with the reserva-
9. _____ tion as it stands.

       g. The Indians may want to continue living on the reservation, but with their own tribal councils.

       h. The island, they asserted, had all the features of a reservation: dangerously uninhabitable buildings, no fresh water, inadequate sanitation, and the certainty of total unemployment.

       i. Despite the implications of this demonstration, however, the Indians do not want to do away with the reservation.

Task 5 Paragraph Organization Game

The following sentences are the scrambled third paragraph of an example essay in this book. The essay's proposition is "The best way tutors can help struggling students is by maintaining a relaxed and warm relationship with them."

Read the sentences aloud in the order that they appear here. Then number them in an order that seems to make the paragraph coherent. Read them aloud again in that order to check your results.

1. ＿＿   a. Again, I speak from experience.

b. In these cases, I have found that once the tutor breaks

2. ＿＿   through that feeling of tension and discouragement by chatting informally, students are able to loosen up and

3. ＿＿   their thoughts flow more freely.

c. On the contrary, tutors begin to serve as faithful friends

4. ＿＿   or as relaxing-agents whom struggling students know they can rely on in time of need.

5. ＿＿   d. The tutor may then find it unnecessary to offer so many suggestions.

6. ＿＿   e. This attitude can become an enormous obstacle to progress.

7. ＿＿   f. In this case, I was the one who profited from working in a relaxed and warm atmosphere.

8. ＿＿   g. Students become so obsessed with the idea that they are incapable of writing.

9. ＿＿   h. But tutors are not the only people who benefit.

i. This is not to say that tutors come to play an unimpor-

10. ＿＿   tant role.

j. In the two months I have spent as a tutor I have met

11. ＿＿   many students who have begun to believe that they will never be able to write a passing paper without help.

k. They begin to realize that they know more about writing than they thought they did, and many times they can find their own mistakes.

Task 6   *Reorganizing a Paragraph*

Read the following passage aloud. Then rewrite it. Begin the revision with the first sentence of the paragraph as given. Make that sentence the topic sentence of your revision. In analyzing the paragraph, use these questions as a guide:

1. What belongs in the paragraph and what does not?
2. What, if anything, should be added?
3. How should the sentences be rearranged to make the paragraph more unified and coherent?

[1]In Israel today, one cause of the difference between the way European-American people and Afro-Asian people raise their children is the great difference in the family structures of these two groups. [2]As a general rule, Afro-Asian families tend to be closer than European-American families. [3]The Afro-Asian woman marries at a very young age. [4]She usually has an average of five or six live births during her lifetime. [5]The European-American woman has an average of two or three live births. [6]A great many women of European-American descent put their children in nursery schools and go out and work to supplement their family incomes. [7]Afro-Asian families tend to be very religious and old-fashioned. [8]Very few of their women work outside the home. [9]Because their families are so large, Afro-Asian people make up the poorer segment of the Israeli population. [10]They live in far-off villages, farm areas, or the slum areas of the major cities. [11]Statistics have shown that there is a higher divorce rate among European-American couples, even though they tend to marry at an older age compared to Afro-Asian couples. [12]Until recently there was very little intermarriage among these two groups. [13]In fact, these two groups rarely mix socially.

"But Why Can't I Write a 'Conclusion'?"

Of course you can write a "conclusion"—that is, put an ending on your essay—eventually. But please, not right now.

There are three reasons you should avoid "conclusions" in the early stages of learning about formal organization in writing.

One reason is that you may have been misled into thinking that a "conclusion" is just a summary of your argument. You may have been taught the venerable principle: Tell them what you're going to say, say it, then tell them what you've said. A summary that tells them what you said can sometimes be useful at the end of a very long essay. But a summary tacked onto the end of a short essay is the least useful way to end it.

Another reason to avoid writing a "conclusion" at first is that writing an effective ending for an essay is a unique problem in itself. An effective ending is not part of the explanation or defense of the paper's proposition, although it may extend the paper's exploration of the implications of that proposition. An effective ending is part of the way the essay packages its proposition. Paragraphs of explanation or defense refer inward to the position taken in the paper's proposition. An ending refers outward to the readers' interests, just as introductions do.

The third reason to avoid writing a "conclusion" at first is the danger that what you "save for the conclusion" might be the whole point of the essay. The formal exercises in this book ask you to make that point not at the end of the essay but toward the beginning: in the last sentence of the first paragraph.

You may find the temptation to write at least a "concluding sentence" overwhelming at first. That is a good sign. It shows that you have already gained a kind of innate formal sense. You feel the need to wrap things up. So, if not writing a "conclusion" is too painful at first, by all means go ahead and write one. Then just leave it off the final version of the paper. This is a kind of ruse, but it may ease the withdrawal process some, and it won't do any harm.

The only thing to make sure of in doing the essay exercises in this book is not to put a formal ending on the final version of the essay. At the end of the explanation or defense, just stop. No "conclusion."

(There is more about how to package an essay effectively in Part Four: Reaching Out to Members of Other Communities, p. 189.)

ASSUMPTIONS

Assumptions are beliefs, facts, or opinions that you take for granted. You usually do not discuss them, explore them, explain them, defend them, or subject them to analysis. You often aren't even aware of many of your assumptions, although every statement you make is based on many of them. They are the premises or biases that you tend not to bring up or mention in conversation with your friends, because you assume (another assumption) that your friends assume what you assume.

As a writer and reader, though, it is important to try to become as aware of your assumptions as you can. As a writer, you cannot assume that all your readers asusme what you assume. If they don't, they may well misunderstand you. As a reader, you may misunderstand what you are reading if you are not aware of the assumptions that underlie it. So when you analyze something to discover its assumptions, you may find out something you may not know about yourself while you are finding out something about your readers or the writer of something you have read.

Sometimes writers come clean and tell us their assumptions. Sometimes they do not. If writers do not tell us what their assumptions are, they are not necessarily being dishonest or devious. They may only be assuming (as we tend to do with our friends) that all their readers share their assumptions. So it is often a good idea to try to discover the assumptions that underlie what you read, the unstated assumptions, just to be absolutely sure that you understand what the essay is getting at and to make sure that it isn't trying to pull the wool over your eyes.

DISCOVERING ASSUMPTIONS

One way to discover a writer's unstated assumptions is to analyze key sentences in the essay to discover the questions that they raise. For example, the undeveloped essay on smog, p. 112, makes several unstated assumptions. Some of these the writer may be aware of, some of them he may not.

¶1   The smog in this city is terrible. We could solve the smog problem by keeping cars out of the city.

¶2   For one thing, cars produce all the worst kinds of air pollution.

¶3   Another reason is that cars produce a greater volume of pollutants than any other source.

The writer could develop the proposition in this example by developing paragraphs 2 and 3. But the proposition cannot be developed completely in this way. The paragraph raises a number of questions. A coherent essay could answer only one of them: "Why will keeping cars out of the city solve the smog problem?" The essay as it is sketched out now cannot answer at least three more questions that the proposition raises. The answers to these questions are among the essay's unstated assumptions.

We could solve the smog problem by keeping cars out of the city.

Who is "we"?

"Who are we? . . ."

How *can* cars be kept out of the city?

Who is "we"? The *we* in this example essay is a rhetorical, or editorial, *we.* By talking about what "we" can do, the essay tries (whether consciously or not) to enlist our sympathy on behalf of the position taken in it. Because the essay's *we* includes us without asking our permission, using the word may be a subtle form of intimidation. The essay assumes the reader's agreement with its position before it has legitimately gained that agreement by exploring, explaining, or defending its position.

"Who are we? . . ." The *we* in the example essay is also a device for suggesting—without stating it explicitly—that engaged, active members of the public have power to effect important changes in the quality of life everyone shares. That is, the essay assumes that "we" have power that some timid or reserved readers might not actually feel. They might say to themselves, "Sure pollution is bad, but who are we to say what ought to be done about it?" The essay tries to enlist our sympathy by assuming that, on the contrary, "we" know what's good for us, "we" have a right to say what we think, and "we" have a right to take action to make things better.

How *can* cars be kept out of the city? Finally, the essay assumes that keeping cars out of the city is technically and politically feasible. Or perhaps, on the other hand, it assumes that how cars are to be kept out is not a matter of immediate concern: it's a problem we can solve when we get around to it. That is, the essay is apparently willing to leave until later the problem of how to put into effect the change it proposes. Maybe the writer will take a position on that in the next essay.

Another example of a proposition that makes unstated assumptions is the proposition of the paper on cars in exercise 5: "Cars may be on the way out as our major means of transportation." This proposition leaves unspecified exactly what it means by "cars" and exactly what it means by the phrase "on the way out." Readers might also want to raise issues such as how long the process of phasing out cars as a means of transportation has been going on, why it began, and how one might be expected to measure such a trend.

Every issue but the central one ("Are cars on the way out?") reveals unstated assumptions that the proposition rests on, assumptions about causes, definition of terms, criteria of measurement, and criteria of judgment. Even the in-out metaphor in which the position is expressed (cars may be "on the way out") may reveal something about the writer's values that is not made explicit anywhere in the essay. For example, we often refer to something being in or out of fashion (jeans are in, saddle shoes are out). So the proposition implies something about our choice of transportation that the essay doesn't really think about, since it doesn't focus on taste but on utility.

ALLOWABLE ASSUMPTIONS

Because every statement you make contains implicit assumptions, it would be redundant and exhausting to explore all the assumptions that writers make. For this reason, every essay's proposition expects readers to accept something on faith for the sake of argument.

Assumptions that readers are willing to accept on faith are allowable assumptions. Writers have to judge which aspects of their subject and which of their assumptions they can leave unexplained, in the belief that readers share and will not question them. Conscientious writers make their more dubious and arguable assumptions explicit, because they want readers to be aware that they are making them.

In this book, for example, the first two paragraphs of the Introduction explain some of the book's assumptions but leave others unexplained in the hope that readers will allow them:

The purpose of this short course in writing is to help students learn to read and write better through collaborative learning. Collaborative learning assumes that reading and writing are not solitary, individual activities, but social and collaborative ones. When we read and write we are never alone, although we may seem to be. We are always in the company of communities of other readers and writers whose language and interests we share.

Collaborative learning places this social, collaborative nature of reading and writing at the center of college and university education. This book, based on collaborative learning principles, turns writing classrooms into collaborative classrooms by making them active, constructive communities of readers and writers and by making students' own writing the most important text in the course.

Most of the assumptions in these two paragraphs are about the nature of collaborative learning and its place and function in college and university education. The paragraphs make one of these assumptions explicit:

> *Collaborative learning assumes that reading and writing are not solitary, individual activities, but social and collaborative ones.*

The paragraphs also assume, less explicitly, that teachers who make their classrooms into "active, constructive communities of readers and writers" in which the "students' own writing" is "the most important text in the course" are actually teaching. Some readers might allow both these assumptions. Others might allow the first but not the second. Still others might regard both of them as nonsense.

To defend these assumptions would go beyond the scope of a writing textbook. So the writer leaves unexplained how readers might arrive at the assumptions he has arrived at. He also leaves unexplored the assumptions that underlie some of the metaphors he uses such as *company, share, center,* even *collaborate.* He assumes, without explanation, that most readers' reflections upon their own experiences as writers and teachers will verify what he assumes. He hopes in any case that, after this reflection, most readers will allow his assumptions, because they are the assumptions on which the rest of the book is based.

When readers refuse to allow a writer's assumptions, or when readers and writers are unaware that their assumptions differ, the inevitable result is misunderstanding. This is what happens when people use the same words to describe different things, or use different words to describe the same thing. When economists talk about *full employment,* for example, they may mean a situation in which only 3 or 4 percent of the labor force is unemployed. To a person who cannot find a job, and is therefore a member of that 3 or 4 percent, an economist's idea of full employment is little better than a bad joke. To unemployed people, full employment occurs when they themselves have jobs and can support their families.

The same sort of difference, which sometimes leads to misunderstanding, occurs between academic disciplines. For example, ask a mathematician, a biologist, an economist, and a historian what they mean by the word *description* and you will get quite a different answer in every case. A mathematician means a graphic action or a kind of equation (as in "describe an arc"). A biologist means a systematic and schematic diagram of a living creature or organ. An economist means a nonchronological generalization based in most cases on accumulated individual decisions, that is, statistical evidence. A historian means a narrative— the story of an event—usually chronological in nature, cut across with analytical discussion that relates one moment with some other moment. Students who face exam questions in different courses in which the word *description* appears have to be aware of the different ways the word is used and the different assumptions underlying its use, or else they risk failing their exams.

DANGER: UNALLOWABLE ASSUMPTIONS

This discussion of unstated or unacknowledged assumptions reveals some startling aspects of writing. Most writers leave assumptions unstated because they take it for granted that their readers agree with them and know as much about the subject as the writer knows. Most writers assume that they and their readers share important values and preconceptions as well as relevant background information. If this agreement is all we discover when we look for writers' assumptions, then we can probably feel relatively safe in their hands.

But some writers may leave their assumptions unstated for less honest reasons. They may not state their assumptions because they are sure (or are willing to bet) that their readers do *not* share their knowledge and values. They hide their assumptions in order to delude or misinform their readers. These writers sense that if they stated their assumptions clearly, readers would reject what they have to say. They leave their assumptions unstated in order to try to con readers into accepting ideas that otherwise, with full knowledge, they would not accept. When you discover writers doing this, you have to read cautiously.

COLLABORATIVE LEARNING

Follow the instructions for working in consensus groups on p. 20.

Task   Discovering Assumptions

Write out the proposition sentence and the first sentence in paragraphs 2 and 3 of an example essay in this book.

1. List the operative words in each sentence. (There is more about finding operative terms in Propositions, p. 85, and What an Essay *Says*, p. 154).

2. Write out as many questions as you can that each of these sentences may raise in the reader's mind. (There is more about the questions that sentences raise in Paragraph Development, p. 111.)

3. Which questions raised by the proposition sentence do paragraphs 2 and 3 of each relevant essay *not* answer? What do you suppose the writer's reasons were in each case for not answering them? Has the writer made only allowable assumptions?

STYLE

Suppose you are reading an essay that defends the proposition, "It is time to abolish capital punishment." The essay begins with these two sentences:

> The most serious method of punishment in human society is the death penalty, the exacting of the life of offenders for their offense. In making use of such means of punishment, society incurs a grave responsibility.

Now suppose that the writer tells you that she's not satisfied with these sentences and asks for our help. If you respond only that you think the sentences are bad or awkward and need to be rewritten, she will be offended as well as justifiably confused. The sentences are rather awkward, although they are perfectly grammatical, and they do need to be rewritten. But if you condemn them out of hand you will not help this writer improve them.

TALKING CONSTRUCTIVELY ABOUT STYLE

You could help her improve them in two ways. One is to show her that in some respects she had done exactly what she should have done. The other is to help her see how she can do those things better. (See Learning to Write Peer Reviews, p. 173.)

There is a lot to praise in the passage. For one thing, it deals with an important topic. Some people, of course, may think that as a topic to write an essay on, the death penalty is old hat, whereas in fact it continues to be a legal and moral issue throughout the Western world. For another thing, the passage approaches that topic in a serious way. Of course, some people may not agree with what the writer seems to be saying about it. But to her, these views on capital punishment may be a real discovery. It may be the first time she has worked out her ideas on the subject and the first time she has realized why she feels as she does about it. In approaching the topic, she has made a decisive value judgment (the death penalty involves human responsibility) and she has accurately defined the key term in the passage, *the death penalty*.

Furthermore, the main clause in the second sentence, "society incurs a grave responsibility," is succinct, readable, and appropriate in tone to the idea expressed. The intent of the opening phrase of the second sentence, "In making use of such means," indicates that the writer is aware of the need to make transitions, in this case linking the definition of the key term to the major value judgment stated in the passage "society incurs a grave responsibility," a statement that will probably lead to the proposition of the paper. Even the serious pun (the death penalty is a "grave responsibility") enforces the point of the passage. These virtues, as well as the rhythm and sound of some parts of the passage, suggest that the writer may have a good native ear for the language.

You could also point out that the writer probably intentionally avoided at least two ways in which she could have improved the passage. The two ways to improve the passage are to make use of rhetorical repetition and break the passage up into shorter sentences. She may have avoided both because she has been told that to repeat words and write short sentences will make her writing repetitious and choppy— that is, they would make her writing seem childish: Dick and Jane writing.

HOW TO IMPROVE AWKWARD STYLE

So one thing you could say to this writer is that in trying hard to avoid childish style, she has obscured the real potential of these sentences. She has tried to make the first sentence say more than any single sentence should be asked to say, or at least more than she is yet able to make a single sentence say:

> The most serious method of punishment in human society is the death penalty, the exacting of the life of offenders for their offense.

The first suggestion you could give her about this sentence is to make it into two sentences, not one:

> The most serious method of punishment in human society is the death penalty. [This is] the exacting of the life of offenders for their offense.

Once she divides the sentence in half, she will probably see right away that she can improve the first of these two new sentences by the simple process of cutting out some words:

> The most serious ~~method of~~ punishment in human society is ~~the~~ death ~~penalty~~.
> The most serious punishment in human society is death.

Also, although it is not necessary and would only provide other ways of saying the same thing, she could rearrange the parts of the sentence:

> Human society's most serious punishment is death.
> Death is human society's most serious punishment.

There are of course other ways she could state the idea just as simply and effectively.

The second sentence, created by cutting the original first sentence in half, became a sentence by giving the unattached phrase a subject and a verb:

> **This is** the exacting of the life of offenders for their offense.

In this form, however, the most important aspects of the idea are un-related to the most important parts of the sentence. The most important parts of most sentences are the subject and verb. To help the writer make the important aspects of the idea and the important parts of the sentence coincide, you could ask her two questions:

> What is doing something in this sentence? A: **Society.**
> What does it do? A: **It exacts.**

Then you could suggest that she turn the answer to question 1 into the subject of the sentence and turn the answer to question 2 into the verb.

> **This is** the exacting of the life of offenders for their offense.
> **Society exacts** the life of offenders for their offense.

In this way, the first sentence of the original passage

> The most serious method of punishment in human society is the death penalty, the exacting of the life of offenders for their offense.

has become by stages two new sentences:

> The most serious punishment in human society is death.
> Society exacts the life of offenders for their offense.

You could also show the writer at this point that she could state the idea expressed in the second sentence allusively, if she wanted to. She could give the idea extra force by referring to a commonly known phrase drawn from the Bible.

Society exacts the life of offenders for their offense.
Society demands an eye for an eye and a tooth for a tooth.

So much for the first sentence in the original passage. Now you could show the writer that the second sentence shows in a different way that she does know what she wants to do but does not know yet quite how to do it:

In making use of such means of punishment, society incurs a grave responsibility.

In the introductory phrase of this sentence

In making use of such means of punishment . . .

she quite properly links the first thing she says in the essay with the second:

Society exacts the life of offenders for their offense. In making use of **such means of punishment** . . .

But in doing so, she confuses two idioms. We usually do not say that we *make use of* means. We usually say that we *adopt* means. We say that we *make use of methods*. But even with this change, the phrase is not entirely satisfactory:

In making use of such methods of punishment . . .

The phrase is euphemistic. It avoids saying something directly and in the way we are most likely to say it when we are talking to each other. It beats around the bush, and it takes too many words to say a fairly simple thing. Other ways to say it are

In punishing people in that way . . .

or

In taking that life . . .

If the writer substituted one of these phrases for the one she began with, the opening of her essay, in thirty-seven words,

The most serious method of punishment in human society is the death penalty, the exacting of the life of offenders for their offense. In making use of such means of punishment, society incurs a grave responsibility.

would finally become the following, in twenty-eight words:

> The most serious punishment in human society is death. Society exacts the life of offenders for their offense. In taking that life, society incurs a grave responsibility.

Now the passage fulfills its original potential. It is succinct and readable. The sentences are a little shorter—at nine, ten, and nine words respectively—than the professional average, which is about fifteen words. But they are varied in form, their structure is uncomplicated, they are well articulated, and they contain no words or phrases used merely to dress up the writing. The passage repeats the key word *society* twice, but this in itself does not make the passage repetitious. On the contrary, it helps make the passage cohere.

The result is simple but in no sense simpleminded. You would have helped this writer toward the kind of unpretentious, economical writing from which her own personal style can grow as she grows.

COLLABORATIVE LEARNING

Follow the instructions for working in consensus groups on p. 20.

Task 1   Simplifying Sentences

Rewrite the following sentences to make them less pretentious and more succinct and readable.

1. Prior to the acquisition of my college diploma, I formulated my goals on the assumption that I would have little difficulty obtaining a remunerative and satisfying position.
2. Upon receiving an aural impression of the detonation, the somewhat overweight officer of the law emerged from the edifice at a rapid pace and apprehended the perpetrator of the disturbance.
3. Security has meant varying pursuits and differing goals for diverse periods of history.
4. His verbal accomplishments notwithstanding, how could the author of *Pilgrim's Progress* hope to find a receptive reader in the present epoch: small the hope indeed if Bunyan were merely one of the many polemicists of the day in whom the spirit of the artist had not fused with the soul of the reformer.
5. The answer to your inquiry is the positive one, Virginia, that the existence of Santa Claus is certain.

Task 2   Muddling Sentences

Rewrite the following sentences to make them as wordy, pretentious, uneconomical, and muddled as you can.

1. Last Saturday I got a terrific bargain on a boat.
2. A farm is a great place to bring up children.
3. If you can't stand the heat, stay out of the kitchen.
4. We could solve the smog problem by keeping cars out of the city.
5. As the sun rose, he kissed her and told her he would never leave her, and then he left.

Task 3   Testing Sentence Length

Here again is the paragraph from Winston Churchill's *My Early Life*. Test the length of Churchill's sentences.

First, guess what you think the average length of Churchill's sentences is, and write down your guess.

Then count the words in each sentence and group the sentences by number in order of length, beginning with the shortest.

Write out the six shortest sentences in order of length.

Figure out the average length of sentences in the paragraph, leaving the longest sentence in the paragraph out of your calculations (because it is extreme and therefore abnormal).

How close did your guess come to the actual average? What does the difference tell you about how long you think your own sentences should normally be?

[1]I continued in this unpretentious situation for nearly a year. [2]However, by being so long in the lowest form I gained an immense advantage over the cleverer boys. [3]They all went on to learn Latin and Greek and splendid things like that. [4]But I was taught English. [5]We were considered such dunces that we could learn only English. [6]Mr. Somervell—a most delightful man, to whom my debt is great—was charged with the duty of teaching the stupidest boys the most disregarded thing—namely, to write mere English. [7]He knew how to do it. [8]He taught it as no one else has ever taught it. [9]Not only did we learn English parsing thoroughly, but we also practiced continually English analysis. [10]Mr. Somervell had a system of his own. [11]He took a fairly long sentence and broke it up into its components by means of black, red, blue, and green inks. [12]Subject, verb, object: Relative Clauses, Conditional Clauses, Conjunctive and Disjunctive Clauses! [13]Each had its color and its bracket. [14]It was a kind of drill. [15]We did it almost daily. [16]As I remained in the Third Form (B) three times as long as anyone else, I had three times as much of it. [17]I learned it thoroughly. [18]Thus I got into my bones the essential structure of the ordinary British sentence—which is a noble thing. [19]And when in after

years my schoolfellows who had won prizes and distinction for writing such beautiful Latin poetry and pithy Greek epigrams had to come down again to common English, to earn their living or make their way, I did not feel myself at any disadvantage. [20]Naturally I am biased in favor of boys learning English. [21]I would make them all learn English, and then I would let the clever ones learn Latin as an honor, and Greek as a treat. [22]But the only thing I would whip them for is not knowing English. [23]I would whip them hard for that.

LEARNING FORMAL ORGANIZATION: THE CRUNCH

Before you have completed the first nine exercises in this book, you may begin to feel impatient and irritable. You may feel that doing these five-hundred word, three-paragraph exercises is futile, perhaps even destructive of your identity and creativity. If you found it easy at first to repeat the three-paragraph form mechanically, you may now discover that you can't do that any longer. And if you found the form hard at first, you may now begin to find it utterly impossible. You may begin feeling that you can't find subjects to write about that seem to fit the form. You may want to tear the book up, drop the course, and forget the whole thing.

This is the writing course crunch. No writing course should be without one.

The writing course crunch is the moment when you face the question, "Am I going to control my words and my ideas, or am I going to go on letting my words and ideas control me?" To choose to control your words and ideas, you may have to undergo a disturbing change. This change involves a change in the way you think about yourself. You may have to become less passive, dependent, and self-deprecating, and instead become more autonomous, self-possessed, and self-controlled.

A change of this sort is necessary because of the deep and complex relationship between language and identity. When you write you tend to feel exposed. Everyone does, because we do expose aspects of ourselves when we write. You began learning language very early in your life, so language is strongly tied into your identity. When you write, your language reveals your thoughts and feelings, some deeply buried in the core of your self, as saplings are buried at the core of mature trees. Your first words, and the feelings you expressed with them, don't go away. They get buried within you. They become part of who you are. As a result, when you write you may feel you are inadvertently revealing aspects of your identity that you are not wholly aware of and that may not be entirely under your control.

That is why criticism of your writing may feel like criticism of your self. In a limited sense, it is. You construct a lot of what you call your *self* with the language you learn in early life. So when someone criticizes the language you use, they are criticizing something that feels as close to you as your self.

It is hard to escape that feeling entirely, but you can at least control how strongly you feel it. You can control your feelings about criticism of your writing by shaping what you write, by giving it form, and in that way distancing it from yourself. Formal control in writing is an act of social adaptation. When you control what you say with formal conventions of the sort that you learn in this book, you adapt your inner thoughts and feelings, derived from the language of communities that you belonged to earlier in life, to the new communities of people that you now address when you write.

Because your inner thoughts and feelings are compounded of the languages of the many communities you have belonged to and that you belong to now, they have a logic of their own. That logic may be so complex that it is hard for other people to understand. Trying to make some of your own particular mix of many languages understandable and accessible to other people when you write can therefore make you feel a little bit apprehensive. Will you be able to get through to them? You can allay some of that apprehension by shaping your ideas in conventional, formal ways.

But allaying your anxiety by shaping your ideas in conventional ways is not always an easy task. The random, associative logic of your inner thoughts is so complex that it sometimes feels like a hodgepodge that is peculiarly and hopelessly your own. You cannot possibly present yourself in that way in writing. No one would understand you. And yet to untangle the knot so that other people can grasp the thread and follow it requires, as one of my students once put it, much mental sweat.

In order to control your thoughts and feelings by giving them some kind of form, furthermore, you have to know what other people's expectations are. You have to know the form that people in the community you are addressing are used to and agree on in order to communicate with each other. The form that this book teaches is one of the forms that the community of educated people agrees on.

But you change your thoughts and feelings when you give them form. So you also change yourself to some extent. While you are making that change, you may feel somewhat unsure of yourself and about the outcome. This uncertainty adds a new element of anxiety to the fear of exposure when you write. When you write, you volunteer to reveal your thoughts and feelings, and by revealing them, change them. At that moment, you are in a sort of no-man's-land between your old self and some unknown new self in the making. Your anxiety in writing results from the fact that you are vulnerable. You are courting exposure during a process of change, a process that would make you feel insecure even if you underwent it entirely in private.

This condition of writing never changes. Writing anxiety is never likely to disappear entirely for anyone. I feel a little nervous even revising this book. Fortunately, however, most of us can reduce that anxiety to the point where it no longer paralyzes us but prods us to do better work.

The best way I know of to reduce writing anxiety is, as Eleanor Gaffney explains in her essay (p. 325), to join a community of fellow writers. To be able to share anxiety often helps allay it. This is one reason that collaborative learning is valuable in learning to write. During the period of change that is involved, you give your student peers sympathy, encouragement, and support, and you expect your student peers to give you sympathy, encouragement, and support as well. It may help if you spend an hour or so in a group gripe session once in a while, talking about how hard writing is, why anyone bothers to write, why essays are sometimes such a pain to write, and what the benefits of writing in a controlled way may be. It often helps to talk about why, as Mark Twain put it, we often hate to write but love having written.

Your teachers can help by reminding you of the practical payoff of controlled writing. The payoff is that you will be able to write clearer, more substantial, and, therefore, more successful examinations and papers in academic courses. Later on you will be able to write clearer, more substantial, and more successful letters, reports, and memos at work. You will be able to discover and formulate an opinion about any subject—academic, political, aesthetic, or whatever, just as Mr. Metzger can in William Perry's essay (p. 343), but more knowledgeably and honestly. In doing that, you also stand to gain more self-knowledge. It is valuable to feel strongly about something, it is more valuable to be able to generalize and formulate what you feel so that you know why you feel that way, and it is even more valuable still to be able to explain what you feel to other people in hopes of leading them to feel the same way.

This is why it is important to remain firm during the writing course crunch. Keep on practicing writing essays in the form the book asks for. You can always write extra essays, if you want to, in any other form you choose.

If you let up on yourself at this crucial moment, and if your peers and your teacher let up on you, you will lose the opportunity that the form offers to confront yourself, your ideas, and your language. To grow as a writer and gain new confidence in your ability to write well and the value of your own ideas, you have to endure the writing course crunch.

PART THREE

Constructive Reading

To be a good writer, you have to be a good reader. The better you can read, the better you can write. Good readers are constructive readers. *Constructive readers* read in order to understand how something they are reading is constructed—how it is put together—as well as what it means.

That is, many good readers are in effect writing something like a descriptive outline in their heads all the while they are reading. They are continuously aware of what something they are reading *does* in relation to the whole essay, as well as what it *says*. That is why you have to be a good reader in order to be a good writer. To control what you write, you have to know what your writing *does* and *says*. You have to read what you write in the same way that you read what anyone else has written: constructively.

There are several reasons to read constructively when you write. One reason is that your first reader is always yourself. You read what you write while you're writing it. When you write something and then read and revise it, you make sense to yourself and other people. **Making sense is constructing sense.** So to make sense you have to be a constructive writer as well as a constructive reader.

The second reason to read constructively when you write is that no one writes in a vacuum. Every time you write you join a conversation already in progress. Other writers write, and sooner or later you write back. You write, and sooner or later someone else writes back. Whenever you feel that you have something to say, you are responding to what other people have already written and said. What you write keeps the conversation going. You read constructively because you want to know whether you are keeping the conversation going in the direction it was already headed or sending it off in an entirely new direction.

Because writing is part of a conversation with other readers and writers, you have to be able to understand what other writers have written. So the third reason to read constructively is that when you are using professional writing as a source, such as textbooks and scholarly articles, you can feel more confident that you understand what they are saying and doing.

Finally, reading constructively helps you find out *how* other writers write, so that you can do the same sort of thing yourself sometime, maybe even better, or at least you can avoid their mistakes. After a lot of practice reading constructively, you may even find yourself reading your own writing more objectively, almost as if someone else had written it. Constructive reading helps you control your writing by making you one of your own peer reviewers.

The purpose of Part Three is to help you read more constructively in all these ways. It explains how reading aloud gets you involved in a community of writers. It explains using descriptive outlines to show how writers construct their essays to make sense. And it explains how peer reviews help you and your classmates improve your writing.

(There is more about communities of writers in Part Four, Reaching Out to Members of Other Communities, p. 189.)

READING ALOUD

Reading is a constructive activity because it is a social activity, just as speaking and writing are social activities. All three are social activities because all three involve language. Language is a social construct. This means that human beings continually make and remake language and learn and relearn language in conversation with each other.

Because language is a social construct, even reading alone is a social process. When you read, you are engaged in conversation with the person who wrote what you are reading. And you are also engaged in conversation with the other people who have read what you are reading, who are now reading it, or who are going to read it. Some of these people are alive. Some of them have been dead for centuries. Some have yet to be born. Dead, alive, or unborn, they are all engaged in conversation with you through what they have written, are writing, and have yet to write; and you are engaged with them in turn through what you write.

WHY READ ALOUD?

Reading aloud is actually a form of publication, like getting your essay printed in a journal or a magazine. In fact, reading aloud is the oldest, easiest, friendliest, and most economical form of publication. Writers have been reading their work aloud for thousands of years. What happens among writers when they read their work aloud is that, right from the start, they begin to get interested in each other and begin to trust each other. They become a community of writers engaged in constructive conversation about writing.

Constructive conversation about writing takes two forms. It can be direct talk, face-to-face. Or it can be indirect talk, talk displaced into writing. Reading aloud is an important part of learning to read and write constructively because it instantaneously transforms one sort of thing (written conversation) into another (face-to-face conversation). Reading aloud puts the ball into play.

Writers sometimes read aloud in order to transform written conversation into face-to-face conversation for the same reason that composers and playwrights perform their work publicly and painters and sculptors display their work in museums and galleries. Knowing how writing sounds when you read your work aloud and hear other writers read their work aloud helps you control language instead of letting language control you. When you hear yourself read what you have written aloud, and when you hear others read aloud, you begin to feel more responsible for what you write.

You begin to acquire this new responsibility when you get the immediate response of a community of sympathetic peers. Sympathetic peers don't necessarily agree with what you write, or even know much about it, but they know how hard it is to write anything at all, and they are willing to listen to you and to talk with you about what you've written. If you know that other people are going to listen to what you are writing and are going to talk about it with you, you will be a lot more careful about what you write and how you write it. Response from other writers diminishes the solitude of writing that encourages carelessness and that makes writing sometimes feel futile and obsessively self-involved.

With time and practice, reading your own work aloud and hearing other writers read their work aloud can also help you become more aware of what is actually down there on the page. You will discover that people can hear relationships, some of which you weren't quite aware of yourself, among the parts of your essays. You will discover that they can respond to what you have written in ways that are really helpful. You will begin to trust those responses and discover that your fellow students respect the helpful responses you are making to their writing. And you will discover that people can even find ideas in what you have written that you hadn't been aware of.

You may also discover that reading aloud gives you new courage by making you more willing to risk writing what you really have on your mind. You will find that other writers really are interested in what you have to say. They will want to talk to you about it and write back. You will find yourself getting interested in what they have to say, too. You will want to talk to them about that and write back. You will collect more topics to write about than you would have time for in a dozen writing courses. And you will discover differences you never knew about between your own interests, ideas, and background and other people's interests, ideas, and backgrounds: between your likes and dislikes and other people's.

Finally, when you read your work aloud and hear other writers read their work aloud, sooner or later you will begin to write "by ear." When you read aloud, you can't help but hear what you have written. So by reading aloud you will eventually learn to hear what you write as you write it, before you read it aloud. That will help you write better, because a lot of awkward, incoherent, pretentious writing results from only seeing writing on the page instead of hearing it there. The more you read aloud and listen to your classmates read aloud, the more likely your own writing will become succinct and readable.

WHEN AND HOW TO READ ALOUD

You can read your work aloud in different ways for different purposes. First, read your work aloud to yourself often while you are writing and revising. That will help you hear your work as you write. It will also get you ready to read clearly and effectively to your classmates.

All the writers in a writing class should read their essays aloud, even if it takes more than one class hour to do it. Every writer should be heard so that every writer gets to publish and every writer gets an idea of what every other writer is doing and thinking about. The class might let someone who is shy off the hook the first time around. But not the second time. Sooner or later, everyone has to read their work aloud. You, your fellow writers, and your teacher can give everyone, even the shyest members of the class, the encouragement they need to be willing to read their work aloud. Say, "I want to hear what you have to say," and mean it.

When you read aloud, both to yourself and to your classmates, read slowly and clearly. Make the major corners in the essay clear too. When you begin a new paragraph, announce it ("paragraph 2 . . .", "paragraph 3 . . ."). When you have finished reading, nobody has to comment, except maybe to say a reassuring thank-you.

After everyone in the class is more or less used to reading aloud, the group can hear fewer papers at one time and learn to analyze by ear and take notes. To do this, writers may have to read an essay more than once and should certainly repeat the proposition and the first sentence of each paragraph, so that people have time to write them down. Sooner or later everyone in the class will be able to tell writers, on the hoof, what each paragraph *says* and *does* and what its relation is to the proposition. (See Descriptive Outlines, p. 152.)

Then writers can compare their own descriptive outlines with what their classmates heard. This comparison can lead to an even more detailed analysis of what each paragraph *says* and *does* to see who understands better how each paragraph is constructed, the writer or the class. It may help to write out the class's descriptive outline on the blackboard. During this discussion the class's most frequent and helpful remark may simply be, "Can we hear it again, please?"

One reason you may have to ask writers to read a passage aloud again, or as a reader you may have to reread it, is that the passage creates expectations that it does not fulfill. It points you in one direction and then goes off in another. This happens when your understanding of the conventions of written language and the writer's understanding of them don't yet match. For the moment, the conversation between you breaks down.

For the conversation to continue, there can of course be a lot of disagreement among people on the issues. If everyone agreed on the issues, there would be no discussion. But everyone does have to agree on one thing: how they will discuss those issues. Community members agree on what they expect, and they agree on how writers ought to fulfill their readers' expectations. The ways in which most readers and writers agree to say and do things are the conventions of written language. You make sense when you organize what you write according to these conventions. You and your readers can follow what you say and understand it. The conventions of well-planned, well-developed position papers are the conventions of unity and coherence. (See Unity and Coherence, p. 116.)

Reading passages aloud repeatedly does not diminish the value of reading aloud as a form of publication. On the contrary, by calling attention to expectations that have not been fulfilled, repetition increases everyone's awareness of the importance of the conventions of written language.

ANONYMITY

Despite these advantages of reading aloud, you may still object to it because it feels like a breach of confidence. You may feel that you write your essays for your teacher, and your teacher is the only person you can trust with your faults and limitations. You may feel that they will embarrass you if you read your essay aloud.

But the whole point of writing is to make your private thoughts available to the people you care about in the form you would most like them to be known. Writing makes your private thoughts public. It is public–ation—the act of entering a conversation with other people. Conversely, your thinking is internalized conversation. When you write, you make public again what was public in the first place, or at least what was originally shared familiarly within a community of people speaking or writing to each other.

So if you are a member of an understanding community of writers, it may turn out that you will not feel embarrassed by your mistakes at all when you read your work aloud. You will simply hear your own and other people's mistakes, talk them over, and learn not to make them again. (See "The Benefits of a Writing Community," p. 325, and "What Tutors Can Learn," p. 308.)

Because writing is a social act, furthermore, reading essays aloud anonymously inhibits collaboration. It makes writing less of a conversational exchange among student peers and instead more of a privileged exchange between you and your teacher, so it increases dependency rather than diminishing it. Anonymity also discourages you from talking about writing with your fellow students, so it inhibits trust among peers rather than fostering it.

In short, anonymity in writing is a form of censorship. Of course there may be some rare situations in which you may want to conceal your identity as the author of an essay because of the personal or controversial nature of its subject matter. But in most cases anonymity has no place in the healthy, coherent, working group that a writing class should be.

DESCRIPTIVE OUTLINES

Descriptive outlines help you become a constructive reader by making you more aware of what writers are doing when they write, as well as what they are saying. So descriptive outlines also help you become more aware of what you are doing when you write. They reveal the parts of an essay that have to work smoothly in relation to each other. Descriptive outlines may be time consuming, but in the long run they can save you a lot of time in writing a well-planned, well-developed essay.

It would be easy to become a self-aware writer if you always had plenty of time. You could put everything you write in a drawer for six months so that when you came back to it you would read it with new eyes. You can just hear what you'd say: "Did I write *this*?" But you don't usually have that kind of time. Most people don't. You have deadlines to meet. So in order to control your words instead of being controlled by them, you have to learn to be two persons at once: writer *and* constructive reader. Writing descriptive outlines can help you gain a measure of this valuable objectivity in writing.

Conventional topic or sentence outlines will not help gain this objectivity. Topic or sentence outlines are supposed to be written before you write the essay. They are plans you are supposed to follow when you write. If you find it hard to plan ahead that way, you are not alone. If you find that you have trouble following an outline even when you have planned ahead, you are not alone. And maybe, when you are supposed to write an outline first and then write the essay, you sometimes write the essay first and then write the outline. You're not alone in that either.

Descriptive outlines ask you to do just that. First you **write the essay.** Then you **write a descriptive outline of it.** And then you **rewrite the essay.**

READING AND REWRITING: DESCRIPTIVE OUTLINES AND HOW TO USE THEM

A descriptive outline is really a tool for constructive reading and for rewriting. It is the closest thing in reading and writing to what mathematicians call a *proof.* You can use it to test whether what you have read is what you think you have read and to test whether what you really have written is what you think you wrote. A descriptive outline sets up a workshop relationship between you and the writer of the essay you are reading, whether that writer is you or a fellow writer. A workshop relationship is one in which you consider an essay as something under construction.

That is, a descriptive outline sets up a workshop relationship between you and your essay's very first constructive reader—yourself. In a descriptive outline you declare what you think you have said and done in your essay. Reading your descriptive outline along with the essay, your readers can look over your shoulder as you work. Writing a descriptive outline of your own essay lets you look over your own shoulder as you work.

A descriptive outline is a kind of aside to constructive readers, a running commentary on what you intended to do as you did it. It calls their attention to parts of the essay that you had difficulty with but couldn't figure out why; to special effects you intended but didn't quite bring off; to special effects you brought off without being aware of it; to things you wanted to do but didn't know how. With this workshop tool you ask constructive readers for help, and they can help you, where you need it most.

Every descriptive outline has two elements. One element is made up of statements that explain what each part of an essay *says.* The other element is made up of statements that explain what each part of an essay *does.* The overall form of a descriptive outline looks like this:

PROPOSITION

    PLAN

PARAGRAPH 1   *says*

            does

PARAGRAPH 2   *says*

            does

PARAGRAPH 3   *says* ·

            does

A *says* statement restates or paraphrases a paragraph in one sentence.

A *does* statement describes a paragraph's relation to the essay's proposition and describes how the paragraph is organized.

The *Proposition* in a descriptive outline is exactly the same as the proposition in the essay. It is a *says* statement for the whole essay. It paraphrases the essay in one sentence.

Similarly, the *Plan* in a descriptive outline is a *does* statement for the whole essay. It explains how the essay as a whole is organized. In effect, it summarizes the *does* statements of all the essay's paragraphs by describing in general how the paragraphs are related to the proposition and to each other.

WHAT AN ESSAY SAYS

Says statements show that a constructive reader of your essay (including its first constructive reader, you) has understood the main point of each paragraph and has therefore read the essay accurately. If an essay's *says* statements are accurate, when you read them consecutively you are reading a concise paraphrase of the essay as a whole. So whenever you have to paraphrase an essay, an article, or even a book, writing a basic descriptive outline of it may be the best way to begin.

An Example

Here is a basic descriptive outline for the essay on cars in exercise 5, p. 44.

    PROPOSITION   Cars may be on the way out as our major means of transportation.

        PLAN   To support the proposition with two reasons.

    PARAGRAPH 1   *says*: Use of cars is at a peak, but there are signs of change.

does: Introduces the proposition by describing the present situation.

PARAGRAPH 2   *says:* Our diminishing oil supply is made worse by the way cars waste gas.

does: Develops the first reason by citing comparative statistics.

PARAGRAPH 3   *says:* Cars waste time and human energy.

does: Develops the second reason by telling an anecdote.

If you omit the *does* statements from this outline, you are left with the essay's proposition plus a *says* sentence that paraphrases each paragraph:

PROPOSITION   Cars may be on the way out as our major means of transportation.

PARAGRAPH 1   *says:* Use of cars is at a peak, but there are signs of change.

PARAGRAPH 2   *says:* Our diminishing oil supply is made worse by the way cars waste gas.

PARAGRAPH 3   *says:* Cars waste time and human energy.

If you rearrange this series by moving the proposition from its place in the outline to its place in the essay—at the end of the first paragraph—these *says* statements paraphrase the whole five-hundred word essay in fifty-one words:

The use of cars is at a peak, but there are signs of change. Cars may be on the way out as our major means of transportation. One reason is that our diminishing oil supply is made worse by the way cars waste gas. Second, cars waste time and human energy.

In some cases, the best *says* statement for a paragraph may be its topic sentence or transitional generalization: the sentence at the beginning of the paragraph that most clearly states the main point. If a paragraph does not have a topic sentence or transitional generalization, then make up a *says* statement that paraphrases the paragraph. Better still, if the essay is your own and you discover that one of its paragraphs doesn't have a transitional topic sentence, write one. Then include it in the descriptive outline as the paragraph's *says* statement. Doing that, you will already have used your descriptive outline for one of its intended purposes: it has helped you to spot a flaw in your essay and correct it.

Testing Says *Statements*

There are several ways to test your *says* statements to see if they are accurate. For example, here is paragraph 2 of the example essay "Kingsgate High School," p. 240.

> ¹The two most troublesome features of Jim's reality this fall seem to be geometry and football. ²The first month of Mr. Trager's plane geometry course has left Jim very much behind. ³He has a weekly quiz average of 68, and Trager says that Jim is inattentive in class, hands in his homework irregularly, and makes thoughtless errors in class recitation. ⁴His performance puzzles Trager because he taught Jim algebra last year and knows that the boy is potentially very good in math. ⁵On the surface, it seems that the cause of Jim's difficulty in geometry may be the fact that he is trying out this fall for quarterback on the football team. ⁶But Coach Tolland says that Jim spends more time joking with the other boys than he spends practicing passes and signals. ⁷Tolland thinks Jim will probably not make Junior Varsity quarterback, and he thinks Jim knows that Billy Fazio, who moved to Hobart just this summer, is the more likely choice.

If you read this paragraph quickly, you might think that its main point is Jim's relation with Mr. Trager and Coach Tolland. Or that Jim is doing poorly in football because he is having so much trouble with geometry. Or the reverse.

Suppose you decided to write a *says* statement based on one of those readings:

> PARAGRAPH 2   *says:* Jim had trouble coping with reality this fall because he has had to reevaluate his abilities.

One way to test this *says* statement would be to see if the paragraph develops the operative words in the *says* statement you have written and to compare those operative words with the essay's proposition. *Operative words* are working words: words that the paragraph or the essay as a whole keeps referring to, defining, and explaining. One or more of the operative words or their synonyms in most paragraphs— and therefore one or more of the operative words in the *says* statement for the paragraph—will be operative words in the essay's proposition too. Here is the proposition of the "Kingsgate High School" essay.

> PROPOSITION   Jim's major problem at the moment seems to be that he is having a little trouble coping with reality.

The operative words in that sentence are *problem, trouble, coping,* and *reality*. Another look at the second paragraph of the essay shows that two of these terms, *trouble(some)* and *reality* do appear in the paragraph's transitional sentence.

> ¹The two most troublesome features of Jim's reality this fall seem to be geometry and football.

They also appear in our *says* statement for the paragraph.

> PARAGRAPH 2   *says:* Jim had trouble coping with reality this fall because he has had to reevaluate his abilities.

These and other operative words in the proposition keep turning up in the essay because they are central to the position the essay takes. (There is more about operative words in Propositions, p. 85.)

But in some cases the operative words test is inconclusive, so it is often worthwhile to test the accuracy of *says* statements in another way as well. One alternative is to look at the way the paragraph is organized. Understanding a paragraph's organization helps you write accurate *says* statements because it helps you avoid mistaking subordinate points for major ones. You examine paragraph organization when you write *does* statements. So you can test the accuracy of the *says* statement for each paragraph in a descriptive outline by comparing it with the *does* statement for that paragraph.

In the "Kingsgate High School" example, although the first sentence in paragraph 2 mentions the reality of geometry and football and tells you that they are both part of Jim's problem, it doesn't say explicitly what the nature of that reality is for Jim. So the first sentence in the paragraph does not state the main point of the paragraph. In fact, the paragraph never states its main point explicitly. It only implies that point.

You discover that implication only when you begin to write a *does* statement for the paragraph. Then you notice that the paragraph has two main parts, sentences 2 through 4 and 6 through 7. Each part is about a different activity (geometry and football) but both parts relate Jim to those activities in the same way: Jim's trouble with geometry and football is a result of another problem, a deeper one. He is disappointed in both cases, and in both cases his disappointment results from being forced by his difficulty with football and geometry to reevaluate his abilities. Jim is discovering that he is not quite as good as he thought he was going to be at everything he undertakes.

So, on the basis of this analysis of the paragraph's organization, if you wrote a *says* statement for the paragraph it might read like this:

> PARAGRAPH 2   *says:* Jim had trouble coping with reality this fall because he has had to reevaluate his abilities.

If you were writing this descriptive outline for another writer and you told him that this is what you think the main point of the paragraph really is, he might infer—correctly—that he ought to revise the paragraph. He would probably decide to make this point at the beginning of the paragraph. He would no longer begin the paragraph this way:

> END OF   . . . Jim's major problem at the moment seems to be
> PARAGRAPH 1   that he is having a little trouble coping with reality.
>
> PARAGRAPH 2   ¹The two most troublesome features of Jim's reality this
>   fall seem to be geometry and football. ²The first month
>   of Mr. Trager's plane geometry course has left Jim very
>   much behind. . . .

Instead, he would probably begin the paragraph something like this:

> END OF   . . . Jim's major problem at the moment seems to be
> PARAGRAPH 1   that he is having a little trouble coping with reality.
>
> PARAGRAPH 2   ¹The most troublesome feature of Jim's reality this fall
>   seems to be his discovery that he is not quite as good
>   at sports and math as he thought he was. ²The first
>   month of Mr. Trager's plane geometry course has left
>   Jim very much behind. . . .

If you had written the essay yourself, checking the *says* statement you had written for the paragraph by comparing it with the detailed *does* statement that you had written for the paragraph could have tipped you off too. You too could have revised the paragraph accordingly.

Still another way you can check the accuracy of *says* statements is to examine the assumptions of each paragraph and of the essay as a whole. In this example, examining the assumptions of the essay would confirm the revised *says* statement you wrote. The introduction implies some of the writer's assumptions about people's attitudes toward themselves. Our attitudes do not derive so much from what we can or cannot do as from the way we feel about what we can or cannot do. The "Kingsgate High School" essay is not so much about Jim's abilities as it is about his feelings. (There is more about assumptions beginning on p. 132.)

WHAT AN ESSAY DOES

What you usually want as a reader, naturally enough, is to find out what an essay *says*. You read mainly to join conversations already in progress, find out what people are talking about, and talk about it with them. That is, if you are going to join any conversation actively, you have to be ready to talk back. Whenever you read, you are in some way getting ready to write, just as whenever you write you are getting ready to read what you write and then write more.

So you have read constructively in order to be sure that you understand what you are reading. To be sure that you understand an essay you are reading, you have to pay attention to how it is organized and how its parts fit together. To be able to follow what something you read *says*, it helps to be aware of what it *does*. Otherwise you are likely to get lost and misunderstand. So it turns out that you can learn something from writing descriptive outlines both as a constructive reader and as a constructive writer.

Since you normally read first for what an essay *says*, when you are first learning to write descriptive outlines, *says* statements seem easier to write than *does* statements. Yet in some respects *does* statements are the more important of the two. *Does* statements help make you aware as a reader and writer that words on a paper are always *doing* something as well as saying something.

This awareness gives you greater control when you write and gives you greater control over your response to what you read. Until you discover that language really does do something instead of just somehow existing passively in its own realm of meaning, you tend to read and write as if language is magic. You are writing magically when you hope your readers will be enthralled or mystified rather than interested, edified, or convinced. And you are reading magically when you are enthralled or mystified by what you are reading rather than interested, edified, or convinced.

In short, the *does* statements in a descriptive outline can help you control words instead of being controlled by them.

Descriptive outlines come in two flavors, **basic** and **detailed**, depending on how detailed and thorough their *does* sections are.

Does statements in both basic and detailed descriptive outlines

- state how each paragraph is related to the essay's proposition and
- describe briefly the unity and coherence of each paragraph as a whole.

In addition, *does* statements in detailed descriptive outlines also describe in detail

- the function each part of the paragraph serves in the paragraph and
- how each part of the paragraph is related to all the other parts and to the paragraph's topic sentence or transitional generalization.

In the short run, writing basic descriptive outlines is a step on your way to writing detailed ones. If you are just learning how to write descriptive outlines, begin by writing basic descriptive outlines. But make it your goal to learn also to write detailed descriptive outlines that capture every aspect of the organization of every paragraph.

The reason for learning to write both basic and detailed descriptive outlines is that in the long run they have different uses. You can use detailed descriptive outlines for examining the paragraph structure of shorter essays or a few crucial paragraphs in a long essay. You can use basic descriptive outlines for analyzing longer essays and books, where the details of paragraph organization would be cumbersome and distracting. To write a detailed descriptive outline of a book, you'd have to write another book.

Basic Does *Statements*

The descriptive outline for the example essay on cars in exercise 5, p. 44, is a basic descriptive outline. Its *does* statements describe each paragraph's relationship to the essay's proposition and its overall organization.

PROPOSITION	Cars may be on the way out as our major means of transportation.
PLAN	To support the proposition with two reasons.
PARAGRAPH 1	*says:* Use of cars is at a peak, but there are signs of change.
	does: Introduces the proposition by describing the present situation.
PARAGRAPH 2	*says:* Our oil supply is going, and this is made worse by the way car motors waste gas.
	does: Develops the first reason by citing comparative statistics.
PARAGRAPH 3	*says:* Cars waste time and human energy.
	does: Develops the second reason by telling an anecdote.

You could use a basic descriptive outline like this one to check the unity and coherence of the essay as a whole. For example, if you compare a basic descriptive outline with the essay it describes you might find out that the proposition stated in the essay is not the proposition that the essay actually explores, explains, or defends. Or, as in the case of the "Kingsgate High School" essay, it could reassure you that the proposition stated in the essay is the proposition that the essay actually does explore, explain, and defend.

It may seem odd that you could write a proposition in a descriptive outline that differs from the one you wrote in the essay. But that often happens, because writing descriptive outlines is one way of reading and writing constructively. When you write an essay and then write a descriptive outline of it, you are not doing two different things. You are doing the same thing in different ways. When you write a descriptive outline of an essay, you are still writing the essay.

As a result, sometimes you may not discover what you really want to say until after you have finished the first draft of the essay and are working on the descriptive outline. If that does happen, great! It means that writing a descriptive outline has done one thing it is supposed to do. Just decide which proposition you like better, the one you put in the essay or the one you put in the descriptive outline. Then, if necessary, revise the essay.

Comparing a basic descriptive outline with its essay could also tell you that there is no transitional generalization at the beginning of a paragraph to be explored, explained, or defended, or that a paragraph in the essay doesn't actually explain or defend the transitional generalization that appears at the beginning of that paragraph (as in the case of the paragraph from the "Kingsgate High School" essay). Or the comparison could tell you that the way you have described the organization of a paragraph isn't quite the way the paragraph is actually organized. It might even suggest a better way to support the proposition than the way the essay actually supports it.

When your comparison of an essay with the basic descriptive outline you have written turns up discrepancies like these, if the essay was one you had written yourself you could improve it by changing it to agree with the descriptive outline. If the essay was one a fellow student had written, you might be able to suggest some ways to improve it. And if the essay was a professional article in a journal or a textbook, you might be justified in wondering if the writer is really not a very good writer after all, or else was trying to pull the wool over your eyes (see Danger: Unallowable Assumptions, p. 136).

So a basic descriptive outline can help you understand and improve the unity and coherence among paragraphs. But it isn't much help in understanding and improving the unity and coherence within paragraphs. For that, you have to learn to write detailed descriptive outlines.

Detailed Does Statements

The *does* sections of a **detailed** descriptive outline identify the parts or subdivisions of each paragraph and explain their relation to each other and to the paragraph's transitional generalization. You may find it easier to understand what goes on in detailed *does* statements if you think of them dramatically. Imagine you are a teenager who wants to use the family car this weekend.* What do you *do*? Naturally, you ask. To ask, you have to *say* something. What do you say? You say, "Dad, may I use the car this weekend?"

WHAT EACH OF YOU *DOES*	WHAT EACH OF YOU *SAYS*
You **ask**.	"Dad, may I use the car this weekend?"
He **refuses**.	"No."
You **beg**.	"Aw, Dad, please let me use the car."
He refuses again, but he **shows signs of weakening**.	"Well . . . no."
You **offer to do something in return**. (That is, you **offer to negotiate**.)	"If you let me use the car, Dad, I'll clean out the garage."
Finally, he **agrees**.	"Well, ok."
You **thank** him.	"Gee, thanks, Dad."
But he **expresses concern**.	"But you've got to drive carefully."
You **reassure** him.	"Sure, Dad, I'll be careful."

Notice that the highlighted words in the left column of this analysis have nothing to do with cars, fathers, or garages. They are all about language: the kind of language that people are using in the dialogue in the right column, and the way they are using it. That is, the terms in the left column describe the kind of "work" that the remarks in the right column do in the conversation between a father and his teenage offspring. They describe what each remark *does*. So a *does* statement for the teenager's part in that conversation would run something like this:

First, the speaker asks someone for something and intensifies the request by begging for it. Then the speaker begins to negotiate, offering to do something in return if the negotiation is successful. Finally, after reaching agreement, the speaker thanks the person the speaker has been negotiating with and reassures him.

---

*I am indebted to David Liss for this example.

In a detailed descriptive outline, the *does* statement for each paragraph talks about the language of the paragraph in this way. It does not talk about the subject matter of the paragraph. Specifically, the *does* statement explains in detail how the paragraph is organized. For example, here again is the second paragraph of the "Kingsgate High School" essay, this time with the new first sentence that you wrote for it earlier in this section, p. 158:

. . . Jim's major problem at the moment seems to be that he is having a little trouble coping with reality.

^{1}The most troublesome feature of Jim's reality this fall seems to be his discovery that he is not quite as good at sports and math as he thought he was. ^{2}The first month of Mr. Trager's plane geometry course has left Jim very much behind. ^{3}He has a weekly quiz average of 68, and Trager says that Jim is inattentive in class, hands in his homework irregularly, and makes thoughtless errors in class recitation. ^{4}His performance puzzles Trager because he taught Jim algebra last year and knows that the boy is potentially very good in math. ^{5}On the surface, it ssems that the cause of Jim's difficulty in geometry may be the fact that he is trying out this fall for quarterback on the football team. ^{6}But Coach Tolland says that Jim spends more time joking with the other boys than he spends practicing passes and signals. ^{7}Tolland thinks Jim will probably not make junior varsity quarterback, and he thinks Jim knows that Billy Fazio, who moved to Hobart just this summer, is the more likely choice.

The paragraph's *says* statement would remain the same whether you wrote a basic or detailed *does* section:

PARAGRAPH 2   *says:* Jim had trouble coping with reality this fall because he has had to reevaluate his abilities.

If you wrote a **basic** *does* statement for the paragraph it might read like this:

PARAGRAPH 2   *does:* Supports the proposition by analyzing two causes of the problem stated in the proposition.

If you wrote a **detailed** *does* statement for the same paragraph it might turn out something like this:

PARAGRAPH 2   *does:* Supports the proposition by analyzing two causes of the problem stated in the proposition. Sentence 1 makes a transition from the first paragraph of the essay by repeating two key words, *trouble* (as in *troublesome*) and *reality*, and it introduces the paragraph by stating a probable cause of the problem. The rest of the paragraph is divided into two parts, each of which relates the probable cause stated in the proposition to a specific activity. Sentences 2, 3, and 4 explain the relationship of the probable cause to the first activity by citing an authority, by giving details of a person's character traits and performance, and by making a historical comparison. Sentence 5 makes a transition to the next part of the paragraph by comparing two aspects of the situation. Sentence 6 refutes that comparison by citing another authority. And sentence 7 explains the relationship of the probable cause of the problem to the second activity by giving evidence to support a prediction of future events.

This detailed analysis of paragraph organization explains how the first sentence in the paragraph, the transitional generalization, connects the paragraph to the proposition of the essay (by repeating key words), and how that sentence also sets up the terms of the paragraph's argument (by listing a probable cause of a problem). Then it outlines how the rest of the paragraph is organized (it is divided into two parts). The rest of the *does* statement describes in detail how each of these two parts is organized.

It is worth pointing out again that neither the basic nor the detailed *does* statement for this paragraph mentions anything about what the paragraph *says*. In neither *does* statement do Jim, geometry, or football ever appear. *Does* statements describe organization and coherence, how paragraphs are constructed, as much as possible without reference to content. This distinction between form and content is artificial, but it is a useful analytical tool.

Because the distinction between form and content is artificial, some *does* statements cannot entirely avoid referring to content. When they do have to refer to content, however, they **generalize** it or refer to it as a **type.** For example, in this detailed *does* statement, Jim's lack of attention in class, his failure to turn in homework regularly, and his 68 average are generalized to the type of observations that these are: "details of a person's character traits and performance." Mr. Trager's comparison of Jim's work this year in geometry with his work last year in algebra becomes "a historical comparison." And Coach Tolland's belief that Billy Fazio, not Jim, will become junior varsity quarterback becomes "a prediction of future events."

GETTING READY TO WRITE A DETAILED DOES STATEMENT

In order to write a detailed *does* statement, you have to find out how the paragraph is organized. The best way to find out how a paragraph is organized is to "map" it.

To map a paragraph, first **number the sentences** by marking them lightly in pencil in front of the first word of each sentence. Then **read the whole paragraph** to yourself, preferably aloud.

Second, **subdivide the paragraph.** The first time through, just guess or follow your intuition. If sentences 1 through 4 seem to hang together, call them part 1. If sentences 5 through 8 seem to hang together, call them part 2. Continue in this way. Each subdivision will be a series of sentences that seem to be more strongly related to each other than to the sentences that precede or follow. Sometimes a single sentence can constitute a part.

Third, test your intuitive division of the paragraph by asking the following questions about each part of the paragraph and about the paragraph as a whole:

- **Who or what** are the sentences in each part about?
- At **what level of generality** do the sentences in each part talk about the subject? (For example, some parts may talk generally about the traits of canines—dogs, foxes, wolves—whereas other parts may talk concretely about the traits of Rover and Spot.)
- Is there any kind of sequence or "story" involved in the paragraph? (For example, are things arranged in **numerical order:** one, two, three? **temporal order:** now as opposed to then? **causal order:** this resulted from that? **problem-posing order:** problem plus solution? **inductive order:** evidence leading to an inference? **deductive order:** a principle applied to experience, leading to a conclusion?) If there is such a sequence in the paragraph, what role does each part of the paragraph play in this sequence?

Fourth, think of an appropriate name or label for each part of the paragraph. The terms you use should describe or explain succinctly the purpose or function of each part. In thinking up names for the parts, you might find some of the following questions helpful:

- How do the parts differ from each other?
- How are the parts connected or related to each other?
- How is each part related to the main point of the paragraph?
- What role does each part play in the paragraph?

If necessary, based on your answers to these questions, adjust the boundaries that you drew intuitively.

Fifth, write a *does* statement based on your division of the paragraph into parts and the terms you devised for labeling them. The statement should name the relation of the paragraph as a whole to the essay's proposition. Then it should describe in as much detail as possible how the paragraph is organized and how it works.

Here are some of the many things a paragraph *does*.

- **tells a story** (See "Homer's Use of the Gods in the *Iliad*," paragraph 2, p. 340, and "Going Back to School," paragraph 2, p. 324.)
- **lists** (catalogue, itemize, enumerate; See "*The Sea Gull*: A Great Play Makes a Bad Movie," paragraph 2, p. 63.)
- **shows how something is done** (See "Family and School," paragraph 2, p. 319.)
- **reasons** (syllogistic, inductive, dialectical; See "To Number or Not To Number," paragraph 2, p. 56.)
- **describes** (See "The Role of Planning in Making Films," paragraph 2, p. 27.)
- **explains** (See "Stock Options," paragraph 1, p. 327, and "Mitosis," paragraphs 2 and 3, p. 334.)
- **compares** (See "*The Sea Gull*: A Great Play Makes a Bad Movie," paragraph 3, p. 63.)
- **defines a term** (See "Family and School," paragraph 3, p. 320.)
- **gives examples** (See "Stock Options," paragraphs 2 and 3, p. 328, "Project Head Start," paragraph 3, p. 76, and "The Pluralist Model of Power and Modern Society," paragraph 2, p. 333.)
- **analyzes** (takes something apart; See "The Role of Planning in Making Films," paragraph 3, p. 27, and "What Should Patients Be Told?", paragraph 2, p. 220.)
- **synthesizes** (puts two or more ideas together showing the relationship between them; See "Homer's Use of the Gods in the *Iliad*," paragraph 2, p. 340.)
- **cites** (refers to an authority; See "Drug Testing in Sports," paragraph 2, p. 331, "Gene Manipulation and Huxley's *Brave New World*," paragraphs 2 and 3, p. 337, and "No One Knows Anything," paragraphs 2 and 3, p. 338.)
- **evaluates** (explains how good something is or what it's good for)
- **offers a hypothesis** (makes an educated guess)
- **gives a history**
- **projects the future**

(There is more about what a paragraph *does* in Organizing for Coherence, p. 123. If you would like to compare another pair of basic and detailed descriptive outlines, the example essay "Project Head Start" on p. 75 has both. Other example essays have basic descriptive outlines, and still others have detailed descriptive outlines. And some have no descriptive outline at all. You can use the essays with no descriptive outline to practice writing descriptive outlines.)

COLLABORATIVE LEARNING

Task 1   Practice Descriptive Outline: Short Essays

Follow the instructions for working in consensus groups on p. 20.

Complete the detailed descriptive outline for "Kingsgate High School," p. 240, begun on p. 163 by writing *says* and **detailed** *does* statements for paragraphs 1 and 3.

Task 2   Practice Descriptive Outline of a Paragraph

Follow the instructions for working in consensus groups given on p. 20.

Read aloud to the group this paragraph from Robert C. Chanaud's "Aerodynamic Whistles." Then write a *says* statement for it and two *does* statements, one **basic**, the other **detailed**.

[1]Class I whistles are the most widely encountered, perhaps because so many of them occur naturally. [2]This category includes telephone wires, tree limbs, and aeolian harps singing in the wind. [3](The aeolian harp is an ancient Greek instrument consisting of a set of strings stretched over a sounding box and set in motion by the wind or the breath.) [4]This kind of Class I whistle, called an aeolian-tone generator, basically consists of a long, thin cylinder in a stream of air or some other kind of fluid. [5]Above a certain speed there will develop behind the cylinder two symmetrically placed vortexes that are stable and steady. [6]If the speed of flow increases above a second threshold and one of the vortexes is disturbed by a sound pressure wave, the vortex will oscillate around its stable position and ultimately break away from the cylinder and move downstream. [7]The breaking away of this vortex causes the opposite vortex to become unstable, and it too breaks away. [8]Another vortex forms in the place of the first one and it in turn becomes unstable. [9]The feedback appears to be entirely hydrodynamic: each vortex gives rise to instability in the other directly, without any intervening agent such as a sound wave. [10]As a result of the influence of one vortex on the other a chain of alternating vortexes soon stretches downstream from the cylinder. [11]As the vortexes develop they generate a sound field with a maximum at right angles to their path.

Task 3   *Writing Descriptive Outlines by Ear*

For this task work with a small group or with the whole class. One person choose an example essay from the book and read it aloud once slowly, then again, pausing to repeat the proposition and the first sentence of each paragraph so that people have time to write them down.

Work toward a consensus on what each paragraph *says* and a detailed statement of what each paragraph *does*. (See Descriptive Outlines, p. 152.)

One person in each group keep a record of how the group describes the essay. In doing this task with the class as a whole, the recorder can work at the blackboard.

Read passages aloud as often as necessary until the description is complete.

Task 4   *Practice Descriptive Outline: Long Essays*

Work in pairs or groups of three. First, each person write a descriptive outline independently. Then confer. Compare the descriptive outlines you have written, discuss the differences between them, and try to decide on a single descriptive outline that you agree on.

Write a basic descriptive outline of John Fischer's "Substitutes for Violence," p. 367, or Walter Lippmann's "The Indispensable Opposition," p. 353; or choose another article from a magazine, journal, or essay anthology.

For convenience, number the paragraphs of the essay lightly in pencil before you begin. If the essay you choose is longer than seven or eight pages, treat clusters of related paragraphs as units, describing in your outline how each cluster of paragraphs fits into the essay as a whole.

Then confer.

Use the following guide:

1. **What is the central point or proposition of the essay?** What position does it take? Using your words or the essay's, state the essay's proposition in one sentence.

   (If you are not sure at first what the essay's main point or proposition is, write down two or three possibilities and complete parts 2 through 5 of this task. Then decide, after working out what each part of the essay *does* and *says*, which possible proposition you wrote down seems correct.)

2. **Describe the essay's introduction.** Where does it end? How many paragraphs are in it? What does it *do* to introduce the essay? What does it *say*?

3. **Describe the essay's ending.** Where does it begin? How many paragraphs are in it? What does it *do* to end the essay? What does it *say*?

4. **Describe the essay's explanation or defense of its position.** What does it *do* to explain or defend that position? What does it *say*?

5. What is the essay's overall plan?

6. Revise your original statement of the essay's proposition.

Task 5   Descriptive Outline Conference

Work in pairs (groups of three are also possible, but may be logistically more difficult).

Exchange essays with a classmate. Number the sentences in the essays lightly in pencil, but do not otherwise mark it up.

Write a **detailed** descriptive outline of each other's essays. Do not evaluate the essay.

Then confer. Compare descriptive outlines of each other's essays. Ask each other if what you said each paragraph *does* is what you intended to do. Ask each other if what you said each paragraph *says* is what you intended to say.

After the conference if you would like to revise your essay go right ahead.

(This task is the first step in peer review.)

PEER REVIEW

One purpose of reading aloud is to make both writing and learning to write more actively collaborative. That is also one purpose of writing descriptive outlines. In writing descriptive outlines and conferring about them, you learn the language that is most useful when, as a reader and writer, you talk constructively about reading and writing.

Peer review combines these two activities. It is a social relationship in which you read each other's writing constructively and write and talk to each other constructively about it. Learning peer review introduces you to the *constructive conversation* that goes on all the time among writers, among readers, and between writers and readers. As peer reviewers of each other's writing, you join that constructive conversation indirectly by corresponding with each other, writing descriptive outlines and written evaluations. And you join it directly when you confer with each other about your essays.

Both kinds of constructive conversation, corresponding and conferring, have advantages. **Corresponding**—writing to each other about reading and writing—is more exacting and rigorous than conferring. **Conferring**—talking with each other about reading and writing—is more immediately responsive to a writer's needs than corresponding. The most helpful kind of constructive conversation combines the two, conference and correspondence. So in peer review you write to each other about your essays first, and then you talk about them.

WHAT PEER REVIEW IS NOT: GRADING VERSUS EVALUATION

Evaluative judgment of some sort is always involved in peer review. Sometimes peers explicitly evaluate each other's essays during peer review, telling each other what is done well in the essay and what needs improvement. Other times peers do not evaluate explicitly. Instead, they evaluate each other's essays only implicitly, by describing them in detail. Learning to make sound evaluative judgments about each other's writing and explain them effectively is what peer review is all about.

People tend to understand the term *evaluation* in different ways. As a result, people tend to understand the purpose of peer review in different ways as well. But understanding what peer review is not is just as important as understanding what it really is. For peers working together, **evaluating** each other's writing **does not mean grading** each other's writing.

Grading is of course related to evaluation. Grades are an administrative convenience used to simplify record keeping in schools, colleges, and universities. Teachers have to reduce complex evaluative judgments to a single quantity, a grade (A, B, C, 92, 81, 75), so that keeping a record of the evaluation of many people taking many courses can be done efficiently. Grading, an institutional function, is part of a teacher's job as long as the teacher is employed by an educational institution that requires grades, as most do, and as long as students need a record of their work in the simplified form that employers and professional schools ask for.

When your teachers give grades, they think about many factors other than the details of the work itself. For example, they consider your level of development, your progress, the type of institution you are at, and the level of the course you are taking. Because as a student you are not in a position to consider all of these factors, you cannot grade each other's work accurately and responsibly.

But as a student you can evaluate each other's work. You can learn to evaluate skillfully, responsibly, and helpfully. And being in a position to evaluate without grading actually increases your usefulness to each other as peer reviewers.

Evaluation is something you do every day. You make evaluative judgments as consumers, citizens, workers, professionals—even at play. Which new dress or suit should you buy? Why? Which candidate should you vote for? Why? Which stock option should you choose, how good a job have you done, which concert or movie should you go to, which first baseman is good enough to make the all-stars, should you sell Boardwalk or hang on to it for a while? And why?

It may be, in fact, that the most important lesson you can learn from a college or university education is the ability to make evaluative judgments like these in a way that makes your own life and each other's lives better, safer, and more responsible.

WHAT IS PEER REVIEW?

Writing peer reviews of writing is one way to learn to make effective, responsible evaluative judgments. Through peer review, you learn how to help other students become better writers by describing and evaluating their writing and then by writing and talking helpfully about it. You do that in order to learn how to become a better writer yourself by describing and evaluating your own writing and by writing and talking about it.

Peer review does not of course make your teachers' evaluative judgment any less useful to you. Teachers represent the community of mature writers and readers that you are trying to join. Part of their job is to tell you how far you have gone toward gaining full membership in that community. That's what teachers do when they evaluate your work and grade it.

Peer review is an additional kind of evaluation that can sometimes be even more helpful to you and your classmates than evaluation by a teacher. If teachers tell you that they can't understand what you have written, you may feel . . . well . . . you know how teachers are. They never quite understand what you're trying to say. But if other students tell you that *they* can't understand, the criticism sticks. And naturally you sometimes feel safer knowing that your mistakes have been noticed first by a sympathetic peer who doesn't wield the power to grade what you have written.

To be a helpful peer reviewer, you have to suspend judgment about what an essay *says* while you are trying to understand what it *does*. You have to find language to describe writing accurately. You have to learn to evaluate tactfully so that other writers can accept what you say and make changes accordingly, emphasizing what is well done as well as what needs improvement. You have to explain your evaluative generalizations and support them with details. You have to learn to trust each other's judgment.

That trust comes hard. No one reviews someone else's writing well the first time. And since every essay you read is different from the last one, every peer review you undertake is in some way a new beginning. At first you may feel a little afraid of evaluating another student's work.

It may feel as if you are ratting on a friend. And you may feel a little afraid at first of having your own work evaluated by other students. Will the teacher take advantage of something negative they say about your essay and lower the grade?

You may also feel wary at first about how other students will treat you. You may think that they will be harder on you than the teacher would be. You can usually count on teachers to be kinder to you than your peers, to tell you only part of the truth and tell it tactfully. Only a mean or vindictive teacher is likely to tell you everything that is wrong with your work all at once. Your student peers may not exercise that kind of professional restraint. They may let you know it straight between the eyes.

Finally, and most importantly, you may find it hard to believe in your authority to evaluate another student's work and in another student's authority to evaluate yours. When you read another student's essay you may feel like saying, "What right do *I* have to tell you what's good or bad about your work?" And when another student reads your essay, you may feel like saying, "What right do *you* have to tell me what's good or bad about my work?"

Sometimes this fear of peer review is realistic. You have learned in traditional, competitive classrooms that everyone knocks the competition given half a chance. You also learned on the playground to fear peer review. Kids know what they'll hear from other kids if they bobble an easy grounder to third, because kids know what to say when another kid bobbles one.

But you can overcome these competitive gut responses. The way to overcome them is by learning how to work together collaboratively and by learning a systematic, constructive approach to evaluating each other's writing. Constructive reading establishes constructive relationships among student peers. You will learn to respect each other's evaluative judgment of each other as you learn to read and write constructively. And as you learn to read and write constructively you will also learn to respect your own evaluative judgment and assume some responsibility for other students' improvement as writers, a self-respect and responsibility that you may never have felt before.

This new collaborative relationship with your peers involves learning a new kind of language, the language that people use to converse constructively about reading and writing. Learning a new language is never easy. For a while you may find that corresponding and conferring with each other about writing is some of the hardest work you have ever done in school. It is such hard work because you have three immediate and demanding audiences. The first audience is yourself. Somehow, you have to tell the truth as you see it. The second audience is the teacher, who will evaluate your written peer review and grade it for its thoroughness, accuracy, insight, tact, and writing quality.

The third and most important audience is the writer of the essay you are reviewing. As a peer reviewer you have to be tactful, constructive, sympathetic, and firm all at once. You have to avoid alienating your peers. At the same time, you want your peers to respect you enough to want to write equally careful, helpful reviews of your essays in return. In short, peer review writing is some of the most *real* writing you will ever do in school. That's why you can learn so much from writing peer reviews.

(I am indebted to a Brooklyn College peer tutor, Christopher Guardo, for this analysis of the peer reviewer's three audiences. See p. 305.)

LEARNING TO WRITE PEER REVIEWS

Peer reviewing requires three different kinds of constructive reading: descriptive, evaluative, and substantive. You don't normally separate these ways of reading in your mind. But as peer reviewers (and as writers as well) you will have to learn to separate them so that you can read constructively one way at a time.

The first kind of reading you will learn to do as a peer reviewer is descriptive. To **describe what you're reading**—that is, to write a descriptive outline of it—you set aside explicit evaluation for the moment. You avoid pointing out what you think is well done in the essay and what you think needs to be improved. And you also set aside whether or not you agree with the position the essay takes. You avoid taking issue with the essay.

Second, as a peer reviewer you will learn to read descriptively and evaluatively. You will describe the essay—write a descriptive outline of it—**and explain what you think is well done and what needs improvement.** But you will still set aside whether or not you agree with the position the essay takes. You will still avoid taking issue with the essay.

And third, you can also learn to read descriptively, evaluatively, and substantively all at once if you are in a course that lends itself to learning all three. A course lends itself to substantive peer review if everyone in the class can write on the same topic or has a working knowledge of the topics that everyone else is writing on. In that case, **you will describe the essay, explain what you think is well done and what needs improvement,** *and* **comment on the topic of the essay and on the position it takes on that topic.**

COLLABORATIVE LEARNING

You can approach learning peer review in three phases that correspond to the three kinds of constructive reading. Begin each phase by writing an essay and a descriptive outline of the essay. Read your essay aloud to other students and exchange essays, keeping the descriptive outline you wrote for your own essay. If you can, exchange essays with different people each assignment, so that you get different opinions about your work.

For each task, answer the peer review questions carefully and accurately. Write a draft of your peer review and revise it. Treat other writers' work with the respect you want from them when they read your work.

Task 1   *Practice Descriptive Peer Review*

Write a detailed descriptive outline of the following essay. Check your descriptive outline twice against the essay, and revise the outline until you are confident that it represents the essay accurately. (Detailed descriptive outlines are explained on p. 153.)

In groups of two or three, compare descriptive outlines. Where they don't match, try to find out why. Negotiate a description of the essay that all of you can agree on.

☐ EXAMPLE ESSAY ─────────────────────────────

Acting Is Believing

Joyce Bresnick Slevin

[1]One of the first assignments in my Introduction to Acting course was to make believe I was an animal of my choice. [2]So I went home and watched my cat Isis for an hour. [3]When I returned to class, I simply imitated all her actions. [4]I licked my chops, cleaned my paws, and chased my tail. [5]Obviously, seeing a woman as a cat required some imagination from myself and the audience. [6]Yet the class was convinced that I was a cat, because I did exactly what the assignment called for: I *made believe* I was a cat. [7]That is, I did not just *pretend* to be a cat. [8]I made myself actually *believe* that I was a cat and did what I would do if I were one. [9]This technique will work for any type of character portrayal, not only that of an animal. [10]As a rule, actors have to believe what they are doing in order to be successful in a role.

[1]The best way for actors to believe in a role is to concentrate on simple physical actions. [2]In *The Actor Prepares* Stanislavsky, the famous Russian actor and director, frequently emphasized that "small physical actions, small physical truths and the moments of belief in them . . . acquire a great significance on the stage." [3]In fact, he developed a practical technique called "making a score of the

role," in which an actor makes a sequential list of the specific physical actions he will perform in a scene. [4]For example, for a scene in which an actor must wait nervously for an appointment he could list the following actions: (1) enter room carrying a newspaper, (2) sit down and read newspaper, (3) stop reading and place newspaper on table, (4) cross legs, (5) uncross legs, (6) look at watch. These actions are tangible, controllable, and repeatable. [5]They give the performer something to fall back on in order to sustain belief. [6]While an actor may not be able to "be nervous" on cue, he can perform the actions that a nervous person would perform.

[1]Besides physical actions, actors can use "verbal actions" to help them believe the role they are playing. [2]A verbal action is not the actual line an actor delivers. Rather, it is the intention behind the words. [3]For example, when Hamlet says, "To be, or not to be," his verbal action is to decide whether or not to kill himself. [4]Actors must have a verbal action for every line they utter in order to make themselves believe their own role. [5]This requires a full understanding of characters and their intention. [6]As with physical actions, a verbal action is more *doing* than *being*. [7]When actors write down verbal actions in the margins of a script, they use verbs of action rather than states of being. [8]The actor playing Hamlet would use the verbal action "to decide" instead of "to be confused." [9]A state of being is not acceptable, because it provides nothing specific to do and leaves the actor stuck with a general emotion. General emotions are elusive and unpredictable. [10]If an actor begins by thinking about emotions and tries to squeeze them out, the result will be distorted and forced. [11]If an actor begins with verbal actions, emotions will come as a result of the actor's own belief in the role. □

Task 2   *Essay Exchange and Descriptive Peer Review*

Exchange essays with a classmate (preferably not one you have exchanged with before). Writing lightly in pencil, number the sentences in the essay you have received in exchange for your own. Don't write anything else on the paper. On a separate sheet write a detailed descriptive outline of the essay. Check your descriptive outline twice against the essay, and revise the outline until you are confident that it represents the essay accurately. (Detailed descriptive outlines are explained in this section, on p. 153).

Confer with the writer whose essay you have read and who read your essay. Compare descriptive outlines. Where they don't match, try to find out why. Negotiate a description of both essays—yours and your partner's—that the two of you can agree on.

The purpose of this first collaborative peer review task is to help you treat an essay as something someone has constructed, like a chair—

something designed, organized, and put together to serve a purpose. The purpose of a chair is to hold people up when they sit on it. To do that well, the chair has to be well constructed. A poorly constructed chair won't serve that purpose. It will collapse when someone sits on it. The essays written for the exercises in this book have a purpose too. It is to state a position and then explore, explain, or defend it. To do that well an essay has to be well constructed, just like a chair. An essay that is poorly constructed won't serve its purpose. Its position won't hold up any better than a poorly constructed chair.

If you describe an essay accurately, you may not be able to avoid implying that the essay does (or does not do) what the writer intended it to do, or whether or not it says what the writer intended it to say. If that happens, so be it. Implicit evaluation of this kind can sometimes be more effective than explicit evaluation. **But for this peer review task, don't evaluate the essay explicitly.** Let your descriptive outline speak for itself. **And do not take issue with any of the opinions expressed in the essay.**

Task 3   *Accepting Authority in Evaluative Peer Review*

Follow the instructions for working in consensus groups on p. 20.

1. A student wrote the following notes in a process log when the first descriptive and evaluative peer review was assigned. Her entries raise at least two issues: **authority among peers** and **social relations among peers**. Explain the writer's attitudes toward each issue.

Log Entries

4/8 I don't feel right judging someone else's work.

4/15 I don't feel adequate trying to gauge anyone else's work. Who am I to tell other students what's wrong with their writing? Grammar and spelling are one thing. Sentence structure, paragraph structure, arrangement of ideas, even the ideas themselves—they're something else entirely.

I don't take well to criticism myself. And I don't know how to review someone else's work effectively without hurting their feelings by being obviously critical.

4/17 I asked Fran to look at a draft of my essay, because she knows how to criticize, and I trust her judgment. But I simply do not want to criticize anyone else's work. It takes more time than I've got. And anyway, I'm very critical of myself. I don't think it's fair to apply the standards I apply to myself to anyone else.

2. In light of your discussion of the previous log entries, explain the attitudes toward the same issues, authority among peers and social

relations among peers, in the following remarks from another student's log.

Log Entry

4/19 I really appreciate the way Steven explained to me how to revise my second paragraph. I didn't want to ask him, because in high school everybody says you shouldn't ask another student anything. If you do, they'll think you're dumb. Or they'll think you're cheating and trying to make them cheat. That really stunk. This year, the teacher told us over and over again that we could ask other people in the class anything. So I did.

Task 4 *Analysis of an Example Descriptive and Evaluative Peer Review*

Have one person in your group read the essay and the descriptive outlines and evaluative peer review that follow it to the rest of the group. Then arrive at consensus answers to the following questions:

1. Notice that the descriptive outlines written by the writer and the peer reviewer do not exactly match. One of the issues that the two students involved would have to negotiate in a peer conference would be why their understanding of the essay's organization differs. Which parts of the two descriptive outlines (*says* and *does*) do you think most accurately represent the essay as written?

2. How would you rewrite the peer reviewer's evaluation to make it more complete, accurate, and acceptable to the writer?

3. How would you rewrite the essay to improve it?

EXAMPLE DESCRIPTIVE AND EVALUATIVE PEER REVIEW

☐ EXAMPLE ESSAY ─────────────────────────

The Issues Surrounding Electronic Music

Kerri Weiss

In *Electronic Music*, Elliott Schwartz, traces some of the important musical developments that led historically to electronic music. He provides a basic introduction to the way various studio systems work using computers to generate sound. With computers, the composer "programs every facet of the sound by means of his instruction to the computer" (Schwartz 89). He controls his music by selecting the "instruments" and dictating, note by note, his entire composition. Since there are many advantages to this process, the number of active computer studios is steadily increasing. Therefore, the main issue that concerns most writers on electronic music is the impact of computer technology on the future of music.

Many writers agree that computers have opened doors to greater opportunities in the music industry. They have "unlocked a universe of musical sounds," ideally allowing composers to produce a very different kind of music (Grey 14). The computer offers composers "incredible power" and "options that never existed in a standard recording setup" (Van Gelder 43). For example, with the proper software, a musician can create new sounds, compose a piece with those sounds, and perform it, all while seated at a computer keyboard (Grey 16). Composers are able to maintain more control over the way their recordings sound than they ever have before, since they can work directly with their material in this way. The costs involved are also reduced, since inexpensive equipment is now readily available. Popular music today reflects these advances. Variations, repetitive rhythmic patterns, and built-in sounds have combined "to transform the very form and content" of pop music (Holden 22). This technology continues to increase the number of possibilities for even greater changes in music in the future.

Although many writers agree that computerization is purely beneficial, others argue that computer technology also has its downside. Purists and traditionalists insist that the "villain . . . is computer-driven tunes," and they "want to smash those dark, satanic music mills" (Pareles 28). They complain that "machines produce music of such plastic perfection that it could have been produced by R2-D2" (Van Gelder 44). Computer music, they say, lacks physical presence and seems cold, impersonal, and unnatural. It threatens the quality and character of music. It has also "thrown a wrench into musical careers" (Newton 19). This is because computers are taking over jobs once performed by live musicians. Officials from the American Foundation of Musicians note that computers have already replaced studio musicians on many movie sound tracks and in the advertising jingle business (Newton 19). This trend, many fear, is the beginning of a technological nightmare, "the final victory of the Machine over Man" (Schwartz 3).

WORKS CITED

Grey, Harold. "Computer Music: Unlocking a New Universe of Musical Sounds." *Brooklyn College Magazine* March 1989: 14–17.

Holden, Stephen. "Why the Melody Doesn't Linger On." *New York Times* 14 Feb. 1988, sec 2: H22.

Newton, James S. "What's New in Music Technology." *New York Times* 1 March 1987, sec 3: F19.

Pareles, Jon. "Just Give Me a Chip Off the Old Bach." *New York Times* 10 Jan. 1988, sec 2: H28.

Schwartz, Elliott. *Electronic Music.* New York: Praeger, 1973.

Van Gelder, Lindsy. "Enjoying the Brave New World of Computer Music." *Ms. Magazine* Oct. 1987: 42–45.

DESCRIPTIVE OUTLINE

PROPOSITION   The main issue that concerns most writers is the impact of computer technology on the future of music.

PLAN   To discuss an important issue that concerns most writers on the topic by summarizing two views. To explain how the book relates to the issue.

PARAGRAPH 1   *says:* The number of active computer studios is growing since the studio creates many advantages for composers.

does: Introduces the proposition by providing background information. The paragraph is divided into two main parts. The first section, sentences 1 through 4, can be subdivided into two more parts. Sentences 1 through 2 introduce the subject matter with a general overview of a book. Sentences 3 through 4 describe a specific aspect of the subject by explaining a process. The second section of the essay, sentences 5 through 6, has two functions. Sentence 5 makes a transition from the first part of the paragraph by showing the result of the process. The last sentence in the paragraph (6) is the proposition, which relates an important issue to these ideas.

PARAGRAPH 2   *says:* Computer technology increases the number of opportunities for positive changes in the music industry.

does: Supports the proposition by summarizing one point of view. The paragraph is divided into three main parts. Part One (sentence 1) makes a transition by expanding the issue presented in paragraph 1. The second part, sentences 2 through 6, can be subdivided into three subsections. Sentences

2 through 3 integrate quotations from magazines to support the point of view. Sentence 4 provides an example that explains the quotations. Sentences 5 through 6 show two additional benefits and the reasoning behind them. The third part (7 through 9) describes a new form that reflects the other ideas.

PARAGRAPH 3   *says:* The use of computers in the music industry has many negative consequences.

does: Supports the proposition by summarizing the alternative point of view. The paragraph is divided into four main parts. The first sentence makes a transition by developing opposition to the view stated in paragraph 2. The second part (sentences 2 through 5) presents some negative aspects of a new technology. This section can be subdivided into two more parts. Sentences 2 and 3 both integrate quotations that vividly describe faults of the new technology. Sentences 4 through 5 list additional problems. The third part (6 through 8) describes the conditions that a specific group of people is facing as a result of these problems. The last sentence (9) makes a general statement that reinforces the importance of the issue.

☐ EXAMPLE PEER REVIEW

Reader: Eric Miller
Author: Kerri Weiss

DESCRIPTIVE OUTLINE

PROPOSITION   The main issue that concerns most writers is the impact of computer technology on the future of music.

PLAN   To support the proposition by summarizing the two main positions on the issue.

PARAGRAPH 1   *says:* Composers can now write music in an entirely new way, by using computers.

does: Introduces the proposition by giving background information about a book. The paragraph is divided into three parts, one that gives general background information about the book, one that states a specific topic discussed in the book, and one that relates the book to the proposition. Sentence 1 gives a general summary of the book. Sentences 2 through 4 explain a specific topic discussed in the book. Sentences 5 through 6 relate the book's content to the paper's proposition.

PARAGRAPH 2   *says:* Computers have opened the doors to greater opportunities in the music industry and changed the form and content of popular music.

does: Summarizes the first position on the issue as stated in the proposition. The paragraph is divided into three parts. Sentences 1 through 2 introduce the first position on the issue. Sentences 3 through 6 state and explain three benefits of using a system. Sentences 7 through 9 explain the effects of the system on a modern art form and state the possible future effects of the system.

PARAGRAPH 3   *says:* Some writers argue that computerization is not beneficial because computer music seems impersonal and because computers have taken jobs away from musicians.

does: Summarizes the second position on the issue. The paragraph is divided into four parts. Part 1 (sentence 1) introduces the second position on the issue. Part 2 (2 through 3) explains two complaints about the system made by two different groups of people. Part 3 (4 through 5) explains two more complaints. Part 4 (6 through 9) discusses an injustice caused by the system for a particular group of people.

EVALUATION

On the whole, your essay is a pleasure to read. You state your position clearly and simply. Everything in the essay explains and defends this main point. The essay is coherent. All the paragraphs, as well as the sentences within them, are in the right order. Most transitions, especially between paragraphs, are effective. The essay is well developed too. Everything you set out to say is fully and carefully explained. Your writing style is clear. The essay is intelligently written, and yet in talking about a difficult subject that most people don't know much about, you do not rely on obscure or technical words. Finally, the essay's mechanics are excellent. Your grammar, spelling, punctuation, and citation form are almost all very good.

It seems to me, though, that a few changes would make the essay more effective.

1. Although the proposition is clear and quite adequate as is, it could be a little more succinct and more firmly attached to the introduction. You make one transitional word, *therefore,* do more work than it may be able to bear. In place of it, you could pick up the idea of *increase* from the foregoing sentence, maybe something like

. . . the number of active computer studios is steadily increasing. This increase raises an important issue in the minds of many writers: the impact of computer technology on the future of music.

2. Some transitions between sentences within paragraphs can use some strengthening too. Right now, your second and third paragraphs seem a little like lists of benefits or faults of computer music. Instead of listing items, you might try grouping them into categories. On the other hand, it may just seem like you've just listed items instead of grouping them because your inter-sentence transitions are hard to locate. More effective sentence transitions would overcome this "listing" effect and create the groups of items I mentioned, so that the paragraphs would flow better.

3. The word *downside* in paragraph 3, sentence 1, seems to me to be an unfortunate choice. *Flaws* or *faults* might fit better.

4. I may be a punctuation nitpicker, but it seems to me that the comma after *Schwartz* in paragraph 1, sentence 1 is unnecessary.

All in all a very good job. I learned a lot. □

Task 5   *Practice Descriptive and Evaluative Peer Review*

Write an evaluation of the essay you wrote a descriptive outline for in task 1, "Industrialization and Modernization in Two Latin American Countries," p. 313. Follow this format:

- **Explain the essay's strengths.** What do you like about the essay? What do you think is well done?
- **Explain what you think could be done to improve the essay.** How exactly do you think the writer can go about doing that?

Plan your evaluation carefully using the following criteria. They are listed in order of importance, with the most important first.

Unity: Is the proposition of the essay clear? Is it stated as concisely as it could be stated? Does everything in the essay defend or explain that proposition, not some other? (See Unity and Coherence, p. 116, and Propositions, p. 85.)

Coherence: Are the paragraphs in the essay in the right order? Does each paragraph begin with an effective transitional generalization? Are the sentences within each paragraph in the right order? Are there transitional elements that relate the sentences? (See Unity and Coherence, p. 116.)

Development: Is everything the essay sets out to say fully explained? Does the essay tell you everything you feel you need to know to understand the main point of the essay? (See Paragraph Development, p. 111, and Introductions, p. 81.)

Style: Is the essay's position expressed and explained as clearly and simply as possible, with no apparent effort to impress by using big words, long sentences, or elaborate word order? (See Style, p. 137.)

Mechanics: Is the essay written in standard written English with generally accepted grammar, spelling, and punctuation? Is it presented neatly, with a good general appearance? (Refer to a standard writer's handbook.)

In evaluating the essay, respond as an honest, demanding, but sympathetic reader—as a constructive reader. Try to make your evaluative comments tactful, but also make them direct, detailed, and helpful.

To strike the right tone in your evaluative comments, keep in mind that you are writing to three audiences. One is the writer. **You want the writer to feel that you are trying to help, not hurt.** The second is your teacher, who will read your peer review to see how carefully, tactfully, and thoroughly you have written it. And the third audience is yourself. You want to say what you really think, as honestly as you can.

Tactfully expressed peer reviews are a sign that reviewers respect writers and understand their problems. Other writers respond positively, just as you do, to thorough, detailed, carefully and kindly worded reviews, both positive and negative. Tactfully worded reviews make writers feel that reviewers really care, have their best interests at heart, and want to help them improve.

If you withhold your comments, positive or negative, from other writers you may keep them from knowing something they need to know in order to improve. Your answer to the first evaluative question, "What is well done in the essay?", is just as important as your answer to the second, "What could be done to improve it?" So a complete and helpful review explains *both* evaluative questions fully. **Writers have to know what they are doing right** in order to keep doing it, just as much as **they have to know what to change in order to improve their work.**

Explaining carefully what is done well is not just an opportunity to be comforting and supportive. **Tell writers what you really do think is good about their work.** Don't be afraid to be obvious. What seems obviously good to you may not be so obvious to everyone, especially the person who wrote the essay. Besides, everyone likes a genuine compliment on something they've done well, even if they already know it's pretty good.

It is also important, of course, to explain fully and in detail what the writer can do to improve an essay. Notice that the question does not ask you to tell writers what you think is bad about their work. Instead, it asks you to tell them something else: what one thoughtful, constructive reader (you) thinks they could do to make reading easier. As you explain what to improve and how to improve it, help the writer set some priorities if you can. Some problems are more troublesome and harder to deal with than others. Try to suggest what you think the writer should work on first.

The *way* you explain what you think is well done, what could be improved, and how to do it, is as important as *what* you say. Pay careful attention to how you express your views. **Explain every generalization you make, and give examples.** If you say that the proposition is wordy, give some examples of what could be cut out. If you say the paragraph transitions are good, point out the words or phrases that make them effective.

In any case, don't worry about pushing other writers around with your peer review. No one has to do what you suggest. Writers can choose to do it or ignore it. But they cannot make that choice if you don't tell them what you think, if you say what you think tactlessly, or if you don't explain it carefully. Detailed explanation of the points you make in your peer review will help writers understand what you're getting at. Try to be as thorough, straightforward, practical, and helpful as you can.

Task 6 *Essay Exchange and Descriptive and Evaluative Peer Review*

Exchange essays with a classmate (preferably not one you have exchanged with before). Number the sentences in the essay you have received in exchange for your own. Write lightly in pencil. Don't write anything else on the paper.

Then, first, on a separate sheet write a detailed descriptive outline of the essay. Check your descriptive outline twice against the essay, and revise the outline until you are confident that it represents the essay accurately. (Detailed descriptive outlines are explained beginning on p. 153.)

Second, write an evaluation of the essay following the format used in task 5, p. 182.

This peer review exercise begins with a descriptive outline for two reasons. One is to reassure yourself that you understand how the essay is written and that your evaluation is accurate. The other reason is to reassure the writer that you have read the essay carefully.

While you are writing your descriptive outline, you may begin to notice some of the essay's strengths and some things you think the writer could do to improve it. Make a note of these responses, but don't include them in your descriptive outline. Save them for your evaluation. Then plan your evaluation carefully using the criteria given in task 5, p. 182.

In evaluating an essay, respond as a constructive reader. Make your evaluative comments tactful, practical, detailed, and helpful.

Task 7   *Essay Exchange and Descriptive, Evaluative, and Substantive Peer Review*

This advanced peer reviewing task involves three students in constructive conversation about each essay. It requires two exchanges, so that each essay has two different peer reviewers. The writer gets to respond twice: between the first and the second peer reviewer and at the end of the sequence.

The task can be done only in courses in which everyone can write on the same topic or in which everyone has a general knowledge of what other people are likely to write about, such as subject matter courses or peer tutoring courses (in assignments where the topic is peer tutoring and related subjects). Also, this task should be done only after everyone has practiced doing entirely descriptive and evaluative reviews.

In this task, peer review takes another step in developing your ability to read constructively. The first peer reviewing task asked you to describe but not evaluate or comment on substance. The second asked you to describe and evaluate but still not comment on substance. **This task asks you, as a peer reviewer, to describe, evaluate, *and* comment on substance.** It asks you to reply to the positions taken in the essays you read in a way that takes into account the assumptions made in those essays. As a writer, furthermore, this task asks you to help your classmates improve their work as peer reviewers by evaluating the peer reviews they write. Make your evaluation of other students' peer reviews as helpful as you would like theirs to be of your own.

First peer reviewer

Write a descriptive and evaluative peer review of the essay as you did for tasks 5 and 6. Then add to it an evaluation of the issue raised in the essay, the position the essay takes on that issue, and the assumptions it makes.

First, write a descriptive outline of the essay.
Second, evaluate the essay's writing technique.

- What is effective and well done in the essay?
- What could be done to improve it?

Third, evaluate the essay's content:

- Do you agree with the essay's main point?
- Do you accept the essay's assumptions? Explain why. (See Assumptions, p. 132.)
- If you do not agree with the essay's position, or if you do not accept one or more of its assumptions, what position would you take on the issue yourself? What assumptions would you make? How would you defend your position, and how would you refute the main point of the essay in question?
- If you do agree with the essay's position, do you think the essay makes the best possible argument supporting it? How would you strengthen that argument? What would you change, add, or omit? Why?

Writer's response

Evaluate the first peer reviewer's evaluation of your essay.

- You may defend your essay, if you like.
- More important, explain how each part of the review affects you as a writer.
- From the point of view of a writer, what is well done in the review? How could it be improved?

Second peer reviewer

First, mediate between the writer and the first peer reviewer:

- In what respects is the first peer reviewer's evaluation of the essay tactful, thorough, detailed, and helpful? In what respects could it be improved?

- Is the writer's response to the first evaluation reasonable? Is it tactful, thorough, detailed, and helpful?

Second, evaluate the essay from your own point of view:

- Explain where you agree or disagree with the first peer reviewer.
- Add anything that you think would help the writer see what is well done in the essay and how to improve it.

Writer's second response
The writer gets the last word:

- **First, reevaluate your essay** in light of the peer review it has received.
- **Second, evaluate both peer reviews.** In what respect has this conversation about your essay been constructive? Has it helped you to improve the essay? If so, how? If not, what would have helped more?
- **Third, evaluate the whole peer review process** from the point of view of both a writer and a peer reviewer. What effect, if any, has the process had on your attitude toward writing and on the way you write? Add anything else you would like to say.

PART FOUR

Reaching Out to Members of Other Communities

Whatever you read, you want to feel it's worthwhile. Everyone feels that way. It's the most compelling reason to read. And whatever you write, you want your readers to feel that what you have written is worthwhile. You want them to understand your position. Everyone feels that way. It is the most compelling reason to write.

But readers sometimes reject what they read before they give it a chance. You may do that yourself sometimes. You know what it's like. You feel bored. You squirm and yawn. You have an irresistible urge to do something else—anything else—rather than keep on reading. You think "this writer doesn't speak my language." You say "baloney" or something worse, and you quit.

That may happen for two reasons. Sometimes you reject what you read because you haven't suspended judgment long enough to understand it. Sometimes you reject it because the writer hasn't worked hard enough to make you want to understand. Either way, you stand to lose. You are rejecting something that might be worth your while to know.

So the question is, what can you do about it? How can you be sure when you read that you are giving the writer a chance? And when you write, what can you do to interest readers so they don't reject what you're saying?

Just stating your position and exploring, explaining, or defending it won't do the trick. That is the insides of an essay. It will interest a few readers who already care about what you have to say, but it probably won't catch the interest of anyone else. In order to interest other readers, besides making parts of the insides relate to each other, you have to show how the insides are related to something outside. You have to make the insides of your essay accessible to readers beyond the boundaries of the community of like-minded people you belong to.

When we talk about ourselves as readers and writers it is helpful to call communities of like-minded people language communities or **discourse communities.** What distinguishes true language or discourse communities is that their members talk with each other about the same sorts of things in the same sorts of ways. Baseball fans talk with other baseball fans about batting averages, pitching techniques, and league standings. Surgeons talk with each other about successful procedures, anatomy, new equipment, and fees. Discourse communities are groups of people who are distinguished by the fact that they "speak the same language."

Discourse communities are also distinguished by the fact that the language they speak with each other is *not* the language that the members of *other* language communities speak. Baseball fans do not normally talk with each other about surgical procedures and surgeons do not normally talk with each other about batting averages. If two surgeons do talk about batting averages, they are not talking as members of the community of surgeons. They are confirming their common membership in another discourse community, the community of baseball fans.

Surgeons sometimes talk baseball with their patients, too, in order to explain to them the surgery they are going to perform or to put them at ease before surgery. If your surgeon talks with you about batting averages, striking out, and hitting home runs, it is true that he is confirming his common membership with you in the discourse community of baseball fans, but he is likely to be doing so for a particular purpose. What the two of you, a surgeon and a patient, are really talking about is surgery, not baseball. So your surgeon is using baseball language in an unusual way, at the boundary between the discourse community he normally belongs to, the community of surgeons, and the discourse community you belong to, the community of patients. He is trying to make it possible for you to accept and understand the experience that the two of you are going to be sharing in such different ways.

That is what people do at community boundaries. They try to make what they have to say accessible to members of other communities of like-minded people, other discourse communities, so that the members of those different communities can understand each other and get along. They do that by negotiating differences in language and by translating from one community language into another. Baseball talk between you and your surgeon is a negotiating gesture, a common language which he is using to help him translate between two languages, the language of his discourse community and the language of yours.

As a writer, that's what you have to do, too, in order to catch the interest of readers who are members of communities other than your own. To interest readers in other communities, you have to show them how the topic you are writing about and the position you are taking on it affect their opinions, involve their experiences, or touch their feelings. You have to find terms that are familiar to both of you and that you both understand in pretty much the same way. You have to show your readers that you can speak their language.

SPEAKING OTHER PEOPLE'S LANGUAGE

It is important to learn how to show your readers that you can speak their language, because most of the readers whose interest you would like to catch probably do not quite speak *your* language. On any topic you write about there is a lot of difference between the opinions, experience, and feelings of people like you and those of people who are different from you. What you talk about with your friends and the way you talk about it in the discourse communities that you belong to differ at least a little bit, and in some cases a great deal, from what members of other discourse communities talk about and the way they talk about it. Even some of the people you think you know pretty well may differ from you in ways that you are not aware of, because they belong to discourse communities that you are not aware they are members of.

You have already discovered some of these differences if you have done exercise 1 in this book: a reminiscence, a family story, or an account of change. Read any story based on your private or family experience to other people, and you will notice that most of them have a lot of questions to ask before they feel that they understand what happened. Look to the left and right of you in any classroom and you are looking at people who differ from you and from each other in many ways, because they belong to different discourse communities. They root for different baseball teams, take different courses, eat different food, do different things before they get to class and after they leave it, have different jobs, strive toward different goals in life.

If people differ even in these simple, everyday ways, you can imagine how much more they differ in more complex and serious aspects of life than sports, school, food, jobs, and goals. No other member of your class was brought up quite as you were brought up, in quite the discourse communities you were brought up in. Probably none of them is a member of your family. Most don't come from your neighborhood or hometown. Some may not even have been born in your country. They or their parents do different things for a living and have different incomes. Some may be quite a bit older or younger than you. Some are of a different race, religion, or ethnic background. Probably half of them are different in gender. Some may differ from you in all these ways at once.

And the differences don't stop there. Not only do you and your classmates differ in experience, background, and gender. All of you also differ in how you feel about yourselves, how you feel about each other, and how you feel other people feel about you.

All these differences affect the way you read and write. Are you someone who knows nothing about baseball who is reading something written for baseball fans, or are you reading it as a baseball fan yourself? Are you a woman writing to other women, a woman writing to men, or a woman writing to both men and women? Are you a small-town person reading something written by a city slicker? Are you an environmentalist writing to deer hunters, or a deer hunter writing to environmentalists? Are you a farmer reading something written by a white-collar suburbanite, or a white-collar suburbanite reading something written by a farmer? Or maybe you are a scientist writing to other scientists, a scientist writing to nonscientists, or a nonscientist writing to scientists. Are there Protestants in your audience? Jews? Catholics? Muslims? How many of your readers are African-Americans, Italian-Americans, Asian-Americans, white middle-class Americans of no easily discernable ethnic background (but certainly of *some* ethnic background)?

Differences of all kinds affect you as a reader trying to understand what other people write and as a writer trying to write so that other people will understand you. They determine whether or not you feel that a writer you are reading speaks your language, and they determine the way you try as a writer to speak the same language that your readers speak.

In short, thinking about differences, between you and the writer you are reading or between you and the people who will read what you are writing, comes down to thinking about differences in language. Men tend to use different language to talk with each other about their feelings, their families, their bodies, their interests, and their jobs than women use. Chemists use different language to talk with each other about the natural world than physicists use. People in different discourse communities talk differently about their religious beliefs, their jobs, what they know, who they know, who they are, where they are, and where they're going. The language people use to talk about things, and the people they talk about those things with, define the ethnic, religious, professional and other kinds of groups they belong to.

So differences in language can be both serious and complicated. They can even cause wars. Just as people who don't understand each other can wind up fighting, nations that don't understand each other can wind up fighting too. Even at the very best, differences in language can break up friendships, keep you from learning things you need to know or would like to know, and deprive you of the pleasures of variety—which everyone knows is the spice of life.

TALKING ABOUT ELEPHANTS

To help you understand how complicated differences in language can be when you try to write across community boundaries, and understand what may be involved in thinking about those differences, consider this updated version of the story of the blind men and the elephant.

As the story goes, once upon a time a king who had heard of elephants but had never seen one wanted to explore new energy resources and thought that maybe elephants could help. So he established a task force to examine an elephant and tell him what elephants were really like. To this task force he appointed three blind men.

Duly appointed and charged, the blind men went off, found themselves an elephant, and began their investigation. The first blind man stepped up to the elephant, felt its side, and said that an elephant was like a wall. The second blind man felt the elephant's trunk and said that an elephant was like a snake. The third blind man felt one of the elephant's legs and said that an elephant was like a tree.

From the point of view of the three blind men, this research completed their investigation. They submitted a report to the king and went back to their work and their private lives.

The king, however, after one look at their report, called them back for another try. The blind men were puzzled and a bit miffed by the king's response. Each of them had reported his experience honestly in the language he normally used when he talked with people he knew. But what neither the blind men nor the king realized was that although the three task force members had a great deal in common, in many more ways they were quite different.

True, they were all blind, they were all royal appointees, none of them had ever touched an elephant before, and they had all just recently touched one. But in ways that turned out to be crucial for the task that the king assigned them to do, they were very different people indeed. The least of these differences was that each one, unknown to the others, touched a different part of the elephant. Much more important was the fact that they had never before engaged in conversation with each other about anything at all, much less elephants. Each of them was a member of a different set of discourse communities.

They all seemed to be speaking the same language—in this case, English. But in fact each one spoke a different version of English, because each one was a member of a different profession. The first blind man was a plasterer. He normally talked mostly with other plasterers. Conversation with plasterers was what he had internalized as thought. To plasterers a vertical flat surface is a wall. As a result, when the first blind man touched the side of the elephant, he thought "wall." If instead of being a plasterer he had been, say, an artist, he might have thought something quite different. Artists talk with each other a lot about the materials they use, so he might have said that an elephant was like a stretched canvas.

The second blind man was a zookeeper, and what he had internalized as thought was the conversation of zookeepers. To him a long, soft, flexible cylindrical object must be a snake. If he had been an electrical engineer instead of a zookeeper, he might have said an elephant is like a coaxial cable, or if he had been a sailor, a rope.

It is obvious by now that the third blind man was a gardener. He was not, say, an architect, in which case he would not have said that an elephant is like a tree. He would probably have said that an elephant is like a classical column, most likely Doric.

In his work on the elephant task force, each blind man used words drawn from the conversation of the professional discourse community he belonged to. So each one spoke a slightly different language. That's why their report didn't tell the king as much as he wanted to know about elephants. What it did tell him was that, so far, his task force on elephants was still a loose aggregate of political appointees talking past each other. They understood the task, but they didn't yet understand *each other* well enough to be able to make sense out of their mutual experience: touching an elephant.

To make sense out of that experience, in fact, they had to begin to talk with each other about touching the elephant. They had to discover and negotiate their differences, especially differences in the way they were using language, and arrive at some sort of consensus. They had to stop talking like plasterers, zoologists, and gardeners. They had to start talking like members of the king's task force on elephants.

So that's what they did. They talked with each other and got to know each other. Gradually their relationship changed. By talking with each other, they began to build a collective conversational history of plasterers, zookeepers, and gardeners. Each one began to remember how the others had talked before about elephants, in a variety of conversational situations. They negotiated their differences. And out of this developing conversational history they constructed a composite language common to their own particular working group: the king's task force on elephants.

They continued to use many of the words that they had been using right along, of course. But by negotiating, translating, and making conversational adjustments and compromises at the boundaries of the communities they normally belonged to, each one changed the way he used those words. And as their language and their relationship changed, so did what they knew about elephants.

Here, for example, is how their conversation went at one stage. The first blind man was still insisting rather boringly that an elephant was like a wall. He was still using the word *wall* just as he had used it in his part of their first report to the king. That is, he was using it as plasterers normally use it, to refer to the vertical flat surfaces they work on. But by now the two other blind men were listening harder and remembering more.

"Oh, I get it," said the third blind man, "you mean that this elephant-wall you're talking about is flat and smooth like a plastered wall."

"Right," said the first blind man. Then, thinking it over for a moment, he continued, "Well, uh, not exactly. An elephant-wall is different. It's, well, sort of bristly."

"Oh, I see," said the second blind man, "bristly like my snake."

"And like my tree?" said the third.

"Say," said the first, "I didn't know your tree and snake were bristly. That's odd. The trees and snakes I've touched around home aren't bristly, any more than the walls I plaster are."

"That's true, come to think of it," said the second. "Trees and snakes aren't bristly around my place either. Very odd. Listen, my elephant-snake is wrinkled as well as bristly. Is your elephant-wall wrinkled, too?"

"My elephant-tree is," interrupted the third.

"Well, maybe," answered the first blind man, ignoring the interruption. "It depends on what the wrinkles on your elephant-snake are like. My elephant-wall sure is wrinkled. But its wrinkles run from side to side. The wrinkles on most of the trees I've ever touched, like oak trees, run up and down."

"Come to think of it," said the third, "the wrinkles on my elephant-tree run side-to-side too."

"Wait a minute," said the second, "my elephant-snake's wrinkles also run side-to-side. Or, to be precise about it, they run around the snake, not from end to end." "Hmm," he said, "do you suppose that what really makes an elephant is bristles and side-to-side wrinkles? No wonder the king rejected our report."

"Nonsense," said the third, his nose still a little out of joint at being ignored. "It is obvious to me that, wrinkles or no wrinkles, bristles or no bristles, an elephant *is* like a tree."

"Pardon me," said the first, "but don't you mean that an elephant is like a wall, a snake, and a tree all at once?"

"Well, all right," conceded the third, mollified that the other two were finally paying attention to what he had to say.

"Hey," said the second, "I think you've really got something there. What an elephant really is, *is* a wall and a tree and a snake all at once, *with* bristles and wrinkles from side to side. What about that?"

"Well, maybe," said the third, not quite following. "By the way," he threw in, "how thick is your wall?"

"*Thick?*" said the first. "I've never thought about thickness before. How thick is your tree?"

And so on. Now this conversation among the three blind men may seem a little silly. But something is going on in it that is crucial to the task that they were assigned. Each one is getting to know how the others use certain key words (*wall, snake, tree*), and they are all learning to use those words in new ways. They are constructing a conversational history and a composite, boundary language common to themselves.

In the process, the social relationship among them is changing. By erasing some of the community boundaries among themselves, they are becoming a new, coherent discourse community, a community of knowledgeable peers. The change in their social relationship occurs as they strive to reach a consensus about what elephants are. How the blind men are related socially, how they talk with each other, and what they know about elephants all change at the same time. It is impossible to distinguish their knowledge, their social relationships, and their language.

Starting off as an aggregation of people who made very little sense to each other or to anyone else because they were members of different language communities, the three blind men gradually became a cohesive new community of people who speak the same language. They made sense to each other—that is, they constructed sense with each other—in this case about elephants. Maybe in time they will make sense about other things too.

WRITING ACROSS COMMUNITY BOUNDARIES

As a writer, that is just exactly what you want to happen when you try to interest members of other language communities in the position you are taking in an essay. You want your readers to put aside for the time being the differences between you and them that are based on the fact that you belong to different language communities. Instead, you want them to agree for the time being to translate the language you are using into language that they normally use. You are inviting them to help you negotiate the community boundaries between you and to become, for the time it takes to read your essay and talk about it, a coherent discourse community with its own composite working language and its own conversational history.

Thinking about both the similarities and the differences between the discourse communities you belong to and those that other people belong to can be crucial to how well you get across. Members of the communities you belong to—your family, your friends, your religious or ethnic group, and so on—are likely to understand your position in one way. Members of other communities are likely to understand it quite differently, if they take enough interest in it to understand it at all. How hard you have to think about these differences depends on what you are reading or writing about, the position taken on the topic, and the depth or sensitivity of the differences you have to deal with.

If your writing course is set up collaboratively so that you can talk with other students regularly about writing, you have an opportunity to discover and negotiate differences among you that are very much like the ones that the three blind men had. You can engage in conversation directly with your readers, many of whom do not belong to the language communities you belong to, so that you can discover the differences among you and negotiate them.

But of course you may not always have that opportunity. And in some cases as a writer you may have to deal with some differences that are more serious and complicated than the differences the blind men encountered. Imagine how much more complicated and contentious their conversation would have been if they differed in other, more complex and deeply personal ways such as ethnic or religious background or in gender.

These deeper differences would certainly not make agreement impossible, but it could make it a lot harder. Everyone engaged in the conversation would have to think more carefully about the differences in language among them and the differences in experience, background, and gender that those differences in language implied.

That is exactly the kind of thinking you have to do when you try to relate the insides of an essay you are writing, to readers whose interests and opinions differ from yours. It is the kind of thinking you will have to do for most of the essays you will ever write. Most of your readers are not going to belong to all the discourse communities you belong to. Not only will they use different words, worse still they may use some of the same words you use, but in different ways. Where you talk about trees, they may talk about snakes or walls. Or where you talk about trees as growing things that bear leaves, they may talk about trees as something you stick into shoes to keep their shape.

The purpose of Part Four is to help you learn how to relate the insides of an essay you write to diverse readers. It will help you write at the boundaries between the discourse communities you belong to and the discourse communities that your readers belong to. It will help you relate what you know and value, what you think on the topic you are writing about, and what you have experienced to what other people have experienced, what they think on the topic, and what they know and value. That is, it will help you place the position you take in an essay into a context of sharable concerns, or a context of issues.

CONTEXTS OF ISSUES, SHAREABLE CONCERNS

Exercise 4 (p. 31) defines an *issue* as a *shareable concern*. Issues are the sort of things that you talk about with people you know, that people you know read about, and maybe that all of you together would like to do something about. Issues grow out of the concrete experiences that you have had in common, that you talk a lot about with each other, or maybe that you hardly ever talk about but just assume.

An issue can be expressed as a noun phrase or as a question that makes specific one or more of the relationships implied in the noun phrase. An example of an issue stated as a noun phrase is *water pollution*. This phrase may also be stated as several specific questions: "What materials are polluting the oceans? Where do these materials come from? What can we do to keep the oceans clean?" (see p. 31).

The **context of issues** of any essay you write is made up of concerns related to the position you are taking in the essay that are shareable by two or more discourse communities. One way to interest members of other discourse communities in that position is to describe, outline, or, better still, dramatize concerns that you think other people may share with you, even though they may have backgrounds and interests that differ from your own. If your readers become aware of those shared concerns, they will be more likely to consider the position you are taking, read what you have to say about it, and give it some thought even though they don't agree with it. If you point out concerns that you and your readers share, they are more likely to feel that what they are reading is worthwhile, and they are more likely to understand what you are getting at.

For example, suppose you decided to write an essay about an experience you had last summer at the beach. When you went for your first walk on the beach with some friends on the day you arrived, you saw an oil slick on the water and a "No Swimming" sign posted at your favorite place to swim. You and your friends felt really disappointed and angry. Then you came across a dead sea gull covered with a thick, sticky, tarlike substance, and you began to feel even worse. Suddenly your vacation seemed a lot less happy than you expected it to be.

Later, you noticed a poster advertising a meeting of commercial fishermen to discuss declining catches due to the oil slick, and you ran into an Audubon Society member organizing teams to save sea birds overcome by oil. Learning about the interests of both these groups made you realize that the experience you shared with your friends on the beach was not just an instance of personal misfortune and disappointment. It made you members of a much larger discourse community made up of people who are concerned for different reasons about the same issue.

This larger community included the fishermen and the Audubon people. It included the region's water commissioners. It included everyone who eats fish, drinks water, or swims in the sea. All those people, however different in other ways, have a common interest when it comes to keeping the oceans clean. So they talk with other members of their own local community about some of the very same things that members of the other communities talk about with each other, although they talk about those things for different reasons and in different ways. The fishermen talk with each other about the oil slick on the ocean because it reduces their catch, the Audubon people because it kills birds, the water commissioners because it affects the drinking water supply, you and your friends because it affects swimming.

The differences in the way the members of these communities talk with each other about keeping the oceans clean—their differences in language—are related to differences in their experience and background. The fishermen are working people living on worker's wages who talk about business in the local dialect. Audubon Society members tend to be well-paid professional or business people who talk bird watching in the dialect of the college-educated middle-class. Fish eaters and swimmers can of course be anyone who talks salmon or surf in any dialect at all, in fact in any native language.

So, when you set out to write an essay based on your vacation experience with the oil slick, the closed beach, and the dead bird, you had a large number of potential readers in a number of different discourse communities who share a concern about clean oceans. Who would you want to read the essay? Who would you want to think about the topic you are writing about and the position you are taking on that topic? Certainly the friends who walked with you along the beach that day. But they already share your interest and your feelings, and they share it in very much the same terms. You all speak more or less the same language.

How much more worth your while it would be to write the essay so that many more people than just that small group of friends would want to read it. To address more people than your immediate friends, you would have to show how it affects the interests of people in other communities besides your own. To write as a fellow beach lover to your beach-bum friends, describing the curl of a breaker and the sun on the sand would certainly make them feel the importance of what you have to say. But how would the fishermen, the Audubon Society members, and the fish eaters be likely to respond?

There is a good chance that they would reject your position out of hand without trying to understand it. They would feel that you aren't someone who speaks their language. To interest them in your position you would have to show them that you are addressing concerns that you all share by finding language that negotiates the boundary between your community and theirs. You would have to talk about declining catches swimming beyond the breakers, endangered species flying above them, and the rich taste of bluefish steaming on the beach to perfection.

Consider another example. Suppose you are a child psychiatrist writing an essay about a scene you witnessed in which two children were fighting in front of a candy store. You want to explain what the fight was all about not just to other child psychiatrists but also to parents of young children and members of the American Association of Candy Store Owners. How would you negotiate the boundaries among these three discourse communities so that few readers in these groups would reject what you say without trying to understand it?

The way you interest members of other discourse communities in what you have to say depends on your understanding of the language they normally speak. Although the members of these three groups may all talk about children, they differ widely in the language they use when they talk about them. Child psychiatrists talk with other child psychiatrists in the language of Freudian or behavioral psychology about how to treat troubled children. Parents talk with other parents about how to deal with children who misbehave in the language of parental hope and despair. Candy store owners talk with other candy store owners in the language of profit and loss about how to sell children more candy.

Given the great diversity of interest and language of these three communities, can you possibly find anything at all that child psychiatrists, parents, and candy store owners have in common? Maybe. Child psychiatrists want the troubled children they treat to behave differently. Parents want their children to behave well in public. Candy store owners want the children who visit their shops to behave politely so that the parents of potential customers will feel comfortable letting their children go there.

So, to interest members of all three groups you might try to show that knowing what any fight is all about can help control it. For example, if you know that a fight in a boxing ring between two men in shorts and puffy gloves is a profit-making business, you know that it can be controlled the way other businesses are controlled: with laws requiring that products be genuine, fairly priced, and as safe as possible for both producers and consumers. In contrast, a fight between bride and groom on their wedding day may result from nervousness or from changing their minds at the very last minute. To control that fight requires knowing something about the personal history and character of the man and woman involved and what led them to decide to marry.

If you can show this relationship between understanding any fight and controlling it, then it is likely that at least some members of all three groups—child psychiatrists, parents, and candy-store owners—would be willing to consider your position that to control a fight between two children in front of a candy store requires understanding what it is really about. Child psychiatrists, parents, and shopkeepers would all feel that you speak their language.

WHAT AN INTRODUCTION DOES

As a writer, it is sometimes possible to try to interest members of other discourse communities in what you have to say by showing that you understand the language they normally speak while you are exploring, explaining, or defending your position. But that is hard to do without confusing both your readers and yourself. You have to bring into your explanation or defense some material that, strictly speaking, does not either explain or defend your position. Mixed with the explanation or defense, it can seem extraneous. It can spoil your essay by destroying its coherence.

Trying to interest members of other discourse communities in what you have to say at the very beginning and at the very end of the essay is a lot easier. An introductory paragraph at the beginning of an essay provides an immediate or limited context of issues for the position you take, so that readers will see how your position is related to their own experience, interests, or knowledge and to those of the discourse community they are members of. (See Introductions, p. 81.)

For example, in an introduction you might have written for the position paper on cars discussed in exercise 5, p. 44, you could have placed the proposition ("Cars may be on the way out as a major means of transportation") in any one of several immediate or limited contexts: the number of cars on the road, air pollution, governmental investigations of car safety, and so on. You would decide which context to use by thinking about the interests and backgrounds of the people you were writing to.

For example, suppose you expect your readers to be the other students in your class. What do you know about their background and interests? Do they drive? Do they have to fight traffic jams on the city streets or on the freeways? Have they or their friends had a car accident recently? Are they worried about the air pollution that cars produce?

If you drew a diagram of the car essay with these interests in mind, you might show that essay as a box placed in a set of possible frames or packages. The diagram might look something like the one on page 202.

In this diagram, the essay's insides are those three little boxes inside the larger context boxes on the left (proposition and two paragraphs of explanation or defense). The diagram makes these insides look less important than their context by exaggerating the difference in size between them. That is of course not the case in the essay itself, as the blown up version of the diagram on the right shows. Context and position are roughly equal in importance. In most essays, what you have to say can be only as effective as the reception it gets by people whose interests differ from your own.

For example, it is not hard to imagine that some people might be almost totally indifferent to the proposition, "Cars as we know them

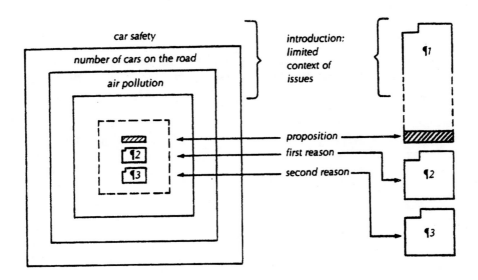

may be on the way out." Ho hum, they might say. People who feel that way are likely to belong to discourse communities in which members seldom talk with each other about cars. To interest members of those communities you have to try to understand the language that they normally speak. The position you take will make sense to them if the introduction shows that the topic, cars, and the position you are taking on that topic address one or more immediately related context of issues, that is, if the introduction shows that the topic and your position on it affect their interests, opinions, and feelings.

Or let's return to the example of the oil slick on the beach (p. 198). Suppose you wrote an essay taking the position that we should put an end to oil spills. And suppose you defended that position with two reasons: Oil spills hurt ocean wildlife (gulls, geese, and terns), and they cripple ocean-dependent industry (fishermen, lobstermen). But the people you wanted most to interest in your position were not Audubon Society members, fishermen, and lobstermen, whom you believe are already convinced that the problem is serious. The people you wanted most to interest in your position this time are some of your ecologically indifferent beach-bum surf-and-sun friends. They're the people you really want to stir up.

Since you know that your friends took a vacation walk along a polluted beach just as you did, you could establish a context of issues by reminding them about finding the "No Swimming" sign and the dead bird. That's a story that you could probably tell with a good deal of feeling. You would probably make it a compelling introduction to the position you want to take in the essay.

Now suppose you found out that you had convinced your beach-bum friends and you knew, of course, that the Audubon people were convinced of the need to put an end to oil spills. Instead, it is the local lobstermen and fishermen's cooperative who have lost interest in the issue. In this case you would have to guess that their background might make them become interested again in keeping the oceans clean. You would have to introduce the essay now in another way. Maybe you could tell a story that one of the fishermen told you at that meeting you attended—the story about coming home with an almost empty boat after twelve hours fishing. Or you could present some figures that show increased unemployment in the fish canning industry due to small catches. Or you could talk about how wary people are becoming about eating fish that they feel may be polluted.

In any case, what you would try to do is develop an immediate or limited context, choosing language that touches the boundary between your discourse community and the communities that the readers belong to, whom you hope to interest. And you would make that context as vivid and striking as you can. You would try to write it in a way that is likely to involve or interest people with backgrounds and interests that may overlap your own but are also somewhat different from your own.

For example, the example essay on cars takes the position that we are not going to use what we think of as cars much longer. Readers who believe that cars are a necessity of human life are not going to find an argument like that very attractive. The introduction at the beginning of that essay looks as if it was written to capture the interest of just such people.

introduction   Cars seem to be everywhere today. We find them in the desert and the mountains, the forests and the plains. They jam the city streets. They flow like rivers along our superhighways. There are more cars on the road today than ever before. Yet, there are signs that people are not entirely happy with this situation. We complain about air pollution and high accident rates. We worry when we read the news that even though domestic cars have improved a great deal in recent years still another manufacturer has had to recall thousands of cars because the brakes are defective or the gas line leaks. More and more people are traveling by plane and train. Bicycles are increasingly popular in many cities and towns. Some two-car families are selling their second car because they simply can't afford the cost of insurance and upkeep. Of course, it is hard to imagine how we could get along without cars entirely. But it is certainly reasonable to speculate that as people choose other ways of getting around, travel by car may have reached its high-water mark and has begun to recede. It seems fantastic *proposition*   and unlikely, yet it is now possible to say that in the future the trend will be for people to use cars as we know them less rather than more. In fact, it looks as if cars may be on the way out as our major means of transportation.

But people who believe cars are a necessity of human life may not be the only people whose interest you want to capture if you wrote the essay on cars. Instead, you might want to interest people who think that today's cars are unique. For that purpose you could conceivably begin the essay with an entirely different introduction that goes something like this:

introduction   Chevys, Fords, Toyotas, VWs, Buicks, Jeeps. Dozens of kinds of cars. And dozens of models: convertibles, range rovers, sporty two-door jobs, four-door family models, pick-ups. Each one seems to have its own special purpose and own history. As different as they are, though, all of them really have a single purpose and a single history. They can all be traced back to the old Model T. Henry Ford did not invent the automobile. But he did invent the family car, the everyday workhorse, the common travel convenience. True, the cars we see on the road today don't seem to look much like the old, rattling, clattering black box on wheels that Ford cranked out by the thousands in the early decades of the twentieth century. But take away the fancy trimmings, the devices added for special purposes, and of course the increase in power and you'd find that the differences between Ford's Tin Lizzy and your own is pretty small. Both run on gasoline fueling an internal combustion engine. Both can go anywhere you want to drive them, when they don't get stuck in the mud. They pervade our lives as though no one had ever thought of an alternative to them. But alternatives do exist, and recent, rapid changes in the world we live in may make these alternatives very attractive indeed. In fact, it looks as if cars may be on the way out as our major means of transportation.

proposition

COLLABORATIVE LEARNING

These collaborative tasks are about acknowledging people's differences in background and coping with those differences.

Task 1   Acknowledging Differences

Divide the class according to birth order: oldest children in the family, youngest children, middle children, only children. One person in each group records the views expressed in the group and the consensus that the group arrives at collaboratively. Try to arrive at an answer to each of the following questions that most people in the group can live with, but make sure that the group's recorder makes note of differences of opinion and dissent from the consensus. Finally, review the recorder's notes. Make sure that they state accurately what the group has decided and include differences of opinion and dissent. When you have finished the task, the recorder will report the results of the group's discussion to the rest of the class.

What was it like being a child in your birth order?

How has being a child of that birth order affected your life after childhood?

In plenary session (the whole class together), recorders should report by listing answers in what the group agrees is their order of importance.

Task 2   Doing Something About Differences as a Reader

Return to birth-order groups.

1. Reach consensus on what you think is the *worst* aspect of being in that birth order and why.

2. Report to the class as a whole. Everyone takes careful notes on what all the other groups report.

3. Record your collective responses as a birth-order group to the other groups' reports. If you feel sympathetic to what another group has reported, explain why you feel that way. If you feel unsympathetic, that's okay too. Just explain why.

Then concentrate on the statement made by another group that brought out your group's most unsympathetic collective response. Suppose that a statement like that turned up in something you were reading. What could you do to make sure that you understand that statement as completely as possible *before* you reject it?

4. Report on your discussion to the class. In the class as a whole, list what seem to be the best ways to try to understand statements you respond to unsympathetically.

Task 3   Doing Something About Differences as a Writer

Return again to birth-order groups and list three experiences, attitudes, goals, or fears that you had as a result of being born in that birth order and that you think would be hard to explain to people whose birth order was different from yours. For example, list three experiences, attitudes, goals, or fears that you had as a result of being an only child and that you think middle children would find hard to understand.

Then decide how you would approach people in each of the other birth-order categories to try to help them understand how you feel on each of those topics.

1. How would you get their interest or make them feel it would be worth their while to listen to what you have to say on that topic? (For example, what could oldest children say to engage the interest and get the sympathy of youngest children?)

2. How would you try to make them care about your position or feel sympathetic to it? (For example, what could middle children say to gain the sympathy of only children?)

After each report, people in each birth-order category explain their reaction to each of the suggested approaches.

This whole set of "difference tasks" may be repeated with other kinds of differences in escalating levels of stress: for example, favorite holidays, why they like (or dislike) their jobs, gender differences, ethnic differences, religious differences, racial differences. To discuss topics like these in a classroom takes increasing amounts of courage, restraint, tact, tolerance, and trust on everyone's part. And yet it is just such topics as these that are most likely to divide us when we try to agree with each other or even just try to get along. Furthermore, if writers are insensitive to differences such as these, they may lose some of their readers.*

WHAT AN ENDING DOES

These issues that directly touch the lives of the members of a few communities of readers, and that you might refer to in an essay's introduction, are often called "limited" issues. There are other issues you could also refer to that affect the members of many more communities, but touch them less directly and in more general ways. Issues of that type are often caled "larger" issues. The place to show how your position is related to these larger issues is in the essay's *ending*.

For example, in contrast to the limited issues of the necessity and the uniqueness of today's cars, the position taken in the essay on cars also has several larger contexts: our changing sense of distance and space, the increasing urbanization of the world, conservation of natural resources, the need for alternative means of public transportation, concern for the environment as a whole, and so on.

*I am indebted to Alex Gitterman for this nonthreatening difference task involving birth order.

If you wanted to place your position in the context of one of these larger issues you would not raise it in the first paragraph, because it is probably too abstract to grab anyone. And you would not raise it while you are exploring, explaining, or defending your position in paragraphs two and three, because it would get in the way. You would devote a fourth paragraph to it. For example, if you diagrammed the car essay again, you could show its insides as three small boxes in the middle (proposition and two paragraphs of explanation) between two concentric sets of issues. The inner set of three issues are the limited ones that your introduction might refer to. The outer set of four issues are the larger ones that your ending might refer to.

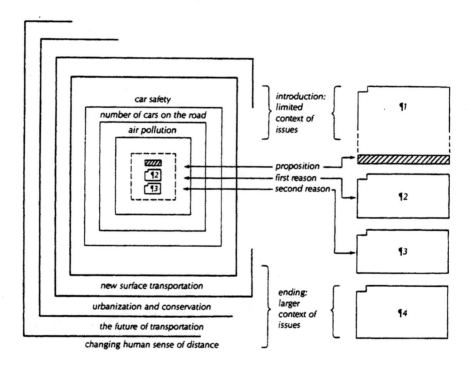

Suppose you decided that the larger issue that affects most people today is the changing sense of distance and space that almost everyone in the world now experiences through satellite-linked TV. To relate the fourth paragraph firmly to the position you take in the essay, first you would refer to the issue you brought up in the introduction. That would remind readers where they started and how your position is related to their more immediate concerns. Then in the ending you would explain the implications of your position to the larger issue. The essay (beginning with the introduction about the necessity of cars) might read something like this:

introduction	Cars seem to be everywhere today. We find them in the desert and the mountains, the forests and the plains. They jam the city streets. They flow like rivers along our superhighways. There are more cars on the road today than ever before. Yet, there are signs that people are not entirely happy with this situation. We complain about air pollution and high accident rates. We worry when we read the news that even though domestic cars have improved a great deal in recent years, still another manufacturer has had to recall thousands of cars because the brakes are defective or the gas line leaks. More and more people are traveling by plane and train. Bicycles are increasingly popular in many cities and towns. Some two-car families are selling their second car because they simply can't afford the cost of insurance and upkeep. Of course, it is hard to imagine how we could get along without cars entirely. But it is certainly reasonable to speculate that as people choose other ways of getting around, travel by car may have reached its high-water mark and has begun to recede. It seems fantastic and unlikely, yet it is now possible to say that in the future the trend will be for people to use cars as we know them less
proposition	rather than more. In fact, it looks as if cars may be on the way out as our major means of transportation.
¶2 transition	And it is high time they were. The world oil supply, which cars depend on for fuel, has been diminishing at the rate
last sentence in ¶2	of. . . . But we travel these super routes at speeds that threaten our lives no matter how safely our cars may be built.
¶3 transition	Cars will become less important in the future not only because they waste fuel and are dangerous, but also because they waste time and human energy. The man I worked for last
last sentence in ¶3	summer. . . . There are millions of conservative travelers like this in mid-century America now taking to the air.
ending *¶4 transition* *reference to introduction (limited context of issues)*	My conservative old friend would be shocked to find out how really up with his times he is. It is all those people jamming the nation's highways who are behind. This is an age in which you can get to London quicker than it takes me to write one of these essays. They no longer show full-length movies on some transatlantic flights. The movies last longer than the few hours it takes to get there. And now we can see things going on in Asia and Europe and Africa, anywhere in the world where they have electricity to run a TV camera, not weeks, months,
leads to a larger context of issues	or days after it happens but the very second it happens. This means that people's sense of distance and space has undergone a big change in the last hundred years. My grandfather went to church on a horse. It was the fastest way to get there. It

another
reference to
the
introduction

took him an hour to go five miles. Those people crawling along our highways at fifty-five miles an hour and sending letters by mail are almost as backward. A man-made satellite goes two-thirds of the way around the earth in the same time. We can fax a letter to Tokyo in minutes, and we can fly from New York to Boston in an hour by jet. The sacred car: How can it compete? It is already little more than an expensive luxury, and in ten years a car may be just a convenience to take vacations in, once you've gotten off the plane in Ankara and rented one for a week's safari into the bush.

On the other hand, you might have chosen to end the essay by relating your position to the interests of some other large community that is affected by some other larger context of issues. For example, you might have related it to the most concrete of the larger contexts, the need for new surface transportation. In this case, the essay would end quite differently, and this ending would catch the interest of the members of an entirely different, and much larger, set of discourse communities. Then the end of the essay might read something like this:

introduction

Cars seem to be everywhere today. We find them in the desert and the mountains, the forests and the plains. They jam the city streets. They flow like rivers along our superhighways. There are more cars on the road today than ever before. Yet, there are signs that people are not entirely happy with this situation. We complain about air pollution and high accident rates. We worry when we read the news that even though domestic cars have improved a great deal in recent years, still another manufacturer has had to recall thousands of cars because the brakes are defective or the gas line leaks. More and more people are traveling by plane and train. Bicycles are increasingly popular in many cities and towns. Some two-car families are selling their second car because they simply can't afford the cost of insurance and upkeep. Of course, it is hard to imagine how we could get along without cars entirely. But it is certainly reasonable to speculate that as people choose other ways of getting around, travel by car may have reached its high-water mark and has begun to recede. It seems fantastic and unlikely, yet it is now possible to say that in the future the trend will be for people to use cars as we know them less

proposition

rather than more. In fact, it looks as if cars may be on the way out as our major means of transportation.

¶2 transition

And it is high time they were. The world oil supply, which

last sentence in
¶2

cars depend on for fuel, has been diminishing at the rate of. . . . But we travel these super routes at speeds that threaten our lives no matter how safely our cars may be built.

¶3 transition

last sentence in ¶3

ending

¶4 transition

reference to introduction

leads to larger context of issues

Cars will become less important in the future not only because they waste fuel and are dangerous, but also because they waste time and human energy. The man I worked for last summer. . . . There are millions of conservative travelers like this in mid-century America now taking to the air.

Despite this new rash of private flying, though, my old boss is not really as ahead of his times as he thinks he is. People have been flying on business trips for years. The shuttle from Washington to New York is an example of the great amount of fast, daily air travel that is already lessening by thousands the number of cars on the road even in this peak year of car travel. But this tendency has held back the most important innovation that must occur soon, before our country, especially in the large urban centers, becomes one hot, smelly traffic jam. That innovation is cheap, clean rail transportation traveling at very high speeds. We must have a way of transporting masses of people medium distances, say from fifty to four or five hundred miles. The governmental machinery is already set up for this kind of transportation, and in places like Japan such systems have been in effect for several years. As soon as these trains begin running regularly and safely, the passing of the car may be inevitable. Cars may be relegated to the position of expensive luxuries. Eventually maybe, automobile transportation will be used only for vacations and Ford will be selling only one line of sedan, three lines of sports cars, and a dozen lines of station wagons—all of them run by electricity.

In the example about oil spills, in which you tried in several different introductions to get several different groups of readers to think about their personal experiences with ocean pollution, the larger context of issues that you might raise in the ending might be the effect of water pollution in rivers and lakes as well as oceans and the effect of pollution on the quality of life in general. Or stewardship: the fact that we are drinking the same water that the dinosaurs drank, but they didn't pollute it, we did. So we have a duty to clean it up.

The difference between this larger context of issues in the ending and the more limited context of issues in the introduction is not that readers are likely to feel one more deeply than the other, although of course they might. The difference is that the introduction shows the essay's relation to the interests of a limited number of discourse communities by spelling out an everyday kind of knowledge and experience and some familiar assumptions and implications (summer vacation, swimming, fishing, family income, the disappearance of favorite birds).

The ending, in contrast, shows the essay's relation to the interests of a broad range of larger discourse communities by spelling out less obvious kinds of knowledge and experience and some less familiar assumptions and implications (the need to control the environment as a whole, pollution of rivers and lakes eventually winds up in the oceans), and to systems of knowledge and value that readers may not yet be fully aware of (environmental studies, the delicate interdependence of all living beings).

In short, introductions are "why bother" paragraphs, whereas endings are "so what" paragraphs. In an *introduction* you answer the reader's question, "Why should I bother reading on?" In an *ending* you answer the reader's question, "Now that I've read all that, so what?"

The two exercises in Part Four are intended to help you learn to write endings that will affect the members of a greater number of larger discourse communities. Exercise 10 asks you, as an experiment, to write two alternative fourth paragraphs for a three-paragraph essay that you have already written. That experiment will show you how different endings can make your position accessible to different sets of larger language communities. Exercise 11 asks you to start from scratch writing a four-paragraph essay: introduction with proposition, two paragraphs of exploration, explanation or defense, and an ending.

(William Perry's "Examsmanship and the Liberal Arts," p. 343, talks about how to engage the interest of members of certain academic communities, those whom your teachers represent, such as English, history, chemistry, sociology, mathematics, and so on. Perry talks about how the language of facts and ideas is related to the language of conceptual frames of reference that gives them meaning for those communities. You may find it interesting to read and discuss this article while working on exercises 10 and 11. See also Unity and Coherence, p. 116, and Assumptions, p. 132.)

▷ EXERCISE 10   EXPERIMENT IN ENDING

The purpose of this exercise is not to produce a polished product. It is to learn something about the difference between the insides of an essay (your position explored, explained, and defended) and what's outside it, the interests of members of other language communities than your own. That is, one purpose is to learn something about the difference between taking a position and putting your position into a context of issues or shared concerns. Another purpose is to help you see that the way you end an essay can affect how seriously people take the whole essay, and for that matter whether or not they are willing to take it seriously at all.

Choose a three-paragraph essay that you wrote for essay exercises 5 through 9. Read it and list all the issues you can think of that are related to it.

Then choose two of these issues and write two alternative paragraphs, each of which could serve as an ending to the essay.

Add a section to the descriptive outline for that essay. Explain what each alternative final paragraph *does* and *says*.

To do this exercise well, you may have to change the last sentence or two of the essay as you originally wrote it. You may also have to change the introduction a little in order to give yourself the kind of phrase you need to refer to in order to write a transition to the two new endings. If you like, you can revise the whole essay.

Don't worry, though, if the product doesn't satisfy you. You started it as a three-paragraph essay. Anything you add now will almost inevitably seem tacked on. One of the alternative endings you write will probably seem better than the other, and you may never like either of them very much.

But that will be alright, because the point of this exercise is not to write a first-rate essay. The purpose is to understand the relation between your position and the several issues it may be related to. Another purpose of the exercise is to help you see that, depending on the circumstances, you always have several options for ending an essay. You always have several possible contexts of issues to choose from that will engage the interest of members of quite different language communities. You make that choice depending on the differences you are aware of between what interests you to talk about and the language you use to talk about it and what interests them and the language they use.

COLLABORATIVE LEARNING

Task 1 *Practice Alternative Endings*

Working in groups of two or three, choose an example three-paragraph essay from this book. Read it aloud.

Describe the essay's introduction. What immediate context of issues or shared concerns does the introduction raise? What community or communities of readers does the introduction set out to interest in the essay's position?

Describe a possible or hypothetical ending for the essay. What possible larger contexts of issues are relevant to the position taken in the essay? How are those larger issues related to the more limited issues raised in the introduction?

Draft two alternative endings to the essay. (Writing these alternative endings could be done individually as a homework assignment. In that case, the members of the collaborative working groups should reconvene in the next class, read their alternative endings to each other, and compare how each writer went about the task.)

Task 2 Reading Aloud

Follow the instructions for reading aloud on p. 55.

☐ EXAMPLE ESSAY ————————————————————

The People's Health

Antonio Rambla

Hardly a day goes by that the news does not carry a story of human drama and suffering that resulted at least in part from poor health care or lack of elementary medical knowledge or medical facilities. Urban minorities, the ghettoized—rural and urban, the jobless, the underpaid, the poorly educated in this country are constantly cheated of the bare essentials of modern health care. Unlike the rich and the middle class, who can afford private medical insurance and private doctors, these people are barred from advanced methods of treatment and from fast, efficient medical service. In a TV ad we are told by the hemophiliac son of a wealthy family that he can survive his disease because his family can afford the huge cost of regular injections of the clotting factor. In the same ad, we are told by a hemophiliac son of poor parents that his chances of obtaining the precious serum are nil. Oddly enough both these young men are equally deprived members of our advanced society. One is as neglected as the other. Both depend on private sacrifice—one by his rich parents, the other by sympathetic and generous strangers. In the end, though, you know who is most likely to survive. This inherent inequality in our system illustrates one of the many spots of social decay that now fester dangerously. To heal this sore, the prescription is simple, but painful and expensive. The remedy is free, government-sponsored national health insurance that gives us total, just, and equal health care for everyone.

Just and equal health treatment, as most city dwellers know as well as those who live deep in the rural countryside of America, is exactly what we do not have. In the country, hospital care is often simply not available at all. In the city, the poor and needy flock to public hospitals in search of care, only to be placed in long waiting lines. Doctors are overworked. Facilities and equipment are overloaded. Quality gives way to quantity. In spite of its good intentions, the medical profession cannot give proper treatment to all the people who need it under these conditions. For lack of room, patients cannot be admitted to hospitals when they need help. Care is delayed and illness aggravated. In sheer human terms, the suffering left unattended by our present medical system is untold.

Beyond the needs of individuals and the organizational, social, and moral problems raised in every local instance by the lack of medical care, there is a larger problem. That is the question of the duty of government to the people governed. Government today must begin to reassess its responsibilities, or, in the fashionable term, its priorities. We believe that one of the main purposes of government is to "promote the general welfare," as the United States Constitution puts it. One interpretation of that phrase is that a government created by a people has a duty to that people. The government is responsible for the preservation of each member of society, as well as the society in general. Of the rights that the Declaration of Independence specifically mentions, "life, liberty, and the pursuit of happiness," the first is life. Life does not mean bare subsistence. It means hale and healthy life, otherwise liberty is useless and happiness impossible to pursue. Hence one of the first duties of modern government is to ensure the health of its people, regardless of social strata or economic means. Anything else falls short of just and equitable treatment for all people, and is an abrogation of duty.

Alternative ending number 1
This abrogation of duty in health care at present is not, however, the only sore that needs healing. Everything that can be said about health can be said about education, shelter, even recreation and transportation. These are necessities of decent human life in a modern, civilized world. They are not luxuries. They are necessary services. And they are services that in fact everyone supposedly pays for through taxes. Taxes go up, bureaucracy expands, expense accounts fatten, and services decline. Politicians continually accuse each other publicly of graft and mismanagement, favoritism, and unfair practices, and yet none of them seem to grasp the central idea: their job, the purpose we elect them to office to fulfill, is increasingly left unfulfilled. In this fix, what are we to do? The answer, finally, may be to undertake a complete restructuring of governmental services. If that's what it takes to guarantee ourselves life, as monumental a task as it may seem, we may just have to do it.

Alternative ending number 2

But it is of course not just "they" who are not doing their duty. Governments can only be as good as the citizens who elect them. The real problem lies in the values of the people themselves. So long as people continue to think of doctors as members of a special social class, instead of fellow participants in a society in which all people are equally and mutually dependent, and think of medical care as a privilege instead of an essential service, the attitude of those who govern those people will not change. Today, medical students learn, in subtle but persuasive ways, that a Fifth Avenue address and a Southhampton summer practice are the proper goals of a self-respecting physician, not making house calls in Harlem or manning a county clinic. It's minding the bank account, not mending the poor, that motivates doctors today. Until we can change the values of those who enter that profession from self-seeking to service to mankind, we will continue to lack responsible health care. □

BASIC DESCRIPTIVE OUTLINE

PROPOSITION   The remedy is free, government-sponsored national health insurance that gives us total, just, and equal health care for everyone.

PLAN   Develop two reasons in defense of the proposition.

PARAGRAPH 1   *says:* Many people in this country do not get good medical care.

does: Introduces the proposition by describing a national public problem and by telling an anecdote.

PARAGRAPH 2   *says:* Public hospitals give poor treatment because they are overcrowded and the personnel are overworked.

does: Supports the proposition by describing the effect of the problem on individuals.

PARAGRAPH 3   *says:* Government has a duty to ensure the life of the people—meaning healthy life.

does: Supports the proposition by explaining the government's responsibility to solve the problem.

ALTERNATIVE ENDING NUMBER 1

PARAGRAPH 4   *says:* Because poor health service is just one of many poor services our government performs, we may have to restructure the government.

does: Shows the relationship of this problem to other governmental problems.

ALTERNATIVE ENDING NUMBER 2

PARAGRAPH 4   *says:* Health care will not change until the public's attitude toward the medical profession changes.

does: Puts the problem into the context of public attitudes toward the relevant profession.

(The difference between basic and detailed descriptive outlines is explained in Part Three: Constructive Reading. See also the example basic and detailed descriptive outlines written for the same essay on p. 77.)

▷ EXERCISE 11   FOUR-PARAGRAPH ESSAY

This essay should be six hundred to seven hundred words long and should be written in four paragraphs: an introductory paragraph ending with a proposition, two paragraphs of defense, and a final paragraph that places the position taken in the essay into a larger context of issues. And of course a descriptive outline.

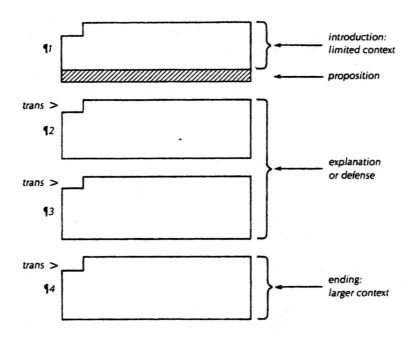

You might prepare yourself to write this essay by reviewing invention exercises 1 through 4, to find a topic closely related to your own experience and knowledge. Also, take a minute to review the instructions for exercise 5. Remember that the place to start, once you have decided on a topic, is the proposition. Then think through a way to explore, explain, or defend the position you take in that proposition. In this exercise you can use one of the forms you learned in essay exercises 5 through 9:

Two reasons

Nestorian order

Opposition plus refutation

Opposition and refutation plus one reason

Opposition and concession plus one reason

Write this essay as you wrote those three-paragraph essays. The only difference now is that you are going to plan ahead for a fourth paragraph—an ending that tries to interest members of larger, more encompassing communities. Write the ending after you have written the introduction. Think of the essay as a single working unit:

Think of a subject.

Think of a tentative proposition.

Think of a defense or explanation.

Write a proposition and defend or explain it.

Write an introduction.

Write an ending.

Check the transitions.

Write a descriptive outline and make adjustments.

Read the essay aloud and revise it.

Make the final copy.

COLLABORATIVE LEARNING

Task 1 Reading Aloud

Follow the instructions for reading aloud on p. 55.

Task 2 Essay Exchange and Peer Conference

Follow the instructions for essay exchange and peer conference on p. 75.

Proteins and Health

Sharon Owens

Protein molecules are large, complex organic compounds composed of carbon, oxygen, hydrogen, nitrogen, and sulfur. These five elements are found in all naturally occurring protein molecules. Proteins are made up of smaller units called amino acids. Hundreds of amino acids make up one protein. Just as railroad cars can be joined to make up one train, so can different amino acids be joined to make up one protein. These amino acids are classified as either essential or nonessential. Essential amino acids are those that we have to include in our diet to maintain life and promote growth. The other amino acids found in proteins are classified as nonessential. This designation tends, unfortunately, to imply that they lack importance in the body, which is not the case. Proteins containing all the essential amino acids are called "complete" proteins, and those containing an inadequate amount of one or more of the essential amino acids are called "incomplete" proteins. Proteins, both complete and incomplete, play an important part in maintaining our health.

One way proteins help maintain our health is by forming body regulators. These regulators include enzymes, hormones, antibodies, and antigens. Enzymes are complex materials that play an important part in digestion and in speeding up chemical reactions in our bodies. Enzymes are present in all cells. Without them, cells could not live. Hormones are chemical substances made by the body that control important functions, such as growth, development, reproduction, and metabolism. Antigens are proteins from other organisms that, when present in the body, may cause illness. The body fights off antigens by producing antibodies, which are substances made by living cells to combat infection.

Besides forming these body regulators, proteins also supply material for the formation of new tissues, which include epithelial, muscular, connective, and nervous tissue. Epithelial tissues are coverings, such as the skin. The skin is the tissue that covers the outside of the body. Muscular tissues allow the body to contract and relax, thus enabling movement throughout the body. Connective tissues that are fibrous, elastic, or bone bind different parts of the body together. Nervous tissues are made up of cells that carry electrochemical impulses from one part of the body to another. Whenever many of these tissues are lost due to stress, burns, or illness, the body's proteins replace them.

Proteins, therefore, are a source of our physical life. When our protein intake is low, our cells begin to waste away and we produce fewer antibodies. As a result, we are more likely to be attacked by infection. To avoid this deterioration, we should eat foods that provide substantial amounts of protein. Generally speaking, protein is found in both animal and plant foods. Animal protein sources include beef, veal, pork, lamb, fish, eggs, milk, and cheese. Plant protein is found in soybeans, navy beans, lima beans, pinto beans, and red beans. Our bodies renew themselves with the life-giving protein they get from these animals and plants. □

DETAILED DESCRIPTIVE OUTLINE

PROPOSITION	Proteins, both complete and incomplete, play an important part in maintaining our bodies.
PLAN	Develop two reasons supporting the proposition, plus an introduction and an ending.
PARAGRAPH 1	*says:* Proteins are made up of smaller units called amino acids.
	does: Introduces the proposition by defining the main term in the proposition and describing the composition of the substance it denotes. Defines another term related to the topic. Distinguishes two main categories of the substance.
PARAGRAPH 2	*says:* One way proteins maintain our bodies is by forming body regulators.
	does: Supports the proposition by explaining one function of the substance. Lists four ways that the substance works to perform this function. Explains each of the four in detail.
PARAGRAPH 3	*says:* Another way proteins maintain our bodies is by supplying material for forming new tissue.
	does: Supports the proposition by explaining another function the substance serves. Lists four products of the substance and explains the purpose of each product in detail.
PARAGRAPH 4	*says:* Because lack of proteins can make us vulnerable to sickness, we must eat enough proteins to keep up our protein supply.

does: Ends the paper by placing its scientific information into the context of maintaining life. Explains the results when the substance is lacking or when it functions improperly. Explains what to do to avoid this result, and, briefly, why.

(How to write detailed descriptive outlines is explained beginning on p. 153.)

☐ EXAMPLE ESSAY ─────────────────────────────

What Should Patients Be Told?

Terry Hayes

In 1977, writer Susan Sontag, while recovering from a mastectomy, began to explore the ways society conceptualizes illness. Sontag was charting unknown waters, the sort that were once labeled "Here lie Dragons" on old maps. The result of her exploration was *Illness as Metaphor*, a brief, fiercely literate analysis of how and why we create myths that obscure the reality of certain fatal diseases. Although a new book by Sontag never enters the literary world unremarked, this one created waves of greater-than-usual magnitude. The overwhelming attention the book received cannot be attributed solely to the combined effects of innovative ideas and a controversial author. At a deeper level *Illness as Metaphor* speaks to us all because it is about a disease that scares us all, cancer. In our highly technological age, every one of us must eat, drink, and inhale carcinogens. As a result, one out of four people alive today will develop cancer (Epstein 8). It has therefore become more practical than fatalistic to familiarize ourselves with the old, much-debated issues surrounding this disease. How will we be treated if we contract cancer? What constitutes proper patient care? Unfortunately, there are no easy answers to such questions as these. The professionals whom we would depend on for care continue to debate, their solutions changing with the character of the times. Consequently, even the basic issue of how much to tell cancer patients about the disease remains unsettled.

Most cancer researchers and clinicians, called *oncologists*, simplify the issue by consistently taking one of two extreme positions.

These positions can be stated briefly as (1) tell all, and (2) tell nothing (Goodfield 224). The first, and for some time the most prevalent opinion, is that patients have a right to as much information about their condition as the doctor can supply: what illness they have, how they will be treated, and how long they can expect to live. Specialists who hold this view feel that whereas nothing can be gained by withholding bad news, telling patients the truth is at least potentially beneficial. Informed patients, they reason, can prepare themselves better for the course of the disease and can cooperate more fully with doctors. Interestingly enough, the growth of this opinion among professionals coincides not only with the increased focus on individual rights that is characteristic of the past few decades, but also with the increased incidence of cancer itself, which is reaching epidemic proportions. The second extreme position, that patients should be told nothing about the disease, is far less frequently encountered today than in the past. But physicians who still adhere to this opinion—and they are not all old-fashioned general practitioners—steadfastly maintain that the less patients know, the less they worry, and, consequently, the more energy they have to fight the illness. This attitude was fashionable during the first half of the twentieth century, a period during which the individual was expected to focus more on others, and during which cancer was less widespread.

Recently, alongside these two extremes, a third, more moderate position has emerged. This position takes into account the cancer victim's individual needs and individual rights (Abrams 44). It is an attitude held by a growing number of physicians who feel that to take a rigid stance at either extreme would be unethical, since different patients have different psychological responses to information about their cancers. Some patients do, in fact, want to know everything, and these people adjust to the disease most successfully when they are given details. Other patients prefer to know as little as possible, and may become severely depressed if told too much. And although patients will probably not state their preference explicitly, by "listening between the lines" the doctor can usually determine which message is being sent (Abrams xxii). Of course, this approach requires more of the doctor, who must listen harder and make tougher decisions. But against the clamor of our times it strikes a hopeful note. Perhaps scientific specialization and personalized attention are not as mutually exclusive as many of us had feared. At any rate, if intelligently put into practice, the moderate attitude is very good news indeed for cancer patients, who are treated in accordance with needs that are theirs and theirs alone (Abrams xxiii). □

WORKS CONSULTED

Abrams, Ruth D. *Not Alone With Cancer: A Guide for Those Who Care.* Springfield, Ill.: Thomas, 1974.

Epstein, Samuel S. *The Politics of Cancer.* San Francisco: Sierra Club, 1978.

Goodfield, June. *The Siege of Cancer.* New York: Random House, 1975.

Levit, Rose. *Ellen: A Short Life Long Remembered.* San Francisco: Chronicle, 1974.

Sontag, Susan. *Illness as Metaphor.* New York: Farrar, Straus, and Giroux, 1977.

Winick, Myron, ed. *Nutrition and Cancer.* New York: Wiley, 1977.

DETAILED DESCRIPTIVE OUTLINE

PROPOSITION Even so basic an issue as how much to tell cancer patients about their disease remains unsettled.

PLAN Explain two extreme views of an issue, one important and the other less important, and then explain the most important third view.

PARAGRAPH 1 *says: Illness as Metaphor* received attention because it's about cancer.

does: Introduces proposition by describing a relevant book: why it was written and what it's about. Analyzes the book's reception. Isolates the most influential of three contributory factors. Cites facts and statistics to establish the importance of the subject matter to any reader. Names two related issues and narrows one of them.

PARAGRAPH 2 *says:* Some cancer specialists tell patients everything so that they can cope better with reality and cooperate more fully during treatment; others tell patients nothing in order to prevent unnecessary worry.

does: Supports the proposition by supplying two contrasting views of the issue. (1) Summarizes the most popular position and gives three reasons (one negative, two positive) in support. Then relates the prevalence of this position to two factors characteristic of our time. (2) Summarizes a less popular opinion and gives one positive reason in support. Relates the former prevalence of this view to two factors characteristic of the times in which it was favored.

PARAGRAPH 3   *says:* Still other doctors hold that the issue must be decided differently for different patients, taking into account their individual psychological needs.

does: Supports the proposition by describing a third view of the issue. Gives one important reason for its growing popularity by contrasting possible effects of the most popular view. Names two drawbacks of this view. Suggests a possible meaning of this new view in terms of modern society. Makes a conditional value judgment about general benefits of this opinion.

OTHER WAYS TO END AN ESSAY

There are several other ways to end an essay besides relating the position you take in the essay to a context of issues.

One common ending in very long essays is to **summarize.** A summary might be useful if you think that your readers may need help remembering and fitting together the several parts of your exploration, explanation, or defense and relating them to your position. And the conventional format for some kinds of papers in the sciences and social sciences requires a summary. But in most short essays, anything up to ten or twelve pages, ending the essay with a summary is a waste of time and paper.

Other options are more constructive. One of these is to **refine the proposition.** In this case, you use your exploration, explanation, or defense of the position you take at the beginning of the essay to suggest another way of stating that position. What you are saying is that, in light of the way you have been explaining your position, another way of phrasing it may seem more accurate, more useful, or more far reaching. For example, an ending that refined the proposition of the essay on cars might say something like this.

introduction	. . . It seems fantastic and unlikely, yet it is now possible to say that in the future the trend will be for people to use cars
proposition	as we know them less rather than more. In fact, it looks as if cars may be on the way out as our major means of transportation.
¶ 2	. . .
¶ 3	. . .
ending	In light of the complexity of all these rapid changes in the way we live, it may oversimplify the situation to say that cars
refining the proposition	may be on the way out. It may make more sense to say that the way we use cars will change so much that what we call cars then won't look at all like what we call cars today. In a

hundred years we may no longer use private vehicles to get around. Instead we may use . . .

If you like, you can prepare your readers for an ending that refines your position in this way with a proposition that is hypothetical ("It may be true that . . . ," or "If X is true, then Y"). Then your ending can restate the proposition more positively.

introduction	. . . It seems fantastic and unlikely, yet it is now possible to say that the future trend will be for people to use cars as we
proposition	know them less rather than more. If our way of life changes as much in the next hundred years as it has in the hundred years just past, cars as we know them may be on the way out.
¶ 2	. . .
¶ 3	. . .
ending *proposition* *restated* *positively*	So it looks as if our lives are going to continue to change just as rapidly as they have been changing for a century or more. That being the case, it oversimplifies the situation to say that cars may be on the way out. It makes more sense to say instead that we may . . .

Similar to an ending that refines a hypothetical proposition is one that chooses one of several alternatives offered in the proposition. In this case, the proposition doesn't state one position but states two similar but alternative positions ("Either . . . or . . ."). In this case, the ending settles on one of the alternatives as preferable, more reasonable, more practical, and so on, in light of what you have said in your exploration, explanation, or defense.

introduction	. . . It seems fantastic and unlikely, yet it is now possible to say that in the future the trend will be for people to use cars
proposition	as we know them less rather than more. Either most of the technological change we are capable of has already occurred so that we will continue transporting ourselves indefinitely pretty much as we do today, or else our lives will continue to change and cars as we know them will simply disappear.
¶ 2	. . .
¶ 3	. . .
ending *alternative* *selected and* *restated*	So it looks as if technological change is not going to stop. Our lives are going to continue to change just as fast as they are changing now. That being the case, then it seems inevitable that cars as we know them will disappear. In the future we are much more likely to . . .

In another kind of ending you can **evaluate the essay**. This kind of ending is useful if it turns out that you cannot explore, explain, or defend your position conclusively, or if you see that you could explore, explain, or defend it in two or more ways. For the essay you are writing you choose one of these ways rather than the other. For example, you take a personal or social approach instead of a political or scientific one.

Then, in the ending, you defend the way of exploring, explaining, or defending your position that you chose; you defend the evidence you used; or perhaps you even defend your decision to write the essay at all.

Or instead, an evaluative ending might evaluate the essay in terms of the timeliness of its argument or its position. You might want to say that the position you have taken is true at the present moment, but since all the evidence is not yet in, the situation may change. So the position you have taken is subject to change.

introduction	. . . It seems fantastic and unlikely, yet it is now possible to say that in the future the trend will be for people to use
proposition	cars as we know them less rather than more. If fact, it looks as if cars may be on the way out as our major means of transportation.
¶ 2	. . .
¶ 3	. . .
ending	In light of the complexity of all these rapid changes in the way we live, of course it oversimplifies the situation to say
evaluating the essay	that cars may be on the way out. Trying to predict the future in this way is always futile. No one has a crystal ball. There is some value in trying to predict the future, however, because even though we can't know the future, we always have to plan for it. . . .

An ending may also **suggest other possible approaches or solutions** to the problem that you have addressed in the essay, evaluating these alternative approaches or solutions in light of what you have written.

introduction	. . . It seems fantastic and unlikely, yet it is now possible to say that in the future the trend will be for people to use
proposition	cars as we know them less rather than more. If fact, it looks as if cars may be on the way out as our major means of transportation.

¶ 2   . . .

¶ 3   . . .

ending   Of course, using a few statistics provided by the major oil companies and some personal anecdotes is not the only way to go about making an important prediction like this. There are less direct but probably just as reliable means, and these may suggest different answers. For example, within half a century or so dozens of what we now call underdeveloped countries will be well on the way to being fully developed. In those countries millions more people will have more money to spend, and one thing they are going to want to spend it on is going places. . . .

Finally, and rarely, depending on your self-confidence as a writer and your command of the subject, the end of the essay may be the place to **go out on a limb and speculate.** You might try guessing what might happen in the future based on what you have said, or what might result from a course of action or thought implied in the position you have taken in the essay.

introduction   . . . It seems fantastic and unlikely, yet it is now possible to say that in the future the trend will be for people to use
proposition   cars as we know them less rather than more. If fact, it looks as if cars may be on the way out as our major means of transportation.

¶ 2   . . .

¶ 3   . . .

ending   So suppose it turns out that cars are on the way out as our major means of transportation—what then? Interviewed ten years ago, the president of the Ford Motor Company was asked what he thought Ford would be making in the year 2050. He didn't know, he said, but it won't be cars. So, facing the possibility that cars are on the way out, what we do is think
speculation   of what is likely to replace them. What is most likely to replace them is . . .

However wild in substance, a conservatively worded speculation that maintains the essay's topic and tone can sometimes demonstrate very effectively your ability to think through an issue.

NOTES FOR PART FOUR

PUTTING POSITION PAPERS TO GOOD USE

WRITING ESSAY EXAMS

Once you understand the form that this book requires, *Short Course* form, you will grasp some of its practical implications. The most obvious of these is that the basic element in *Short Course* form (proposition plus exploration, explanation, or defense) can be useful in answering questions on essay examinations.

The first sentence (or two) of an exam answer should be a clear, succinct generalization that answers the question fully. This generalization is your proposition. Then in the rest of the answer you explore, explain, and defend your generalization by explaining its operative words and the key relationship it draws among those words. (See Propositions, p. 85, and Paragraph Development, p. 111.)

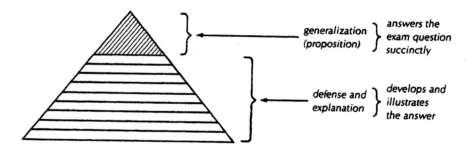

Used without an introduction in this way, *Short Course* form resembles the standard form of newspaper articles:

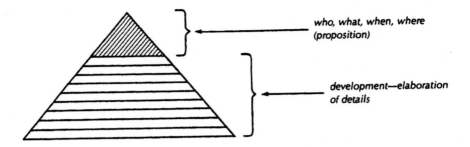

This resemblance between *Short Course* form and newspaper form is not accidental. The pressure you would feel as a newspaper reporter and the pressure you feel as an exam writer are similar. Reporters and exam writers both have limited time and space. Both have to write quickly and intelligibly.

Both also have to write in a form that will suffer the least damage if it has to be cut short abruptly and arbitrarily for lack of time or space. Reporters write in pyramid form so that the editor can snip the article off at any point to fit the space available in the newspaper, yet not lose the main point of the article. When you are writing an exam, you write in a similar form so that if the bell rings and you have to quit when you are only halfway through the essay, your answer will not lose its point. You will already have made your point, right up there at the beginning.

Short Course form without an introduction will not work for every essay exam question you write, but it will work for most of them. Also, there are hitches. One is that you may sometimes change your mind halfway through writing an exam essay, so that the proposition you wrote at the beginning no longer says what you want to say.

Of course you might change your mind no matter what form you write in, and in fact you are less likely to change your mind using *Short Course* form because the form itself encourages you to think through your answer carefully before you begin to write. You have to think through your answer to some extent in order to write a proposition sentence to begin your answer. If you do change your mind, you can still go back if you have time, scratch out the proposition you wrote in the first place, and write a new one.

One way to think through an exam answer is with an imaginary dialogue or an imaginary topic interview. Before you set pen to paper, imagine yourself explaining to a friend the answer you have tentatively decided on. Silently "talking over" the answer in this way lets you write a first draft in your head where you can change the answer without penalty. (See Topic Interviews, p. 30.)

Another hitch you may run into in using *Short Course* form for writing essay exams is that, because it makes clear what you know to both your teacher and yourself, it may also make it harder for you to hide what you do not know from both the teacher and yourself. That is a measure of self-awareness that can be painful or satisfying, depending on the way you look at it.

Short Course form leads you to discover what you know and what you don't know because the form requires you to be specific and concrete. You write an initial statement (your proposition) that can be stated as generally as the question is stated. Then you write a detailed, specific development that explores, explains, and defends the position you have taken in that initial statement.

The form is useful, therefore, because no matter how generally an examination question may be stated, it always requires a specific, concrete answer. But it means that you have to know those specifics and you have to have thought them through in order to arrive at some of the generalizations that they may suggest. In short, if you plan to use *Short Course* form to write an exam, you've got to prepare yourself well to take the exam.

Finally, if you do use *Short Course* form and if you have time, you can add an ending to your answer that places it in a context of issues. One of the most effective endings you can write to an exam question suggests that you are aware of your answer's limitations and the limitations of the operative words you have used in it. These qualifications tell your teacher not only that you understand the subject matter of the course but that you also understand the way that conversation about that subject matter is carried on in the relevant discourse community.

(See Talking About Elephants, p. 193, and William Perry's "Examsmanship and the Liberal Arts," p. 343. Perry talks about relationships between what you know and the academic communities that your teachers represent, such as English, history, chemistry, sociology, mathematics, and so on. See also Unity and Coherence, p. 116, and Assumptions, p. 132.)

EXAMPLE ESSAY EXAM

Question: Gene Sharp's *Social Power and Political Freedom* is about relationships between political freedom and governments regarded as hierarchies of power. He argues that in hierarchies of political power, the people at the top are placed in that position by those at the bottom. People get the government that they deserve, that they want, or that they need. Describe the arguments that have been made against Sharp's position by political writers we have read this term and explain them.

☐ EXAMPLE ESSAY ANSWER ─────────────────────

Sharp's *Social Power*

Theresa Montoya

Several of the political writers we read this term say that, contrary to Sharp's position, people obey political rulers for reasons that are anything but voluntary.

The reasons explaining people's obedience are varied, but they are all related in some way to their psychological makeup. Bertrand de Jouvenel claims, for instance, that habit is a major reason people do what they are told. He concurs with Hume, who wrote that because habit is acquired through culture and experience that we are not fully aware of, many people "never think of departing from that path" laid down by "their ancestors." People obey, de Jouvenel says, largely because they are apathetic, and he talks about "zones of indifference" where people "accept orders without questioning authority." Another reason people obey is because they fear sanctions or punishment, as Thomas Green points out. The state can use the criminal justice system against anyone who defies it, and it can threaten the insubordinate with extreme penalties for petty crimes. Still another reason is self-interest. The state can offer incentives such as elevation in political or social status, jobs, and privileges. Green also points out that people may feel that they gain indirectly from obedience, because obedience makes a government stable so that it can concentrate its energies on raising the standard of living of its people.

But the strongest force making people obey their government according to these writers seems to be the belief that obedience is a moral obligation. This belief may be a basic cultural value of the people being governed, or it may be a product of government indoctrination. In either case, people tend to identify psychologically with the ruler and the state, which they see as extensions of themselves and therefore not to be betrayed. Even Sharp acknowledges the power of this feeling of moral obligation. But Green puts the case much more forcefully than Sharp. He says that people feel that obedience is an individual's contribution to a good society because to resist, that is, not to obey, might bring down "greater evil" on the society and might even make the government collapse. Once again fear plays a role. Most people believe that the state provides personal security, they regard the established leadership as legitimate, whatever its history, and they condone punishment for those who disobey.

Given such strong motives to obey, people who have tried to oppose a government in power have found the belief that obedience is
socially acceptable and morally just hard to undermine. Those who
have used force to oppose a government and bring it down (in, for
example, the French, American, or Russian Revolutions) resort to
inciting fear and outrage against apathy and habit. Those who have
tried to bring a government down or oppose what they regard as
oppressive conditions with disobedience or passive resistance (for
example, Ghandi and King) play feelings of moral justice, self-
interest, even social embarrassment against apathy and habit. In
the end, looking closely at these contests of will, it is hard not to
agree with Sharp that people get the government they need and
want. So, the revolutionary's job is, by hook or by crook, to get people
to want something better for themselves and their children, and
then realize that they don't just want to change it but feel it as a
genuine need. □

ADAPTING SHORT COURSE FORM FOR MANY USES

Essays can be written in many forms. The essay form that this book
teaches you is only one of them. But it is an especially useful one and
it can be adapted for many purposes. It is adaptable because it stresses
the fundamental necessities of all well-planned, well-developed expository writing—focusing on a single idea and expressing relationships
between subordinate ideas. It is also adaptable because it helps you
discover, explore, explain, and defend your ideas.

The previous section, Writing Essay Exams, explains only one way
you can adapt *Short Course* form. You can also stretch it to any length
for term papers and other long writing assignments. And you can use
it as an efficient format for writing letters, reports, and memos in business and the professions.

LENGTH: TERM PAPERS AND OTHER LONG WRITING ASSIGNMENTS

Most essays you write in school or at work have to be a lot longer than
three or four paragraphs and 500 to 750 words. Whenever you write
long essays like that you can apply everything you have learned about
organization in earlier parts of this book simply by stretching *Short Course*
form.

The organizational principles of the form are clear, no matter how
much you stretch it. You can organize a twenty- or thirty-page research
paper with it just as you can use it to organize a two-page, five-hundred-
word essay, because it teaches you explanatory subordination. That is,
it helps you to focus on a single main idea and to make explicit rela-

tionships between that idea and subordinate ideas, and among those subordinate ideas. Whatever the length and complexity of the paper, *Short Course* form helps you discover and explore your ideas and helps you explain and defend them. You may even find that the longer and more complex your writing task is, the more helpful *Short Course* form becomes.

Short Course form is even clear when it is stretched to length of a three-hundred-page book. Imagine writing a book in which chapter one is an introduction that explains the issues addressed in the book and ends with a paragraph that summarizes the book's main point. Then chapters two through five explore, explain, and defend that point. And the last chapter places your position into a larger context of issues. Your book would be an adaptation of *Short Course* form. You would know how to make the book coherent throughout every one of its three hundred pages because you would know from writing transition sentences connecting paragraphs and parts of paragraphs in five-hundred-word, three-paragraph essays how to write transitions linking chapters and parts of chapters to each other and to the main point you are making in the book.

You can organize long essays in the same way, subdividing them into mini-chapters as you divide up a book. For example, you might begin a twenty-page term paper with two or three pages of introduction explaining the issues addressed in the essay, leading to a paragraph that summarizes the essay's main point: the essay's proposition. Then you might write several minichapters of four or five pages each that explore, explain, and defend different aspects of that point. You could organize each of these mini-chapters in *Short Course* form, too. Finally, you could end the paper with two or three pages that place the position you have taken into a larger context of issues.

In writing a long essay like that, you would take care to write transitions linking the chapters and paragraphs to each other and to the essay's main point, just as you have to take care to write transition sentences connecting the paragraphs and parts of paragraphs in a five-hundred-word, three-paragraph essay.

The following example is a research essay written by a student who had learned to write shorter essays in *Short Course* form and who adapted what she learned when she came to be doing the mature undergraduate research that she reports in this essay. Notice that the proposition of the essay occurs at the end of the introductory section of the essay, just before the first subheading, not at the end of the first paragraph (or at the end of the paper). Notice that the essay's ending puts the argument into the larger context of national attitudes toward war and violence. And notice that the essay includes transitional generalizations at the beginning of each section as well as at the beginning of each paragraph. The essay's subtitles at the beginning of each new section also help readers follow the explanation.

☐ EXAMPLE ESSAY

The Inescapable Guilt of Lieutenant Calley

Michele C. Watts

The Vietnam War saw many tragedies and atrocities. One of these stands out for its brutality and scale. On March 16, 1968, Charlie Company of Task Force Barker, under the command of Lieutenant William Laws Calley, destroyed the tiny Vietnamese hamlet that the American Army called My Lai 4 and killed most of its inhabitants, all of them unarmed, twenty-two of them while hiding helplessly in an irrigation ditch.

Calley was subsequently court-martialed and convicted of murder. In his defense, he claimed that he was just following orders when he killed most of the people in My Lai 4, and that he and his men killed in self-defense. But the jury did not find these claims persuasive. They determined that Calley himself was ultimately responsible for what happened.

As always in such a complex and threatening experience as warfare, not just one but many factors contribute to every event. Army Intelligence, having misnamed and confused Vietnamese villages, sent Calley's company to attack the wrong one. Army Intelligence also said the village would be empty of civilians that morning, so that Charlie Company could assume that anyone left there must be enemy personnel. Compounding the confusion, Task Force Barker, of which Charlie Company was a part, was a newly assembled unit with an unclear chain of command. Finally, the Vietnamese surprise attack called the Tet Offensive had just begun.

These are all mitigating factors—the conditions under which the event occurred. But even after considering every one of them carefully it is impossible to disagree with the jury's verdict. The evidence is overwhelming that Calley was responsible for the disaster, because he alone was in command.

BACKGROUND

In order to understand the atmosphere that would allow a My Lai 4 to happen, it is necessary to take a closer look at the conditions under which it occurred. Of these, the Tet Offensive was perhaps the most important, because it was the spark that lit the fire of suspicion and fear of all Vietnamese that motivated My Lai 4. The Vietnamese celebrate the religious holiday of Tet in late January. For the Vietnamese, Tet is like New Year's and Christmas rolled into one. It is a time of great rejoicing and traditionally a time of truce (Everette 11). For this reason, as the Tet season arrived in January 1968, the American troops quite reasonably breathed a sigh of relief. But their relief turned out to be premature. Tet that year marked one of the bloodiest battles of the Vietnam war. The Tet Offensive, as it came to be known, took the Americans almost completely by surprise. First, the North Vietnamese and the Vietcong infiltrated the cities that constituted American strongholds in the guise of holiday travelers, smuggling in ammunition in bodiless coffins (Everette 15, 13). As the Tet festivities began, the Vietnamese and Vietcong troops crept out of hiding, unearthed their ammunition, and attacked.

Overnight, Saigon and other Vietnamese cities went from relatively safe, peaceful enclaves to a battleground. Terror ruled the city streets and the surrounding countryside as the North Vietnamese and the Vietcong swept the cities. It took the Americans several weeks of sustained fighting to recapture hostile territory. In order to regain control, they used napalm, heavy artillery, and bombs (Everette 13). They destroyed every area that the enemy occupied, putting into effect what has been described as the American Army's principle of destroying the village to save the people. It was on this principle that My Lai 4 was destroyed.

After the Tet Offensive, the American troops remained on high alert to avoid another surprise attack of the same sort. All Vietnamese became suspect. American soldiers, already at their nerves' end from jungle warfare, were even more terrified than they had been before the Tet Offensive began. Many of them felt a thirst for vengeance. As one soldier put it, they wanted "a chance to revenge the deaths of our fellow GIs" (Hammer 111). In this atmosphere of hatred, fear, and suspicion, the village of Song My, long a Vietcong stronghold, was targeted for a search-and-destroy mission.

Song My was the base of operations from which, during the Tet Offensive, the Vietcong attacked the city of Quang Ngai, the headquarters of the second division of ARVN, the American-South Vietnamese coordinated military force (Hammer 11). The search-and-destroy mission aimed at Song My was to be carried out by the Eleventh Brigade, part of Task Force Barker of the Americal Division. Task Force Barker was "a tiny ad hoc unit composed of one company from each of the three divisions in the brigade" (Hersh 22).

This fact is significant because, newly established, Task Force Barker was a mélange of units from several independent divisions and still lacking a firm chain of command. As orders came down from above, they remained unclear, neither direct nor detailed enough to prevent them from being misconstrued. Interpretation of commands was frequently left to those in subordinate positions. This lack of clarity in the chain of command was the condition of uncertainty in which Calley could misinterpret a command and take it on himself to order his unit to kill the civilian inhabitants of My Lai 4.

Not only was Task Force Barker new, but almost all of the soldiers in its Charlie Company were green. Calley's Sergeant had been in combat before, but none of the other men in the unit, including Calley, had. They had gone straight from training in Hawaii to the bush of Vietnam and the proximity of a Vietcong stronghold. They did not know what to expect. Then, for days on end, they saw little combat and as a result became frustrated and tense. Charlie Company finally saw real action in My Lai 4. There, they overreacted because they were inexperienced, frustrated, and scared (Sack 29–30).

Army Intelligence added to Charlie Company's problems by reporting that, on Saturdays, most of the villagers at My Lai 4 would either be in the rice fields or at the market. So the attack was planned for a Saturday morning (Hammer 60). But this pattern was broken on the morning of March 16. What Army Intelligence called My Lai 4 was a subdivision or hamlet in the village of Song My. The night before, many villagers had returned to Song My after years in refugee camps because the government had told them that Song My was now safe (Hammer 115). On that Saturday morning many people did not go to work in the rice fields but stayed home to get resettled.

Army Intelligence also confused the hamlets that made up Song My, with the result that they aimed the mission at the wrong hamlet. When it arrived at My Lai, Charlie Company did not find a Vietcong emplacement and munitions dump. Instead, it found "exactly three rifles . . . some ammunition, and a couple of grenades (Hammer 144). This error occurred in part because Army Intelligence renamed hamlets in Song My to suit its own convenience, giving them instead names that were easier to recognize and classify. In place of their Vietnam place names, it labeled the several little hamlets that made up Song My village My Lai 1 through My Lai 6. Intelligence then compounded the confusion by nicknaming the six My Lais "Pinkvilles," because they were colored pink on the maps. Partly as a result of this compound confusion, Charlie Company was sent to attack Xom Lang, renamed My Lai 4, instead of My Khe, renamed My Lai 1, which was the true target of the American search-and-destroy mission that morning (Hammer 11). Ironically, the Vietnamese name for the hamlet where the mission was actually carried out, Xom Lang, means The Place Where Trouble Does Not Come (Hammer 11). Due to American arrogance and incompetence, Xom Lang turned out to be the place where trouble indeed did come.

CALLEY ON THE STAND

Despite all the errors, shortcomings, and suspicions of the American Armed Forces, however, the Army charged Lieutenant Calley, the leader of Charlie Company, with ultimate responsibility for what happened at My Lai 4. Calley was detained and charged under Articles 32 and 118 of the Uniform Code of Military Justice with 102 counts of murder. Article 32 states that with sufficient cause and after sufficient investigation, a suspect may be charged and detained. Article 118 states that a person who has "premeditated design to kill" is subject to the death penalty or life in prison (*Title 10*, United States Code 191). It was then up to Calley to defend himself against this charge.

The prosecution argued that Calley was responsible for two reasons. First, he was in command. His misinterpretation of his orders led him to order his troops to kill all the civilians they encountered and to kill them himself. And second, even if it were true that Calley was following orders, however he construed them, that fact does not excuse his actions. The universal norm accepted even in military courts martial is that it is wrong to take another person's life unless your own life is threatened. Self-defense does not excuse the slaughter of over one hundred unarmed civilians.

Calley's defense against these arguments was twofold. First, he did plead self-defense, because although in fact the My Lai villages were not armed, he believed, and had good reason to believe on the basis of Army Intelligence reports, that they were either Vietcong or Vietcong sympathizers, and as such they counted as the enemy. His task, as he understood it, was to kill the enemy in order to save American lives. And second, Calley testified that he was following orders, because, on the witness stand, he recalled specifically asking his superior officer, Captain Medina, "Do you mean [to kill] women and children too?" and remembered that Medina replied, "I mean everything" (Sack 89). In support of this argument and in Calley's defense, another soldier remembered hearing Medina utter similar words in a preattack pep talk. Vernardo Simpson, a member of Medina's company, stated that Medina told the men to "kill or burn down everything in sight" (Hammer 111).

Unfortunately for Calley, not every witness was so favorable to his case. Paul Meadlo, who was at Calley's side when he shot the villagers, was the witness most destructive to Calley's defense. Meadlo testified twice that he saw Calley reload his magazine "between ten and fifteen times" (Everette 148–149). Meadlo made no mention of the order that Medina had supposedly issued about killing everything. Meadlo's testimony was so harmful to Calley's case, in fact, because he claimed that Calley alone initiated the massacre. Another major witness for the prosecution was equally destructive. Captain Ernest Medina himself took the stand to testify against Calley. Medina firmly denied ever giving such an order as Calley credits him with (Everette 182–183). Following Medina's testimony, several more witnesses corroborated Meadlo's and Medina's stories, totally destroying Calley's defense.

CONVICTION, SENTENCE, AND THEIR IMPLICATIONS

The jury convicted Calley of twenty-two counts of murder. They did not convict him of all of the 102 counts he was charged with, because they thought that there was not enough evidence to link him directly to all the killings. The direct link that the jury decided had been established was the twenty-two people shot in an irrigation ditch. After convicting Calley, the jury had to sentence him as well. They had the choice of death or life in prison. They chose the latter, but through appeals and commutation of the sentence, in the end Calley served a total of only three years in prison.

The story of My Lai 4 and Lieutenant Calley is therefore a tragic one not only for 102 murdered Vietnamese villagers and their families and friends, but for Calley, his fellow soldiers, and for the citizens of the United States of America on whose behalf the American Army acted in Vietnam. As is always the case, many factors contributed to the atrocity. In American memory, My Lai takes its place along with a long history of atrocities perpetrated by American military and police personnel against supposed enemies: Native Americans, African Americans, trade unionists, and war protestors. It now brings to mind another atrocity of the Vietnam War much nearer home, the death of four Kent State University undergraduates at the hands of Army National Guardsmen three years later. And for those who witnessed them, Calley's trial evoked recollections of Nazi war crimes trials in Nuremberg.

But the message of My Lai and other such atrocities is not clear. Were not Calley and his men victims too, their lives destroyed by a war America never meant to wage and, waging it, never meant to win? Vietnam put the nation under enormous pressure. But more to the point it put the American men it sent to Vietnam under enormous pressure. Men under pressure can break. Armed men under pressure who break are all too likely to break others. A jury rightfully convicted Lieutenant Calley of murder. But given the chance, of what would a jury convict the nation that sent him there? □

WORKS CONSULTED AND CITED

Contesta, David R., and Robert Muccigrosso. *America in the Twentieth Century—Coming of Age.* New York: Harper and Row, 1988.

Everette, Arthur, Katheryn Johnson, and Harry F. Rosenthal. *Calley.* New York: Dell, 1971.

Hammer, Richard. *One Morning in the War.* New York: Coward-McCann, 1970.

Hersh, Seymour H. *My Lai 4—A Report of the Massacre and Its Aftermath.* New York: Random House, 1970.

Sack, John. *Lieutenant Calley—His Own Story.* New York: Viking, 1971.

United States Code, *Title 10.* Washington: Government Printing Office, 1983.

EFFICIENCY: WRITING IN BUSINESS AND THE PROFESSIONS

Because *Short Course* form teaches you to take a position clearly and in a conspicuous place in your writing, no matter what the situation or topic, anyone who reads an essay that you write in that way can get the point right away. It also teaches you to focus your ideas and make clear relationships among supporting factors and ideas and between them and the main point of the essay. This means that the form helps you yourself understand better what you have to say, as well as helping your readers understand it. It makes it less likely that you will write nonsense—or, rather, it makes it more likely that you will be able to detect the nonsense you have written before the boss does.

So *Short Course* form is an efficient form for professional or business writing as well as for essay exams and term papers. And it is also a good form for writing articles for publication in most academic journals.

Here's how the form might work, for example, if you were a professional asked to serve as a consultant to an institutional administrator. Suppose you are a guidance counselor in a high school. The parents of one of the students in the school (we'll call him Jim) have called the high school principal and told her that they are worried about their son's performance in school. They ask her why Jim is doing so poorly in his courses. The principal tells him that she will look into the problem and will call them back.

Then she calls Jim's guidance counselor. That's you. She asks you to write her a letter about Jim. She wants you to explain what you think is going wrong, so that she can explain the problem to Jim's parents. That's your professional "writing assignment."

You get ready to write the letter by doing a little research. You look over Jim's records, you interview him, and you talk to his teachers. Then you sit down to think over what you have learned, and you begin to generalize it, much as you did in the invention exercises in exercise 4. You decide that Jim's main problem is that at this time he is having some difficulty coping with reality.

You formulate this generalization and express it as the tentative proposition of your report to the principal: "Jim's major problem at the moment seems to be that he is having a little trouble coping with reality." This is the position you are taking about Jim, your judgment about him as a professional guidance counselor.

But you can't leave it at that. Your professional responsibility requires you to do more than formulate an opinion. It also requires you to explain and support your opinion so that other people will understand and accept it. To explain your judgment in this case, you express it as the proposition of your report on Jim and divide your explanation into two parts, what your proposition *assumes* and what it *asserts*. This division gives you the basis of the second and third paragraphs of your report.

Your judgment, that "Jim's major problem at the moment seems to be that he is having a little trouble coping with reality," *assumes* knowledge of the reality that Jim faces. The principal and Jim's parents may not be aware of that reality. Let's say that Jim faces new competition on the football team and is having trouble learning the first principles of plane geometry. Paragraph 2 of your letter would outline these problems and the pressures that they are likely to bring to bear on a high school student's life.

Based on this assumption, your generalization also *asserts* that Jim's present way of trying to cope with this reality is inadequate. Perhaps because he did well in first-year mathematics without working very hard, Jim is trying to get by in plane geometry in the same way, putting off his homework until the last minute and then rushing through it to get the answers without thoroughly understanding the principles involved. Maybe he is trying to deal with new competition on the football team with boasting and bravado instead of facing his limitations and trying out for another position. Paragraph 3 of your report would describe Jim's behavior and explain why it is preventing him from developing as he should.

Having taken a position and explained it, you would then write an introduction. Paragraph 1 of your letter, the introduction, might outline a conceptual context. You might discuss generally what a boy of Jim's age might be expected to accomplish and to what degree a boy of his age might be expected to understand himself and the problems he faces. You might also refer to conditions at the school or in the culture at large that might be expected to make life somewhat difficult for high school students like Jim. This introductory paragraph would end with your one-sentence evaluation of this particular boy in this particular situation. This sentence would be the proposition of your report that takes a position on "Jim's major problem at the moment."

These three paragraphs—introduction and two paragraphs of explanation—would complete the task the principal assigned you. If you also felt that the principal would appreciate some suggestions about what the school and Jim's parents might do to help him through this difficult time, you might add a fourth paragraph outlining some steps they might take. Paragraph 4 would give your report an ending by placing its proposition, a judgment based on your professional expertise, into the context of possible cooperative or individual action, as you learned to do that in What an Ending Does, p. 206, and in Other Ways to End an Essay, p. 223.

The result of organizing your letter in this way would be a well-focused essay very much like the essays that the exercises in this book ask you to write. One version of the report you might have written follows. Following that is an example report in a business situation written in *Short Course* form.

☐ EXAMPLE ESSAY MEMO ─────────────────────────────

KINGSGATE HIGH SCHOOL
86 Oakwood Road
Hobart, Illinois

Counseling Department

Dr. Jean Corey, Principal
Kingsgate High School
86 Oakwood Road
Hobart, Illinois

Dear Jean,

You have asked me to respond to questions Jim MacReady's parents have asked about Jim's difficulties in school this fall. I don't think the problems are terribly serious, and they can be fairly easily solved. Jim is sixteen, and a sophomore. His junior high school record is above average. He did well at Kingsgate last year. He plays basketball and football, seems very interested in science and English, and is socially active. His class elected him treasurer last spring. At sixteen, though, he is in a very difficult stage of development. He is likely to have a chaotic emotional life, a great deal of uncertainty about his relationships with girls, and still rather strong dependence on support from home. At the same time, he may have a tendency to resent that dependence. He probably wants to try new things, and prove himself by succeeding in them, and he may feel very impatient if that success is slow to come. Most of these characteristics can be found in Jim's personality at this time. The result is that, in my view, Jim's major problem at the moment seems to be that he is having a little trouble coping with reality.

The two most troublesome features of Jim's reality this fall seem to be geometry and football. The first month of Mr. Trager's plane geometry course has left Jim very much behind. He has a weekly quiz average of 68, and Trager says that Jim is inattentive in class, hands in his homework irregularly, and makes thoughtless errors in class recitation. Jim's performance puzzles Trager because he taught Jim algebra last year and knows that the boy is potentially very good in math. On the surface, it seems that the cause of Jim's difficulty in geometry may be the fact that he is trying out this fall for quarterback on the football team. But Coach Tolland says that Jim spends more time joking with the other boys than he spends practicing passes and signals. Tolland thinks Jim will probably not make Junior Varsity quarterback, and he thinks Jim knows that Billy Fazio, who moved to Hobart just this summer, is the more likely choice.

These two pressures on Jim's life at the present time have left him rather confused. In our talk yesterday morning, Jim admitted that he was afraid Billy would make quarterback. I asked him how he felt about that. He acted cocky and said that Fazio is not half as good a quarterback as he (Jim) is. If Fazio makes it, Jim said, it would be through favoritism. He couldn't tell me why he thought Tolland favored Fazio. As for geometry, I asked Jim if he liked Mr. Trager as a teacher. He brightened up at this. He said he liked Trager, and he liked algebra a lot last year. Algebra all seemed to make sense, it all fit together. When I asked about geometry, Jim became quiet. He complained that all those axioms are too hard to memorize. None of it makes sense to him. I asked if he put as much time into his homework this year as last year. He said he did—just as much, but it didn't do any good. He knew he was going to fail geometry anyway. Half an hour of homework was enough for algebra, he said, and it should be enough for geometry too. If not, he couldn't be bothered doing more.

The new reality Jim is facing here is not just the difficulty presented by these two new subjects—geometry and quarterbacking. Both have confronted Jim with higher hurdles then he has ever had to jump before, and this has led to a bit of a crisis in Jim's self-evaluation. Surely Jim can pass geometry if we can get him to realize that it is a different sort of mathematics from algebra, and requires a different approach and more study. Trager will help him with this. Jim's parents can help too. I suggest that they call Trager and talk it over with him. Football is another kind of problem entirely. Jim is a good player, but (according to Tolland and some of the boys on the team) Fazio is more than good—he's talented. Here Jim is up against real limitations in contrast with the other boy's strengths. He is going to have to learn to accept that fact. Tolland thinks that Jim would make a solid halfback, though, and he has an opening on the team in that position. He has mentioned that opening to Jim, but Jim just mumbled something and walked away. In this case it may help to remember that Jim's father got his letter as a quarterback in his day at Kingsgate. We may be able to turn that fact to advantage in helping Jim accept the situation if we talk it through together. I suggest a meeting next week with Coach Tolland, Jim's father, and myself.

Yours sincerely,

Clinton Marley
Counselor

☐ EXAMPLE ESSAY MEMO

McKAY, TREPP Inc.
Industrial Consultants
One East Livingston Street
Remsen, California

Memorandum   Date: May 30, 1992

To: Frank Pierrepont, President
           Lisa Hicks, Vice President—Operations
           Pierrepont Manufacturing Corporation
           Basset, Illinois 97654-3210
From: Lucille McKay
Subject: Production Problems, East Basset Plant

Background

On April 12, 1992, Frank Pierrepont, President, Pierrepont Mfg. Corp., ordered a review of production methods and organization at Pierrepont's East Basset plant. McKay, Trepp was hired on May 23, 1992, to visit the plant, examine its procedures, and interview its personnel. What prompted this review was the fact a significant decrease in production at the East Basset plant during November–February, 1991–92 (see accompanying charts). Reports from managing officers at the plant did not seem to justify the slowdown. A visit to the plant by the company president in January elicited very little useful information and failed to increase production. An educated guess by the president in consultation with the vice president for operations was that the principal cause of the poor production record might be personal friction among managerial and production personnel at the plant. Investigation by McKay, Trepp Inc. has shown, however, that although some personal problems exist, a complicated mix of internal and external factors was the main cause of the slowdown.

Causes

Our observations and interviews at the East Basset plant suggest that there has in fact been some friction among plant personnel this winter. None of it seems serious enough in itself, though, to cause the production slowdown, and most of it can be easily resolved. The major conflict occurred between the supply manager and the production line foreman over unboxing parts and supplies. This issue, however, is not just a problem of deciding who is responsible for the task. It is complicated by the possibility of increased corrosion of the surfaces of some parts if unboxed too early and left standing too long exposed to the air. Along with this technical problem, which became unnecessarily a problem in personnel relations, another personnel problem also helped cause the winter slowdown: illness. Several important highly skilled workers came down with the flu during the first week in December. This interruption not only brought production almost to a halt for that week, but also set off a chain of production difficulties lasting well into January. Then heavy snows and a boiler breakdown in January further slowed production that month.

Despite these difficulties, production should have been only slightly less than normal this winter. The major cause of the slowdown occurred not during the winter but well before winter began: the trucking strike last October. As a result of the strike, the plant ran low on several crucial supplies toward the end of November. Faced with this shortage, plant personnel behaved nobly. Pierrepont management had reason to be especially grateful, for example, to one junior manager, Mervyn Fox, who learned of a small stock of the crucial supplies set aside in the storehouse of a recently bankrupt firm in Toledo, drove there early in December to negotiate their purchase, and brought them back in his car in a single working day. At the same time, East Basset plant managers and foremen might have been somewhat more resourceful in reorganizing production around these short supplies for the time being, and thereby saving expensive downtime on production machinery.

Recommendations

Given these causes, the solution to the East Basset plant production problems lies mainly in the hands of central management. We recommend that the vice president for operations examine the corrosion problem in consultation with suppliers and make a decision about responsibility for unboxing based on the vulnerability of the materials involved. Plant management and foremen should discuss and decide upon contingency plans to minimize the effects of brief interruptions in the flow of supplies and parts. Central management should consider computerizing supply control so that plant managers and foremen can get supplies-on-hand updates and have the opportunity to revise their requisitions once a week rather than once every two weeks. Finally, we suggest that Pierrepont hire an assistant to the vice president for operations to keep management informed of impending events and trends in the economy, labor relations, and government regulations that could affect production and other company operations in the foreseeable future.

PART FIVE

Research and Research Writing

WHAT IS RESEARCH?

People do research because they are curious about something or they need to know something. The need for research begins with a question. Why didn't your car start this morning? What did other readers think of the book you just read? Why is production down at the East Basset plant? Where was baseball invented? Should I really be eating food with less cholesterol in it? What's the shortest route from here to Toledo?

Questions like these drive you to do research. In some cases you research the question yourself. In other cases you ask someone else to research it for you. You would probably ask your mechanic to find out why your car wouldn't start this morning, and you'd ask your doctor about cutting down on cholesterol. If your teacher asks you to find out what the reviewers said about the book you've just read, you look them up yourself. And if your boss asks you why production is down at the East Basset plant, you hustle right on down there to find out. On these or any other subject you would try to think of some way to find out what you want to know. What makes you want to do research is having a question to answer.

But you don't begin to do research with a question. You begin research with a hunch about what the answer to the question might be. Some people call guessing what the answer might be *formulating a hypothesis.* Your mechanic says he thinks he'll check the fuel line first. He has a hunch that your car didn't start because the fuel line was plugged with condensation. You guess that the reviewers said the book you read is badly organized. On the way to the East Basset plant you formulate a hypothesis that production is down because the foreman there doesn't know what he's doing. You suspect that baseball was invented in New York City. You bet your doctor will tell you to cut down on cholesterol. Your hunch is that the northern route is the shortest way to Toledo.

In each case, research begins with one of these hunches. You, your mechanic, or your doctor guesses the answer and then sets out to see if the guess is correct. All of you want to see where your hunches will lead if you follow them up.

With this beginning, research can go in many directions. It is impossible to make up a cast-iron list of rules for research. But in most cases the next step after a hunch is to figure out some ways you might go about checking to see if your hunch is right. This is known as deciding on a procedure or a method.

The method that most research follows involves a complex mix of analysis (taking things and ideas apart to study them) and synthesis (putting them back together again in the same or different ways). To learn when and where baseball was invented you have to look at the historical record. To decide whether or not you should cut down on cholesterol, your doctor has to read conflicting medical opinions, think them over, and decide how they apply to you. To figure out how to get to Toledo you have to be able to read a map and interpret the confusing directions your friends have given you. To fix your car, your mechanic has to take apart your car's fuel system, and (you hope) put it back together again so that it works. To report on the reviews of your book, you have to find them, read them, and figure out what they have in common and why they differ. To please your boss, you're going to have to look over the records at the East Basset plant, talk to people there, and watch how they go about their work. All of that qualifies as research.

What generally happens is that researchers turn their first hunch into a series of progressively more refined, better educated hunches as they become better informed. Arriving at a confirmed hunch, a position that you feel you can explain and defend, depends on how complicated the issue is and how good a detective you are. Sometimes you can settle the issue. Sometimes you change your mind over and over again. Sometimes you have to leave the issue up in the air. For example, you would find it pretty easy to arrive at a confirmed hunch that, as far as anyone knows now, baseball was invented in New York. And, after looking at a map, you would decide without too much trouble on the northern route to Toledo.

But your mechanic's hunch is harder to confirm. In fact, he winds up disconfirming it. He finds out that his original hunch was wrong. He discovers (after a morning of research on your car at the going hourly rate) that it wasn't condensation at all that kept it from starting. You need a new carburetor. Your doctor says that in your case the evidence is somewhat ambiguous. He tells you that on the whole it might be a good idea if you cut down on cholesterol, but you don't have to avoid high cholesterol foods entirely. As you read the reviews of the book you have read you begin to realize that you must have missed something, so you go back to reread it. And you find out that the situation at the East Basset plant is a lot more complicated than you thought.

Sooner or later most research involves reading and writing. To find out about the beginning of baseball, you read some histories of baseball and write a letter to Cooperstown. Your doctor reads the latest research papers on cholesterol. You study a map of Ohio and write out an itinerary. You read the reviews of your book and write an essay explaining what they say. After reading the records of the East Basset plant, you write a memo to your boss explaining what you found there. (A memo of the kind you might write is on p. 242.) Your mechanic has to consult a parts catalogue and the repair manual for your brand of car, and he has to write up a bill to explain what he did to your car and convince you that it was worth the price.

Three motives keep you going while you are doing all this research and research writing. One is your curiosity and the desire to find out how clever you are: how close did your hunch come to what turns out to be the case? Research is a kind of detective game in which you compete against yourself.

Another motive that keeps you going in research is your desire to learn something new. With the help of the reviewers, you really are going to understand that dratted book after all. You will have the satisfaction of knowing more baseball history than all of your friends. You won't worry any more about cholesterol, because you're going to be doing something about it. Your boss may give you a raise for your wonderful work in East Basset. Your car may start tomorrow, and with any luck at all you will make it to Toledo.

The third motive that keeps you going while you are doing research and writing it up is less clear-cut and more subtle than either curiosity or new knowledge. Yet in the long run it may be the strongest of the three. It is the satisfaction of talking with people you haven't met before, contributing to conversations going on in communities you haven't been a member of before, and working with other people and taking a hand in what is going on.

Of course, in doing research you may not always feel that you are involved with other people. A lot of the time you will seem to be working alone. You will find yourself in a dorm room or your room at home, in the library or lab, or in the office of the East Basset plant long into the night. Your mechanic will spend most of the hours he bills you working alone too, with his head stuck under the hood of your car.

But even when you seem to be working alone you will in literal fact be involved in *indirect* conversation with other people. You will be carrying on your conversation with them in the displaced ways that we call reading, writing, and thinking. Your mechanic makes contact with other mechanics and suppliers by reading the parts catalogue and repair manual. Your doctor gets involved in the ongoing, unresolved conversation about how bad cholesterol is for us when she reads research articles on the subject. In East Basset, you engage in both direct and indirect conversation with accountants and managers when you evaluate what you find in the company's books and on the floor of the plant. And you join the ranks of the company executives who hired you and trust you when you think about the situation and report on it in your memo to the boss.

In short, what makes research interesting and fun is that you get to have your cake and eat it too. Research work is both *in*dependent and *inter*dependent. Your independence comes from the fact that you decide how to go about the task, you do it on your own, and you decide when you're finished. Your interdependence comes from the community-defined limits you work within. *Community-defined limits* are a discourse community's conventions and rules of conduct and procedure, such as the rules of the Baseball Commission, the course assignments your teachers give you, the materials stress charts that the engineers who designed your car followed, and the plans that your boss's executive committee has decided on for the company's future.

In many cases you may continue to carry on the conversation you begin in research long after the research work itself is over. By doing the research and writing it up you establish your membership in discourse communities that you did not belong to before. Research prepares you for membership in those communities by teaching you how their members, who are knowledgeable on the topic, talk and behave. It also prepares you for membership by giving you a chance to contribute to their discussion. (There is more on discourse communities in Part Four: Reaching Out to the Members of Other Communities, p. 189, and in the Introduction, p. 10.)

RESEARCH WRITING

When you write up your research, you are making a bid to join communities whose members are interested in the subject and knowledgeable about it. You make that bid in two ways: by contributing to their conversation and by acknowledging the sources that they too have drawn on. When you acknowledge their sources you are noticing the fact that they too work within community-defined constraints and are engaged in conversation directly or indirectly with other members of their community by reading and writing.

One of the hallmarks of research writing is the documentation of sources. You document sources by telling readers in parenthetical citations and a bibliography (also called *works cited*) where you got the information you are using and therefore where they too could find it. You document the sources you draw on in order to strengthen what you say. Citations identify your friends and allies. You show that you know what other people have already said on the topic and that you have benefited from reading it. If every essay takes a position and then explores, explains, and defends that position, a *research essay* takes an *informed* position and then explores, explains, and defends that position in an informed way. In any essay you write you have to know what you're talking about. In a research essay you have to *show* that you know what you're talking about.

Research essays can be short and simple, or they can be as long and complex as a book. Length doesn't matter. What matters is that research essays reassure readers that you are not writing off the top of your head. Some of your information may come from secondary sources such as books and magazines. Some of it may come from primary sources and direct, systematic, or experimental contact with the subject matter through surveys, laboratory experiments, exploration, photographs, documents, and recordings.

When you cite these sources, you give your readers the opportunity to refer to them themselves. They may want to refer to one to make sure that the source is reliable, to make sure that you have quoted or paraphrased it correctly and completely, and to see if you have interpreted or explained it sensibly. Or they may want to refer to it because you have interested them so much in the subject that they want to learn more about it.

So, in order to learn to do research and write research essays, you have to learn a certain amount of research technique. One way to start learning research technique is by reading one reliable, well-written book about a topic that interests you and then following up what you learn from that book. To do that there are four steps you should take.

First, make sure that you understand the book.

Second, evaluate the book as a source by finding out what well-informed reviewers had to say about it when it was published.

Third, identify the issues the book addresses and the context of issues within which the book makes sense. You can begin to examine the book's context of issues by rereading the reviews of the book. Because reviewers evaluate books from different points of view, they often explain or imply why the book was written.

Finally, you can take a position yourself on one of those issues, a position that by this time is going to be very well informed.

If you learn research in this way, you will learn some of the satisfactions of research as well as some of its elements and techniques. You will learn how to cite sources and document whatever you say without losing the real purpose of research in a confusion of commas, parentheses, and page numbers. By writing a series of short, related research essays as you go along, you will learn how to keep your style readable while you synthesize the ideas of other writers. And you will learn to shape and reshape your material for different purposes.

Most of all, you will learn that knowledge is not something carved in stone for all time. Knowledge is fluid and changing. In every field, scholars, critics, politicians, mathematicians, and laboratory scientists differ in their views and in their conception of what is correct and true. Sometimes they agree in general but differ in detail. Sometimes their whole conception of what is right and true differs completely from one person to another and from one discourse community to another. But these differences are almost always constructive, because the process of trying to negotiate and resolve them changes our understanding of ourselves and the world we live in. By engaging in research yourself, you learn how to contribute to that lively, exciting process of change by contributing to the conversation that makes it happen.

The Purpose of These Research Exercises

Essay exercises 12 through 16 ask for relatively short, 500- to 750-word essays that are very much like the essays you wrote for exercises 5 through 11. If you have not written at least one or two of these earlier essay exercises, you are likely to find exercises 12 through 16 more confusing and difficult than they should be. Essay exercises 5 through 9 show you how to begin with a topic that interests you, take a position on that topic, and explore, explain, or defend it. Exercises 10 and 11 show you how to begin and end an essay so that members of other discourse communities, people who don't quite "speak your language," will want to consider your position and try to understand it.

Exercises 12 through 16 also begin with your own interests and curiosity. They ask you to choose a book on a subject that interests you, so that you can focus your attention for a while on what one writer has to say on that subject. Then, exercise 12 asks you to read the book more carefully and constructively than you have probably ever read a book before, by writing a basic descriptive outline of it. Exercises 13 through 16 ask you to enlarge the scope of your study. You do that by *evaluating your sources*, beginning with the book you have read and outlined.

You begin evaluating sources in exercise 13 by writing your own review of the book. Then, having met your book and gotten to know it pretty well, you set out to meet some of its family and friends. In exercise 14, by reading reviews of the book in newspapers, magazines, and journals, you find out how other readers with different backgrounds than your own evaluated the book when it was first published, and you synthesize what you have found in an essay that reports on those reviews.

Next, you dig up more of your book's family and friends in order to report on them too. Exercise 15 asks you to enlarge the scope of your study still further by exploring the book's context of issues. You try to discover the discourse communities that the book's author belongs to. That is, you try to discover what authors have read and what they talk about with other members of their profession. To do that, you have to act something like a detective. You assume that people write books because other people have written them before on the same subject or a similar one. You assume that writers have colleagues and professional friends they talk over what they are writing with, just as you talk over with your classmates what you are going to write and what you have written. As a kind of Sam Spade of the library stacks, you try to find out who these other writers, colleagues, and friends may be and what their influence was on the book you have read.

All this information is not so hard to find out as you might expect. Of course you cannot recover writers' direct, face-to-face talk with their friends and colleagues over coffee in the cafeteria. But you can recover their indirect, displaced conversation. You can read what the author of your book read when doing research for the book, and you can read some of the published conversation that went on about the book after it was published. The issues that the book's family talk about together is its context of issues. In writing the essay for exercise 15 you will explain how that conversation went. You will be writing a sort of family history of the book you have read.

After writing this series of reports, in exercise 16 you will finally get to take a position of your own on a topic related to the book you read, and to explore, explain, and defend your position using the new knowledge that you have acquired in your research. In this exercise, the book, its reviews, and other articles that you have been reading become part of your essay's family. They become sources for you to draw upon in writing a well-informed essay.

In short, one thing you may notice about these research exercises is that they move step-by-step away from what they focused on at first, your first source, the book you chose to read. By stages, that book becomes just one among many sources for what another writer has to say on the same subject. That other writer is you.

You may also notice in doing these research exercises that even though the writers you consult in your research may be impressively authoritative—big names who really know what they're talking about—they have not said all there is to say. Reviewers raise doubts about what writers say. One book or article corrects or contradicts another. And once you have prepared yourself through research, you will find that you will quite easily arrive at a judgment of your own on the subject, and you will explore, explain, and defend your judgment knowledgeably. You may also find that you change your mind as you go along, or change the direction of your interests—not a lot, maybe, but some. At the very least, the more you know, the larger the context in which you know it, the less absolute and certain you may become. If you read carefully, you may even be able to see this kind of change happening in the example essays in this section.

The endless conversation that you join when you engage in research and research writing is the means by which human beings construct knowledge. These research exercises show you how to take a hand in that process.

CHOOSING A BOOK

The first step in this set of research exercises is to choose a book on a topic that interests you. Make your own choice according to the following criteria or pick one from the list beginning on page 253. The book you choose will serve as a basic text for the whole set of five essay exercises, 12 through 16.

Not every book you might like to read will work for these research essay exercises, although you can probably find a suitable book on almost any subject. The book has to meet three criteria. First, the book has to be expository. That is, it has to be like the essays you have been writing, although of course much longer. It has to take a position on some issue and explore, explain, or defend that position. Most books that tell a story, such as novels, biographies, autobiographies, and travel books, will not work for these research exercises.

Second, the book has to be respected in its field. That is, people who know as much about the subject as the author does have to think the book is worth reading. The way to tell if a book is respected is to see if it has been reviewed in literary journals (for example, *TLS [The (London) Times Literary Supplement]* or *The New York Review of Books*) and in professional and scholarly journals. If it has been reviewed by professionals, then people who know the subject well probably take the book seriously. They think that the book is worth reading even though they may not agree with the position it takes. Books taken seriously by those who know the subject well may also be reviewed in the popular press (such as the *New York Times, Time Magazine,* and *Newsweek*), but books that have been reviewed only in the popular press will not serve the purpose of these exercises.

The third criterion is that the book must have been published or copyrighted at least two years ago. A book published less than two years ago may not yet have been reviewed in professional and scholarly journals, which often take two years or more to review important books.

To find a book that meets these three criteria, you can ask a friend or a teacher who knows a field that interests you to recommend one. You can consult back issues of a literary journal such as *TLS* or *The New York Review* to find titles that catch your interest. A review published in one of these literary journals may also give you some idea whether the book in question is important and substantial enough for these exercises. Or you can choose a book from the list below.

Be a little adventurous in choosing a book. Follow your curiosity. You may choose a book in a field you already know something about. But you might also try looking into a subject that is totally new to you but that you're a little bit curious about. If you do that, you may learn something new about yourself as well about the subject.

Once you have chosen the book, the next thing to do is read it. But before you read it straight through from cover to cover, look it over. Skim it. Read the table of contents. Try to get a general idea of how the book is organized and what it is saying. Read the preface, the introduction, and the conclusion if there is one. Read the first paragraph and the last paragraph of each chapter. Try to guess what each chapter as a whole probably says. (Remember, research starts with a hunch.)

Then read the book from beginning to end.

Book List for Exercises 12–16

The following books are a selection among the many that could be used for these research exercises. Some of them have been used before by students doing this set of exercises. All of them fit the criteria for suitable books.

THE ARTS

Baraka, Amiri (LeRoi Jones). *Blues People: Negro Music in White America.* New York: Perennial, 2002.

Biel, Steven. *American Gothic: A Life of America's Most Famous Painting.* New York: Norton, 2005.

Brownlow, Kevin. *Behind the Mask of Innocence: Sex, Violence, Prejudice, Crime: Films of Social Conscience in the Silent Era.* Berkeley: University of California Press, 1992.

Cook, Nicholas. *Music, Imagination, and Culture.* New York: Oxford University Press, 1992.

Cooper, Barry. *Beethoven and the Creative Process.* New York: Oxford University Press, 1995.

Florescu, Radu R., and Raymond T. McNally. *Dracula, Prince of Many Faces: His Life and His Times.* Boston: Little, Brown. 2005.

Hollander, Anne. *Seeing Through Clothes.* Berkeley: University of California Press, 1993.

Sublette, Ned. *Cuba and Its Music: From the First Drums to the Mambo.* Chicago: Chicago Review Press, 2004.

HISTORY

Anderson, Virginia DeJohn. *Creatures of Empire: How Domestic Animals Transformed Early America.* Oxford University Press, 2004.

Burrows, Edwin G., and Mike Wallace. Gotham: *A History of New York City to 1898.* New York: Oxford University Press, 2000.

Carson, Rachel. *Silent Spring.* Boston: Houghton Mifflin, 2002.

Davis, David Brion. *The Problem of Slavery in Western Culture.* New York: Oxford University Press, 1988.

Egnal, Marc. *A Mighty Empire: The Origins of the American Revolution.* Ithaca, N.Y.: Cornell University Press, 1988.

Foner, Nancy. *From Ellis Island to JFK: New York's Two Great Waves of Immigration.* New Haven, Ct.: Yale University Press, 2002.

Ling, Roger. *Pompeii: History, Life and Afterlife.* Gloucestershire, UK: Tempus Publishing Ltd., 2005.

Manville, Philip Brook. *The Origins of Citizenship in Ancient Athens.* Princeton, N.J.: Princeton University Press, 1997.

Maraniss, David. *They Marched into Sunlight: War and Peace Vietnam and America October 1967.* New York: Simon & Schuster, 2004.

Slatta, Richard W. *Cowboys of the Americas.* New Haven, Ct.: Yale University Press, 1994.

MEN, WOMEN, AND CHILDREN

Bulliet, Richard W. *The Case for Islamo-Christian Civilization.* New York: Columbia University Press, 2005.

Collingham, Lizzie. *Curry: A Tale of Cooks and Conquerors.* New York: Oxford University Press, 2006.

Crone, Patricia, and Michael Cook. *Hagarism: The Making of the Islamic World.* Cambridge: Cambridge University Press, 1978.

Diamond, Jared. *Guns, Germs and Steel.* New York: Norton, 2005.

Egan, Timothy. The Worst Hard Time: *The Untold Story of Those Who Survived the Great American Dust Bowl.* New York: Houghton Mifflin, 2005.

Friedan, Betty. *The Feminine Mystique.* New York: Norton, 2002.

Geertz, Clifford. *Interpretation of Cultures.* New York: Basic Books, 2000.

Gutschow, Kim. *Being a Buddhist Nun: The Struggle for Enlightenment in the Himalayas.* Cambridge, Mass.: Harvard University Press, 2005.

Harris, Marvin. *Cultural Materialism.* Walnut Creek, Calif.: AltaMira Press, 2001.

Honore, Carl. *In Praise of Slow: How a Worldwide Movement Is Challenging the Cult of Speed.* London: Orion, 2005.

Marmot, Michael. *The Status Syndrome: How Social Standing Affects Our Health and Longevity.* New York: Owl Books, 2005.

Moore, Charlotte. *George and Sam* [autistic children]. New York: Viking, 2005.

Nolen, Stephanie. *Promised the Moon: The Untold Story of the First Women in the Space Race.* New York: Four Walls Eight Windows, 2003.

Rokeach, Milton. *The Three Christs of Ypsilanti: A Psychological Study.* Guildford, UK: Columbia University Press, 1981.

Sacks, Oliver. *Seeing Voices: A Journey into the Land of the Deaf.* New York: Vintage, 2000.

Saunt, Claudio. *Black, White, and Indian: Race and the Unmaking of an American Family.* Oxford: Oxford University Press, 2005.

Shattuck, Roger. *The Forbidden Experiment: The Story of the Wild Boy of Aveyron.* Tokyo: Kodansha International, 1994.

Van Schaik, Carel. *Among Orangutans: Red Apes and the Rise of Human Culture.* Cambridge, Mass.: Harvard University Press, 2004.

Williams, Kayla. *Love My Rifle More Than You: Young and Female in the U. S. Army.* New York: Norton, 2005

Wray, T. J., and Gregory Mobley. *The Birth of Satan: Tracing the Devil's Biblical Roots.* New York: Palgrave Macmillan, 2005.

PUBLIC AFFAIRS

Critser, Greg. *Fat Land: How Americans Became the Fattest People in the World.* Boston: Houghton Mifflin, 2003.

Davis, Mike. *The Monster at Our Door: The Global Threat of Avian Flu.* New York: New Press, 2005.

Diamond, Jared. *Collapse: How Societies Choose to Fail or Succeed.* New York: Viking, 2005.

Forer, Lois G. *Criminals and Victims: A Trial Judge Reflects on Crime and Punishment.* New York: Norton, 1980.

Gebissa, Ezekiel. *Leaf of Allah: Khat & Agricultural Transformation in Harerge Ethiopia 1875–1991.* Athens, Ohio: Ohio University Press, 2004.

Gray, Colin S. *Another Bloody Century: Future Warfare.* Suffolk, UK: Weidenfield & Nicholson, 2005.

Lemann, Nicholas. *The Promised Land: The Great Black Migration and How It Changed America.* New York: Knopf, 1991.

Lewis, Tom. *The Hudson: A History* [of New York's river]. New Haven, Ct.: Yale University Press, 2005.

Litwack, Leon F. *Been in the Storm So Long: The Aftermath of Slavery.* New York: Random House, 1981.

Maslowski, Peter, and Don Winslow. *Looking for a Hero: Staff Sergeant Joe Ronnie Hooper and the Vietnam War.* Lincoln, Neb.: University of Nebraska Press, 2005.

Miller, Michael B. *The Bon Marché: Bourgeois Culture and the Department Store, 1869–1920.* Princeton, N.J.: Princeton University Press, 1994.

Monmonier, Mark. *Rhumb Lines and Map Wars: A Social History of the Mercator Projection.* Chicago: University of Chicago Press, 2004.

Nestle, Marion. *Food Politics: How the Food Industry Influences Nutrition and Health.* Berkeley: University of California Press, 2002.

Rogers, Heather. *Gone Tomorrow: The Hidden Life of Garbage.* New York: New Press, 2005.

Russell, Sharman Apt. *Hunger: An Unnatural History.* New York: Basic Books, 2006.

Sampson, Anthony. *The Seven Sisters: The Great Oil Companies and the World They Made.* London: Coronet, 1993.

Vaitheeswaran, Vijay V. *Power to the People: How the Coming Energy Revolution Will Transform an Industry, Change Our Lives, and Maybe Even Save the Planet.* New York: Farrar, Straus and Giroux, 2003.

SCIENCE

Cohen, I. Bernard. *Benjamin Franklin's Science.* Cambridge, Mass.: Harvard University Press, 1996.

Davis, Philip J., and Reuben Hersh. *The Mathematical Experience.* Boston: Houghton Mifflin, 1998.

Forbes, Scott. *A Natural History of Families.* Princeton, N.J.: Princeton University Press, 2005.

Gallagher, Shaun. *How the Body Shapes the Mind.* Oxford: Oxford University Press, 2005.

Goodall, Jane. *Through a Window: My Thirty Years with the Chimpanzees of Gombe.* London: Phoenix, 2000.

Gross, Alan G. *The Rhetoric of Science.* Cambridge, Mass.: Harvard University Press, 1996.

Kaku, Michio. *Einstein's Cosmos: How Albert Einstein's Vision Transformed Our Understanding of Space and Time.* New York: Norton, 2004.

Lamb, Simon. *Devil in the Mountain: A Search for the Origin of the Andes.* Princeton, N.J.: Princeton University Press, 2004.

McPhee, John. *Basin and Range* [geology]. New York: Farrar, Straus and Giroux, 1981.

Miller, Jonathan. *The Body in Question.* London: Pimlico, 2000.

Rozwadowski, Helen M. *Fathoming the Ocean: The Discovery and Exploration of the Deep Sea.* Cambridge, Mass.: Harvard University Press, 2005.

Thomas, Lewis. *The Lives of a Cell: Notes of a Biology Watcher.* New York: Penguin, 1986.

▷EXERCISE 12   BASIC DESCRIPTIVE OUTLINE OF A BOOK

After you have read the book you have chosen, write a basic descriptive outline of it.

The purpose of writing a descriptive outline of the book you have read is to be sure that you understand it. Writing a descriptive outline of anything you read can help you understand it better by making you a constructive reader. Becoming a constructive reader sets up a "workshop" relationship between you and the writer. The two of you in effect get to talk over what the writer has written and negotiate an understanding between you. As a constructive reader, you are more aware of the distinguishable parts of what you are reading and of the significant relationships among them. You stand a greater chance of being able to follow the writer and less chance of getting lost. You have greater control over your responses to what you read.

It is important to follow the writer of the book you have chosen and to control your response to the book, because you are reading it in order to be able to put your own response to it in writing. You are getting ready to join a conversation already in progress by finding out what other people are talking about (the writer of the book you are reading and his or her friends and colleagues) so that you can talk about it with them indirectly by writing about it. You are reading the book and doing this set of exercises about it to get ready to write a well-informed essay on the same or a related topic yourself, the essay you will write for exercise 16.

To read well enough to prepare yourself in that way, it can help to do as a reader what you have been doing as a writer: pay close attention to how the text is organized and how its parts fit together. When you write, you have to remember how the things you say near the beginning of an essay set up terms that you use all the way through the essay. You have to be just as aware of organization when you read. Books and articles set up terms at the beginning that they use all the way through. You have to be able to remember them, what they mean, and how they fit in. (There is more about constructive reading in Part Three beginning on p. 147.)

Your descriptive outline will probably be easier to write if you buy a paperback copy of the book you are reading so that you can mark it up, number the paragraphs, and so on. But many books suitable for these exercises are not available in paperback. So the chances are that you will be using a library book. Take very good care of library books. Don't mark them up or damage them. If you do, you will deprive other people of the tools they need to do their work. Instead, learn to take notes on organization and substance (*does* and *says*) by indicating page and paragraph numbers with a simple code (for example, you could indicate page 10, line 2 with a code 10-2).

WRITING A BASIC DESCRIPTIVE OUTLINE OF A BOOK

To write a basic descriptive outline of a book, begin by mapping it chapter by chapter.

Follow these steps for mapping a book.

First, read again in sequence the chapter titles and the first paragraph of each chapter.

Write a *says* statement for each chapter.

Read your chapter *says* statements in sequence and revise them so that they make sense when you read them consecutively. Together, they should add up to an accurate paraphrase of the book.

Then write out the position that you think the book takes: its main idea or proposition. If the book does not seem to have a succinct position statement, write one out yourself. Or if you are not sure which of several passages might state the book's main point, write out two or three alternatives.

Since you are dealing with a book, not a five-hundred-word essay, the proposition may amount to several sentences, not just one. After working out what each chapter of the book *says* and *does*, you will have a chance to decide which possible proposition you wrote down is correct.

Second, decide how the chapters are arranged. For example, are they in numerical, temporal, or causal order (phase one, phase two, phase three; later as opposed to earlier; X resulted from Y)? Do they seem to pose a problem and then offer a solution to it? Do they seem to have some logical order? For example, does evidence lead to inferences inductively, or is a principle applied to experience deductively?

Decide what role each chapter plays in the sequence. Think of an appropriate label for each chapter that names what it *does:* the function it serves in the book. In thinking up labels for the chapters, it will help to decide

- how the chapters differ from each other,
- how they are connected or related to each other, and
- how they are related to what you understand to be the main point of the book.

Write a *does* statement for each chapter. Base your *does* statements on the labels you have given the chapters.

Third, subdivide each chapter. If the writer has already subdivided the chapter with subheadings, use those. If not, divide the paragraphs into sequences yourself, depending on what role you think each sequence plays in the chapter, how it is related to the other paragraph sequences, and how it is related to the main point of the paragraph.

Give the subdivisions labels and use them to complete your *does* statements by describing how each chapter is organized.

Fourth, if the book has an introduction, subdivide it and write a *does* statement for it. What does it *say* to introduce the book? What does it *do* to introduce it?

Fifth, if the book has a clearly defined ending, subdivide it and write a *does* statement for it. What does it *say* to end the book? What does it *do*?

Sixth, *reread* the outline you have written in the following two ways:

1. Reread your *says* statements in sequence along with the tentative proposition statements you wrote to begin with. Decide which one is closest to your understanding of the book now that you have finished your analysis of it. If none of them seems to say very accurately what you now think the book is about, find another proposition statement in the book, or write one yourself.

2. Then reread your *does* statements in sequence. Revise them so that they say clearly and readably how the book is organized.

You can leave your descriptive outline in descriptive outline form, or you can revise it into paragraphs that describe the book and explain what it says.

Finally, add an informational note to your descriptive outline. The note should identify the primary sources that the writer used in writing the book and the most important secondary sources.

Primary sources are in most cases original documents that the writer dealt with, drew upon, and interpreted firsthand. *Secondary sources* are articles or books that synthesize and interpret primary sources. Primary sources are firsthand information. Secondary sources are secondhand information.

For example, suppose you were trying to find out what went on at Judy's party last week. John and David were there. They wrote home describing what they saw going on. Those letters are primary sources. Virginia and Vivian didn't go to the party, but they both talked to a lot of people who were there and they read the letters that John and David wrote home. Then each of them wrote you a note explaining what she thinks went on. The notes that Virginia and Vivian wrote are secondary sources, because they synthesize and interpret primary sources.

There are also tertiary sources. *Tertiary sources* are two steps removed from primary sources. The report that the policeman wrote about what went on at Judy's party, after he read the notes that Virginia and Vivian wrote, is a tertiary source. He was not there. He didn't talk to someone who was there. His information is thirdhand. His report synthesizes and interprets someone else's interpretation of other people's firsthand accounts. The book you have read for these research essay exercises is a secondary source. It draws on primary sources. The reviews of the book are tertiary sources. They interpret a secondary source: the book they review. Textbooks (such as this one) are also tertiary sources, because they synthesize secondary sources for use by teachers and students.

The informational note that you add to your descriptive outline should also list and explain the book's special features, if it has any, such as maps, charts, illustrations, appendices, important acknowledgments, an index, and so on.

(There is more about writing descriptive outlines in Part Three: Constructive Reading, p. 147. See also Practice Descriptive Outline: Long Essays, p. 168.)

☐ EXAMPLE DESCRIPTIVE OUTLINE OF A BOOK ─────────

Descriptive Outline of
Austin T. Turk,
Political Criminality

Eugene Benger

Political Criminality: The Defiance and Defense of Authority by Austin T. Turk defends the writer's position that a political crime is behavior that conflicts with the views of government officials who are empowered to define what crime is. That is, political criminality is a relative concept that is defined mainly by those in power, and every government's definition of what constitutes a crime is politically motivated. Turk states this position in the preface of the book and characterizes his purpose as being objective inquiry, not support of a particular view. In Chapter One he outlines his assumptions, the abstract principles on which his study is based. He defends his position in Chapters Two and Three. Chapter Four defends the rationale behind the studies presented in Chapters Two and Three and thus indirectly supports the book's position. Chapter Five concludes the book with another broad discussion of the issue.

Chapter One outlines abstract ideas rather than defending the writer's position directly and concretely. Many of the concepts introduced here are explained more fully in later chapters and used there to support Turk's position. First, the chapter sketches an ideal model of political organization explaining its purpose and processes. It also discusses the elements of a system of government that are responsible for establishing authority. Among these are "established jurisdiction" and "institutionalized policing." Turk uses both of these concepts later in the book to support his position by showing how they contribute to defining someone as a criminal. The chapter closes with a brief discussion of the difference between conventional, or civil and criminal, offenses and political offenses. This distinction too is given greater attention in later chapters. Chapter One, like all the other chapters, ends with a brief restatement of its contents under the subheading "Summary."

Chapter Two deals with the legal aspect of political criminality. It begins to defend the writer's position by illustrating a distinction between civil and criminal laws, such as incitement to riot and trespassing, and political criminal laws, such as, in the United States, the Alien and Sedition Acts and the Smith Act. Both of these laws outlawed statements and behavior that opposed established government policy. More importantly, however, besides demonstrating the overtly political aims of some laws, in this chapter Turk presents many examples showing that throughout history governments have even misinterpreted civil and criminal laws in order to punish people whose political views were in conflict with authorities.

Chapter Three focuses specifically on one aspect of the writer's position. Here Turk presents a catalogue of social deviance and lists characteristics of people involved in deviant behavior. The end of the chapter further illustrates his position by briefly stating the relationship between authorities and subjects, the two groups involved in the definition of criminality. The end of the chapter also serves as a transition to the next chapter by raising the issue of a government's response to resistance. The writer states his belief here that the way a government responds to resistance—in particular, the way it uses its police force—is the key to understanding political criminality.

Chapter Four discusses political policing at considerable length. The chapter describes different methods of policing. It gives many examples of the methods and effects of policing techniques such as terror, information control, and intimidation. Turk contends in this chapter that understanding policing is fundamental to understanding political criminality, because the way the government responds to deviant behavior is what labels someone who holds opposing views a political criminal. Consequently this chapter supports indirectly the position taken in the book.

Finally, Chapter Five puts much of the information given in the previous four chapters into a larger context of issues. Turk predicts the future success and failure of political organizations, possible changes in what motivates people to resist the government, and changes in methods of political policing. The chapter also adds to the summary sections at the end of each of the previous chapters a separate subheading entitled "Conclusion." In this final section, Turk returns to the broad, abstract discussion of society and civilization that he began with in Chapter One. □

▷EXERCISE 13   BOOK REVIEW: EVALUATIVE JUDGMENT

Write a five-hundred-word, three-paragraph review of the book you have read addressed to the other students in your class.

The reason for writing a review of the book is to consolidate the understanding you gained in writing a descriptive outline of it. Writing a review will also give you a better sense of what reviewers do, before you begin reading the work of professional reviewers for exercise 14. It will make you a better critic of the critics.

A good book review

1. tells what the book is about,
2. makes a judgment of the book's worth, and
3. defends that judgment.

Beyond this, some reviews also

4. introduce readers to the background of the book, the history of the subject, or the context of issues the book is related to.

Of course, you do not know as much about the subject of your book as the writer or as professional reviewers know. Some professional reviewers know the book's subject almost as well as the person who wrote the book.

But even though you don't know much more about the topic than you have learned in reading the book, you can still give your audience, the other students in your class, a fair estimate of the book based on careful reading.

The proposition of your review should evaluate the book. That does not mean that it should simply assert your opinion that the book is good or bad. To say that a book is good or bad only indicates whether or not you liked it. That is a factor in your opinion. But it is a statement of taste, not of judgment. You can defend it only by referring to yourself—what there is about you that would make you like or dislike it.

Instead, try to imagine what the other students in your class might want to know about the book or what they might get out of reading it. They want to know whether the book is interesting, useful, reliable, up-to-date, well organized, and well written. They may want to know if it will be reliable for a long time or will go out of date quickly. They may want to know if it is a complete and coherent study of the subject or treats only part of it or treats it in a fragmentary or incoherent way. They may want to know if the book supports its position thoughtfully and uses convincing evidence to explain or defend its position, or if it is shallow and thin.

Address the proposition of your review to questions like these. Then explore, explain, or defend your position by referring directly to the book itself.

In paragraph 1, introduce the proposition by describing the book and telling what it is about. Paraphrase the book's main points and explain briefly how the book is organized. For both, draw on your descriptive outline of the book.

COLLABORATIVE LEARNING

Task 1   Reading Aloud

Follow the instructions for reading essays aloud, p. 55.

Task 2   Review Exchange and Peer Conference

Follow the instructions for essay exchange and peer conference on p. 75.

☐ EXAMPLE BOOK REVIEW ────────────────────

Aspects of Political Crime

Eugene Benger

As its title suggests, Austin T. Turk's *Political Criminality: The Defiance and Defense of Authority* investigates how people have resisted governmental authority and how governments have defended their authority against that resistance. Political criminality, in Turk's view, does not describe actions of individuals. Rather, it describes the perceived threat that actions may pose to those in authority. To defend this position, Turk first explains various forms of authority, how they are asserted, and how they are legitimized in the eyes of people subject to them. Then he explains how governments use civil and criminal laws for political ends and stereotype those who challenge their authority by labeling them anarchists, rebels, and terrorists. Turk's most crucial point in defense of his position is that people who resist government authority do not possess a single unifying characteristic. All they have in common is that some governmental body labeled them criminals by reacting to them with force. But in discussing the political use of force—that is, using the police for political purposes—Turk's objectivity and fairness seem to take a back seat. He begins to manipulate evidence to support his anti-establishment position. Thus, although the book succeeds in presenting with great clarity a new point of view on the subject, its one-sided discussion of government motives in establishing and enforcing a legal system is unconvincing.

Turk's initial discussion of the reasons that human beings establish political organizations, or governments, is detached, logical, and rational. He begins with the contention that "people are inevitably involved in intergroup struggles over who shall have what resources in a finite world" (35). Governments exist to distribute limited resources. The legal system of every government, furthermore, can be divided into laws that define social crimes—civil and criminal law—and laws that define offenses against the government—political crimes. Turk then outlines the aims and wide-ranging powers of laws pertaining to political crimes. In this outline, his facts are well established and his evidence dismaying. Then he makes the charge that all governments misuse civil and criminal laws in order to persecute or punish individuals who hold anti-government opinions. Turk provides many examples of misuse. He cites the history of the United States labor and civil rights laws; England's Black Act of 1723, which made trespassing, poaching, looting, and smuggling capital offenses; legalized racism in South Africa; and the practice in the Soviet Union and elsewhere of labeling dissenters insane and locking them up. All these are clear examples of how governments use basic laws against civil and criminal offenses to achieve political ends (41–51). With these examples, Turk convincingly supports his view that the definition of political criminality depends on a government's response to deviant behavior.

His argument begins to go astray, though, when he insists that "there simply is nothing empirically distinctive about *all* political 'criminals'. . . . Their only common attribute is that they are targets of political policing" (114). Here Turk begins his assault on institutionalized policing in very broad terms, while portraying all criminals as political criminals and therefore as unfortunate victims of government cruelty and rigidity. Indeed, the very first sentence of Chapter Four declares flatly that "All policing is political" (115). Throughout the rest of Chapter Four, Turk portrays police units of various kinds as agents of the state involved in control functions such as gathering intelligence, controlling information, intimidating the general public, and neutralizing offenders (117). Turk would presumably defend this portrayal as simply "accurate," but it is by no means unbiased. To his credit, he does include opposing views. But he presents them half-heartedly, and dismisses each one quickly with the use of more evidence to the contrary. With the strong bias shown in this technique and in the wild, sweeping accusation that all governmental authorities are concerned with controlling people rather than serving them, Turk begins to lose his audience. If we were to adopt his bleak and pessimistic view of government, and of human beings, his readers are likely to say to themselves that there is no point of anyone protesting, petitioning, voting, or in any other way participating in public life.

WORK CITED

Turk, Austin T. *Political Criminality: The Defiance and Defense of Authority.* Beverly Hills: Sage, 1982.

▷ EXERCISE 14   REPORT ON A REVIEW OF THE REVIEWS: SIMPLE SYNTHESIS

Write a five-hundred-word, three-paragraph essay in which you report what the reviews had to say about the book you have read.

In exercises 12 and 13 you focused entirely on the book that you have read, first by outlining it and then by reviewing it. In this exercise you are beginning to move away from the book you have read by examining its context. But since the part of the context you are examining is the way the book was received, the focus of your attention still remains very close to the book itself.

You can now begin to see how this series of research exercises progressively assimilates and synthesizes knowledge by enlarging the scope of the conversation. You began in exercises 12 and 13 by paying close attention to your original source, the book you chose to read. In this exercise you take the first of two steps toward finding that source a place as one among many sources for what you yourself will have to say on the same or a related subject.

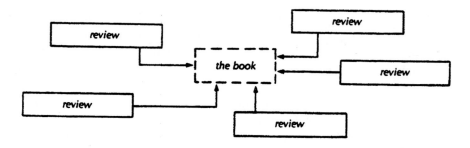

RESEARCH: READING THE REVIEWS, GETTING READY TO WRITE

To collect reviews of the book you have read, consult standard bibliographical works in print or online. A reference librarian will help you make the best use of these basic tools. (See p. 273 for sources listing book reviews.)

When you do any kind of research, get into the habit of recording basic information about a source even before you read it. Before you read each review, write down the following:

- the reviewer's name if it is given, and spell it correctly
- the title of the review if it has one, complete and correct
- the title of the periodical in which the review appears
- the date of the issue
- the inclusive pages on which the review appears (that is, the number of the first and last pages of the review)

Then read each review twice. The first time you read a review, don't take notes. Get the gist of it: the position that the review takes and the way it supports that position. While you are reading it the first time, try to answer the following questions:

1. **What are the reviewer's qualifications** for reviewing a book on this topic? Some review publications include a note giving the reviewer's qualifications. If there is no note, maybe you can find the writer's name online. Try Google.

2. **What kind of audience did the reviewer have in mind?** Was the review written for readers who already know quite a bit about the subject of the book, or was it written for readers who probably don't know much about it?

3. What kind of publication was the review written for? Does the review or the source it appears in have a political, religious, or intellectual slant that might affect the way reviewers might evaluate a book on this topic? How can you tell? Is the source published for a particular professional audience? Is it published for the general public?

4. Does the review stick to reviewing the book, or does it go off on tangents? If it does digress, can you discover why?

5. Does the review agree with other reviews you have read? If two or more of the reviews you have found take opposing positions on your book, can you account for that difference of opinion? If two or more agree, can you decide why?

In light of your answers to these questions, read each review a second time. The second time you read the review, take notes. Use a separate note card for each note. On the first card, write out the name of the reviewer, the source the review appears in, the date of the issue, and the pages the review appears on. Then on other cards copy out accurately any passages in the review that you think are interesting or revealing, and, most important, copy out the passage that you think states most succinctly the reviewer's evaluation of the book. Also copy passages that support the reviewer's position. Label each of these cards with the reviewer's name (or the name of the source) and the page where the passage you quote or refer to appears.

Finally, make some notes about what the reviewer says or seems to imply about the context of issues in which the book was written.

Why does the reviewer think the book was written?

What questions or problems does the reviewer think the book addresses?

What questions does the reviewer think the book leaves unanswered?

If you label each card with the reviewer's name or the name of the source and the page, you will be able to cite the source of the passage if you decide to use it in anything you write. You will also be able to go back later and check to make sure that you have quoted accurately.

SYNTHESIS: WRITING A REVIEW OF THE REVIEWS

Up to this point you have been gathering material. The next step is to decide on a tentative proposition for your review of the reviews. Your proposition should say how the book was received.

To write this proposition, reread the notes you wrote when you were reading the reviews. Sort them out according to ideas and attitudes. This sorting will be a lot easier if you have made each note on an individual card or slip of paper instead of notebook pages.

Classify your notes. Try sorting them in several different ways to see which seems to make most sense to you. Are the reviews generally favorable or are they all generally unfavorable? Do the reviewers criticize details in the book or do they criticize the book's basic position? Perhaps there is a majority opinion about the book that most reviewers agree on, and a minority opinion that only a few of them express.

Your proposition should synthesize the reviewers' responses, as you see them. It should state your view of the reviews, how it seems to you that the book was received. The position you take should be one that you can explore, explain, and defend with the material you have gathered from reading the book and its reviews.

Use one of the forms of defense and explanation that you learned in essay exercises 5 through 9. Drawing on the notes you have taken, document what you say with references to the book and to the reviews. For the rules of documentation, use a standard guide, such as the *MLA Handbook for Writers of Research Papers*, the *Publication Manual of the American Psychological Association*, or the instructions on documentation in a standard writer's handbook.

In paragraph 1 of your review of the reviews, introduce your proposition by describing the book more or less as you did in the introduction to your own review for exercise 13. But this time you can go a bit beyond just paraphrasing the book and describing how it is organized. Now you can also say something about the book's context of issues and the writer's qualifications for writing it.

Give your essay the kind of finished quality that you learned in writing earlier exercises:

- Check the transitions.
- Write a descriptive outline and make adjustments.
- Read the essay aloud and revise it.
- Make the final copy.

USING QUOTATIONS

Why use quotations? You usually quote what other writers have written in order to support the position you have taken in your own essay. So it is important to explain why the quotation you are using is relevant to the point you are making.

To make this relevance clear,

1. introduce the quotation,
2. quote it accurately,
3. cite the source of the quotation, and
4. explain how it is related to what you are saying.

When you introduce a quotation, tell your reader what to look for in it by saying briefly what the relationship is between the quotation and what you are saying at that point in the essay. After you have given the quotation, explain that relationship in greater detail.

You will use quotations better if you see them from the reader's point of view. As a reader, when you see a quotation coming, you wonder why you should take the trouble to read it. You feel that you have a right to know how it fits in and what idea you should keep in mind while you are reading it. After reading the quotation, you want to be told what the quotation's significance is in the essay you are reading, so that you will feel that reading the quotation was really worthwhile. All three of these elements should be present in some form whenever you quote.

Generally speaking, there are four ways to use quotations. The simplest and easiest way to use quoted evidence is with **full formal reference.**

Suppose, for example, you are writing an essay explaining this writing textbook, *A Short Course in Writing,* and you want to use some material from the book's introduction. In fact, you want to quote some passages from the first two paragraphs in the introduction:

The purpose of this short course in writing is to help students learn to read and write better through collaborative learning. Collaborative learning assumes that reading and writing are not solitary, individual activities, but social and collaborative ones. When we read and write we are never alone, although we may seem to be. We are always in the company of communities of other readers and writers whose language and interests we share.

Collaborative learning makes this social, collaborative nature of reading and writing central to college and university education. This book, based on collaborative learning principles, turns writing classrooms into collaborative classrooms by making them active, constructive communities of readers and writers and by making students' own writing the most important text in the course.

To make full formal reference to parts of these paragraphs, introduce the material, quote it, cite the source, and explain its relevance. Indicate anything you leave out of the quotation with an ellipsis (. . .), and indicate anything you insert into the quotation or any other change you make in it with square brackets ([]). Here is how your paragraph might read.

introducing the quotation	In order to help students learn to read and write better by working collaboratively with their peers, *A Short Course in Writing* assumes "that reading and writing are not solitary, individual activities, but social and collaborative
insertion	ones." "Based on [the author's] collaborative learning
	principles," the book helps turn "writing classrooms into
ellipsis	collaborative classrooms by making them . . . communi-
citation	ties of readers and writers" (Bruffee 1). This statement of
explanation	the book's underlying assumption is important because it
	places the book in the context of the recent developments
	in educational thought that regard knowledge as a social
	construct rather than a mental entity.

WORK CITED

Bruffee, Kenneth A. *A Short Course in Writing.* 4th ed. New York: Pearson Longman, 2007.

Another way to make a formal reference is to integrate a quotation into a sentence of your own. Introduce or explain the quotation and quote important parts of it as part of a single sentence.

introducing integrated quotations	In order to help students learn to read and write better, *A Short Course in Writing* assumes that reading and writing are "social and collaborative" activities. The
ellipsis	book's assumption that "reading and writing are . . . social, collaborative acts" shows its relationship to recent developments in educational thought that regard knowledge as a social construct rather than a mental entity
citation	(Bruffee 1).

You can also present quoted evidence in the form of a **partial paraphrase**. In a partial paraphrase you quote some material and paraphrase the rest in your own words. In this case, the three elements—introduction, quotation, and explanation—may be hard to distinguish. Their effect, however, should still be clear.

introduction	*A Short Course in Writing* teaches students to write by organizing them to work together. By making "reading
partial paraphrase	and writing . . . social and collaborative acts" in that way, the book demonstrates that it is part of recent developments in educational thought based on the view that
citation	knowledge is a social construct rather than a mental entity (Bruffee 1).

You can also refer in passing to passages in material you have read, without quoting or paraphrasing them. You are likely to refer to material in passing when you are making a subordinate point or when you merely want to make an assertion without explaining or defending it further. In this case, you cite the relevant passage with a page number or some other designation, so that readers can find the passage you are referring to if they want to follow it up.

reference in passing	*A Short Course in Writing* contributes to recent developments in educational thought based on the view that knowledge is a social construct by organizing students to
citation	work together as readers and writers (Bruffee 1).

Whenever you quote, use only as much of the passage as you really need in order to make your point. If your readers have to wade through a long quotation only to discover that only a few words of it are relevant to what you are saying, they are likely to lose interest.

Make sure that you explain the quotation's relevance to what you are saying. Nothing you quote is valuable for its own sake. No quotation says what you want to say better than you can say it. If it doesn't help you make your point, don't quote it.

(See example essays on pp. 220, 232, and 279.)

CITATION GUIDE

A *citation* is a statement, usually abbreviated or in code, that refers to the source of the passage you have quoted or paraphrased. Whenever you quote or paraphrase what someone else has written in an essay of your own, you have to tell readers where it came from. That is, you have to cite your source.

The general rule for citing the source of any quoted or paraphrased passage is this:

> *At the end of the sentence in which the quotation occurs, put in parentheses the writer's last name and the page number of the source. At the end of the essay, list alphabetically by the writer's name the books and articles you have referred to in parentheses.*

This general rule has to be varied in many ways under different conditions. Standard form manuals such as the *MLA Handbook of Research Papers* or the *Publication Manual of the American Psychological Association* explain these variations in detail.

For example, in the following paragraph, every parenthetical citation refers to an item in the list that follows the paragraph.

Attempts to apply collaborative learning to teaching writing (for example, Bruffee, *Short Course* 1) originate with an effort in Britain during the late 1950s to help medical students learn diagnostic judgment through conversation (Abercrombie 112–115). The basic idea is that we learn judgment by learning first how to converse about choices and decisions, and then we internalize that kind of conversation as thought. Many writing courses based on collaboration assume that writing, like other communication media is social, not private, and is therefore related to conversation. Many collaborative writing courses also assume that because writing is a social activity it plays an important role in liberal education (Bruffee, "Liberal Education" 109–110). Many of the ideas underlying collaborative learning are traceable to those of John Dewey and Thomas Kuhn, but probably the most pervasive influence is Richard Rorty's notion that "we understand knowledge when we understand the social justification of belief" (Rorty 170).

WORKS CITED

Abercrombie, M. L. J. *The Anatomy of Judgment* Harmondsworth: Penguin, 1969.

Bruffee, Kenneth A. *Collaborative Learning: Higher Education, Interdependence, and the Authority of Knowledge.* 2nd ed. Baltimore: Johns Hopkins University Press, 1999.

———. "Liberal Education and the Social Justification of Belief." *Liberal Education* 68, no. 2 (1982): 95–114.

———. *A Short Course in Writing.* 4th ed. New York: Harper-Collins, 1993.

Rorty, Richard. *Philosophy and the Mirror of Nature*. Oxford: Blackwell, 1990.

Notice that each citation in parentheses includes only enough information for readers to find the relevant source listed in the works cited.

HOW TO FIND BOOK REVIEWS

To locate reviews of a particular book, you need to know

- the full name of the author,
- the exact title of the book, and
- the year the book was originally published.

To find a book's publication or copyright date, look on the front and back of the title page. If both a publication and a copyright date are given, and they differ, use the earlier date. If you do not have the book with you, check your library's catalogue or ask a librarian for help in finding it.

Once you have the author's name, the correct title, and the publication or copyright date, look the book up in more than one index, because you cannot count on any index to be complete. Since indexes differ a lot in the way they are organized, you may need to read the introduction to each one you choose to find out how to use it.

Many book reviews can be located in online periodical indexes. There are a number of online book review indexes, such as the *Book Review Digest*. Furthermore, many general or subject-specialized periodical indexes, such as *Academic Search Premier* or *Social Science Abstracts*, include book reviews either as citations or full text.

ONLINE SOURCES

Most students know how to make Internet search engines do what they want them to do. But many students still have a lot to learn about how to make search engines give them what they need. Students need reliable sources. The Internet can provide many reliable sources. But it can also provide many unreliable sources. Everybody knows that the Internet is full of nonsense, because it is a free medium. Anybody can put almost anything online.

One reliable way to be sure that the sources you use are reliable is to ask for help from a reference librarian. Reference librarians know what book reviews, books, and other paper and online sources the library holds. They also know how to go about discerning reliable from unreliable online sources. Whenever you think you may not quite know what you're doing, ask a reference librarian for some help.

Those of us who aren't trained reference resource librarians can learn the basics of telling reliable sources from unreliable ones. To do that, we need to know what makes a reliable source "reliable" and what makes an unreliable source "unreliable." One way to learn how to answer questions about the reliability of sources is to compare some of the hundreds of reliable sources available online. What do they have in common. In what respects do they differ?

Here are a *very* few of the hundreds of popular, reliable sources accessible on the Web.

GENERAL SOURCES

These are sources that many people turn to first. Much of the information they provide is the kind that might be found in an encyclopedia or other tertiary source. They may be online or published in book form.

Academic Search Premier (EBSCO Host)
The New York Times Book Review Index, 1896–1970
The New York Times Index, 1970–current
The New York Times Historical Edition 1851–2002, *through* ProQuest
The *New York Times,* full text, *through* LexisNexis
Book Review Digest
Book Review Index Plus
Readers' Guide to Periodical Literature [1890–1982]
Book reviews in the academic disciplines (English, chemistry, psychology, etc.): ask a reference librarian to direct you to these.

Another way to take a cursory first look at a topic before moving on to scholarly sources is to read some nonscholarly sites that tend to be carefully written. An example is the reviews that accompany many of the books on Amazon.com. But don't stop there. Once you have a general idea of what some readers think about the book, move on to scholarly data bases. They will lead you to scholarly reviews and to other scholarly sources.

SPECIALIZED SOURCES

Many subject and research areas have periodical databases that include book reviews. Here are a few in fields that undergraduate students might be likely to research.

American History and Life
Anthropology Abstracts
Alternative Press Index
Art Index
Biological and Medical Sciences
Contemporary Women's Issues
ERIC (education and related issues)
Film Literature Index
Health Reference Center
Historical Abstracts
Medline (medicine)
RILM (abstracts of music)
Sociological Abstracts

For more sources in these and other academic disciplines ask a reference librarian.

You can improve your ability to distinguish reliable online sources from unreliable ones by becoming familiar with the scholarly research tools your library provides. Look at two scholarly sources and ask yourself how they differ and what they have in common. For example, *American History and Life* and *Biological and Medical Sciences* differ in that one contains citations to research articles in history and allied fields, while the other contains citations to research articles in biology and medicine. But while they are about very different fields of study, they both contain citations to scholarly research articles, they both link to full text when it is available, and they are both subscription sources and require authentication outside the library. These scholarly sources differ from a general Web search (for example at Yahoo or Google) in that the search results are limited to only citations to full-text articles, while a general Web search will give you some scholarly results along with a large number of sites that vary a great deal in their accuracy and authority.

Please keep in mind as you learn to use online scholarly sources that any list of sources can become outdated overnight. Some people say that we live in the "information age." What we know and how we understand and use what we know changes rapidly and constantly. Often that new data is instantly available electronically. As you work on a research project, consult a resource librarian frequently to make sure that you haven't missed something.

Sources such as those listed here also have other uses. Besides locating reviews of important books, they can lead you to periodical literature—that is, journal articles published by academic and professional associations. Recent issues of these journals can tell you what has been going on in scholarly studies and scientific research for many years in the past, and they can also bring you up to date on what's going on in the field right now.

Take, for example, Betty Friedan's famous book *The Feminine Mystique*. You can read the book. You can read reviews of the book written when the book was first published. You can read reviews of the book written for the twenty-fifth anniversary of the book's publication, a quarter-century later. You can also find scholarly studies of the issues that the book raised, such as military, religious, medical, and political careers for women. You can find out how people felt about those issues many years ago. And you can find out how attitudes toward them, social behavior, and goals have changed since the book was first published.

COLLABORATIVE LEARNING

Task 1   Using Bibliographic Resources

Working in a group of two or three, list the online sources available in your library that are relevant to group-members' topics. Each group pick one source as a sample and write a short paragraph about it. The paragraph should

1. state the format of the source (the kind of source it is—print, CD-ROM, mainframe, online, etc.);
2. list the kinds of bibliographical information it provides (subject-specialized or general, citations or full text, etc.); and write out a brief sample of each kind.

Task 2   Finding Book Reviews

Working in a group of two or three, choose one book that is relevant to a group-member's topic.

1. Working together, write a short paragraph that states the full name of the author, the complete, exact title of the book, and the year the book was originally published.

2. Using the author's name, the book's title, and the book's publication date, look the book up in Info Trac and two relevant specialized indexes. Working together, write a short paragraph comparing the information that the three indexes provide. Since indexes
differ in the way they are organized, the index introductions may
help you use them. Your librarian can also help.

3. Group recorders read aloud to the class the information each
group has collected and groups respond to questions.

Task 3   Reading a Review

Working in groups of five or six, have one person read aloud a review
that one student in the group has found (or a review chosen by the
teacher, or the example review given in this section).

Then work toward a consensus in answering the following questions:

1. What are the reviewer's qualifications for reviewing a book on
this topic?

2. Who is the audience of the review? Does it seem to be written for
readers who already know quite a bit about the subject of the
book, or is it written for readers who probably don't know much
about it?

3. Does the review (or the publication it appears in) have a political, religious, or intellectual slant that could affect the way reviewers might evaluate a book on this topic? How can you tell?

4. Does the review digress or go off on tangents, or does it stick to
reviewing the book? If it does go off on tangents, can you guess
what the writer's motive might have been?

5. What is the reviewer's evaluation of the book? Underline the
passage that states the reviewer's evaluation of the book most
succinctly. Describe how passages that support the reviewer's
position are organized. Then answer each of the following questions in a single sentence:
   • Why was the book written?
   • What questions or problems does it address?
   • What questions does it leave unanswered?

6. What does the review say or imply is the book's context of issues? Underline passages that state or imply the book's context
of issues.

Finally, have the recorder for each group read aloud the answers that the group has given to each question. The groups should then negotiate differences among these answers and try to arrive at a consensus that satisfies the whole class.

Task 4   Reading Aloud

Follow the instructions for reading essays aloud, p. 55.

Task 5   Review Exchange and Peer Conference

Follow the instructions for essay exchange and peer conference on p. 75.

☐ EXAMPLE REVIEW OF THE REVIEWS —————

Reviews of Austin Turk's
Political Criminality

Eugene Benger

The chief concern that Austin T. Turk's *Political Criminality* addresses is what Turk regards as the unending struggle between authority and resistance to authority. In investigating this phenomenon, Turk, a professor of sociology and criminology, argues that living and surviving inherently involve conflict between members of a society, because every person in a society tries to control as many of the scarce resources (land, food, water) as life offers. In order to distribute these resources more fairly and thus maximize the possibilities of life, people form political organizations or governments. As Turk points out, however, simply forming a government does not in itself solve the problem of equitable distribution. As a result, people who don't see their chances in life improving under the prevailing government may defy its authority. As Turk demonstrates with historical evidence, governments try to maintain their authority by suppressing resistance. He investigates who resists, how they resist, and how governments respond to their resistance, in particular how they use police. He concludes that political policing often involves illegal methods. But he also concludes that governments that allow resistance—that is, democratic governments—are the most likely to survive. Because it supports this conclusion thoroughly, *Political Criminality* received positive reviews.

An important reason for the generally favorable response to Turk's book is his effective use of examples. He takes his evidence from a broad range of sources, including "illustrations from class, racial, and civil libertarian struggles" (Jeffery 551). Some critics focus on the way Turk's examples support the various parts of his argument. One remarks that his examples are "carefully selected" to illustrate "how civil and criminal laws . . . have been used to suppress political activity" (Moran 429). Another critic comments on another successful way Turk uses his data: he "provides useful reviews of the empirical evidence concerning the demographics or dissent, disobedience, evasion, and violence, and the techniques of what he calls political policing" (Sarat 516). Thus, Turk makes both his general statement of important concepts and his argument that civil and criminal laws have been used for political purposes more effective by extensive illustration. It is this use of illustration in particular that leads one critic to applaud the book as "remarkably lucid" (Moran 429).

In addition to the book's clarity and specificity, critics also point out the importance of Turk's theme. They all agree that he "provides a rich theoretical discussion of a highly significant subject" (Lee 233). Indeed, Turk's basic premise is rooted deeply in theoretical concepts such as the human effort to improve one's lot in life, the reasons that human beings form governments, and the relationship between governments and the governed. In this respect, he "provides a useful summary of the familiar conflict perspective in political sociology" (Sarat 516). Turk's critics agree with him that this "conflict perspective" is important because "political organization inevitably generates unequal life chances among different groups of people, and struggle over authority is a constant" in every society (Jeffery 551). The book's thematic importance, clarity, and firm theoretical basis lead his critics to conclude that, as one of them puts it, "Turk has succeeded well in his aim 'to promote the scientific investigation of political criminality, rather than . . . partisan commitment' " (Jeffery 552). □

WORKS CITED

Jeffery, Ina A. Rev. of Austin T. Turk, *Political Criminality: The Defiance and Defense of Authority. The American Political Science
Review* 77 (1983): 551–552.

Lee, Alfred McClung. Rev. of Austin T. Turk, *Political Criminality:
The Defiance and Defense of Authority. Annals of the American
Academy of Political and Social Science* (1983): 232–233.

Moran, Richard. Rev. of Austin T. Turk, *Political Criminality: The
Defiance and Defense of Authority. Contemporary Sociology* 12
(1983): 428–429.

Sarat, Austin. Rev. of Austin T. Turk, *Political Criminality: The Defiance and Defense of Authority. Journal of Politics* 45 (1983):
515–517.

Turk, Austin T. *Political Criminality: The Defiance and Defense of
Authority.* Beverly Hills: Sage, 1982.

▷EXERCISE 15   REPORT ON THE CONTEXT OF ISSUES: COMPLEX SYNTHESIS

Write a five-hundred-word, three-paragraph essay in which you report on the context of issues of the book you have read.

Like exercise 14, this exercise enlarges the scope of your research by
examining other aspects of the book's context.

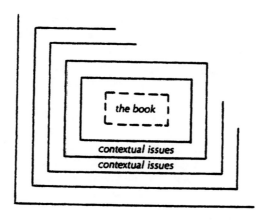

In exercise 13 you explained how one reader (you) responded to the book. In exercise 14 you explained how some other readers (those who reviewed it) responded to the book. In exercise 15 your job is to explain what many of those who decide to read the book may have on their minds before they read it, and the direction their thinking may take as a result of reading it. That is the role this exercise plays in the progressive assimilation and synthesis of knowledge taking place in this series of research exercises. It is the second step in enlarging the scope of the conversation that began in exercise 14. It is another step toward making your first source, the book you chose to read, just one among several sources you can draw upon when, in exercise 16, you write about the same or a related subject.

One purpose of the exercise, therefore, is to give you another chance to synthesize diverse material. To synthesize means to give form to disorganized facts and ideas. You synthesize diverse material by focusing on a single way of looking at it, a way that, from your particular point of view, points to similarities and relationships. This exercise is also related to exercises 10 and 11 because it is concerned with the way a statement (whether it is a single sentence or a whole book) gains significance when it is related to a context of issues. To understand the purpose of exercise 15 from this point of view, it may help to reread Speaking Other People's Language, p. 191, and also William Perry's "Examsmanship and the Liberal Arts," p. 343.

In order to determine what the book's readers may have on their minds while they are reading it—its context of issues—you will have to examine a variety of sources. These sources include the reviews of the book that you used for exercise 14. But they also include sources that the writer of the book acknowledges in the book's preface, notes, and bibliography or works cited section. In examining these sources, you are enlarging still further your acquaintance with the book's "family," the community of readers and writers who engage in conversation about topics related to the book's topic, and who talk about those topics in the kind of language used in the book.

For example, suppose you chose to read a book about waste disposal: sewage and trash. Any book on waste disposal has to face several questions that people are likely to have on their minds. One is, If we recycle, what do we do with all those newspapers, cans, and bottles when we get them collected? Another is, What are we going to do with all the rest of the trash we produce that we can't recycle? And a third is, What effect is the vast expense involved in controlling waste and disposing of it safely going to have on our economy?

The broadest context of issues implied in these questions includes (1) relations between any government and the individuals it governs (issues such as freedom, duty, and personal integrity), and (2) relations between one government and another (since trash is an international problem).

The reviews of the hypothetical book you read on waste disposal would probably praise or condemn the book at least in part according to the way it addresses questions like these. That is, in the course of evaluating a book, reviewers often give you a good idea of its limits and the implications of what it says, what it didn't say that the reviewer wanted it to say, and what it made the reviewer think further about. So for this exercise you should draw upon your knowledge of the issues that you gained in reading the reviews.

But you also have to go beyond the reviews to look at other sources. This is where you get to act most like a detective. Begin your sleuthing with the acknowledgments page or preface of the book you have read. If the writer names a book that influenced him or her before writing the book, find that book and skim it. To *skim* a book, you read the table of contents carefully, read the first few paragraphs of each chapter to get the gist of what the book is about, and then read the chapters that you think are particularly relevant to your purpose, in this case, relevant to the book you read for this set of exercises. The question to answer while you are skimming is, What is there about this book that might have influenced the writer of the book you read?

If the writer of your book lists other influential writers but doesn't mention what they wrote, see if you can find out what they have written that may be relevant to your book. Decide what there is about what they say that might influence someone to write further on the topic.

Then read through the footnotes or endnotes of the book you read. Sometimes writers mention their debts in notes instead of in acknowledgment pages. Even more interesting from the point of view of a detective is that in their notes writers sometimes contradict other writers, argue with them, or attack them. If you find conflict of this sort you may have discovered some negative influences as well as some positive ones. Your book may not have been written just to extend or fulfill some other writer's work. It may also have been written in part to attack or correct some other writer's work. The plot thickens.

There are two ways you can write the essay for this exercise. One way is to explain the issues that pertain to your book and how writers tend to differ on those issues. In your introduction, classify the issues and choose one of them as the most important one.

In paragraphs 2 and 3 explain the conflicting views on that issue. If there seem to be two main points of view on the issue, explain one point of view in paragraph 2 and the other in paragraph 3. If there seem to be many points of view on the issue, use Nestorian Order to explain what you think are the less important or weaker positions in paragraph 2 and the most important or strongest position in paragraph 3.

Or, if you prefer, you can explain how the issues that pertain to your book may be subdivided or classified. In your introduction, explain several ways the issues might be classified. Then choose one of these as the most suggestive or informative way to classify them. In paragraphs 2 and 3 explain why.

Whichever alternative you choose, keep in mind that what you are doing is *reporting* on the issues. You are not taking a position of your own on one of the issues. You will be able to do that in the next essay, exercise 16. In this essay report the positions other writers take on the issues. For example, if *Political Criminality* was the book you had read for these exercises, your essay exercise 15 would not say what you think about why people tend to resist the policies of established governments. You would save that for exercise 16. Instead, your exercise 15 essay would explain, as the example essay does, what other writers think about that issue.

COLLABORATIVE LEARNING

Task 1   Reading Aloud

Follow the instructions for reading essays aloud, p. 55.

Task 2   Report Exchange and Peer Conference

Follow the instructions for essay exchange and peer conference on p. 75.

☐ EXAMPLE ESSAY ───────────────────────

The Issues Surrounding
Political Criminality

Eugene Benger

Most people today would agree that some form of structured, formal government is necessary for survival. Without some way to control people's emotions and actions, life would be chaotic. But although most people support the institution of government, they also support, with equal enthusiasm, individual liberty. In this seeming contradiction lies a basic problem faced by many modern societies: how to reconcile individual rights with the rights of society as a whole. In his book, *Political Criminality*, Austin Turk investigates the history, politics, and sociology of several theories of individualism and the state, and he makes some important points about the nature of political organization. Since the resources needed to sustain life are limited, he says, human beings are continually engaged in conflict over controlling the distribution of those resources. We form governments in order to make that distribution as equitable as possible. But true equity is hard to attain. So the conflict continues, not so much among individuals as between two clearly defined forces, established governments and those who do resist their policies. People resist the policies of established governments, promoting their own aims, because they feel left out: they do not see much chance of their own lives improving as a result of those government policies. If we are to cope at all effectively with this tendency of people to resist the policies of established government, we at least have to understand the issues that underlie it.

One way to understand these issues is from the point of view of individual liberty. Western history and tradition provide a basic definition of this hard-to-define term. Traditionally, individual liberty means that human beings have inherent freedom of action which, if allowed free reign, will produce a free society. But this generalization usually leads to two questions. First, to what extent, if any, can the state limit individual liberty for the sake of society as a whole? In answering this question, some say that individual interests are usually selfish and arrogant. They should be sacrificed when necessary to satisfy the needs of society at large. Opposing this point of view, others, such as the nineteenth-century British statesman and philosopher John Stuart Mill, believe that individual liberty should be limited only if in exercising it a person would harm another person. Mill supports this broad notion of individuality and diversity because "mankind are greater gainers by suffering each other to live as seems good to themselves, than by compelling each to live as seems good to the rest" (155). This belief, however, raises the second question: Can a better society as a whole result just from benefiting individual members of that society? Those who answer yes say that "something truly new and magnificent can only be a product of great individuality" (Szczepanski 465). Individuality leads to creativity, because people's morals and ideas are so diverse that creative ideas are almost inevitable. The more ideas and the greater variety of ideas, the greater the benefit to society. The purpose of governmental power is to guarantee individual liberty so that this process of fertile growth can occur.

The other way to understand the conflict between the individual and society focuses on the institutionalized form of society we call government or the state. In practice, it says, the real purpose of government is never to guarantee individual liberty but to stay in power. Writers who support this view use historical evidence to show that older forms of political organization gave power to established, institutionalized groups such as churches or ruling families. And they show that modern governments transfer power to the individual as a citizen of the state only to make the individual "the object of state activity," so as to use individual independence and freedom "like other objects of value" (Mayer 193, 195; Meyer 67). This happens because even in democratically elected governments, "actions, decisions, and behavior flow from [the rulers'] internal, personal characteristics and not situations, structures, or relationships" (Hall 90). As a result, even modern governments that preach the gospel of individuality turn it into a self-deceiving, "distorting, alienating, and self-defeating" force (Hall 92). In support of this position, writers cite, for example, a classic study of blue collar workers who, even when they recognize that they have had no influence on the decision that their lives will not change, blame themselves for not moving up on the social and economic ladder (Hall 91). □

WORKS CITED

Hall, Peter M. "Individualism and Social Problems: A Critique and an Alternative." *Journal of Applied Behavioral Science* 19 (1983): 85–94.

Mayer, Karl Ulrich, and Urs Schoepflin. "The State and the Life Course." *Annual Review of Sociology* 15 (1989): 187–209.

Meyer, J.W. "The World Polity and the Authority of the Nation State." In G. M. Thomas, et al, *Institutional Structure: Constituting State, Society, and the Individual*. Newbury Park: Sage, 1987. Quoted in Mayer, 194–195.

Mill, John Stuart. "On Liberty." In *Essays on Politics and Society*, Collected Works of John Mill, vol. 8, ed. J. M. Robson. Toronto: Univ. of Toronto Press, 1977. Quoted in *The Shaping of the Modern World: From the Enlightenment to the Present*, 2nd ed. New York: Brooklyn College Press, 1987.

Szczepanski, Jan. "Individuality and Society." *Impact of Science on Society* 31 (1981): 461–466.

Turk, Austin T. *Political Criminality: The Defiance and Defense of Authority*. Beverly Hills: Sage, 1982.

▷ EXERCISE 16   ESSAY: JUDGMENTAL SYNTHESIS

Write a seven-hundred- to eight-hundred-word, four-paragraph essay (introduction, two paragraphs of exploration, explanation, and defense, plus an ending). In this essay, take a position of your own on a topic related to the book you have read or to its context of issues, and draw on your reading to defend your position.

In this exercise, as in exercises 14 and 15, your first source, the book you chose to read, becomes one among several sources for what you want to say yourself on the same subject or a related one. In exercises 12 and 13 you focused on reading and evaluating one source. In exercise 14 you continued to evaluate that source, but did so by drawing together and synthesizing what other people had to say about it—the reviewers. In exercise 15 you explored some of the concerns that many of those who decide to read the book might have on their minds before they read it and the influence that reading the book might have on their thinking. Step-by-step you have assimilated and synthesized knowledge that was new to you by enlarging the scope of the conversation that you became involved in when you read the book that you chose.

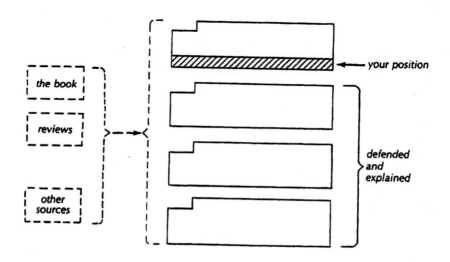

The four-paragraph essay you write for this exercise is similar in form to the one you wrote for essay exercise 11. The major difference is that this time you are far better informed about your topic than you were then. For that essay you drew on what you already happen to know. For this essay you have been researching related topics for several weeks. You not only have more information at hand, but you also know a good deal about how that information is shaped by different contexts of issues and what the different points of view are that people can take toward it.

For this essay you may reuse any material you have already used in the essays you wrote for exercises 13 through 15. You will notice that the writer of the example essay "Has Individuality Run Amok?" (p. 289) has done this. He has formulated a position of his own on one of the issues that arose in his reading for this series of exercises. As a result, his final essay is quite different from the earlier essays in the series. It accomplishes quite a different purpose, and it demonstrates that the writer's views have changed and have become much better informed as a result of his research reading and writing.

Just as you are finding new ways in this essay to use the research that you have already done, you may want to do some more reading and find some new material. Footnotes and acknowledgments in the books and articles you have read so far can lead you in new directions and provide new evidence and new ideas to draw upon. For this essay, use anything you know or can find out that will help make your position interesting and convincing.

Write a well-organized, well-expressed essay on a subject you have become very familiar with in the past several weeks. Because you are taking a position of your own, and because you know a great deal about the subject, you may find this essay the most interesting and exciting to write of all the essays you have written so far. You will find yourself writing with a good deal of confidence and self-assurance.

Keep in mind, though, that you now know quite a bit about something your readers probably do not know much about. Explain your position clearly and readably. Teach your readers what you know. Explore your experience and knowledge, draw generalizations, explain and defend your position in a way that will make it interesting and meaningful to other people. Relate your ideas clearly, linking sentences to other sentences, paragraphs to other paragraphs, and everything in the essay to your proposition. Think hard, write well, and document what you say thoroughly and accurately. And remember the process of writing from the inside out that you have learned:

Decide on a subject.

Decide on a proposition.

Defend or explain the proposition.

Write an introduction.

Write a meaningful ending.

Check the transitions.

Write a descriptive outline and make adjustments.

Read the essay aloud and revise it.

Make the final copy.

COLLABORATIVE LEARNING

Task 1   Reading Aloud

Follow the instructions for reading aloud on p. 55.

Task 2   Essay Exchange and Peer Conference

Follow the instructions for essay exchange and peer conference on p. 75.

☐ EXAMPLE ESSAY ────────────────────

Has Individuality Run Amok?

Eugene Benger

Philosophers, social scientists, and the general public have often contemplated the nature of society and government and their relationship to the individual. A key area of concern for them all is the relationship between the individual and authority. This relationship involves concepts such as natural liberty, collective security, and the individual's purpose in a collective body, that is, society. The greatest point of disagreement on these issues is the question of rights: the individual's rights versus society's rights. Surprisingly, the two basic points of view that most people take on this issue can be stated quite simply. One sees the individual as a complete, autonomous system that need not and should not yield to the desires of society as a whole. The other sees the individual as selfish, arrogant, and unconcerned with the welfare of the whole. Who's right? In my view, the collectivists are. The rights of a society, as a collective body, must outweigh the rights of its individual members.

Those who oppose this view heap scorn on it as being un-American. They argue that this country was founded on the idea that individual liberty is sacred. Liberty, in the sense they mean it, guarantees every person the opportunity to express his or her views and pursue his or her goals. Indeed, the power of individuals acting alone to make effective changes in society has allowed this country to adapt to an enormous variety of ideas, norms, and policies. Clearly, then, allowing individuals to upset the status quo has led to many peacefully attained, lasting benefits for American society as a whole. Those who believe in the importance of individual liberty and the efficacy of individual action stress also the negative consequences of government suppression of individual rights. They point to the many attempts by governments throughout history to limit individualism. As a result, they keenly oppose attempts to coerce individuals to sacrifice their views in favor of society's demands.

This individualist argument is a persuasive one. As an American, everything about it appeals to me. I find the values it is based on deeply ingrained in myself. But at the same time, it also strikes me that much of the reasoning in the argument is based on theory and abstract ideas. As a result, in practice the argument is not quite so convincing. The history of the United States is a history of subordinating individuals to a central authority. This is evident in the earliest Puritan settlements, in our constitutional form of government, and in the power that the federal government wields over people's lives on many issues, such as, today, civil rights, the purity and availability of food and water, and even the national 55-mile-an-hour speed limit. These examples represent a paradox in our history. We preach individuality as an ideal, but in reality we readily conform in order to benefit society as a whole. We deny in practice what we maintain in theory. We have to. No nation of the size and complexity of the United States could exist otherwise. In fact, no family however small could otherwise exist for very long without collective agreement and action. Modern democratic societies as a whole are not oppressive giants. They are formal, structured collections of the ideas, norms, and morals of millions of individuals who have agreed, and who for the most part continue to agree, to act as a collective body for their mutual benefit. Both rulers and subjects are members of this body, so they are both responsible for the well-being of all of its members.

This collective responsibility often seems missing in American culture today. It is missing because the strong traditional view that the individual is central to American life actually presents us today with a distressing problem: citizens who abuse the privilege because they somehow feel it is okay to be selfish, self-interested, and self-serving. Instead of cooperating with each other, individuals and society confront each other. Lifting their own problems from what they feel to be their overburdened shoulders and placing them instead on the ample shoulders of the largest possible group, American society and government, individuals let somebody else do the job, and then complain when they do. We see this avoidance of responsibility in small events every day. Never mind big-time crime. When was the last time you saw someone give up a seat on the bus, stop when the light turned yellow because a pedestrian wanted to cross, or return a lost wallet or purse? Other peoples in other countries seem to help each other and care more about each other from day to day. Why not here? The reason, it seems to me, is that too many of us grow up with the attitude "get yours because you deserve it" instead of "we're all people, so why not help each other out?" Clearly, individuality has a role in society, but it is a role that has to take into account the reality that the rights of the whole surpass the rights of the one. □

WORKS CONSULTED

Hall, Peter M. "Individualism and Social Problems: A Critique and an Alternative." *Journal of Applied Behavioral Science.* 19 (1983): 85–94.

Mayer, Karl Ulrich, and Urs Schoepflin. "The State and the Life Course." *Annual Review of Sociology.* 15 (1989): 187–209.

Mill, John Stuart. "On Liberty." In *Essays on Politics and Society,* Collected Works of John Mill, vol. 8, ed. J. M. Robson. Toronto: Univ. of Toronto Press, 1977. Quoted in *The Shaping of the Modern World: From the Enlightenment to the Present,* 2nd ed. New York: Brooklyn College Press, 1987.

Szczepanski, Jan. "Individuality and Society." *Impact of Science on Society.* 31 (1981): 461–466.

Turk, Austin T. *Political Criminality: The Defiance and Defense of Authority.* Beverly Hills: Sage, 1982.

A Course for Writing Peer Tutors

The purpose of Part Six is to help students understand what is involved in peer tutoring and to help instructors and administrators responsible for college and university peer tutoring establish sound new programs and refine programs already in effect. It explains the purposes that peer tutoring serves and how students may become good writing peer tutors. It shows how collaborative activities may be integrated into peer tutor training programs through a credit-bearing course in advanced composition. And it demonstrates that such a course can be a rigorous, educationally significant addition to any college or university curriculum.

The course for writing peer tutors described in Part Six incorporates the collaborative principles and many of the collaborative tasks and practices found in this book, and it draws on the socially constructed understanding of knowledge explored in the book's Introduction and in several items listed in its Bibliography.

WHY PEER TUTORING? WHY A PEER TUTORING COURSE?

Peer tutoring in writing is an educationally valuable academic service. It is the form of collaborative learning in which undergraduates tutor other undergraduates. Some peer tutoring is done in writing centers, labs, or workshops. Some is done in classrooms where peer tutors team up with the faculty member teaching the course. Peer tutoring can be adapted to benefit underprepared basic writers. But the greatest benefit of peer tutoring is to potentially high-achieving students and the vast middle 50 percent of the college and university population.

Peer tutoring is more, however, than just a service to those students. It is a way to involve them in each other's intellectual, academic, and social development. It personalizes education in the face of high student-teacher ratios and institutional expansion. And it applies two principles teachers have known for ages: that we sometimes learn things from each other that resist the direct instruction of classroom teachers, and when we teach other people we sometimes learn more than those we teach.

The best way to learn to be a peer tutor is in a credit-bearing writing course designed to teach peer tutoring as a collaborative process. A collaborative learning course in peer tutoring is important to a peer tutoring program because it improves the reading and writing of both the tutors and the students they tutor. It provides an alternative to the normal authority structure of classroom teaching. And it makes available to colleges and universities a pool of knowledgeable undergraduates who understand student problems and academic issues from the ground up. Peer tutors are in a position to grasp the collaborative, constructive understanding of knowledge and learning that is essential today to significant educational change.

Such a course also has some long-range benefits. When peer tutors graduate, they take with them into business, government, and the professions several significant strengths. They can work effectively with their peers. They understand how, in every field of human endeavor, most judgments are made. They are aware of the way knowledge is constructed socially and aware of their responsibility to contribute to that constructive process. They have a strong sense of the social utility and social value of knowledge. And (very much to the point) those who become teachers themselves take with them a grass roots understanding of collaborative learning.

Perhaps most of all, a writing course for peer tutors is important in both the short and long run to a college or university peer tutoring program and to the tutors themselves because it ensures that the peer tutors will keep on writing.

WHY SHOULD WRITING PEER TUTORS WRITE?

In *Look Homeward, Angel*, Thomas Wolfe describes a peer tutoring incident and celebrates its effects. He says that as a child he had trouble learning to write—that is, forming words with a pencil on paper. Dramatizing himself as the novel's hero, Eugene, he says that finally a friend of his looked at his scrawl, said, "That ain't writin'," and showed him how to form the words. Suddenly then, Wolfe says, "the line of life, that beautiful developing structure of language that [Eugene] saw flowing from his comrade's pencil, cut the knot in him that all instruction failed to do, and instantly he seized the pencil, and wrote the words in letters fairer and finer than his friend's."

Besides illustrating the direct and immediate educational effects that peer tutoring can have, this incident also illustrates the common experience of all teachers, that they must keep learning or fall behind the people they teach. Having helped Eugene leap ahead, his friend had to redouble his efforts or be left behind himself. What this means for peer tutoring is that to continue to grow both as writers and tutors, peer tutors themselves have to keep on writing.

There are two reasons for this. Both have to do with awareness. When tutors write, they stay in touch with the difficulties of writing, so they remain sympathetic with the students they tutor. For example, struggling right now to write these paragraphs on why peer tutors should write makes me feel just how hard a task I give my students when I ask them to write. I cannot forget that my readers will judge me when they read this, just as I judge my students and they, as peer tutors, judge each other when they write peer reviews of each other's writing. Tutees, the students whom peer tutors tutor, face the same ever-present feeling of risk in writing. Peer tutors who write face that risk too, and facing it helps maintain their peership with their tutees. To write takes courage as well as skill, a fact that no writing tutor (and no writing instructor) should ever forget.

So, besides maintaining a healthy awareness of the difficulty of writing, tutors who write also develop another kind of awareness: the social awareness of the community of people in which they work. This new social awareness places peer tutors in a position to explore the hundreds of social, political, cultural, personal, and academic issues alive on every college campus today. They read and listen to what other students are saying, and they help students say what they feel that they cannot or dare not say. As writers of essays and of tutoring logs themselves, tutors reflect upon what they experience and what they learn. As writers and tutors both, therefore, peer tutors contribute to the growth of their institution.

RESULTS

Experience in teaching and supervising peer tutors through a course such as the one described below suggests that it brings peer group influence to bear on students' intellectual growth and their personal, social, and intellectual development. Many students begin to understand for the first time how they think and formulate their ideas. They do not in most cases understand these issues in philosophical or psychological terms. They understand them instead on the hoof, as they see them emerge in each other's work and in their own.

They become aware, for example, of some of the possible varieties of logical contradiction and some of the patterns of resistance to learning and verbal expression that regularly occur. They learn to identify these problems in other people's work and help other writers resolve them. Eventually they begin to identify the same problems in their own writing and resolve them. As one peer tutor, Hung Chan, put it, the writing problems he confronted in reviewing his fellow tutors' essays and in peer tutoring "seemed to be a mirror image of my own."

This student drew an example from his tutoring that shows the practical level at which peer tutors become engaged with ideas. "I recall one student I tutored," he wrote,

> who avoided detail like the plague. He was writing a report on the book *Dibs: In Search of Self*, which is about a troubled boy who closed himself off from the world, and about the way his teacher brought him back. In writing this paper, the student did nothing but generalize. He was worried that the details of the book were too tedious and irrelevant to use in his paper. But together we delved into the book and extracted the details he needed for a solid support of the point he wanted to make. From [working on this paper] both of us realized that it was just those "tedious" details that made the book enjoyable. It was mainly the ability of the author to relate her thoughts to concrete detail that made her writing good.

The apparent simplicity of the writing problem in this example should not obscure the fact that these two students, peer tutor and tutee, are grappling with a sophisticated issue: the relationship between specific and general, concrete and abstract. They are also confronting another frequently ignored problem that may underlie the difficulty many students have in trying to understand that relationship. The tutee's overgeneralized writing and his worry about "those tedious details" reveal a desire to find a level of discourse appropriate to academic writing and to talking about ideas. That is, it reveals an anxiety common among students that highly generalized, abstract expressions are necessarily more significant (less "tedious") than simpler, more concrete expression. (See Style, p. 137.)

This peer tutor also illustrates how the collaborative effort of two students puzzling together over a complex writing problem can affect the intellectual growth of both of them. "It was not just the importance of detail that I learned from the experience," he continues,

> I also learned something more valuable. I learned something about the actual process of learning. Such a realization occurred to me from the conglom-

eration of all my tutoring experiences. This process of learning is not easily described. Learning is grueling work done with much mental sweat. And you never really know how to learn until you actually have to apply what you have learned by teaching it. Peer tutoring has given me this teaching experience, and it has taken me a long way down the road of learning how to learn.

These accounts of rigorous collaborative activity show how it can bring to the surface the social nature of knowledge and learning. As peer tutors and as peer reviewers of each other's writing, students deal with ideas not fully formulated and complete but in a fluid, incomplete state of change. Ideas as they deal with them are unequivocally social constructs, cobbled together in social exchange. Through peer review and tutoring peer tutors also confront the deep personal interest and proprietary attachment to their own ideas that everyone feels, especially when we put those ideas down in writing. So peer review and peer tutoring make students more intensely aware than most undergraduates ever are of the fragility, uncertainty, and excitement of intellectual work.

In this course, peer tutors also experience, many for the first time, power of two kinds: the power of ideas, their own as well as others', and the power latent in the relationship between student and teacher. As one tutor, Gail Olmstead, put it, through peer review and peer tutoring she became

conscious that I have a tendency to want others to adopt my values. . . . Power, I have found, is something I like having. For example, a classmate of mine came to the Writing Center to meet with his teacher. He saw me there in my role as a tutor. The next day in class he asked my advice about his English paper. I enjoyed his asking my advice. The fact that he values my opinion makes me happy. What makes me unhappy is realizing that in exercising that power I sometimes do to others what I've always hated others doing to me—just evaluate their work, not help to make it better.

This frank confession suggests how much self-esteem and self-awareness students can derive from peer tutoring. It also suggests the danger hidden in this self-esteem. Peer tutors may easily begin to see themselves as "little teachers," puppets of the academic regime.

An important goal of the course described here is to help peer tutors avoid turning into "little teachers." It helps them become conscious of the institutional status that they share with the students they tutor. And it helps them maintain that status equality by making sure that their tutees understand it. In effect, through continual interaction and reference to each other over intellectually challenging course-related, writing-related, and tutoring-related issues in this course, students form a semiautonomous tutorial community of their own in which they develop expertise and judgment that is at once interdependent and independent.

In all these ways, the course helps distinguish peer tutoring based on collaborative learning from one of its predecessors, the hierarchical "monitor" system used in nineteenth-century British schools. Monitors were older students whom teachers appointed to teach and guide younger students. Instead, in many cases, monitors bullied the students they were responsible for. This abuse occurred because monitors were agents of hierarchical academic governance—they were "little teachers"—but they lacked the academic training, personal responsibility, and stake in the outcome that is expected of teachers. A peer tutor training course based on collaborative learning provides students with all three by developing their judgment—academic and personal—in the way judgment is always most effectively developed, in collaboration with others.

TEACHING PEER TUTORS

A course in peer tutoring works best when the tutors-in-training tutor other students in authentic tutorial situations, write essays themselves, and write peer reviews of each other's essays throughout the term. When tutors write essays and review each other's writing while they are beginning to tutor, their tutoring and their writing become more sophisticated and expert. When they actually begin to tutor while they are writing essays and reviewing each other's writing, their discussions of tutoring become more immediately practical and less merely conceptual or theoretical.

That is, peer review is the collaborative classroom counterpart of peer tutoring. It turns the peer tutor-training classroom into a kind of tutoring workshop or lab, where tutors meet mock tutees who are really their colleagues in tutoring, equally aware of the issues and stresses that they are all encountering as tutors. The course should therefore include a final peer review exercise that formalizes this evaluative exchange. (See Essay Exchange and Descriptive, Evaluative, and Substantive Peer Review, p. 185).

Since a peer tutor training course based on collaborative learning makes tutors continually aware that they are writing students themselves, they learn to maintain peership with the students they tutor and to avoid the role of institutional agent or "little teacher." Maintaining peership is important because peership is the key to the educational effectiveness of peer tutoring. Peership cuts the knot that all instruction may fail to cut.

The collaborative peer tutoring course outlined here divides the school term—whether quarter or semester—roughly in two. Throughout the term tutors address each other in a series of essays and collaborative tasks. During the first half of the term they concentrate on learning the language of describing and evaluating writing. During the second half, they concentrate on unresolved issues in peer tutoring.

The course maintains continuity during this divided term with a series of essay exercises. The essays differ in two ways: the range of topics tutors are asked to write on, and the intensity and complexity of collaborative work that the essays involve. The collaborative work includes topics interviews, reading aloud, descriptive outlines, evaluating other tutors' work, and peer conferences. As a result of this extensive collaboration, the course asks tutors to write only four essays. But the collaborative work on each essay makes up for the number of essays and their length.

Tutors choose their own topics for all four essays, but within a gradually narrowing range of possibilities. The topic of the first essay is entirely free. The second and third essays are on academic issues drawn from the content of courses that tutors are currently taking, first the content of a course other than their peer tutoring course and then aspects of the peer tutoring course itself. The fourth essay is devoted to any aspect of peer tutoring, including the organization, administration, procedures, and goals of the tutoring program as a whole, the peer tutoring course, and the tutors' experiences during the term as tutors and writers.

Collaborative work increases in complexity as the term goes on. Following the first essay exercise, exercise 5, p. 44, tutors exchange essays twice and write two descriptive peer reviews of fellow tutors' essays. (See Essay Exchange and Descriptive Peer Review, p. 175.) Then all the tutors revise their essays.

Revision is built into the first essay assignment for two reasons. First, revision is what most peer tutoring in writing is all about. All tutors should have the opportunity to consider directly and in some detail what their tutees' experience may be when asked to revise. Second, this is a writing course that assumes that even the best writers still have something to learn. Tutors who are writing essays in *Short Course* form and descriptive outlines for the first time will need a chance to work on basic elements of organization. Those who have already mastered formal writing will have a chance to pay more attention to nuances of transition, stylistic detail, and so on.

Some tutors may even revise the first essay a second time, and most will want to revise other essays that they write during the term. In most cases these subsequent revisions will be held off until the end of the term. At that time, drawing on the advances they have made as writers and tutors during the term, tutors will have a compelling sense of how much they have learned.

The second essay assignment allows a choice of form (essay exercises 5 through 9) but restricts the topic to subject matter drawn from other courses that the tutors are taking or have taken. (See Recalling Something You Have Learned, p. 25.) Once again, tutors exchange essays twice (preferably not with the people they exchanged with last time) and write two descriptive and evaluative peer reviews. (See Essay Exchange and Descriptive and Evaluative Peer Review, p. 184.)

Class discussion about writing and about the students' first experiences as peer tutors accompanies the first two assignments. With two essay exchanges, peer conferences, and revision, the first two essay assignments take the course nearly to the middle of the term. Two essays take so long because of the intensive collaboration that occurs on each one. Writing each essay takes a week or so. Each peer review exchange takes two classes: first a class in which tutors read their essays aloud, and second a class spent peer conferencing. And revisions may take a week, especially at this stage, if students have difficulty catching on to *Short Course* form or descriptive outlines.

The second half of the term begins with the third and fourth essay assignments. (In a quarter system, the pace will have to be faster.) Tutors again choose the form they will use: for the third essay, three paragraphs (essay exercises 5 through 9); for the fourth essay, four paragraphs (exercise 11). The topic of the third essay is a substantive issue related to the peer tutoring course and tutoring, such as difficulties writing peer reviews, the complexities of peer conferencing, the authority of peer tutors, and the responses of tutees. (See Peer Tutors on Peer Tutoring, p. 307.) In their collaborative work on the third essay, tutors continue to practice evaluation, again exchanging their essays twice and writing two descriptive and evaluative peer reviews.

The emphasis in topics for the fourth essay broadens somewhat. Tutors may write about issues relevant to the peer tutoring course or about larger issues such as the nature and source of their own authority as peer tutors, the nature of a teacher's classroom authority, and so on. They may write about problems and responses of their tutees or the causes of some of the particular difficulties of tutees that they have encountered, the place and function of peer tutoring in their institution, and so on. Or, they may write about their difficulties writing peer reviews, or they may write about what peer reviews and peer conferences have revealed to them about the nature of writing or of peer tutoring or of the educational system they are a part of. (See Peer Tutors on Peer Tutoring, p. 305.)

And while describing and evaluating each other's fourth essays, tutors now evaluate each other's work as peer reviewers (and therefore each other's work as tutors) by writing a descriptive, evaluative, and substantive peer review (p. 185). This collaborative exercise, the most complex in the series, entails two exchanges as well as replies by writers, who evaluate their peer reviewers.

Tutors should be invited to interpret these topics broadly, and there is no need to be too strict about the order in which topics occur between the third and fourth essays. Sometimes tutors use these last two essay assignments to suggest changes in the course or in the institution's tutoring system, complain about the limitations and failures of peer tutoring, or propose solutions to problems they encounter as students and as tutors. Some tutors write two related essays—in effect, two "chapters" of one longer essay—taking up two aspects of the same general topic. The introduction to the example essay "What Tutors Can Learn" (p. 308) shows, for example, that it is the second in a series of related essays that the tutor wrote about what he was learning from being a peer tutor.

Any topic is fair game that has to do with peer relations, academic life, education in general, the purpose of writing, the difficulties of writing, *Short Course* form, writing descriptive outlines, what has been going on among the tutors or between them and the teacher, the collaborative procedure recommended in this book for training peer tutors, or for that matter, anything else of interest about the book, the course, the program, or the college or university as a whole.

The value of asking tutors to write on these topics is twofold. It involves them intellectually in issues relevant to peer tutoring, such as the role of academic writing in their own and their tutees' education and the contribution peer tutors can make to their college or university. In addition, they are writing on topics that everyone in the class is familiar with. As a result, in peer conferences on the third and fourth essays the tutors' collaboration with each other can advance to discussion of the substance as well as the technique of the essays they read.

Peer tutors normally find issues of this sort of considerable interest. Their interest will be even greater if throughout the course they keep a journal of their experiences as student and tutor in the form of a double-entry process log. (See p. 304.) A class list of names, addresses, and phone numbers is also a useful convenience that helps cement the coherence of the class.

A SAMPLE SYLLABUS

The following syllabus was developed and used in a semester calendar of two seventy-minute classes twice a week for a total of twenty-eight meetings. It can be adapted to three one-hour classes a week or to a quarter calendar.

CLASS 1   Purpose and requirements of the course: the aims of tutoring. Collaborative learning tasks: introductions,

Why are you here? What does a peer tutor do? Assignment: read exercise 5 (p. 44).

CLASS 2   Assignment: the first essay, due in class 5. Form: exercise 5. Topics: open. Topics due next time. Collaborative learning tasks: How do students typically feel when a teacher assigns a paper? What could a peer tutor do to help them deal with that response?

CLASS 3   Discuss topics for the first essay. Distinguish topic and proposition. Collaborative learning task: topic interviews (see p. 30).

CLASS 4   Collaborative learning task: practice descriptive outline (Churchill paragraph, p. 125). Assignment: begin double-entry process logs (p. 304).

CLASS 5   First essay due. Writers read their essays aloud (p. 54). Discuss descriptive peer review (p. 174). Assignment: first exchange and descriptive peer review.

CLASS 6   First exchange due. Collaborative learning task: practice descriptive outline (p. 152). Assignment: second exchange: repeat descriptive peer review with another student's essay.

CLASS 7   Second exchange due. Peer review (see collaborative learning exercise, p. 173). Collect and read essays and peer reviews.

CLASS 8   Return first essay and peer reviews. Assignment: revisions of first essay, due in class 9. Collaborative learning tasks: How do students typically feel when a teacher asks them to revise an essay? What could a peer tutor do to help them deal with that response?

CLASS 9   Revisions due. Collaborative learning task: practice descriptive outline of an example essay chosen from the Anthology of Student Essays (p. 319). Assignment: second essay, due in class 11. Form: choose from essay exercises 5 through 9. Topic: something you learned in another course. Topics due next time (invention exercise 3, p. 24). Assignment: logs due next time.

CLASS 10   Logs due. Topic interviews (p. 30) and topic conferences (students in pairs for collaborative topic inquiry).

CLASS 11   Second essay due. Read aloud (p. 54). Assign first exchange: descriptive and evaluative peer review (p. 177).

CLASS 12   First exchange due. Assignment: second exchange (descriptive and evaluative peer review repeated). Collaborative learning task: First Essay for Peer Tutoring Practice (p. 313).

CLASS 13   Second exchange due. Peer conferences. Assignment: third essay, due in class 16. Topics: writing, peer tutoring, tutor training, institutional role of peer tutors, what's wrong (or right) with this course, etc. Topics due next time.

CLASS 14   Topic interviews. Collaborative learning tasks: unity and coherence exercises (p. 126).

CLASS 15   Collaborative learning tasks: unity and coherence exercises (p. 126).

CLASS 16   Third essay due. Read aloud. Assignment: first exchange: descriptive and evaluative peer review.

CLASS 17   First exchange due. Collaborative learning task: What are the most difficult problems you face as peer tutors? Assignment: second exchange (descriptive and evaluative peer review repeated).

CLASS 18   Second exchange due. Peer conferences.

CLASS 19   Collaborative learning task: Second Essay for Peer Tutoring Practice, p. 316.

CLASS 20   Assignment: fourth essay, due in class 22. Form: four paragraphs, exercise 11. Topic: issues raised by peer tutoring, the program, and the course. Topics due next time. Discuss context of issues. Reading assignment: Perry, "Examsmanship," p. 343, and Part Four, p. 189.

CLASS 21   Discuss beginnings and endings and introductions, establishing relevance, and reaching out to members of other communities. Collaborative learning task: suggest alternative endings for an example essay (exercise 10, p. 211).

CLASS 22   Fourth essay due. Read aloud. Assignment: first exchange: descriptive, evaluative, and substantive peer review (p. 185).

CLASS 23   First exchange due. Assignment: writer's first response. Discuss issues and problems in peer tutoring.

CLASS 24   Writer's first response due. Assignment: second peer reviewer's mediation and review. Discuss issues and problems in peer tutoring.

CLASS 25   Peer reviewer's mediation and review due. Assignment: writer's second response. Discuss issues and problems in peer tutoring.

CLASS 26   Writer's second response due. Peer conferences. Assignment: logs due next time.

CLASS 27   Logs due. Discuss issues and problems in peer tutoring.

CLASS 28   Retrospective discussion of term's work.

NOTES

In addition to course work, students should be tutoring two to three hours a week.

The **final grade** in the course should be based on students' essay and review writing and on the way they have fulfilled their responsibilities as tutors. The faithfulness and fullness with which students have kept their logs is relevant to their grade, but the quality of their writing in the logs is not.

Punctuality is extremely important in completing writing assignments, because the peer review process involves exchanging papers frequently. Late papers inconvenience other students and may affect the quality of their work and their grade. Because peer reviews are the classroom counterpart of tutoring, punctuality in meeting deadlines in class is the classroom counterpart of reliability in meeting peer tutoring appointments and assigned hours.

A **double-entry process log** serves the same purpose in this course as it does in research work. In fact, it makes the peer tutoring class into a kind of research course in which the subject of research is the tutors themselves. It is an informal record of students' personal experience as writers, tutors, and peer critics, and student life and work in general. And it is a place to blow off steam in an otherwise tightly scheduled and rigorous course that combines writing formal essays with the pressures of tutoring and writing peer reviews. Tutors should keep a dated daily record of their work and tutoring on the lefthand pages of their logs and regularly comment personally on their work on the opposite righthand pages, carrying on a conversation with themselves about what is going on. Their comments should be unrevised, uncorrected, random, rambling, and not self-conscious as to correctness and form.

The teacher should read students' logs once early in the term (the sample syllabus suggests about the fifth week of a semester calendar). The purpose of this reading is not to evaluate the logs but to allay students' anxiety about doing it right. In marginal notes, the teacher can enter into the conversation that students are having with themselves in their logs, encouraging them to explore aspects of their experience as students, writers, peer reviewers, and peer tutors that they may not have considered before. The teacher's comments can also guide students' log writing by encouraging them to write more fully about their experiences as tutors and students and help them steer clear of issues that are too intimate or personal. Once the teacher has read the logs early in the term, students' writing in them usually loosens up a good deal, and they begin using the log more appropriately.

The purpose of reading the logs at the end of the term is to give the teacher an opportunity once again to enter into the conversation students are having with themselves with comments and annotations. In reading logs at the end of the term the teacher sometimes finds out what has "really" been going on in the course, veiled (as it should be) by the unusually high degree of autonomy that typically develops (as it should) among tutors as a peer group.

Revision is important in this course, since one of its goals is to improve the tutors' writing and another is to make them aware of how writing, and writers, change. During the last three or four weeks of the term, students should be invited to revise for a better grade one or two essays from their term's work. Revising early work at this late stage of the course demonstrates to both students and the teacher how much they have developed as writers during the term.

☐ Peer Tutors on Peer Tutoring —————————————————

Learning to Write Peer Reviews

Christopher Guardo

One of the things that makes Tutor Training a unique course is its use of peer reviews. No other class I have taken uses a structured system that enables its members to criticize and comment on each other's writing. As a result, students in Tutor Training learn new ways to look at their peers' writing, as well as new ways to look at their own. This change is a challenge in itself, but it is one that is overshadowed by an even greater challenge. Not only must students discover new perspectives on writing, but they must also learn how to transform what they see into clear, tactful language that benefits both their peers' and their own understanding of writing skill. The ability to write a good peer review is one that is developed only gradually, with practice, throughout the term. Simply stated, learning to write peer reviews takes time.

Potential peer reviewers do, after all, have a lot to learn when they enter the course. Students in the course have to agree first on a common language if they are to understand each other. We are in effect introduced to a whole new vocabulary. Words like *unity, coherence,* and *focus* become all-important. The word *proposition,* once considered harmless (if a trifle risque), is soon moaned over and even wailed in sleep, the subject of many a student's nightmare. Students in Tutor Training also have to learn how to distinguish among various ways of looking at an essay. Peer reviewers have to understand clearly the difference between reading a paper for structure, content, or grammar, if they expect to be of any help to their friends in class. In addition, reviewers have to learn to determine which characteristics of another student's essay are priority items, and which are less important and can therefore remain safely unremarked upon. In short, students have to learn what to look for in writing peer reviews, and like most complicated things, learning what to look for is not an overnight affair. It comes as a result of practice and patience, over a considerable period of time.

Not only do peer reviewers have to invest themselves with new "eyes" for their craft, but they must also somehow come up with a wealth of diplomatic skill. They have to learn what to say, how to say it, and what is best left unsaid. The problem is that they are playing to three different audiences. First, peer reviewers have to please the teacher. They have to say something worthwhile that will earn them an A. At the same time, they have to try not to alienate their fellow students by coming off as tactless, harsh, or insensitive. And, through it all, they have to manage somehow to please themselves by getting down on paper an honest and helpful assessment of their classmate's work. All this is no easy task, and it is one that we naturally approach with more than a little hesitancy at first. If it is difficult to learn the technical aspects of peer reviewing, it is even more difficult to learn the diplomatic. Likewise, if it takes time to acquire an eye for error, it takes even more time to acquire the openness, confidence, and tact necessary to give effective, constructive criticism.

But the time invested in peer reviewing is time well spent. The skills needed to be a good reader are helpful throughout life. Learning to give and to accept constructive criticism graciously, to circumvent emotional reaction, and to navigate successfully around different personalities are time-learned skills, but they are useful in virtually every human relationship. Learning to be open, honest, and confident of one's opinions is a lifelong struggle, and it is part of the process of growth. The challenges offered by peer reviewing are opportunities to develop skills that can enhance the quality of a student's whole life. □

The Hardest Part of Tutoring

Harold E. Grey

As a peer tutor manning the reception desk of the Writing Center, I have seen some strange and funny things happen on the other side of the open door. One day I happened to notice two young women struggling in the hallway. At first I thought they were fighting. As it turned out, one of the women was trying to convince her friend to go into the Writing Center and get some help. The friend was saying she didn't need any help. But with one strong push, she was convinced otherwise. This incident exemplifies a common attitude among writers and explains why students tend to under-use this valuable service. The common attitude of many writers is that, despite the low grades they are getting on their papers, they need no help with their writing. This attitude has many causes. Whatever the cause, though, it is an obstacle to improved writing. Admitting that a weakness exists is often the hardest part of improving your writing.

Admitting weakness is hard because of the human tendency to attribute failure to things other than our own ability. More than once I have heard tutees say, "The teacher doesn't like me," or "He's such a tough marker," in trying to account for their grade of C or D. Educational psychologists call this tendency *finding an external locus of control*. A locus of control is where students place, psychologically, the cause of their success or failure. Students with an external locus of control feel that outside forces always determine how they do on a paper or exam. If students with this attitude do happen to venture into the Writing Center, the first thing a tutor has to do is show them that they themselves are solely responsible for earning a good grade. I have found that describing my own writing experiences helps students accept this responsibility. My experience has been that when I've written a bad paper, I've gotten a bad grade, and when I've written a good one, I've usually gotten a pretty good grade. Often when I show tutees my own graded papers it helps them attack their own writing with renewed enthusiasm. As a peer tutor, I use my position as a student to show tutees that I face many of the same problems that they feel they are up against themselves.

Another barrier that keeps students from admitting weakness is pride. I often feel that my writing is an extension of myself. Other students feel the same way. Many students whose writing is weak, therefore, feel that by coming to the Writing Center they will be exposing more than just weaknesses in their writing. They feel that they will also be exposing weaknesses in themselves. Many students fear showing their personal shortcomings, of course, and they see exposure as a blow to their pride. But this fear keeps them from reaping the benefits that the Writing Center offers. Many tutees I have worked with have been cautious about what they are willing to expose about their writing. Looking at the paper they are currently working on is hard enough, but it may only be the first step to real improvement. I usually ask tutees to show me earlier papers that their teachers have already marked. This way I can see what errors have been recurring. The answer I usually get to this request is, "Oh, you don't want to see *those*." The tutees who finally do show me their old papers have to swallow a certain amount of pride. It isn't easy to look at papers marked up in red pen, but that is of course the only way to find out what went wrong. Students who can suffer this small indignity have a much better chance of improving their writing. □

What Tutors Can Learn

Thomas Seghini

In my last paper I took the position that peer tutors play a useful role in helping other students to write. One of the reasons I gave in support of this position was that peer tutors could inspire other students' confidence in their writing. But this exchange or learning process does not go in just one direction. Peer tutors themselves learn by helping other students. I have been able to help most of the students I have tutored, but sometimes I have had trouble seeing just what the problem was or, when I saw the problem, what tack to take in trying to solve it. Then I asked for help from another tutor or from a faculty member. There was always someone there to help me help the tutee. When that happened, of course, I learned too. But this is only one way in which tutors learn. Tutoring itself can make an important contribution to a tutor's own efforts to learn to write.

Tutoring can help tutors learn to write mainly because tutoring often involves teamwork. For example, a young woman came in for tutoring last week with an assignment for an English literature class. The assignment was to discuss the theme of mutability in English literature from 1400 to 1800. She had to compare the themes in selected poems by fourteen different poets. The task seemed mind-boggling to this student. She had already read all the poems and had picked out the themes in each one. But she said she didn't know how to approach the paper. She had no idea where to begin. I suggested that she group the poems into blocks according to themes. When she did this, we noticed that some of the poems overlapped each other. Then she began to write some possible transitional sentences that would connect the blocks of poems to each other. Here she went beyond my ability to help. Her transitions were smooth and logical, far better than I could have written. I could help her see the connections among the poems, but I could not find words to express those connections. So working as a team, we had both learned something practical about gaining coherence in an essay.

Another way tutoring helps tutors is by teaching them to read more objectively. Take the problem I still have writing paragraph transitions. When I started to tutor I couldn't spot the lack of transitions in someone else's essay, let alone my own. Now I have no trouble spotting this problem in someone else's paper, and if I concentrate hard enough I can sometimes spot a missing transition in one of my own papers. Being objective when reading your own writing is difficult, because telling yourself what's wrong is ego shattering and tedious. Also, it's relatively easy to pick out mistakes in other people's work. If you don't understand what they are saying, there is probably something wrong with the way they are saying it. In your own work, you already understand what you're saying, or you think you do. So you really have to know what to look for before you can do a good job of correcting your own work. And that's one thing tutoring teaches you: what to look for.

Tutoring has helped me to learn to write better because tutoring, like writing, is a process of conscious communication. Many people think writing requires a special inborn talent, simply because they have never taken the time to learn how to write clearly. That is how I looked at writing in high school. I write more clearly now, but I still haven't become entirely conscious of what I am doing when I write. I am not yet fully aware of what I am writing and how clearly I am conveying my message. That awareness is the key to good writing, and in my opinion anyone can acquire it. One way to acquire it is through tutoring. As a result, I have probably gotten as much out of tutoring as my tutees have. This was especially true at the beginning of this semester. And the students I am tutoring now get the benefit of what I have learned. □

The Tutoring Trade

Joyce S. Theroux

Marie is an attractive, friendly native of Haiti who is studying in the United States toward a degree in criminal justice. She is an older student with experience in a variety of occupations both here and in Haiti. But she is also handicapped here, because she has not yet learned all of the intricacies of the English language. I was the writing peer tutor she came to for help with technical writing in English, and I think I helped her quite a bit. But I was also a student in French who was having some trouble with the intricacies of that language. Conversations with Marie showed me that, even though she could not always express herself well in English, she was a very intelligent person. Before long, we made a trade. I would help her with English. She would help me with French. It soon became clear that Marie was a very effective tutor in French.

Not everyone at the college thought it would turn out that way. Some people, both teachers and students, thought it was too risky for me to get help in French from Marie. They thought she wasn't competent to teach French, because she couldn't always understand them when they talked and couldn't always express herself very clearly in English. Others thought that, while she might be intelligent, she was an unlikely candidate for a tutor because she didn't have a firm grasp of the English language. Still others judged her French, a language they didn't know, by evaluating her ability to speak English. They knew that the French she spoke was a Haitian dialect of French, not standard or Parisian French, and told me that her dialect would interfere. So, they said, she wouldn't be able to teach me standard written French.

All this advice from well-meaning people seemed reasonable enough. But I knew they were wrong. I had learned in my tutor-training course why Marie could tutor me well in standard written French. In *The Practical Tutor*, Meyer and Smith say, "Standard written English is a dialect that nobody speaks." No one can know people's competence in standard written English just from listening to their everyday conversation in whatever dialect of spoken English they speak. The same is true of French, and my French professor knew it. When I asked her about Marie's competence as a tutor, she explained that I shouldn't worry about the difference in spoken dialect. It would be like listening to someone from England speak with someone from America. Of course minor differences show up in everyday conversation. But most of them disappear when people write the "unspoken dialect" of standard written English. Standard written French is the same whether the writer speaks Haitian French, Canadian French, African French, or Parisian French. And that's the way it turned out. Marie's knowledge of written French was accurate and sophisticated. As Haitian as she might be in her spoken French, her written French was as Parisian as if she had lived her whole life on the banks of the Seine.

When I decided, despite all the warnings, to take the risk and accept her help with my French course, our tutor trade worked.

Marie became my tutee in standard written English; I became her tutee in standard written French. This experience made me realize that on our campus, and probably on campuses all over the country, there must be other Maries fluent in French, Spanish, Russian, Chinese, Japanese, and other languages that American students want to learn, and who would be delighted to trade their expertise for help learning English. Many of these foreign students are stereotyped as incompetent by their difficulty speaking and writing English. In a tutor trade between English speakers and foreign language speakers, both students can provide the kind of conversational exchange, the kind of listening and speaking, reading and writing in the languages they want to acquire, that is far more valuable than repetition of traditional drills and rote grammatical material. They can also explain tricky verb tenses and other points of grammar, and they can provide better firsthand information on their own culture than any textbook. It seemed to me that I had discovered a rich, untapped resource. I recommend that other people tap it. □

The Proper Atmosphere

Anette-Marie Skjerdal

When my Freshman Composition instructor asked me if I would be willing to participate in a peer tutoring program, I was flattered and I quickly agreed to give it a try. But my feeling of ecstasy did not last very long. I began to think that I could never measure up to this new obligation. After all, what did I know about tutoring? Where would I begin once I sat down with my first tutee? These fears were quickly set aside once I began my work at the Writing Center. Through my experiences there I have learned what it means to be a peer tutor. I might even venture to say that I have stumbled upon the most important contribution that peer tutors can make to their tutees' writing. A lesson in grammar? Help in organization? No. The best way peer tutors can help struggling students' writing is by maintaining a relaxed and warm relationship with them.

I came to this conclusion during my first session with a tutee. As I sat there wondering if I'd ever be able to help anyone with a writing problem, I apparently made it quite obvious that I was nervous. No sooner had we begun to discuss the problem, when Mike (my tutee) asked me if I was feeling well. I suppose I had not been much help up to then, and I found myself confessing to him that this was actually my first experience as a peer tutor. Expecting him to gather up his books and head for the nearest exit, I was surprised when he gave me an understanding smile instead and told me not to be so nervous. He explained that he had a lot of experience as a tutee, and he assured me that I was doing a wonderful job. This seemed to do the trick. Immediately the tension subsided and I was able to do a better job as a peer tutor. Instead of worrying about how well I was doing, I concentrated all my efforts on the problem at hand, and suggestions came to mind more readily. As a result, Mike left the Writing Center with a better paper, and I left with a feeling of great satisfaction.

In this case, I was the one who profited from working in a relaxed and warm atmosphere. But tutors are not the only people who benefit. More important, tutees benefit too. Again, I speak from experience. In the two months I have spent as a tutor I have met many students who have begun to believe that they will never be able to write a passing paper without help. This attitude can become an enormous obstacle to progress. Students become so obsessed with the idea that they are incapable of writing that they actually do become incapable. In these cases, I have found that once the tutor breaks through that feeling of tension and discouragement by chatting informally, students are able to loosen up and their thoughts flow more freely. They begin to realize that they know more about writing than they thought they did, and many times they can find their own mistakes. The tutor may then find it unnecessary to offer so many suggestions. This is not to say that tutors come to play an unimportant role. On the contrary, tutors begin to serve as faithful friends or as relaxing agents whom struggling students know they can rely on in time of need. ☐

COLLABORATIVE LEARNING

The best kind of practice for peer tutors is doing peer reviews of each other's essays. But to practice peer review and peer tutoring any example essay in this book may be used.

The examples offered in the collaborative learning tasks in this section present two interesting and typical kinds of peer tutoring challenge, each interesting and difficult in its own way. The first is a fairly accomplished draft that the writer can probably revise into a very good essay given the right kind of help. The second is the work of an inexperienced writer who needs many different kinds of help, who can be easily discouraged by the wrong kind of help, but who shows promise of becoming a competent writer given help of the right kind.

The collaborative learning tasks designed for each essay will help peer tutors decide what is the best kind of help to give each writer.

Task 1 *First Essay for Peer Tutoring Practice*

Assume that the following essay is a draft. The student has brought it to you for help before she turns it in to her teacher in an introductory course called "Latin American Culture."

☐ PEER TUTORING PRACTICE ESSAY ——————————

Industrialization and Modernization in Two Latin American Short Stories

G. S.*

[1]Despite attempts by Latin American nations to modernize and industrialize, these nations still have enormous problems to contend with. [2]There is overpopulation, unequal distribution of land, resources, and wealth, unequal control of the means of production, high illiteracy rates, high birth and death rates, and widespread disease and hunger. [3]There is an overdependence on foreign countries and an inability to produce enough food. [4]Nations are run for the most part by self-serving individuals concerned mainly with the preservation of their own interests and who are often influenced by foreigners who care little about the well-being of the people of Latin America. [5]While this small elite group fares very well, for the majority of Latin American people, living conditions are very poor indeed. [6]This plight of the majority has become the subject of many Latin American literary works.

[1]One such work is the short story "El Josco" by Abelardo Diaz Alfaro. [2]On the surface, this story deals with bull breeding. [3]However, not too far below this surface, there lies a thinly veiled commentary on Latin American society. [4]Josco is a black bull who mates to produce cows. [5]He is a strong and proud bull who doesn't back down. [6]He is a symbolic representation of the Latin American people and their society. [7]The owner of the breeding farm decides to import an American bull to "improve" the breed. [8]This American

---

*This essay was given to me anonymously a decade or more ago by the teacher of the course for which it was written.

bull is white, huge, and "impressively sculptured." [9]He is of course a representation of the United States. [10]His coloring is a symbol of white people or North Americans, and his size can be equated with the relative hugeness of the United States, both in physical size and in political power, as compared to the nations of Latin America. [11]Through these descriptions and the statements of the owner of the breeding farm, Alfaro is expressing opposition to the widespread idea that if Latin America is to improve conditions, it must do so by using foreign methods. [12]He believes instead in ideas similar to those held by people like Vasconcelos and the South American revolutionary leaders of the past, that Latin America has a culture just as capable of functioning at a high level and solving its own problems as any other culture of the world. [13]Alfaro is aware that the idea that foreign culture is superior is as old as the colonial period. [14]He knows that people believe that despite foreign help and perhaps because of it, Latin America has not come anywhere near to reaching its potential. [15]The moral of Alfaro's story is that if conditions are to change, the Latin American people themselves must be responsible for these changes.

[1]In another short story, "There's a Little Colored Boy in the Bottom of the Water," by Jose Luis Gonzales, the results of modernization and industrialization serve as a backdrop. [2]The difference between the rich and the poor, or in other terms the unequal distribution of wealth, existing in Latin American is clearly illustrated in the story. [3]Gonzales tells about a family pushed out of their home by new homes built for the well-to-do. [4]They live in the sort of squatter village that is a common sight outside of Latin American cities. [5]The family sleeps on a pile of sacks and is underfed. [6]They cannot improve their condition because there are very few jobs available and they are underqualified due to lack of education for the jobs that do exist. [7]In short there is little hope for these people, who are sadly deprived of what they need to fulfill the basic human needs of adequate food and shelter. [8]Against this picture of abject poverty, there is a reference to highways and motor vehicles and the people traveling in them—a symbol of wealth.

[1]I strongly agree with the points made in both these stories. [2]Cultures cannot be judged qualitatively. [3]They are all different. [4]Comparing cultures of Latin America and the United States is like comparing apples and oranges. [5]It simply can't be done. [6]I also agree that a huge gulf exists between the haves and the have-nots in Latin American societies. [7]In both tales, reflecting on the impact or lack of it of modernization and industrialization, the authors are expressing several more ideas I agree with too. [8]Change and reform are desperately needed. [9]There are real problems that need solutions. [10]These solutions must be found by Latin Americans because

only Latin Americans really care about Latin America. [11]And until such solutions are put into effect, the future of Latin America is extremely limited and its potential will not be reached. □

First, write a descriptive outline of the essay. Check your descriptive outline against the essay, and revise the outline until you are confident that it represents the essay accurately. While you are writing your descriptive outline, you may begin to notice some of the essay's strengths and some things you think the writer could do to improve it. Make a note of these responses, but don't include them in your descriptive outline.

Then, working collaboratively in small groups with other peer tutors, compare descriptive outlines. Negotiate until you arrive at a detailed description that everyone in the group can agree on or at least live with. Then, working collaboratively, write an evaluation of the essay using this format:

Explain the essay's strengths. *What do you like about the essay? What do you think is well done?*

Explain what you think could be done to improve the essay. *How exactly do you think the writer can go about doing that?*

In answering each question, *arrange your comments and suggestions in order of importance,* putting first the comment or suggestion that you think is the most important or that you think the writer should deal with first. Here are some criteria to consider in writing your evaluation.

Unity: Is the proposition of the essay clear? Is it stated as concisely as it could be stated? Does everything in the essay defend or explain that proposition, not some other? (See Unity and Coherence, p. 116, and Propositions, p. 85.)

Coherence: Are the paragraphs in the essay in the right order? Does each paragraph begin with an effective transitional generalization? Are the sentences within each paragraph in the right order? Are there transitional elements that relate the sentences? (See Unity and Coherence, p. 116.)

Development: Is everything the essay sets out to say fully explained? Does the essay tell you everything you feel you need to know to understand the main point of the essay? (See Paragraph Development, p. 111, and Introductions, p. 81.)

Style: Is the essay's position expressed and explained as clearly and simply as possible, with no apparent effort to impress by using big words, long sentences, or elaborate word order? (See Style, p. 137.)

Mechanics: Is the essay written in standard written English with generally accepted grammar, spelling, and punctuation? Is it presented neatly, with a good general appearance? (Refer to a standard writer's handbook.)

Respond to the essay as honest, demanding, but sympathetic readers—as **constructive** readers. Try to make your evaluative comments tactful, but also make them direct, detailed, and helpful.

(There is more on how to make tactful evaluative comments in Peer Review, p. 169, and two collaborative learning tasks that are also relevant to peer tutoring, Accepting Authority in Evaluative Peer Review, p. 176, and Analysis of an Example Descriptive and Evaluative Peer Review, p. 177. See also Part Three: Constructive Reading, p. 147.)

Task 2   Second Essay for Peer Tutoring Practice

Assume that a teacher has sent a student to you with this essay and asked you to give him some help. The student tells you that he wrote it as an impromptu essay in a single class hour. The assignment was to answer the question, "What is reality?"

☐ PEER TUTORING PRACTICE ESSAY ─────────────

Reality*

Reality is what I say it is, I say is to live for "God." It's real or I such say that he is for real and he is more real if you know that your just here on earth for just some time, maybe forty year, fifty, eighty years, but who realy knows. I guest nobody here on earth knows. You know in "good book," I mean the "Bible," it said that there is two kinds of life, this kind of life, that where living on earth and the life where he lives. This is reality to know that I'm just here for a short while because I donn't know when he is coming for me (death & passing away of the body) I'm glad I wont pass away just my body. But I have to take under consideration that there are other people that were born before me and there turn has to come before me. Because its just like a line, your just waiting to be called.

A funny thing happen to me when I went to the A. P. shoping for food. I was with my wife and we got all the food that we can get for

*This essay also appears in Mina Shaughnessy, *Errors and Expectations* (New York: Oxford University Press, 1977), p. 238. It was offered to me by the teacher of the course for which it was written. The name of the writer is unknown.

us to eat for two weeks. Something distriked my eye when I was about to pay for the ideoms. There was a book on the counter by the cash-register and this book (books) where for people to buy. It was published by Readers Digest and it said "How to live a *longer* life in nine easy steps." This was realy funny to me because people of today are trying to prolong life, I mean a lot of people, doctors inventing something like a heart transplant (thats just one ex.). How far can you get. Like in this story of Edgar Allan Poe, Allegory & The Masque of the Red Death & Bartleby the Scrivener. Death comes and there no way in the world that you can stop it because the lord comes he comes like a shadow at night, or the angle of the Red Death.

This is reality if people can see it but thay have eye's but they cannot see & they have ears but they cannot hear. □

Working collaboratively, have someone in the group read the essay aloud to the others. Then, treating the essay as a draft, and still working collaboratively, answer the following set of questions.

1. What is your first, private, gut reaction to the essay? What do you feel but would not reveal to the student?

2. Now imagine that when you first read the essay it was not in the form given above. Instead, the writer wrote it on a computer, ran it through a spelling program, and corrected most of the essay's punctuation and usage errors, so that the surface of the essay was more conventional in appearance. How would your first reaction to the essay differ? How would you account for the difference?

Reality

Reality is what I say it is. I say it is to live for God. It's real, or I say that He is for real, and He is more real if you know that you're just here on earth for just some time, maybe forty years, fifty, eighty years, but who really knows? I guess nobody here on earth knows. You know in the "Good Book," I mean the Bible, it says that there are two kinds of life: this kind of life that we're living on earth and the life where He lives. This is reality: to know that I'm just here for a short while, because I don't know when He is coming for me (death and passing away of the body). I'm glad I won't pass away, just my body. But I have to take into consideration that there are other people that were born before me and their turn has to come before me. Because it's just like a line. You're just waiting to be called.

A funny thing happened to me when I went to the A&P shopping for food. I was with my wife, and we got all the food that we can get for us to eat for two weeks. Something distracted my eye when I was about to pay for the items. There was a book on the counter by the cash-register, and this book was for people to buy. It was published by *Reader's Digest*, and it said *How to Live a Longer Life in Nine Easy Steps*. This was really funny to me, that people of today are trying to prolong life. I mean a lot of people such as doctors inventing something like a heart transplant (that's just one example). How far can you get? Like in the story by Edgar Allan Poe, the allegory "The Masque of the Red Death," and in Melville's "Bartleby, the Scrivener." Death comes, and there's no way in the world that you can stop it, because the Lord comes, He comes like a shadow at night, or the Angel of the Red Death.

This is reality, if people can see it. But they have eyes but they cannot see, and they have ears but they cannot hear. □

3. What do you think the writer of this essay wanted to say most? That is, what position do you think he intended to take or what do you think he intended the proposition or main idea of the essay to be?

4. What differences are most noticeable between paragraphs one and two? How would you account for those differences?

5. Leaving spelling and punctuation aside for a moment (that is, dealing for a moment only with the revised version of the essay), what three points (positive or negative) would you make about the essay if you were trying to help the writer improve his work?

6. How would you express each point so that the writer would be most likely to follow your advice in improving this essay? What would you tell him that you think is well done in the essay? What would you tell him that you think needs improvement and how to improve it?

7. Which of these points you would say first, second, and third? Why would you put them in that order?

8. What could you say that would make it more likely that he would write a better impromptu essay next time?

9. Returning to the original version of the essay, if you were going to comment on spelling and punctuation, where in your list of suggestions would you do it? Why there? And what would you say?

10. Finally, what do you think of "What is reality?" as the topic for a one-hour in-class impromptu writing assignment?

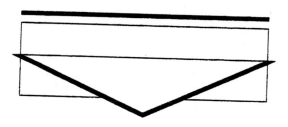

Anthology of Student Essays

Family and School

Frederic Garsson

When students enter college it is often a very different experience than they had anticipated. This is especially true for students who go to a local college while most of their high school friends go to an out-of-state school. Both the students who stay at home and those who go away to school feel alone and afraid sometimes in this strange new environment. But students who stay at home may also find themselves without emotional support. They have lost most of their high school friends, with whom, in the past, the mere act of talking would bring about a feeling of security. And they are not likely to be able to replace these friends quickly, as people are usually able to do when they move into a college dormitory. This feeling of being cut off is serious because of the differences in teaching methods that exist between high school and college. In college, there is the freedom to become lazy about studying. Homework is rarely collected. As a result, students are unsure of how well they will do in college. When this feeling of insecurity overcomes students entering college, there are several ways families can provide them with emotional support so that they can adjust to a strange environment.

First, the family can take over the job of talking with the student. Often, while students are enjoying their senior year of high school, the lines of communication between parents and children are temporarily and unintentionally broken. Students often take their relationship with their families for granted, and it is not until they find themselves without friends that they realize the truth of what their parents have been telling them for years: that friends may come and go, but your family, especially your brothers and sisters, will always be your friends. By renewing the conversation with their families students gain security and reassurance that things will work out well, with schoolwork as well as with meeting people. A student might even find himself forming a real friendship with his little sister, who, until recently, he had totally ignored, or with an older brother who he had always regarded as a bully. The next time his sister asks him to play Old Maid (her favorite card game), or to take her to the mall, the student might accept her offer rather than casually dismiss it as he had done in the past. The next time his brother asks him to shoot baskets, the student might go along cheerfully, even if he knows he'll get trounced.

Another way families can give emotional support to their children in college is through rituals, acts performed on a regular basis that a person can depend on to occur. Rituals tend to put order into a person's life and provide a sense of self-assurance and security. A common ritual is Sunday dinner. No matter what the children in the family are doing, even studying for exams, family rules may require them to eat dinner with the family. In this case the whole family can anticipate this one time of the week, knowing that no matter what, they will be together. It is an event that the whole family, and most important, the children, can rely on and find comfort in. My family first learned about the use of Sunday dinner as a family ritual through a friend of mine. On several occasions, he turned down an invitation to have dinner at my house, explaining to my parents that his father insisted that his whole family eat dinner together on Sunday evenings. My parents thought that this mandatory attendance at Sunday dinner was something that would work well at our house too. At the time I did not understand the psychology behind the plan, but now I think I do. Furthermore, I feel that it has succeeded in achieving its desired effect. It gave my sister and myself a feeling of security that we not only experience every Sunday, but that we also carry with us into the world beyond our family. □

DETAILED DESCRIPTIVE OUTLINE

PROPOSITION   When this feeling of insecurity overcomes students entering college, there are several ways families can provide children with emotional support so that they can adjust to a strange environment.

PLAN   Support the proposition by stating and describing two of the several methods mentioned in the proposition.

PARAGRAPH 1   *says:* When students find themselves in a strange new school environment near home, there are ways their families can provide emotional support to help them adjust.

does: Introduces the proposition by describing an undesirable situation and how it comes about; describes a typical reaction to this situation; suggests that there are ways to remedy this situation.

PARAGRAPH 2   *says:* By constantly talking with the student, families give them a sense of security and constant reassurance that things will work out.

does: States the first method. Explains background, making the method necessary. Describes results in general. Gives the examples of these results.

PARAGRAPH 3   *says:* The use of Sunday dinner as a ritual tends to put some order into the student's life and to bring about a feeling of security.

does: States the second method. Defines the key term. Explains results in general. Gives a concrete example and explains it in detail. Describes the writer's experience with the example and its outcome.

Growing Up on Spock

Elan Katz

Reading child-rearing books has become an obsession, a mania, a cult among parents in our society. The reason is parental insecurity. First-time parents lack knowledge and experience in raising a child. Many don't have their own parents around to answer questions and reassure them, so they look for guidance in child-care books. One of these that has become particularly successful is Dr. Benjamin Spock's *The Common Sense Book of Baby and Child Care*. Thirty million copies of it have been sold since it was first published in 1946. In other words, the book has sold at the rate of one copy for almost every first-child born to an American family (Harvard). Today, child-care books flood the shelves of bookstores, and still Dr.

Spock remains a household name. I myself was raised by the advice of Dr. Spock. My mother devoured the book, following it word for word. She kept my bottles warm (but not too warm, of course). She never forced me to eat vegetables. And when she rebuked me, she also reassured me (Spock *passim*). Reading Spock now myself, it is clear to me why Dr. Spock held my mother and millions of mothers like her so securely in his grip. The book is such a success because it is so comforting.

One thing that makes it comforting is that Dr. Spock obviously knows so much. Spock had been a family physician and pediatrician in and around New York City for many years before he synthesized his knowledge in his book. During that time, he amassed a great deal of information about children and parents. He conferred with other professionals such as sociologists and child psychologists. He filtered their knowledge through his own first-hand experience, so that he could give advice on a broad range of topics, many of which are not, strictly speaking, medical. Some of these are the special problems of working mothers, handicapped children, and adopted children. He also gives advice on issues having to do with emotions and behavior, such as spanking, tantrums, thumb sucking, punishment, and spoiling a child. For parents who know that medical issues are only a part of what they need help with in rearing their children, and who also know that every issue with regard to children is related in some way to every other issue, this evidence of almost universal knowledge can't help but be reassuring (Wegman 1329).

But the book's success isn't just due to Dr. Spock's great knowledge. It is due also to the way he delivers his knowledge. The book is written in a soothing, unruffled style designed to cool down parental panic. It is almost certain that the first thing that catches the attention of young parents is Spock's motto in the very first chapter: "Trust yourself." Imagine doting, terrified parents being told to trust their own instincts, not to "take too seriously all that the neighbors say," and not to "be over-awed by what the experts say." Most importantly, imagine the deep sigh of relief that must greet the advice "trust your own common sense" (Spock 1). As he goes on, Spock confirms this advice and explains it. "All parents do their best," he tells us, "when they have a natural, easy confidence in themselves. Better to make a few natural mistakes than to do everything letter-perfect out of a feeling of worry" (25). With advice like that, parents can realize that the power of successful parenting is inherent, even in parental stumblebums like themselves. □

WORKS CITED

Rev. of Benjamin Spock, *The Common Sense Book of Baby and Child Care. Harvard Education Review.* 43 (1973): 669.

Spock, Benjamin. *The Common Sense Book of Baby and Child Care.* New York: Pocket Books, 1946.

Wegman, Myron E. Rev. of Benjamin Spock, *The Common Sense Book of Baby and Child Care. The American Journal of Public Health.* 36 (1946): 1329.

Going Back to School

Kathleen Wilson

Most of my school years were spent during an era when society, including my family, felt a college education was necessary for a prosperous future. However, while the trend was for everyone, men and women, to attend college, my father maintained society's older values regarding women. He believed that a woman's place was in the home and since a woman would ultimately become a housewife despite a college education, it was not necessary for her to obtain one. But since a man had to become a breadwinner, my father believed an education was integral to the man's future. The quality of that future depended on a college degree. I internalized these values as my own and directed my life toward marriage and that ultimate role of housewife. During my junior year in high school I took courses geared for future homemakers. They included Home Economics and Clothing and Foods. In my senior year I took Advanced Clothing and Foods. All this time, while I was preparing to become a housewife, my three brothers got college degrees. Then my brothers married teachers. All these degrees constantly reminded me that I lacked one of my own. As a result, I always felt inadequate—stupid, really—when I was surrounded by all the professionals in my family. Then, when I hung my husband's sheepskins on the wall, I realized that I was the only member of the entire family who didn't have a degree, the only one who didn't know anything. Finally, thirteen years after I graduated from high school, I applied for admission to college. My acceptance had an immediate positive effect on my self-confidence. Attending college has continued to have this positive effect.

Of course, the big boost I got with my acceptance didn't last. By the time I actually started classes I was extremely nervous. I thought everyone would notice my stupidity. I was so afraid I wouldn't understand anything that I carried a dictionary to each class to interpret the big, alien words I expected to hear. To my surprise and delight I knew more than I gave myself credit for, and even had some abilities I was never aware of. When my first exam was returned with a large A I checked to see if the teacher had made a mistake. I could not believe it was my test paper. I marveled each time I received another A, and when at the end of the semester I received three As and a B in my courses, I was completely awestruck. These achievements helped me to become aware for the first time that I was a competent person. By the end of the first semester I realized I wasn't stupid. This realization tremendously improved my self-confidence.

My newly found confidence gave me even greater courage. I enrolled in courses I once thought I could never pass. I was particularly apprehensive about English Composition. It had been so long since I had taken an English course that I couldn't even remember what a predicate was. I had to rely on my ear to help me through English. I also thought a person had to be born with a talent to write. Eventually, I learned about predicates and a few other things that I had forgotten, and I no longer believe in the myth that writing is innate. Furthermore, the process of learning to write has helped me to improve my vocabulary. In addition to eliminating a lot of diction marks on my papers, having a better vocabulary has become an advantage in my personal life. When I am confronted with problems at home or at work, I am at last able to express myself adequately. □

DETAILED DESCRIPTIVE OUTLINE

PROPOSITION	Attending college has continued to have a positive effect on my self-confidence.
PLAN	To develop two reasons supporting this proposition.
PARAGRAPH 1	*says:* Before attending college I lacked self-confidence and felt stupid because I was surrounded by family members with college degrees.
	does: Introduces the proposition by giving a history that includes examples of past values and attitudes. Updates the history by explaining how the writer became dissatisfied. Finally, explains how correcting this dissatisfaction led to the situation described in the proposition.

PARAGRAPH 2   *says:* These achievements helped me to become aware, for the first time, that I was a competent person; this realization tremendously improved my self-confidence.

does: Develops first reason in support of proposition by describing how past attitudes began to change. Generalizes the writer's achievements and describes how the writer felt about them. Summarizes the paragraph by describing discovery of false past attitude as a result of proposition.

PARAGRAPH 3   *says:* My new confidence gave me the courage to enroll in an English Composition course, which has led to improvement in my writing, vocabularly, and self-expression.

does: Develops second reason in support of proposition by explaining how negative assumptions were corrected by experience. Enumerates negative assumptions and positive experiences. Describes how positive experiences reinforced the proposition.

The Benefits of a Writing Community

Eleanor Gaffney

Writing has always been a deeply personal experience for me. When I write I wrap up a piece of myself and hand it to someone to savor. I expose my feelings, values, or thought processes to someone else's judgment. That gift has never been easy for me to offer. I have always wanted to write well, so I have been sensitive not only about what I am writing but also about how well I am writing. Often this sensitivity has kept me from questioning a professor's grade, even a good grade, because I have been uncomfortable talking about my work. Even when I have asked a friend for help on an assignment, my defenses about my writing have gotten in the way of any kind of productive assistance. Studying writing this semester has helped to break down some of that sensitivity. I have learned that it is good for writers to work in a writing community.

A writing community creates an atmosphere of shared concerns.

Knowing that the other students in my writing class are feeling as vulnerable as I feel has really helped me to relax about my work. I was never sure if anyone else got as anxious as I do. By using my writing class as a working community I have learned that most students feel exposed when they write. During the first weeks of class, when we talked about what writing is like for us, I was relieved to discover that other students experience the same panic and fear I do. I immediately felt less defensive about sharing my work. In fact, I felt that I wanted to comfort my fellow students, so my attention left my own anxieties and focused more on their needs. I think they responded in the same way, with the result that we began working as a community. Just knowing that other students are in the same boat has helped all of us to open up and breathe more easily while talking about our writing.

And once I relaxed about sharing my written work I experienced the full benefits that come from working in a writing community. A fellow writer can see mistakes in my work much more clearly than I can. Once I have gotten used to the way words have been put together in my head, I get stuck and feel frustrated. I cannot seem to develop a clearer way to get my message across. Another writer doesn't have that same block and can often immediately think of suggestions to help me out of the rut. A lot of writing involves making decisions about how much information to share and what kind of information is most important. Fellow writers can be a tremendous help in making those decisions. For example, they can share insights about what they need to know in order to understand someone's message. It always seems so much clearer when someone else shares an outside perspective.

Inviting that outside perspective from other students doesn't mean that writing becomes less risky or less personal. I still feel that I wrap up a small piece of myself when I write. I still feel fearful. But sharing work allows me to break through some of my defenses and welcome insights and suggestions. I can get help directly from my audience and learn to deliver a more powerful message. Writing will never feel quite so lonely again. I intend to find a community to work with for any future writing that I do. I have learned that it is productive to share my work and invite outside insight. I will use this knowledge in my future attempts to share a piece of myself through writing. □

DETAILED DESCRIPTIVE OUTLINE

PROPOSITION   I have learned that it is good for writers to work in a writing community.

PLAN   To state a proposition and defend it with two reasons.

PARAGRAPH 1   *says:* I have always been uncomfortable sharing my writing.

does: States a generalization to describe the experience being discussed. Gives further details about this experience and then discusses consequences of the experience. Offers two instances when the consequences have prevented productivity. Describes a change in the experience and foretells new consequences.

PARAGRAPH 2   *says:* Knowing that other students share some of my anxieties has helped me to be less defensive about my own writing.

does: Supports the proposition by stating a generalization about the subject and then narrows and refines that statement. Offers a concrete example to support the generalization and describes the consequences. Summarizes the paragraph.

PARAGRAPH 3   *says:* Other writers can see mistakes in my work much more readily than I can.

does: Supports the proposition with another generalization. Gives an example from the writer's experience. Explains the consequences and the relation between the example and the main point of the paragraph.

PARAGRAPH 4   *says:* Because a writing community works so well for me, I intend to find a community to work with whenever I write in the future.

does: Refers back to the introduction and compares the new situation with the earlier one. States consequences of the change in perspective. Predicts future action.

Stock Options

David Bugayer

There are many ways to invest money: savings accounts, municipal and corporate bonds, stocks, and real estate. Some of these investments are relatively safe, others are pretty risky. One of the newest and riskiest ways to invest is stock options. A stock option is the right to buy or sell a certain stock for a fixed price before a fixed date. The right to buy is called a *call option*. The right to sell is called a *put option*. Owning stock and owning options differ in an important way. Stocks are relatively low-risk investments because they have neither a fixed price nor a fixed expiration date. Investors buy and sell them whenever they like at the prevailing price. Stock options are high-risk investments for two reasons. First, the value of a stock option depends on its strike price, which is a predetermined price for the stock that the option represents. Second, the value of a stock option expires at a predetermined time, such as 30 days from the purchase date. Once an option expires, it is worth nothing. Despite this high risk, however, for investors who can afford it stock options offer several advantages.

One reason investors may buy stock options is that they can make a great deal more money with them than they can with stocks. For example, if IBM stock is selling for, say, $160 a share, the price of a 30-day option to buy IBM at $160 a share (which brokers call a "$160 IBM call option") would be about $2 a share. Whereas 100 shares of IBM stock itself would cost $16,000, 100 $160 IBM call options would cost only $200. If the price of IBM falls below $160, an option to buy IBM at $160 is worthless. But if within 30 days the price of IBM rises above $160, the price of the option also rises, and at a greater rate. When IBM stock reaches $170 a share, the option to buy IBM at what is now the predetermined bargain price of $160 may be about $12. An investor who sells for $170 the stock he bought at $160 makes a reasonable 6.3 percent profit. But the investor who sells $160 IBM call options at this point makes a whopping 500 percent profit. For investors who can afford to lose their whole investment, the possibility of that kind of profit makes options well worth the risk.

Another reason investors may buy stock options is to protect their investments. Options can serve as an insurance policy on stocks investors already own if the price goes down. For example, say an investor owns 100 shares of GE at $80 a share (total cost, $800). For $200 she buys 100 $80 put options—the right to sell 100 shares of GE stock for $80 a share. The $200 is her insurance premium. If the stock goes up, she doesn't need the insurance, for the same reason that you don't need insurance on your house if your house doesn't burn down. But if the stock goes down, just as if your house burned down, that insurance is well worth the premium. Suppose in this case the price of GE drops from $80 a share to $70. When the investor sells, she loses $100. But the value of her 100 put options on those shares (the right to sell GE stock at the now lucrative predetermined price of $80 per share) has risen to $1200. Selling her put options, she covers the $100 she lost on the stock and the $200 she paid for the options, and she has $100 left over to pay her brokerage fees. Her house burned down, but the insurance she wisely carried on it pays to rebuild it. □

On Revoking the Second Amendment

HyunSoo Cha

On November 3, 1791, the first Ten Amendments to the United States Constitution went into effect. Most of these amendments were, and still are, crucial to the well-being of the nation. They not only endow people with basic rights, but also conserve these rights by promoting further legislation and judicial rulings. With the exception of one of them, the Ten Amendments remain relevant today. The exception is the Second Amendment. This amendment allows the ownership of arms by every citizen and a "well-regulated militia," that is, an army of citizens, in contrast to professional soldiers. The intent of this amendment was to make sure that the central government of the nation did not have a monopoly on arms and the ability to use force. It fulfilled Thomas Jefferson's belief that a free nation needed a revolution every few years to maintain its freedom, and that an established central government alone is not enough to maintain people's freedom. Unfortunately, each passing day renders this amendment obsolete. Today the federal government supports people's rights more effectively than local governments. The misuse of arms by citizens is a much greater danger than misuse of arms by the government. From deliberate shootings to accidental ones, armed citizens pose greater problems than ever before. It is time, therefore, to repeal the Second Amendment.

One reason we should repeal the Second Amendment is that the characteristics of American society have changed tremendously since the Ten Amendments were ratified by the original thirteen states. The early years of the United States were a period of frequent conflict. In the early eighteenth century, newly arrived colonists fought repeatedly against Native Americans for possession of land and the colonies fought for their independence against Great Britain. Later, new settlers in the West fought Native Americans and the

Spanish colonists. Most of the country was rural. Because there were large distances between people, they needed firearms to maintain their security. Owning arms was a necessary part of life. Today, we are not confronted with any of these problems. There is no reason for us to take up arms to fight for our beliefs. We have a stable government and a society in which votes are stronger than bullets. The United States is now a superpower, with an armed force more capable than any other nation's. The rise of huge cities has also made arms obsolete. People maintain their security and collective power by living close together. We protect ourselves against each other with well-organized police departments—our armed militia—making arms owned by individuals obsolete.

But it is not only that the Second Amendment is now unnecessary that it should be repealed. It is also because it now allows incompetent and unworthy people to own guns. The ease of buying guns, coupled with frequent epidemics of drug use and crime, are the greatest problems today. In our big cities—Los Angeles, Chicago, New York—gangs proliferate and with them gang violence and murder. Every year recently these cities have broken their previous year's record homicide rate, and it seems almost certain that the trend will continue. For children this trend is especially dangerous. Last year in New York City, for example, at least ten children were shot or killed, their only fault being that they were innocent bystanders. Urban children at risk in this way are like mushrooms. Fragile and delicate, they must learn to survive in an increasingly hostile environment. What puts them at risk is the ease with which anyone can buy guns. In some states, the only requirement for buying a gun is an ID card and proof of address. In some places it is easier to buy a gun than to rent a movie on videotape. With guns easy for everyone to get, everyone is at risk. □

Drug Testing in Sports

Chris Varney

In the past ten years, drug testing has become one of the most controversial issues in amateur and professional sports. In 1988, the issue really took off when Canadian runner Ben Johnson tested positive for anabolic steroids during the Summer Olympic Games in Seoul. Just before he got caught, Johnson had set a world record in the 100 meter dash. Later, Johnson's trainer admitted that he had injected the runner with the illegal drug. But what has become the hottest issue, during the games and since, is not using drugs but testing for them. Those who want to control the use of drugs in sports believe that testing is the only way to do it. The opposition believes that testing infringes on the players' rights. A close look at the arguments on both sides suggests that drug testing is wrong for a number of reasons.

It is not hard of course to sympathize with the proponents of drug testing. Sports officials feel that they must control athletes' use of drugs before they harm both the players and the game (Duda 32–33). The owners of professional teams have an interest as well. They want the athletes they pay to perform at their peak, and drugs can lower that peak. Officials and owners together feel that testing is needed because educating athletes about drugs doesn't work (Percy 145), whereas sports "that have conducted high quality testing have virtually eliminated the use of stimulants" (Fitch 137). As a result, in 1985, to put pressure on the players' union to accept mandatory testing, Major League Baseball Commissioner Peter Ueberroth instituted a plan to test all baseball employees except players. Robert J. Brodick, team physician of the Montreal Expos approves of the measure. Baseball players, he says, "are role models. They have an obligation to fans and management to perform at their best, and there's no way they can do that when they're on drugs" (Duda 32).

This emotional appeal has a good deal of merit. It is a legitimate question whether pumped up athletes are really athletes at all. But the arguments against mandatory drug testing in sports far outweigh the arguments in favor of it. Testing for drugs is enormously costly. The new, hard-to-detect drugs require new equipment and highly trained technicians (Ryan 132). Testing methods are unreliable. Some drugs that athletes take appear also, for example, in over-the-counter cold pills. Yet "one cold pill containing a small amount of a banned chemical taken by a yachtsman could not possibly influence the outcome of a sailing race, but its detection may disqualify the athlete" (Hanley 134). And testing policy is often faulty. Before Super Bowl XXIV, for example, the NFL executed its drug-testing policy erratically, punishing some players who tested for small amounts of drugs but ignoring the large amounts detected in other players (King 9). But certainly the most important reason for opposing drug testing in athletes is that it is an unconstitutional invasion of privacy (Murray 47) that "constitutes a general search without wrongdoing" (Duda 33). The courts have prohibited drug testing in schools and even in prisons. No other American institution outside of the military allows it (Duda 33). Why should sports? □

WORKS CITED

Duda, Marty. "Baseball's Bold Step: Mandatory Drug Testing." *Physician and Sportsmedicine*, July 1985: 32–33.

Fitch, K. D. "Penalties Are the Best Deterrent." *Physician and Sportsmedicine*, Aug. 1983: 137–140.

Hanley, Daniel F. "Quadrennial Testing Won't Control Doping." *Physician and Sportsmedicine*, Aug. 1983: 134.

King, Peter, ed. "Drug Redux." *Sports Illustrated*, 5 Feb. 1990: 9.

Murray, Thomas H. "Drug Testing and Moral Responsibility." *Physician and Sportsmedicine*, Nov. 1986: 47–48.

Percy, E. C. "Protect Athletes from Hazards of Drugs." *Physician and Sportsmedicine*, Aug. 1983: 145.

Ryan, Allan J. "Drug Testing in Athletes: Is It Worth the Trouble?" *Physician and Sportsmedicine*, Aug. 1983: 131–132.

The Pluralist Model of Power and Modern Society

Jeffrey Sonenblum

In the study of political sociology, there are three major ways to think about power: the class model, the elite model, and the pluralist model. In the class model, power is inherent in those who own the means of production. They constitute a ruling class governing the masses. In the second, or elite model, power is held by a ruling group called the *elite*, a small, tightly knit fraction of the whole population. The elite may or may not own the means of production, but they do control social relations and political decisions. What these two major theoretical models have in common is the idea that power is held by a small, self-serving group. They also agree that under these conditions, the majority of people can have no impact on their own fate. The third model, pluralism, differs greatly from both the class and elite models. In the pluralist model, the majority of people participate directly and indirectly in the political process. Through elections and interest-group activities, people hold political officials accountable and prevent them from favoring the interests of any one group. They have to bargain and compromise in order to please many different factions. It is of course possible to see American politics from both the class and the elite points of view. But today the American political structure most closely resembles the pluralist model of power.

One pluralist aspect of American society is the dispersion of political power among a great number and variety of competing interest groups. These groups make claims both on the government and through it. When dealing with governmental institutions in order to strengthen or protect our interests, we can often get the results we want only through group action. Suppose, for example, that in a residential area of town a rash of traffic accidents occurs at a busy intersection. It is obvious that some sort of traffic control is needed. Individual people living in the area might petition the city council to install a traffic light by writing letters or personally visiting the council. The council, however, would probably not act on the request of these single individuals. It would be much more apt to take action if a neighborhood organization complained. The council would be more responsive to the group's request because the organization represents a large number of people. The organization, then, can achieve politically what persons acting as individuals cannot: a hearing. But to continue the example, at the same time that the citizen's group makes its complaint, some local businessmen might claim that a traffic light at that intersection would slow traffic, inconveniencing commuters, discouraging them from passing through the area, and thereby hurting trade. As individuals, these businessmen might have no better luck pursuing the council than the individual private citizens they oppose. But if the businesses approached the city council through local business and trade associations, they would be more likely to be heard. The advantage of group action by businessmen against the light is just the same as it is for those who want the light installed.

A second aspect of pluralism is that no single group can win every issue, nor are people ever likely to get everything they want. People and groups must bargain and compromise with each other. A pluralist society believes in give-and-take as the fairest and most equitable way of resolving conflict and deciding issues. A good example of bargaining and compromise in our society is what might happen in the case of the neighborhood organization asking for a new traffic light versus the business and trade organizations that oppose the light. So far, the situation is a standoff. To break the deadlock in a pluralist way, the city council would become an umpire, weighing each group's arguments to see which would benefit society more as a whole. Even when the arguments were weighed, there might be no decision for or against the traffic light. Instead, the conflicting parties might be helped to reach a compromise in which the council approved the installation of a stop sign. The sign would tend to prevent accidents, but it would not hold up traffic for long periods of time and hinder trade as a light might do. In this way the private citizens would get most of what they want—a safer intersection. And the businessmen would not feel that their interests were totally ignored. □

Mitosis

David Lepkofker

An important concept of cell theory is that all cells arise from preexisting cells. If this statement is true, then the obvious question is, Where did the first cell come from? According to scientist Stanley Miller, billions of years ago a variety of inorganic compounds formed organic compounds with the addition of energy. Eventually these organic compounds formed the first cells to exist on Earth. These cells reproduced by a process of simple fission. Cells evolved into highly complex organisms and eventually reproduced by a process known as mitosis, that is, one cell produces two daughter cells, each one identical in chromosome number and genetic material. The complex process of mitosis consists of two phases that often, but not always, occur together.

The complete process of mitosis occurs in as little as one hour in some cells. During the first part of mitosis, the karyokinesis phase, the nucleus divides. Chromosomes that contain genetic material enlarge and replicate. As the chromosomes enlarge, the nuclear membrane breaks down. Each chromosome had earlier replicated. The replicates separate and migrate to each pole of the cell. Full sets of chromosomes are then enclosed by new nuclear membranes. This completes the first phase in mitosis.

The next part of mitosis is the cytokinesis phase. During this phase, the cytoplasm divides. In animal cells, the cell membrane indents. This is called furrowing. When furrowing is complete two new cells are created. In plant cells, a cell plate is formed in the center of the cell; eventually, the plate extends to the periphery, providing for division of the cytoplasm. After cytokinesis is complete, the two genetically identical cells perform regular cellular activities before mitosis occurs again.

This process of mitosis is basic to life because the chromosomes that replicate in mitosis are made up of a chemical called deoxyribonucleic acid (DNA), which contains all the genetic material necessary to give humans their characteristics. When an egg cell from your mother and a sperm cell from your father fused together to form the zygote, you attained characteristics from both parents. Sometimes there are mistakes in the transmission of the genetic code of DNA and different diseases can occur while the infant is developing in the mother's body. Today many women who have a history of genetic diseases occurring in their family have amniocentesis done early in pregnancy. This process allows doctors to examine the chromosomes of the unborn infant to determine whether certain genetic diseases might be developing. Also, genetic engineers are studying mitosis and trying to alter the structure of DNA to prevent genetic diseases. According to scientists, they will be able not only to prevent genetic diseases in the future, but also to construct a superior DNA molecule that will create immunity to many diseases. □

DETAILED DESCRIPTIVE OUTLINE

PROPOSITION   Karyokinesis and cytokinesis are the main phases in mitosis.

PLAN   Develop two reasons supporting the proposition, and a conclusion.

PARAGRAPH 1   *says:* Mitosis is the process by which one cell produces two daughter cells, each one identical in chromosome number and genetic material. Mitosis can be divided into two phases: karyokinesis and cytokinesis.

does: Introduces the proposition by raising a question about a theory. Answers the question and defines a process. Then divides the process into two phases. States the proposition.

PARAGRAPH 2   *says:* During the thirty minutes of karyokinesis the chromosomes enlarge then divide and the nucleus enlarges then divides. The new chromosomes and nucleus will be an exact copy of the original. They will also be transferred to the new cell.

does: Develops the first reason supporting the proposition saying how long the complete process takes. Then explains how long the first phase takes and gives a detailed explanation of that phase.

PARAGRAPH 3   *says:* During the thirty minutes of cytokinesis the nuclei cause furrowing and the cytoplasm divides. The cellular membrane pinches off to form two identical cells.

does: Develops the second reason supporting the proposition explaining how long the second phase takes. Explains this phase in detail. Then tells the length of the process and what is happening while the process is not going on.

PARAGRAPH 4   *says:* Sometimes there are mistakes in the genetic code of DNA and diseases can occur. Scientists say in the future they will be able to prevent these diseases._

does: Places the process into the larger context of human propagation. Explains some unwanted results that may occur from the process and what is being done to prevent them in the future.

Gene Manipulation and Huxley's *Brave New World*

Eric Leibowitz

In his novel *Brave New World,* Aldous Huxley writes about a society in which human beings are controlled by a system of eugenics. People are born into categories or classes according to the genetic makeup that has been programmed into them at conception. Eugenics has been a hotly debated topic for many years. We have seen the devastating effects of a system based on eugenics in Hitler's regime. The Nazis sifted out what they regarded as inferior non-Aryan races by killing them, and they tried to breed members of the Aryan race by controlling relations between men and women. This attitude toward selecting, or hybridizing, human beings as if they were farm animals is extremely crude. But something like it potentially exists today in a much more sophisticated form in the science of gene manipulation. As recently as September 1990, an actual experiment involving the insertion of a gene into a human being was performed (Weiss). Many serious issues are raised by this procedure, as they are in many new aspects of medical science, such as recombinant DNA. The issue that most writers on gene manipulation address is whether it causes more harm than good.

Those who object to gene science do so on grounds of morality and ethics. One problem is the fact that it is not a perfect science. There is much room for error. For example, several years ago a doctor did a gene science experiment on a human patient suffering from beta thalassemia without getting permission from the relevant medical watchdog committees. The experiment was unsuccessful and the doctor was reprimanded. His failure supports those who say that much more needs to be done before those responsible for maintaining medical ethics will feel comfortable with gene science (Munson 339). Others believe that we should abandon gene science altogether for religious reasons. They believe that human beings have no right to "play God" by manipulating genes (Arras 403). And yet another question that many people raise concerns the morality of the basic premises of gene science. For example, do we have the right to change people's genes in order to make them enjoy doing menial labor? And if so, what if that trait were passed down to their offspring, as it is in Huxley's novel (Munson 362)? We would then be manipulating traits in people not even born. In other words, we would be forcing constraints on a future generation without their knowledge or consent.

Those who are in favor of gene science, however, stress its medical value. There are many diseases that we may be able to cure through gene manipulation, such as heart disease and certain forms of cancer. So long as this is the case, the argument goes, it is better to save lives than to worry about moral problems (Arras 403). In any case, they argue, if we have the ability to cure people genetically, then it may actually be morally wrong not to cure them (Munson 389), just as it would be immoral not to save a drowning person if we were able to do so. People who hold this position also disagree with the religious arguments against gene science. They argue that gene science is no different from curing a disease by today's common methods. Isn't having tetanus shots "playing God" too? As to the question of causing certain traits to be passed down to someone's offspring, those who take this point of view explain that it is simply not a problem. Scientists cannot manipulate sex cells. Today's gene therapy involves nonsex cells, thereby insuring the trait's extinction when the patient dies. □

WORKS CITED

Arras, John. *Ethical Issues in Modern Medicine*. 2nd ed. San Francisco: Mayfield, 1983.

Huxley, Aldous. *Brave New World.* New York: Harper and Row, 1969.

Munson, Ronald. *Intervention and Reflection.* 3rd ed. New York: Wadsworth, 1988.

Weiss, R. "First Human Gene-Therapy Test Begun." *Science News,* 22 Sept. 1990: 180.

No One Knows Anything

Daniel W. Foley

In the centuries-old debate about whether knowledge and certainty are possible, no one has reached any clear conclusions. Skepticism, the view that human beings can know little or nothing for certain, persists. Since the start of this conflict between skeptics and the rationalists who attack them, philosophers have felt compelled to defend one side or the other. Rationalists try to lay skepticism to rest with arguments that seem airtight, but with little success. Skeptics defend their views by arguing that what the rationalists say about knowledge is unsound. In the words of the prominent twentieth-century philosopher Robert Nozick, "The continuing felt need to refute skepticism, and the difficulty in doing so, attest to the power of the skeptic's position, and the depths of his worries" (197). A critical examination of both sides of the debate may not be enough to convince everyone that skepticism is the more reasonable view of the world to hold. But it should at least persuade anyone that attempts to refute skepticism fail.

Perhaps the most common and initially persuasive argument against skepticism is that it is self-defeating. Skeptics, the argument goes, claim that we know nothing. But if we know nothing, rationalists assert, we cannot know that we know nothing, nor can we argue for the position that we know nothing. Our skepticism renders uncertain any reasons we offer in its defense. George Pappas and Marshall Swain concede the difficulty: "It is not easy," they admit, "to present cogent arguments in [defense] of skepticism" (38). Nevertheless, the rationalist argument outlined here misrepresents the skeptical position. In this as in many such cases, as Keith Lehrer puts it, "The skeptic has been mistreated" (348). Skeptics do not argue that "no one knows anything." They argue that we can never be absolutely certain of anything (347). This argument meets the accusation that skepticism is paradoxical, because it shows that skeptics are not arguing that theirs is the only valid position. The premises of the skeptic's argument, Lehrer remarks, "must not be understood as claims to knowledge, but only formulations of what he believes and hopes we shall concede" (348).

Another argument commonly advanced against skepticism is that we can know "necessary truths," such as mathematical and logical truths, even if we concede that factual propositions about the world around us may be subject to error. Rationalists call the tenets of mathematics and logic "necessary truths" because they seem rock solid. Denying them leads to seemingly nonsensical results. After all, who would deny the Fundamental Theorem of Arithmetic or the Law of the Excluded Middle? Once again rationalists seem to have made their point. But skepticism takes no prisoners in its critique of such claims. First, as Lehrer argues, it is possible to believe a proposition to be necessarily true and yet not know it, because we might believe it for superficial and insufficient reasons. We could easily have some good evidence that it is true, but not enough evidence to be certain of its truth. No matter how strong the evidence may be that a truth is necessary and therefore certain, "we do not know that the logical possibility of error has been excluded" (Lehrer 349–350). Bertrand Russell's comment on mathematics testifies to the strength of Lehrer's position. "It is one of the chief merits of proofs," he wrote, "that they instill a certain skepticism about the result proved" (Kline 315).

The failure of these antiskeptical arguments indicates that rationalists are attacking a straw man. When properly argued, skepticism remains undefeated by their attack. But the persuasiveness of the skeptical position aside, skepticism represents a healthy and honest way of looking at our everyday lives. Skeptics are willing to subject their own views and beliefs to criticism and are willing to change their views if they see that they are incorrect. Skeptics prefer to admit their own ignorance and fallibility, rather than cling to comforting illusions of certitude. The beliefs of skeptics are not dogmatic, not carved in stone. The result is that skepticism can be an extremely useful philosophy, especially in science and technology, where a mistake caused by too much confidence in one's own knowledge and judgment can cost millions, and can sometimes even cost lives. □

WORKS CITED

Kline, Morris. *Mathematics: The Loss of Certainty.* New York: Oxford Univ. Press, 1980.

Lehrer, Keith. "Why Not Skepticism?" In Pappas.

Nozick, Robert. *Philosophical Explanations.* Cambridge: Harvard Univ. Press, 1981.

Pappas, George, and Marshall Swain, eds. *Essays on Knowledge and Justification*. Ithaca: Cornell Univ. Press, 1978.
Turner, Daniel. "Why Skepticism?" In Pappas.

Homer's Use of the Gods in the *Iliad*

Andrew Boyle

Epics are long oral narratives based on myth and composed orally in verse. Unlike a novel, in which the author works out the plot before writing, the plot of an epic is composed during recitation before an audience. Like novelists, composers or performers of an epic, that is, epic poets, may think of things they want to add to the story and changes they want to make in it while they are performing it. For example, if the plot they started with turns out not to fit the theme they want to convey, they will want to change the plot to fit the theme. In writing a novel, this kind of revision is fairly easy to do: simply rewrite. But since an epic is composed orally, poets cannot delete parts of the story that they have already told. They can only change the parts of the story that are left to tell, and they have to try to make those changes fit what went before. This kind of revision seems to explain the way Homer uses the Olympian gods in developing the plot of the *Iliad*.

The Olympian gods were useful to Homer because they helped him make events turn out in ways that, according to what happens at the beginning of the story, might seem to lead to another outcome. For example, the background of the *Iliad* is that Helen's father, Tyndareus, made all her suitors swear that if she were taken away by another man, they would all join her husband to get her back. They agreed, and Helen chose to marry Menelaus. In the meantime, the Olympian goddesses asked Paris, brother of the famous Trojan warrior Hector, to judge a beauty contest among them. All the contestants tried to bribe Paris. Aphrodite's bribe, Helen, appealed to him most. So Aphrodite won the beauty contest, and Paris won Helen. This event sets off the Trojan War, which Homer begins in the *Iliad* at the point where Menelaus and Helen's former suitors, a group of Achaians, attack Troy. Paris offers to fight any Achaian, and Menelaus takes him up on it. Menelaus, clearly the better fighter, seems destined to win. But Homer makes the Olympian goddess Aphrodite intervene just in time to save Paris's life, because if Menelaus should win the battle, the Trojans would have to return Helen. The war would be over, and so would the epic.

Besides using the Olympian gods to patch up the plot as he goes along, Homer also makes the gods use their powers to transform motives and traits of characters that he has already established earlier in the story. For example, Achilles, the best and most feared of the Achaian warriors, refuses to fight in the war because of a dispute with King Agamemnon. When the Trojans seem to be winning the war, Achilles still refuses to fight, but because his own ships are in danger he lets his best friend, Patroclus, use his armor, making him invulnerable. In the heat of battle, the war-crazed Patroclus forgets his orders, which are to fight only until Achilles's ships are safe. He kills many Trojan warriors and drives the rest back into the walls of Troy. Unfortunately, according to the way Patroclus is characterized earlier in the story, this result is unlikely. To make Patroclus's bravery believable, Homer places the Olympian god Zeus on his side. At the same time, however, in order not to shift attention from the central theme of the poem (Achilles's anger, not Patroclus's military prowess) Homer brings in another Olympian, Apollo, to get Patroclus out of the way. Apollo makes Patroclus's armor fall off so that Hector can kill him, thus inflaming Achilles's smoldering anger and sending him on the warpath. This interference by the Olympian gods puts the derailed story back on track. Without the gods, Patroclus would have defeated the Trojans and destroyed the theme of the story. □

DETAILED DESCRIPTIVE OUTLINE

PROPOSITION	Homer uses the Olympian gods to make later episodes in the *Iliad* fit what went before.
PLAN	Two reasons in support of the proposition.
PARAGRAPH 1	*says:* Epics require the poet to develop the story as he goes along.
	does: Introduces the proposition by stating the type of literary work being discussed and describing it. Explains how this type of work is generated and the problems that arise in generating it that way.
PARAGRAPH 2	*says:* The Olympian gods provided a means of developing a plot by affecting the outcome of events that might seem inevitable.
	does: States a generalization in support of the proposition. Defends this generalization by retelling a portion of an epic. Shows the relation between the

generalization and the essay's proposition by explaining what would have happened if the device named in the proposition had not been used.

PARAGRAPH 3   *says:* The Olympian gods also helped develop epic plots by creating new motives.

does: States another generalization in support of the proposition. Defends this generalization, as in paragraph 2, by retelling another part of the same epic. Shows the relationship between the generalization and the proposition by explaining how several points in the work would have changed if the device named in the proposition had not been used.

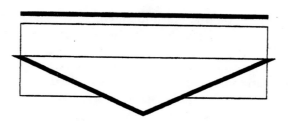

Anthology of Professional Essays

Examsmanship and the Liberal Arts: A Study in Educational Epistemology

William G. Perry, Jr.

"But sir, I don't think I really deserve it, it was mostly bull, really." This disclaimer from a student whose examination we have awarded a straight "A" is wondrously depressing. Alfred North Whitehead invented its only possible rejoinder: "Yes sir, what you wrote is nonsense, utter nonsense. But ah! Sir! It's the right *kind* of nonsense!"

Bull, in this university [Harvard], is customarily a source of laughter, or a problem in ethics. I shall step a little out of fashion to use the subject as a take-off point for a study in comparative epistemology. The phenomenon of bull, in all the honor and opprobrium with which it is regarded by students and faculty, says something, I think, about our theories of knowledge. So too, the grades which we assign on examinations communicate to students what these theories may be.

We do not have to be out-and-out logical-positivists to suppose that we have something to learn about "what we think knowledge is" by having a good look at "what we do when we go about measuring it." We know the straight "A" examination when we see it, of course, and we have reason to hope that the student will understand why his work receives our recognition. He doesn't always. And those who receive lesser honor? Perhaps an understanding of certain anomalies in our customs of grading good bull will explain the students' confusion.

I must beg patience, then, both of the reader's humor and of his morals. Not that I ask him to suspend his sense of humor but that I shall ask him to go beyond it. In a great university the picture of a bright student attempting to outwit his professor while his professor takes pride in not being outwitted is certainly ridiculous. I shall report just such a scene, for its implications bear upon my point. Its comedy need not present a serious obstacle to thought.

As for the ethics of bull, I must ask for a suspension of judgment. I wish that students could suspend theirs. Unlike humor, moral commitment is hard to think beyond. Too early a moral judgment is precisely what stands between many able students and a liberal education. The stunning realization that the Harvard Faculty will often accept, as evidence of knowledge, the cerebrations of a student who has little data at his disposal, confronts every student with an ethical dilemma. For some it forms an academic focus for what used to be thought of as "adolescent disillusion." It is irrelevant that rumor inflates the phenomenon to mythical proportions. The students know that beneath the myth there remains a solid and haunting reality. The moral "bind" consequent on this awareness appears most poignantly in serious students who are reluctant to concede the competitive advantage to the bullster and who yet feel a deep personal shame when, having succumbed to "temptation," they themselves receive a high grade for work they consider "dishonest."

I have spent many hours with students caught in this unwelcome bitterness. These hours lend an urgency to my theme. I have found that students have been able to come to terms with the ethical problem, to the extent that it is real, only after a refined study of the true nature of bull and its relation to "knowledge." I shall submit grounds for my suspicion that we can be found guilty of sharing the students' confusion of moral and epistemological issues.

I

I present as my "premise," then, an amoral *fabliau*. Its hero-villain is the Abominable Mr. Metzger '47. Since I celebrate his virtuosity, I regret giving him a pseudonym, but the peculiar style of his bravado requires me to honor also his modesty. Bull in pure form is rare; there is usually some contamination by data. The community has reason to be grateful to Mr. Metzger for having created an instance of laboratory purity, free from any adulteration by matter. The more credit is due him, I think, because his act was free from premeditation, deliberation, or hope of personal gain.

Mr. Metzger stood one rainy November day in the lobby of Memorial Hall. A junior, concentrating in mathematics, he was fond of diverting himself by taking part in the drama, a penchant which may have had some influence on the events of the next hour. He was waiting to take part in a rehearsal in Sanders Theatre, but, as sometimes happens, no other players appeared. Perhaps the rehearsal had been canceled without his knowledge? He decided to wait another five minutes.

Students, meanwhile, were filing into the Great Hall opposite, and taking seats at the testing tables. Spying a friend crossing the lobby toward the Great Hall's door, Metzger greeted him and extended appropriate condolences. He inquired, too, what course his friend was being tested in. "Oh, Soc. Sci. something-or-other." "What's it all about?" asked Metzger, and this, as Homer remarked of Patroclus, was the beginning of evil for him.

"It's about Modern Perspectives on Man and Society and All That," said his friend. "Pretty interesting, really."

"Always wanted to take a course like that," said Metzger. "Any good reading?"

"Yeah, great. There's this book"—his friend did not have time to finish.

"Take your seats please," said a stern voice beside them. The idle conversation had somehow taken the two friends to one of the tables in the Great Hall. Both students automatically obeyed; the proctor put blue books before them; another proctor presented them with copies of the printed hour-test.

Mr. Metzger remembered afterwards a brief misgiving that was suddenly overwhelmed by a surge of curiosity and puckish glee. He wrote "George Smith" on the blue book, opened it, and addressed the first question.

I must pause to exonerate the Management. The Faculty has a rule that no student may attend an examination in a course in which he is not enrolled. To the wisdom of this rule the outcome of this deplorable story stands witness. The Registrar, charged with the enforcement of the rule, has developed an organization with procedures which are certainly the finest to be devised. In November, however, class rosters are still shaky, and on this particular day another student, named Smith, was absent. As for the culprit we can reduce his guilt no further than to suppose that he was ignorant of the rule, or, in the face of the momentous challenge before him, forgetful.

We need not be distracted by Metzger's performance on the "objective" or "spot" questions on the test. His D on these sections can be explained by those versed in the theory of probability. Our interest focuses on the quality of his essay. It appears that when Metzger's friend picked up his own blue book a few days later, he found himself in company with a large proportion of his section in having received on the essay a C+. When he quietly picked up "George Smith's" blue book to return it to Metzger, he observed that the grade for the essay was A−. In the margin was a note in the section man's hand. It read "Excellent work. Could you have pinned these observations down a bit more closely? Compare . . . in . . . pp. . . . ."

Such news could hardly be kept quiet. There was a leak, and the whole scandal broke on the front page of Tuesday's *Crimson*. With the press Metzger was modest, as becomes a hero. He said that there had been nothing to it at all, really. The essay question had offered a choice of two books, Margaret Mead's *And Keep Your Powder Dry* or Geoffrey Gorer's *The American People*. Metzger reported that having read neither of them, he had chosen the second "because the title gave me some notion as to what the book might be about." On the test, two critical comments were offered on each book, one favorable, one unfavorable. The students were asked to "discuss." Metzger conceded that he had played safe in throwing his lot with the more laudatory of the two comments, "but I did not forget to be balanced."

I do not have Mr. Metzger's essay before me except in vivid memory. As I recall, he took his first cue from the name Geoffrey, and committed his strategy to the premise that Gorer was born into an "Anglo-Saxon" culture, probably English, but certainly "English speaking." Having heard that Margaret Mead was a social anthropologist, he inferred that Gorer was the same. He then entered upon his essay, centering his inquiry upon what he supposed might be the problems inherent in an anthropologist's observation of a culture which was his own, or nearly his own. Drawing in part from memories of table-talk on cultural relativity* and in part from creative logic, he rang changes on the relation of observer to observed, and assessed the kind and degree of objectivity which might accrue to an observer through training as an anthropologist. He concluded that the book in question did in fact contribute a considerable range of "'objective', and even 'fresh'," insights into the nature of our culture. "At the same time," he warned, "these observations must be understood within the context of their generation by a person only partly freed from his embeddedness in the culture he is observing, and limited in his capacity to transcend those particular tendencies and biases which he has himself developed as a personality in his interaction with this culture since his birth. In this sense the book portrays as much the

*"An important part of Harvard's education takes place during meals in the Houses." An Official Publication. [Perry's note.]

character of Geoffrey Gorer as it analyzes that of the American people." It is my regrettable duty to report that at this moment of triumph Mr. Metzger was carried away by the temptations of parody and added, "We are thus much the richer."

In any case, this was the essay for which Metzger received his honor grade and his public acclaim. He was now, of course, in serious trouble with the authorities.

I shall leave him for the moment to the mercy of the Administrative Board of Harvard College and turn the reader's attention to the section man who ascribed the grade. He was in much worse trouble. All the consternation in his immediate area of the Faculty and all the glee in other areas fell upon his unprotected head. I shall now undertake his defense.

I do so not simply because I was acquainted with him and feel a respect for his intelligence; I believe in the justice of his grade! Well, perhaps "justice" is the wrong word in a situation so manifestly absurd. This is more a case in "equity." That is, the grade is equitable if we accept other aspects of the situation which are equally absurd. My proposition is this: if we accept as valid those C grades which were accorded students who, like Metzger's friend, demonstrated a thorough familiarity with the details of the book without relating their critique to the methodological problems of social anthropology, then "George Smith" deserved not only the same, but better.

The reader may protest that the C's given to students who showed evidence only of diligence were indeed not valid and that both these students and "George Smith" should have received E's. To give the diligent E is of course not in accord with custom. I shall take up this matter later. For now, were I to allow the protest, I could only restate my thesis: that "George Smith's" E would, in a college of liberal arts, be properly a "better" E.

At this point I need a short-hand. It is a curious fact that there is no academic slang for the presentation of evidence of diligence alone. "Parroting" won't do; it is possible to "parrot" bull. I must beg the reader's pardon, and, for reasons almost too obvious to bear, suggest "cow."

Stated as nouns, the concepts look simple enough:

cow (pure): data, however relevant, without relevancies.
bull (pure): relevancies, however relevant, without data.

The reader can see all too clearly where this simplicity would lead. I can assure him that I would not have imposed on him this way were I aiming to say that knowledge in this university is definable as some neuter compromise between cow and bull, some infertile hermaphrodite. This is precisely what many diligent students seem to believe: that what they must learn to do is to "find the right mean" between "amounts" of detail and "amounts" of generalities. Of course this is not the point at all. The problem is not quantitative, nor does its solution lie on a continuum between the particular and the general. Cow and bull are not poles of a single dimension. A clear notion of what they really are is essential to my inquiry, and for heuristic purposes I wish to observe them further in the celibate state.

When the pure concepts are translated into verbs, the complexities become apparent in the assumptions and purposes of the students as they write:

> To cow (v. intrans.) or the act of cowing:
>
> To list data (or perform operations) without awareness of, or comment upon, the contexts, frames of reference, or points of observation which determine the origin, nature, and meaning of the data (or procedures). To write on the assumption that "a fact is a fact." To present evidence of hard work as a substitute for understanding, without any intent to deceive.
>
> To bull (v. intrans.) or the act of bulling:
>
> To discourse upon the contexts, frames of reference, and points of observation which would determine the origin, nature, and meaning of data if one had any. To present evidence of an understanding of form in the hope that the reader may be deceived into supposing a familiarity with content.

At the level of conscious intent, it is evident that cowing is more moral, or less immoral, than bulling. To speculate about unconscious intent would be either an injustice or a needless elaboration of my theme. It is enough that the impression left by cow is one of earnestness, diligence, and painful naiveté. The grader may feel disappointment or even irritation, but these feelings are usually balanced by pity, compassion, and a reluctance to hit a man when he's both down and moral. He may feel some challenge to his teaching, but none whatever to his one-upsmanship. He writes in the margin: "See me."

We are now in a position to understand the anomaly of custom: As instructors, we always assign bull an E, *when we detect it*; whereas we usually give cow a D, *even though it is always obvious*.

After all, we did not ask to be confronted with a choice between morals and understanding (or did we?). We evince a charming humanity, I think, in our decision to grade in favor of morals and pathos. "I simply can't give this student an E after he has *worked* so hard." At the same time we tacitly express our respect for the bullster's strength. We recognize a colleague. If he knows so well how to dish it out, we can be sure that he can also take it.

Of course it is just possible that we carry with us, perhaps from our own school-days, an assumption that if a student is willing to work hard and collect "good hard facts" he can always be taught to understand their relevance, whereas a student who has caught onto the forms of relevance without working at all is a lost scholar.

But this is not in accord with our experience.

It is not in accord either, as far as I can see, with the stated values of a liberal education. If a liberal education should teach students "how to think," not only in their own fields but in fields outside their own — that is, to understand "how the other fellow orders knowledge," then bulling, even in its purest form, expresses an important part of what a pluralist university holds dear, surely a more important part than the collecting of "facts that are facts" which schoolboys learn to do. Here then, good bull appears not as ignorance at all but as an aspect of knowledge. It is both relevant and "true." In a university setting good bull is therefore of more value than "facts," which, without a frame of reference, are not even "true" at all.

Perhaps this value accounts for the final anomaly: as instructors, we are inclined to reward bull highly, *where we do not detect its intent*, to the consternation of the bullster's acquaintances. And often we do not examine the matter too closely. After a long evening of reading blue books full of cow, the sudden meeting with a student who at least understands the problems of one's field provides a lift like a draught of refreshing wine, and a strong disposition toward trust.

This was, then, the sense of confidence that came to our unfortunate section man as he read "George Smith's" sympathetic considerations.

II

In my own years of watching over students' shoulders as they work, I have come to believe that this feeling of trust has a firmer basis than the confidence generated by evidence of diligence done. I believe that the theory of a liberal education holds. Students who have dared to understand man's real relation to his knowledge have shown themselves to be in a strong position to learn content rapidly and meaningfully, and to retain it. I have learned to be less concerned about the education of a student who has come to understand the nature of man's knowledge, even though he has not yet committed himself to hard work, than I am about the education of the student who, after one or two terms at Harvard, is working desperately hard and still believes that collected "facts" constitute knowledge. The latter, when I try to explain to him, too often understands me to be saying that he "doesn't *put in enough generalities.*" Surely he has "put in *enough* facts."

I have come to see such quantitative statements as expressions of an entire, coherent epistemology. In grammar school the student is taught that Columbus discovered America in 1492. The *more* such items he gets "right" on a given test the more he is credited with "knowing." From years of this sort of thing it is not unnatural to develop the conviction that knowledge consists of the accretion of hard facts by hard work.

The student learns that the more facts and procedures he can get "right" in a given course, the better will be his grade. The more courses he takes, the more subjects he has "had," the more credits he accumulates, the more diplomas he will get, until, after graduate school, he will emerge with his doctorate, a member of the community of scholars.

The foundation of this entire life is the proposition that a fact is a fact. The necessary correlate of this proposition is that a fact is either right or wrong. This implies that the standard against which the rightness or wrongness of a fact may be judged exists *someplace*—perhaps graven upon a tablet in a Platonic world outside and above *this* cave of tears. In grammar school it is evident that the tablets which enshrine the spelling of a word or the answer to an arithmetic problem are visible to my teacher who need only compare my offerings to it. In high school I observe that my English teachers disagree. This can only mean that the tablets in such matters as the goodness of a poem are distant and obscured by clouds. They surely exist. The pleasing of befuddled English teachers degenerates into assessing their prejudices, a game in which I have no protection against my competitors more glib of tongue. I respect only my science teachers, authorities who *really know*. Later I learn from them that "this is only what we think *now*." But eventually, surely. . . . Into this epistemology of education, apparently shared by teachers in such terms as "credits," "semester hours," and "years of French," the student may invest his ideals, his drive, his competitiveness, his safety, his self-esteem, and even his love.

College raises other questions: by whose calendar is it proper to say that Columbus discovered America in 1492? How, when, and by whom was the year 1 established in this calendar? What of other calendars? In view of the evidence of Leif Ericson's previous visit (and the American Indians), what historical ethnocentrism is suggested by the use of the word "discover" in this sentence? As for Leif Ericson, in accord with what assumptions do you order the evidence?

These questions and their answers are not "more" knowledge. They are devastation. I do not need to elaborate upon the epistemology, or rather epistemologies, they imply. A fact has become at last "an observation or an operation performed in a frame of reference." A liberal education is founded in an awareness of frame of reference even in the most immediate and empirical examination of data. Its acquirement involves relinquishing hope of absolutes and of the protection they afford against doubt and the glib-tongued competitor. It demands an ever-widening sophistication about systems of thought and observation. It leads, not away from, but *through* the arts of gamesmanship to a new trust.

This trust is in the value and integrity of systems, their varied character, and the way their apparently incompatible metaphors enlighten, from complementary facets, the particulars of human experience. As one student said to me: "I used to be cynical about intellectual games. Now I want to know them thoroughly. You see I came to realize that it was only when I knew the rules of the game cold that I could tell whether what I was saying was tripe."

We too often think of the bullster as cynical. He can be, and not always in a light-hearted way. We have failed to observe that there can lie behind cow the potential of a deeper and more dangerous despair. The moralism of sheer work and obedience can be an ethic that, unwilling to face a despair of its ends, glorifies its means. The implicit refusal to consider the relativity of both ends and means leaves the operator in an unconsidered proprietary absolutism. History bears witness that in the pinches this moral superiority has no recourse to negotiation, only to force.

A liberal education proposes that man's hope lies elsewhere: in the negotiability that can arise from an understanding of the integrity of systems and of their origins in man's address to his universe. The prerequisite is the courage to accept such a definition of knowledge. From then on, of course, there is nothing incompatible between such an epistemology and hard work. Rather the contrary.

I can now at last let bull and cow get together. The reader knows best how a productive wedding is arranged in his own field. This is the nuptial he celebrates with a straight A on examinations. The masculine context must embrace the feminine particular, though itself "born of woman." Such a union is knowledge itself, and it alone can generate new contexts and new data which can unite in their turn to form new knowledge.

In this happy setting we can congratulate in particular the Natural Sciences, long thought to be barren ground to the bullster. I have indeed drawn my examples of bull from the Social Sciences, and by analogy from the Humanities. Essay writing in these fields has long been thought to nurture the art of bull to its prime. I feel, however, that the Natural Sciences have no reason to feel slighted. It is perhaps no accident that Metzger was a mathematician. As part of my researches for this paper, furthermore, a student of considerable talent has recently honored me with an impressive analysis of the art of amassing "partial credits" on examinations in advanced physics. Though beyond me in some respects, his presentation confirmed my impression that instructors of Physics frequently honor on examinations operations structurally similar to those requisite in a good essay.

The very qualities that make the Natural Sciences fields of delight for the eager gamesman have been essential to their marvelous fertility.

III

As priests of these mysteries, how can we make our rites more precisely expressive? The student who merely cows robs himself, without knowing it, of his education and his soul. The student who only bulls robs himself, as he knows full well, of the joys of inductive discovery—that is, of engagement. The introduction of frames of reference in the new curricula of Mathematics and Physics in the schools is a hopeful experiment. We do not know yet how much of these potent revelations the very young can stand, but I suspect they may rejoice in them more than we have supposed. I can't believe they have never wondered about Leif Ericson and that word "discovered," or even about 1492. They have simply been too wise to inquire.

Increasingly in recent years better students in the better high schools and preparatory schools are being allowed to inquire. In fact they appear to be receiving both encouragement and training in their inquiry. I have the evidence before me.

Each year for the past five years all freshmen entering Harvard and Radcliffe have been asked in freshman week to "grade" two essays answering an examination question in History. They are then asked to give their reasons for their grades. One essay, filled with dates, is 99 percent cow. The other, with hardly a date in it, is a good essay, easily mistaken for bull. The "official" grades of these essays are, for the first (alas!) C+ "because he has worked so hard," and for the second (soundly, I think) B+. Each year a larger majority of freshmen evaluate these essays as would the majority of the faculty, and for the faculty's reasons, and each year a smaller minority give the higher honor to the essay offering data alone. More interesting, a larger number of students each year, while not overrating the second essay, award the first the straight E appropriate to it in a college of liberal arts.

For us who must grade such students in a university, these developments imply a new urgency, did we not feel it already. Through our grades we describe for the students, in the showdown, what we believe about the nature of knowledge. The subtleties of bull are not peripheral to our academic concerns. That they penetrate to the center of our care is evident in our feelings when a student whose good work we have awarded a high grade reveals to us that he does not feel he deserves it. Whether he disqualifies himself because "there's too much bull in it," or worse because "I really don't think I've worked that hard," he presents a serious educational problem. Many students feel this sleaziness; only a few reveal it to us.

We can hardly allow a mistaken sense of fraudulence to undermine our students' achievements. We must lead students beyond their concept of bull so that they may honor relevancies that are really relevant. We can willingly acknowledge that, in lieu of the date 1492, a consideration of calendars and of the word "discovered," may well be offered with intent to deceive. We must insist that this does not make such considerations intrinsically immoral, and that, contrariwise, the date 1492 may be no substitute for them. Most of all, we must convey the impression that we grade understanding qua understanding. To be convincing, I suppose we must concede to ourselves in advance that a bright student's understanding is understanding even if he achieved it by osmosis rather than by hard work in our course.

These are delicate matters. As for cow, its complexities are not what need concern us. Unlike good bull, it does not represent partial knowledge at all. It belongs to a different theory of knowledge entirely. In our theories of knowledge it represents total ignorance, or worse yet, a knowledge downright inimical to understanding. I even go so far as to propose that we award no more C's for cow. To do so is rarely, I feel, the act of mercy it seems. Mercy lies in clarity.

The reader may be afflicted by a lingering curiosity about the fate of Mr. Metzger. I hasten to reassure him. The Administrative Board of Harvard College, whatever its satanic reputations, is a benign body. Its members, to be sure, were on the spot. They delighted in Metzger's exploit, but they were responsible to the Faculty's rule. The hero stood in danger of probation. The debate was painful. Suddenly one member, of a refined legalistic sensibility, observed that the rule applied specifically to "examinations" and that the occasion had been simply an hour-test. Mr. Metzger was merely "admonished." □

The Indispensable Opposition

Walter Lippmann

Were they pressed hard enough, most men would probably confess that political freedom—that is to say, the right to speak freely and to act in opposition—is a noble ideal rather than a practical necessity. As the case for freedom is generally put today, the argument lends itself to this feeling. It is made to appear that, whereas each man claims his freedom as a matter of right, the freedom he accords to other men is a matter of toleration. Thus, the defense of freedom of opinion tends to rest not on its substantial, beneficial, and indispensable consequences, but on a somewhat eccentric, a rather vaguely benevolent, attachment to an abstraction.

It is all very well to say with Voltaire, "I wholly disapprove of what you say, but will defend to the death your right to say it," but as a matter of fact most men will not defend to the death the rights of other men: if they disapprove sufficiently what other men say, they will somehow suppress those men if they can.

So, if this is the best that can be said for liberty of opinion, that a man must tolerate his opponents because everyone has a "right" to say what he pleases, then we shall find that liberty of opinion is a luxury, safe only in pleasant times when men can be tolerant because they are not deeply and vitally concerned.

Yet actually, as a matter of historic fact, there is a much stronger foundation for the great constitutional right of freedom of speech, and as a matter of practical human experience there is a much more compelling reason for cultivating the habits of free men. We take, it seems to me, a naïvely self-righteous view when we argue as if the right of our opponents to speak were something that we protect because we are magnanimous, noble, and unselfish. The compelling reason why, if liberty of opinion did not exist, we should have to invent it, why it will eventually have to be restored in all civilized countries where it is now suppressed, is that we must protect the right of our opponents to speak because we must hear what they have to say.

We miss the whole point when we imagine that we tolerate the freedom of our political opponents as we tolerate a howling baby next door, as we put up with the blasts from our neighbor's radio because we are too peaceable to heave a brick through the window. If this were all there is to freedom of opinion, that we are too good-natured or too timid to do anything about our opponents and our critics except to let them talk, it would be difficult to say whether we are tolerant because we are magnanimous or because we are lazy, because we have strong principles or because we lack serious convictions, whether we have the hospitality of an inquiring mind or the indifference of any empty mind. And so, if we truly wish to understand why freedom is necessary in a civilized society, we must begin by realizing that, because freedom of discussion improves our own opinions, the liberties of other men are our own vital necessity.

We are much closer to the essence of the matter, not when we quote Voltaire, but when we go to the doctor and pay him to ask us the most embarrassing questions and to prescribe the most disagreeable diet. When we pay the doctor to exercise complete freedom of speech about the cause and cure of our stomachache, we do not look upon ourselves as tolerant and magnanimous, and worthy to be admired by ourselves. We have enough common sense to know that if we threaten to put the doctor in jail because we do not like the diagnosis and the prescription it will be unpleasant for the doctor, to be sure, but equally unpleasant for our own stomachache. That is why even the most ferocious dictator would rather be treated by a doctor who was free to think and speak the truth than by his own Minister of Propaganda. For there is a point, the point at which things really matter, where the freedom of others is no longer a question of their right but of our own need.

The point at which we recognize this need is much higher in some men than in others. The totalitarian rulers think they do not need the freedom of an opposition: they exile, imprison, or shoot their opponents. We have concluded on the basis of practical experience, which goes back to Magna Carta and beyond, that we need the opposition. We pay the opposition salaries out of the public treasury.

In so far as the usual apology for freedom of speech ignores this experience, it becomes abstract and eccentric rather than concrete and human. The emphasis is generally put on the right to speak, as if all that mattered were that the doctor should be free to go out into the park and explain to the vacant air why I have a stomachache. Surely that is a miserable caricature of the great civic right which men have bled and died for. What really matters is that the doctor should tell *me* what ails me, that I should listen to him; that if I do not like what he says I should be free to call in another doctor; and that then the first doctor should have to listen to the second doctor; and that out of all the speaking and listening, the give-and-take of opinions, the truth should be arrived at.

This is the creative principle of freedom of speech, not that it is a system for the tolerating of error, but that it is a system for finding the truth. It may not produce the truth, or the whole truth all the time, or often, or in some cases ever. But if the truth can be found, there is no other system which will normally and habitually find so much truth. Until we have thoroughly understood this principle, we shall not know why we must value our liberty, or how we can protect and develop it.

Let us apply this principle to the system of public speech in a totalitarian state. We may, without any serious falsification, picture a condition of affairs in which the mass of the people are being addressed through one broadcasting system by one man and his chosen subordinates. The orators speak. The audience listens but cannot and dare not speak back. It is a system of one-way communication; the opinions of the rulers are broadcast outwardly to the mass of the people. But nothing comes back to the rulers from the people except the cheers; nothing returns in the way of knowledge of forgotten facts, hidden feelings, neglected truths, and practical suggestions.

But even a dictator cannot govern by his own one-way inspiration alone. In practice, therefore, the totalitarian rulers get back the reports of the secret police and of their party henchmen down among the crowd. If these reports are competent, the rulers may manage to remain in touch with public sentiment. Yet that is not enough to know what the audience feels. The rulers have also to make great decisions that have enormous consequences, and here their system provides virtually no help from the give-and-take of opinion in the nation. So they must either rely on their own intuition, which cannot be permanently and continually inspired, or, if they are intelligent despots, encourage their trusted advisers and their technicians to speak and debate freely in their presence.

On the walls of the houses of Italian peasants one may see inscribed in large letters the legend, "Mussolini is always right." But if that legend is taken seriously by Italian ambassadors, by the Italian General Staff, and by the Ministry of Finance, then all one can say is heaven help Mussolini, heaven help Italy, and the new Emperor of Ethiopia.

For at some point, even in a totalitarian state, it is indispensable that there should exist the freedom of opinion which causes opposing opinions to be debated. As time goes on, that is less and less easy under a despotism; critical discussion disappears as the internal opposition is liquidated in favor of men who think and feel alike. That is why the early successes of despots, of Napoleon I and of Napoleon III, have usually been followed by an irreparable mistake. For in listening only to his yes men—the others being in exile or in concentration camps, or terrified—the despot shuts himself off from the truth that no man can dispense with.

We know all this well enough when we contemplate the dictatorships. But when we try to picture our own system, by way of contrast, what picture do we have in our minds? It is, is it not, that anyone may stand up on his own soapbox and say anything he pleases, like the individuals in Kipling's poem ["L'Envoi"] who sit each in his separate star and draw the Thing as they see it for the God of Things as they are. Kipling, perhaps, could do this, since he was a poet. But the ordinary mortal isolated on his separate star will have a hallucination, and a citizenry declaiming from separate soapboxes will poison the air with hot and nonsensical confusion.

If the democratic alternative to the totalitarian one-way broadcasts is a row of separate soapboxes, then I submit that the alternative is unworkable, is unreasonable, and is humanly unattractive. It is above all a false alternative. It is not true that liberty has developed among civilized men when anyone is free to set up a soapbox, is free to hire a hall where he may expound his opinions to those who are willing to listen. On the contrary, freedom of speech is established to achieve its essential purpose only when different opinions are expounded in the same hall to the same audience.

For, while the right to talk may be the beginning of freedom, the necessity of listening is what makes the right important. Even in Russia and Germany a man may still stand in an open field and speak his mind. What matters is not the utterance of opinions. What matters is the confrontation of opinions in debate. No man can care profoundly that every fool should say what he likes. Nothing has been accomplished if the wisest man proclaims his wisdom in the middle of the Sahara Desert. This is the shadow. We have the substance of liberty when the fool is compelled to listen to the wise man and learn; when the wise man is compelled to take account of the fool, and to instruct him; when the wise man can increase his wisdom by hearing the judgment of his peers.

That is why civilized men must cherish liberty—as a means of promoting the discovery of truth. So we must not fix our whole attention on the right of anyone to hire his own hall, to rent his own broadcasting station, to distribute his own pamphlets. These rights are incidental; and though they must be preserved, they can be preserved only by regarding them as incidental, as auxiliary to the substance of liberty that must be cherished and cultivated.

Freedom of speech is best conceived, therefore, by having in mind the picture of a place like the American Congress, an assembly where opposing views are represented, where ideas are not merely uttered but debated, or the British Parliament, where men who are free to speak are also compelled to answer. We may picture the true condition of freedom as existing in a place like a court of law, where witnesses testify and are cross-examined, where the lawyer argues against the opposing lawyer before the same judge and in the presence of one jury. We may picture freedom as existing in a forum where the speaker must respond to questions; in a gathering of scientists where the data, the hypothesis, and the conclusion are submitted to men competent to judge them; in a reputable newspaper which not only will publish the opinions of those who disagree but will re-examine its own opinion in the light of what they say.

Thus the essence of freedom of opinion is not in mere toleration as such, but in the debate which toleration provides: it is not in the venting of opinion, but in the confrontation of opinion. That this is the practical substance can readily be understood when we remember how differently we feel and act about the censorship and regulation of opinion purveyed by different media of communication. We find then that, in so far as the medium makes difficult the confrontation of opinion in debate, we are driven towards censorship and regulation.

There is, for example, the whispering campaign, the circulation of anonymous rumors by men who cannot be compelled to prove what they say. They put the utmost strain on our tolerance, and there are few who do not rejoice when the anonymous slanderer is caught, exposed, and punished. At a higher level there is the moving picture, a most powerful medium for conveying ideas, but a medium which does not permit debate. A moving picture cannot be answered effectively by another moving picture; in all free countries there is some censorship of the movies, and there would be more if the producers did not recognize their limitations by avoiding political controversy. There is then the radio. Here debate is difficult: it is not easy to make sure that the speaker is being answered in the presence of the same audience. Inevitably, there is some regulation of the radio.

When we reach the newspaper press, the opportunity for debate is so considerable that discontent cannot grow to the point where under normal conditions there is any disposition to regulate the press. But when newspapers abuse their power by injuring people who have no means of replying, a disposition to regulate the press appears. When we arrive at Congress we find that, because the membership of the House is so large, full debate is impracticable. So there are restrictive rules. On the other hand, in the Senate, where the conditions of full debate exist, there is almost absolute freedom of speech.

This shows us that the preservation and development of freedom of opinion are not only a matter of adhering to abstract legal rights, but also, and very urgently, a matter of organizing and arranging sufficient debate. Once we have a firm hold on the central principle, there are many practical conclusions to be drawn. We then realize that the defense of freedom of opinion consists primarily in perfecting the opportunity for an adequate give-and-take of opinion; it consists also in regulating the freedom of those revolutionists who cannot or will not permit or maintain debate when it does not suit their purposes.

We must insist that free oratory is only the beginning of free speech; it is not the end, but a means to an end. The end is to find the truth. The practical justification of civil liberty is not that self-expression is one of the rights of man. It is that the examination of opinion is one of the necessities of man. For experience tells us that it is only when freedom of opinion becomes the compulsion to debate that the seed which our fathers planted has produced its fruit. When that is understood, freedom will be cherished not because it is a vent for our opinions but because it is the surest method of correcting them.

The unexamined life, said Socrates, is unfit to be lived by man. This is the virtue of liberty, and the ground on which we may best justify our belief in it, that it tolerates error in order to serve the truth. When men are brought face to face with their opponents, forced to listen and learn and mend their ideas, they cease to be children and savages and begin to live like civilized men. Then only is freedom a reality, when men may voice their opinions because they must examine their opinions.

The only reason for dwelling on all this is that if we are to preserve democracy we must understand its principles. And the principle which distinguishes it from all other forms of government is that in a democracy the opposition not only is tolerated as constitutional but must be maintained because it is in fact indispensable.

The democratic system cannot be operated without effective opposition. For, in making the great experiment of governing people by consent rather than by coercion, it is not sufficient that the party in power should have a majority. It is just as necessary that the party in power should never outrage the minority. That means that it must listen to the minority and be moved by the criticisms of the minority. That means that its measures must take account of the minority's objections, and that in administering measures it must remember that the minority may become the majority.

The opposition is indispensable. A good statesman, like any other sensible human being, always learns more from his opponents than from his fervent supporters. For his supporters will push him to disaster unless his opponents show him where the dangers are. So if he is wise he will often pray to be delivered from his friends, because they will ruin him. But, though it hurts, he ought also to pray never to be left without opponents; for they keep him on the path of reason and good sense.

The national unity of a free people depends upon a sufficiently even balance of political power to make it impracticable for the administration to be arbitrary and for the opposition to be revolutionary and irreconcilable. Where that balance no longer exists, democracy perishes. For unless all the citizens of a state are forced by circumstances to compromise, unless they feel that they can affect policy but that no one can wholly dominate it, unless by habit and necessity they have to give and take, freedom cannot be maintained. □

Aerodynamic Whistles

Robert C. Chanaud

The sound of aerodynamic whistles is familiar as the resonant note of an organ pipe, the shrill peep of a teakettle and the mellow tone of a flute. How are these sounds produced? In such nonaerodynamic devices as a drum, a violin, and a loudspeaker sound is generated when a mechanical system vibrates and disturbs the air. In an aerodynamic whistle the vibrating system is the air itself. Not all aerodynamic whistles whistle in the usual sense of the word. They include, for example, a telephone wire hissing in the wind.

Aerodynamic sound generation has been the subject of experiment and theoretical study for more than a century. In the course of these investigations novel whistles have been discovered and mathematical descriptions have been developed (notably by Vincenz Strouhal of Czechoslovakia and by Lord Rayleigh of Britain). More recent investigation has identified the feedback mechanisms that determine the frequency and intensity of aerodynamic whistles.

Current research in aerodynamic whistles, including my own at the University of Colorado, has been stimulated not only by scientific curiosity but also by important practical considerations. Many machines and structures of modern technology generate whistling sounds that are annoying and even capable of damaging the ear. Such sounds can better be controlled if the generating process is understood. Aerodynamic whistles also serve constructive purposes: they can measure the rate of flow of fluids in manufacturing processes and function as amplifiers in "fluidic" control systems. In oil burners whistles can make combustion more efficient by vaporizing the fuel and even mixing it with air.

Clearly aerodynamic whistles can take many forms. Nonetheless, all aerodynamic whistles work in basically the same way. In every whistle a steady flow of fluid must be established. Below a certain speed the flow is laminar, or smooth and stable. Above that speed some disturbance can cause the stream to form periodically spaced vortexes that give rise to oscillations in the surrounding fluid. If the frequency of the oscillations is between 50 and 20,000 cycles (the range of human hearing), a sound is heard. If the frequency is higher or lower, ultrasonic or subsonic acoustical fields are produced.

This is only a partial description of how whistles work. It neglects the fact that the disturbance amplified by the fluid instability may occur only intermittently. How then does an aerodynamic whistle produce a prolonged, steady tone? Here the concepts of modern theory can be used to describe the whistle mechanism in simple terms. In the language of control theory an aerodynamic whistle is a self-maintained oscillator, analogous to a public-address system that squeals when too much sound from the loudspeaker is picked up by the microphone, reamplified, and then fed back to the speaker.

The basic elements of such a system are (1) a means of amplification and (2) a means of feeding part of the amplified energy back to sustain and control the process. In an aerodynamic whistle a small disturbance in the stream flowing through the whistle is amplified into a large one by the instability of the stream, which permits steady energy to be converted to oscillatory energy. Part of the energy of the amplified disturbance is fed back upstream, where the flow is most unstable, and if it has the appropriate frequency and amplitude, it joins the original disturbance in maintaining the process. After a few cycles of this kind, the feedback controls the input completely. At this point the frequency is determined not by the original disturbance but by the period of the feedback cycle.

In an aerodynamic whistle there is a limited amount of energy in the stream, so that for a given set of conditions the sound reaches a steady amplitude. This steady state is achieved in the course of several feedback cycles. Each time a cycle is completed the amplitude of the sound increases. The rate of increase declines, however, until it reaches zero. At that point virtually all the available energy contained in the steady flow has been diverted into amplifying the original disturbance.

Aerodynamic whistles can be divided into three classes according to the means of feedback. If the whistle's feedback consists primarily of hydrodynamic oscillations (that is, incompressible vortex motion), I call it a Class I or hydrodynamic whistle. If the feedback consists of the sound waves generated by the whistle and fed directly back to the region of instability, it is a Class II or acoustic whistle. Class III whistles are distinguished by the fact that feedback is accomplished by sound waves reflected back to the region of instability by some ancillary structure.

Any classification scheme for aerodynamic whistles is somewhat arbitrary, for two reasons. First, a whistle mechanism can be so complex that it may operate in several classes; the classifications below apply to normally observed operation. Second, the names given the elements of a whistle are only symbolic descriptions applied to the device so that it can be discussed and investigated. They do not correspond to conveniently self-contained "black boxes" such as the components of a public-address system. Each of the components of a whistle is physically intertwined with the others.

Class I whistles are the most widely encountered, perhaps because so many of them occur naturally. This category includes telephone wires, tree limbs, and aeolian harps singing in the wind. (The aeolian harp is an ancient Greek instrument consisting of a set of strings stretched over a sounding box and set in motion by the wind or the breath.) This kind of Class I whistle, called an aeolian-tone generator, basically consists of a long, thin cylinder in a stream of air or some other fluid. Above a certain speed there will develop behind the cylinder two symmetrically placed vortexes that are stable and steady. If the speed of flow increases above a second threshold and one of the vortexes is disturbed by a sound pressure wave, the vortex will oscillate around its stable position and ultimately break away from the cylinder and move downstream. The breaking away of this vortex causes the opposite vortex to become unstable, and it too breaks away. Another vortex forms in place of the first one and it in turn becomes unstable. The feedback appears to be entirely hydrodynamic: each vortex gives rise to instability in the other directly, without any intervening agent such as a sound wave. As a result of the influence of one vortex on the other a chain of alternating vortexes soon stretches downstream from the cylinder. As the vortexes develop they generate a sound field with a maximum at right angles to their path.

The only other type of Class I whistle appears to be the vortex whistle. This whistle can consist of a pipe with air flowing through it. If the air enters the pipe tangentially to the wall or encounters a set of appropriately designed blades in the pipe, it will begin to swirl. When this swirling flow encounters the open end of the pipe (or a widened section of the pipe), the helical flow begins to precess, or rotate around the axis of the pipe, at a definite frequency. The interaction with the exit of the pipe produces a sound field. This mechanism may seem quite different from that of the aeolian-tone generator, but when the precessing flow is viewed in cross section along the axis of the pipe, it resembles the vortex pattern that forms behind a cylinder.

The sound of Class I whistles is a by-product of vortex development; indeed, the vortexes can develop without generating any audible sound at all. A whistle is produced only when the frequency falls in the audible range and the flow speed is high enough. Even then the intensity of the sound is usually low. Sometimes the process of sound generation in an aeolian-tone generator makes the cylinder itself vibrate, as when a telephone wire "gallops" in the wind. This motion can contribute to the sound, but it is not essential to its production.

The precise nature of the feedback in both the aeolian-tone generator and the vortex whistle has resisted efforts to observe or analyze it. Today, after almost a century, we do not know much more about the aeolian tone than Strouhal and Lord Rayleigh did. In 1878 Strouhal observed that no sound was emitted by the flow around a cylinder until a given flow speed had been reached. Above that speed a sound was generated whose frequency was directly related to the speed of the fluid and the diameter of the cylinder. The frequency, Strouhal found, was generally higher for smaller cylinders and lower for larger ones. In fact, the relationship could be described in terms of a constant that is the product of the sound frequency times the diameter of the cylinder divided by flow speed. This number is now called the Strouhal number, and it can be used to describe all whistles.

With sufficient experimental data the behavior of Class I whistles can be predicted, and this can make them useful as flow-meters. The frequency of the sound produced by an aeolian-tone whistle or a vortex whistle is almost directly proportional to the flow speed. Therefore by measuring this frequency one can monitor the rate of flow through a pipe. The precession of helical flow, however, is not always helpful. It can be a serious problem in the combustion chamber of a solid-propellant rocket. Unless it is suppressed the combustion energy will amplify the vortex and the rocket engine will be destroyed.

Class II whistles are more numerous than those of Class I. Some of these whistles have been discovered only recently, and it seems likely that more will be found as the search for whistles that can be adapted to practical purposes is continued. Some of this research has been preventive. Several kinds of Class II whistles can be generated accidentally in jet-aircraft engines. These oscillations are so intense that they can cause metal fatigue and engine failure. Through an understanding of the feedback loop in such whistles ways have been found to disrupt them.

One of the oldest and best-known of the Class II whistles is called the edge tone. The edge tone, which can be generated by flows at both low speeds and supersonic ones, generally has a pure, intense sound that can be painful to the ear. An edge tone is produced when a jet of air emerging from a slit encounters an object downstream. The sheared jet flow is unstable; any disturbance will cause vortex development and hence cause a force to be exerted on the downstream object. The reaction force exerted by the object on the fluid then generates a sound field.

The lines of fluid motion associated with the edge tone sound field resemble the pattern of iron filings around a magnet. As the sound is propagated back toward the slit, where the jet is more unstable, it reinforces the instability by causing a lateral displacement of the jet that gives rise to vortexes downstream; these vortexes encounter the object (generally a sharp wedge) and cause further sound emission. The sound field propagates back to the orifice and the cycle begins again.

Two other whistles in this class—hole tones and ring tones—are generated by a round jet impinging on a round edge or a circular ring. The teakettle whistle is a good example of the hole tone. Such a whistle consists of two holes separated by a small cavity. A whistle sounds when the jet formed at the first hole impinges on the second hole. Like the edge tone, the stream instability causes vortexes to form that generate sound when they encounter the object. The air in the second hole vibrates much like the diaphragm of a loudspeaker. Part of the sound generated by this diaphragm of air travels outward. The rest travels back toward the hole from which the jet issues. Unlike the edge tone, the sound causes slight changes in flow speed that give rise to vortex rings resembling rings of cigarette smoke. These vortexes travel downstream, impinge on the second hole and cause more disturbance in the flow through the hole to complete the feedback loop.

When the second hole in a hole-tone whistle is replaced by a small ring, the weaker ring tone is generated. If the diameter of the cavity between the two holes in the hole-tone generator is reduced to the diameter of the holes, thus forming a straight pipe, there may be a whistling sound called a jet tone. Its mechanism is very similar to that of the hole tone. Human whistling, in which sound is produced at an orifice formed by the mouth, also seems similar to the hole tone, but the mechanism of this whistle has not been studied thoroughly enough to classify it.

The observation of supersonic jet flows has led to the discovery of another Class II whistle called the choked-jet tone. It consists of a high-pressure stream of air flowing through a narrow passage. The intense sound produced by this whistle results from the fact that when air enters a restriction such as a nozzle at a pressure higher than atmospheric pressure, it cannot flow through the nozzle faster than the speed of sound. As a consequence the air cannot return to atmospheric pressure until after it has escaped from the nozzle. When the flow emerges, it suddenly accelerates to supersonic speed and then readjusts to subsonic speed by compression through a shock wave. The process creates a series of diamond-shaped cells of alternate supersonic and subsonic flow.

Such a pattern of cells can be seen in the exhaust of a rocket engine. The shock front at the head of certain cells is so unstable that small disturbances can cause it to oscillate and produce sound. The sound then propagates outward and creates a disturbance at the nozzle that is amplified in the jet to complete the feedback loop. A particularly good photograph of the sound from a choked-jet tone has been made by M. G. Davies of the University of Liverpool.

If Strouhal's observations applied, it could be anticipated that as the flow speed in a Class II whistle is increased the frequency of the whistle would gradually rise. This has been found to be true, but at a certain flow rate the continuous rise is interrupted and the frequency jumps abruptly upward. It then resumes a steady rise with increasing flow speed. This phenomenon, called a frequency jump, can be reversed by decreasing the flow rate. On the way down, however, the pitch will fall abruptly at a flow rate different from that at which it originally jumped up. The complete graph of frequency v. flow speed forms a loop and is analogous to the graph of the hysteresis loop in magnetic circuits.

Most Class I and Class II whistles can be made so that they can be blown with the mouth. Because the frequency depends almost linearly on flow speed, and because it is difficult to maintain a precise flow speed with the mouth, these whistles have never resulted in highly developed musical instruments. They had to be modified to Class III whistles before they were able to produce a constant frequency.

Class III whistles can be distinguished from the other kinds by the fact that a resonant or reflecting structure controls the feedback. A common example in this class of whistles is the flute. The flute whistles when a jet of air from the mouth is blown across a hole in the side of the instrument. The jet impinges on the opposite edge of the hole to create an edge tone. The edge tone, however, makes the column of air in the tube of the instrument resonant at a frequency that is determined by the length and diameter of the tube. The reflected sound waves in the column of air are sufficiently intense to override the normal edge-tone feedback, and thus the frequency of the tone is the resonant frequency of the tube. In a recorder or an organ pipe a resonant tube also controls the frequency. Instead of a round hole, however, a sharp wedge establishes the jet tone by interfering with a jet of air blown across it.

Since the frequency of the tone of an organ pipe or a woodwind is controlled not by the speed of the airflow, as it is in a Class I or Class II whistle, but by the resonant modes of the tube, the flow speed can be altered considerably without affecting the pitch of the instrument. It is this fact that enables organ pipes and woodwinds to function effectively as musical instruments. In order to change pitch, pipes of various lengths can be added to an instrument, as they are in an organ. The pitch of a flute or a recorder is changed by covering or uncovering holes so that the effective length of the tube changes. Because of the dominance of the resonant cavity, consecutive musical notes, each of a constant but different frequency, can easily be blown. Making tube lengths and hole spacings that will produce harmonically related notes is still an art, and it is likely to remain so for some time. When the jet, because of a speed increase, can no longer amplify the first resonance of the tube, it is said to be overblown. The instrument then switches from the first resonance to a second one through a frequency jump.

Police whistles belong in Class III. The Metropolitan Police of London use a small version of the organ pipe. The American police whistle, however, has a cylindrical cavity containing a ball that rotates so that a warbling tone is generated. The controlling element in the feedback for this whistle is still unknown. It may be controlled by acoustical resonance within the cavity; it may also be controlled by the fluctuating recirculating flow inside the cavity. When the jet is deflected inside the cavity, some flow enters that later must reappear at the nozzle exit. This flow may deflect the stream of air and thereby maintain the feedback cycle. The warbling occurs when the rotating ball blocks the hole and stops the tone.

The Class III whistles most useful in industry are descendants of a whistle developed by Sir Francis Galton in 1883 to test hearing ability. The Galton whistle consists of a ring-shaped jet that produces sound when it impinges on the edge of a resonant cavity set coaxially in front of it. The sound can be varied from low frequencies and intensities to high ones. In a modification of the Galton whistle made by Julius Hartmann of Denmark in 1919 a circular jet is substituted for a ring-shaped one. The Hartmann whistle generates a tone by directing a supersonic flow of air into a cavity. If the cavity is located at the correct distance from the nozzle, a traveling shock wave is formed within the cavity. When the traveling wave impinges on the standing shock wave in the jet and immediately in front of the cavity, it causes the standing wave to jump. The jump gives rise to a new wave in the cavity and to sound emission similar to the shock motion in the choked-jet tone. If the airflow is subsonic or even laminar, a Hartmann whistle will still produce a tone, but in these circumstances the amplifier is simply the jet instability.

Another variation on the Galton whistle is the stem jet. The cavity of this device is supported by a rod projecting from the nozzle, and a parabolic reflector fitted around the nozzle focuses the sound. In supersonic operation this jet is similar to the Hartmann whistle in that the jumping of the exterior shock wave generates the sound. The effect of the stem on the flow field is quite large, however, and higher sound levels result.

The Galton whistle, the Hartmann whistle, and the stem jet have all been adapted to practical ends. The Galton whistle was once used as a steam-locomotive whistle. Instead of having a ring-shaped jet of steam impinge on the edge of one big cavity, several smaller chambers of different lengths were assembled to form a supersonic "pipes of Pan" that produced harmonically related sounds. Although this "chime" whistle was pleasant to hear, it was a failure in sounding a strident warning of the train's approach. Today Hartmann whistles and stem jets control combustion by altering chemical-reaction rates and vaporize liquid fuel so that it burns more efficiently in a boiler. They also emulsify liquid mixtures and coagulate smoke and dust. Sonic energy generated by these whistles can hasten drying, clean surfaces, and test rocket materials and components. There are mechanical sirens that can generate sounds intense enough for these purposes, but because whistles have no moving parts they are simpler to construct and maintain.

Not all aspects of the supersonic Class III whistles are understood. The amplifying mechanism is still somewhat obscure, particularly with regard to the role played by the jet instability. Although vortexes must develop in the jet as a consequence of the jet's being disturbed by the strong sound field, they are far weaker than the vortexes found in the subsonic jet whistles.

The detailed study of aerodynamic whistles not only has satisfied scientific curiosity and provided some novel solutions to practical problems but also has opened avenues to the understanding of aerodynamic sound generation. The mechanism of whistles is intimately related to the mechanisms that create the sounds of jet-aircraft engines and air-moving fans. Whistles, although very complex, are still easier to analyze, and hypotheses of sound generation can be more readily tested with them. Further study of whistles should lead to deeper knowledge of sound generated by fluids and perhaps to cures for the myriad noises that are bombarding mankind with ever increasing intensity. □

Substitutes for Violence

John Fischer

Scoundrels and in some cases even ruffians terrified the citizens. Young mothers had to take their babies to Central Park in armored cars. Old women went to the theater in tanks, and no pretty woman would venture forth after dark unless convoyed by a regiment of troops. . . . the police wore bullet-proof underwear and were armed with mortars and fifteen-inch howitzers. . . .
—James Reston: *New York Times*, Oct. 29, 1965.

Like most fables, Mr. Reston's moral tale exaggerates a little. But not much; for all of us are uneasily aware that violence is becoming a central fact of American life. Year after year the official graph for crimes of violence—murder, rape, assault, robbery, and riot—inches a little higher.* Many of these crimes seem to be entirely senseless: a California sniper blazes away at random at passing motorists . . . Bronx youngsters pillage the Botanical Garden and wreck their own schoolrooms . . . a subway rider suddenly pulls a knife and starts slashing at his fellow passengers . . . a gang of roaming teen-agers comes across an old man drowsing on a park bench; they club and burn him to death without even bothering to rifle his pockets.

It is hardly surprising, then, that violence is becoming a dominant concern in our politics, literature, and conversation. Every campaigning candidate promises to chase the hoodlums off the city streets. Murder and mayhem—usually aimless, inexplicable, "existential"—are a growing preoccupation of American novelists: witness the recent work of Norman Mailer, Nelson Algren, and a hundred less-publicized writers. And not only the novelists; one of the most memorable nonfiction books of the past year was Truman Capote's *In Cold Blood*, a factual account

---

*According to the annual reports of the Federal Bureau of Investigation. But its figures are based on voluntary reports by more than eight thousand local law-enforcement agencies, using different definitions of crime and widely varying statistical methods; therefore the FBI does not vouch for their accuracy. In fact, nobody knows precisely how much crime is committed in the United States, or its rate of increase, if any. [Fischer's note.]

of the peculiarly brutal murder of the Clutter family by two young sadists. Significantly, the scene was not a city street but a Kansas farm.

Nor is the carnage limited to the United States. As *The Economist* of London pointed out in a recent article (reprinted in the November issue of *Harper's*), rioting and hooliganism are on the rise in nearly every country, including England, Sweden, and Russia. Bloodshed in the big cities naturally gets most of the headlines, but it seems to be almost as widespread in predominantly rural areas—the Sudan, for example, India, the Congo, and Colombia, where *la violencia* has taken hundreds of thousands of lives during the last two decades.

Explanations for all this are easy to come by, from nearly every clergyman, sociologist, and politician. Unfortunately they are seldom consistent. Some blame the miseries of slum life, others the breakdown of the family, or religion, or our national moral fiber. Racial and religious frictions apparently account for much free-floating hostility—in Watts and Calcutta, Capetown and Hué, even in Moscow and Peking, where African students report a lot of rough treatment from their hosts. Marxists, naturally, explain it all in terms of bourgeois decadence (although that would hardly account for the outbreaks in Prague and Novocherkassk, where the wicked bourgeoisies were liquidated long ago). While the Black Muslims decry police brutality, J. Edgar Hoover is prescribing more policemen, armed with wider powers. The Freudians suggest that sexual frustration may be the root of the trouble, while Billy Graham is just as sure that it is sexual laxity. Nearly everybody points an indignant finger at the dope peddlers, and William Buckley gets cheers whenever he proclaims that nothing will save us short of a universal moral regeneration.

Perhaps there is some truth in all these explanations. But I am beginning to wonder whether, far beneath them all, there may not lie another, more primordial reason. Just possibly the global surge of antisocial violence may result from the fact that nearly all societies—especially those we describe as "advanced"—suddenly have been forced to change a key commandment in their traditional codes of behavior; and many people, particularly the young males, have not yet been able to adjust themselves to this reversal.

That commandment was simple: "Be a fighter." Ever since human beings began to emerge as a separate species, something over a million years ago, it has been our first law of survival. For the earliest men, life was an incessant battle: against the hostile Pleistocene environment, against other mammals for food, against their own kind for a sheltering cave, a water hole, a hunting range, a mate. The fiercest, wiliest, and strongest lived to raise children. The meek, weak, slow, and stupid made an early breakfast—for a local tiger or, perhaps oftener, for a neighboring family, since archaeological evidence suggests that cannibalism was common among primeval man. The result was that "our ancestors have bred pugnacity into our bone and marrow. . . ."*

As civilization began to dawn, fighting became more organized—a community enterprise rather than a family one. In addition to their daily skirmishes with wolves, cattle thieves, and passing strangers, the able-bodied men of the village (or polis, kingdom, or pueblo) normally banded together at least once a year for a joint killing venture. The convenient time for settled farming people was early fall, after the harvest was in; then they had both enough leisure and enough surplus food to mount an expedition. So it was about September when the Assyrian swept down like a wolf on the fold, when Gideon smote the Philistines, when Vikings ravaged the Kentish coast, when the Greeks shoved off for Troy, when the Dorians swept into the Argive plain, irresistibly armed with that first mass weapon, the iron sword. (Because iron ore was much more plentiful than copper, it could be used—once the secret of smelting it was learned—to equip every man in the ranks. The victims of the Dorians, still lingering in the Bronze Age, normally armed only their officers with metal blades; the rest carried flint-tipped spears and arrows.) Tribes in the preagricultural stage sometimes found other seasons more suitable for rapine. The War Moon of the Great Plains Indians, for example, came in May—since the spring grass was then just high enough to graze the horses of a raiding party, and the full moon made it easy to travel fast at night. Regardless of timing, however, warfare was for centuries the main social enterprise, absorbing virtually all of the community's surplus time, energy, and resources. "History," as William James put it, "is a bath of blood. . . . war for war's sake, all the citizens being warriors. . . . To hunt a neighboring tribe, kill the males, loot the village, and possess the females was the most profitable, as well as the most exciting, way of living."

As soon as warfare became socialized, the premium on belligerence was redoubled. Always highly favored by the processes of natural selection, it was now celebrated as a prime civic virtue as well. The Great Fighter was enshrined as the universal hero. His name might be Hercules or Rustum, Beowulf or David, Kiyomori or Hiawatha, but his characteristics remained the same: physical strength, reckless courage, skill with weapons, and a bottomless appetite for bloodshed. From earliest boyhood the males of the community were taught to emulate him. Their training for combat began as soon as they could lift a spear, and by eighteen they normally would be full-fledged warriors—whether in Ath-

---

*As William James put it in his classic essay, "The Moral Equivalent of War," published in 1910. His other comments on this grisly topic will be noted in a moment. [Fischer's note.]

ens or Cuzco—equally ready to defend their city's walls or to pillage a weaker neighbor. Success in battle was the basic status symbol. The best fighters were feted in victory celebrations, heaped with honors and plunder, endowed with the lushest women, both home-grown and captive. The weak and timid, on the other hand, were scorned by elders and girls alike, and in many societies cowardice was punished by death.

For nearly all of human history, then, the aggressive impulse—so deeply embedded in our genes—had no trouble in finding an outlet. This outlet was not only socially acceptable; it was encouraged and rewarded by every resource at society's disposal.

This remained true until roughly a hundred years ago. (When my grandfathers were boys, the martial virtues were still applauded about as much as ever, and both of them marched off to the Civil War with the joyous spirit of an Alcibiades bound for Syracuse.)

Then, with stunning abruptness, the rules changed. Within about a century—a mere eye-blink in terms of evolutionary development—the traditional outlet for violence closed up. Fighting, so long encouraged by society, suddenly became intolerable.

One reason, of course, was the industrialization of war. It not only made warfare ruinously expensive; it took all the fun out of it. Long before the invention of the atom bomb, farsighted men such as William James had come to see that war was no longer "the most profitable, as well as the most exciting, way of living"; and by 1918 the lesson was plain to nearly everyone. In retrospect, our Civil War seems to have been the last in which physical strength, raw courage, and individual prowess could be (sometimes, at least) decisive; perhaps that is why it is written about so much, and so nostalgically.

For there is a certain animal satisfaction (as every football player knows) in bopping another man over the head. By all accounts, our ancestors thoroughly enjoyed hammering at each other with sword and mace; it exercised the large muscles, burned up the adrenalin in the system, relieved pent-up frustrations, and demonstrated virility in the most elemental fashion. But nobody can get that kind of satisfaction out of pulling the lanyard on a cannon, pointed at an unseen enemy miles away; you might as well be pulling a light switch in a factory. Indeed, in a modern army not one man in ten ever gets near combat; the great majority of the troops are cranking mimeograph machines, driving trucks, and tending the PX far to the rear. As a consequence, warfare— aside from its other disadvantages—no longer satisfies the primitive instinct for violence as it did for uncountable thousands of years.

At about the same time—that is, roughly a century ago—the other socially approved outlets for pugnacity also began to close up. For example, so long as our society was mostly rural and small-town, a good deal of purely personal, casual brawling was easily tolerated. When

Lincoln was a young man, the main public amusement seemed to be watching (and often joining in) the donnybrooks which boiled up regularly in the village street; and during his New Salem days, Abe more than held his own. Our literature of the last century, from *Huckleberry Finn* to the story of the OK Wagon Yard, is studded with this kind of spontaneous combat. And our chronicles memorialize the violent men (whether fur trappers, river boatmen, forty-niners, lumberjacks, or cowboys) in the same admiring tone as the sagas of Achilles and Roland. As recently as my own boyhood, fist-fighting was considered a normal after-school activity, like marbles and run-sheep-run; nobody thought of us as juvenile delinquents, in need of a corps of Youth Workers to hound us into docility. A tight-packed urban society, however, simply can't put up with this kind of random combat. It disturbs the peace, endangers bystanders, and obstructs traffic.

As we turned into a nation of city dwellers, we lost another traditional testing ground for masculine prowess: the struggle against nature. Since the beginning of history, when men weren't fighting each other they spent most of their time fighting the elements. To survive, they had to hack down forests, kill off predatory animals, battle with every ounce of strength and cunning against blizzards, droughts, deserts, and gales. When Richard Henry Dana came home after two years before the mast, he knew he was a man. So too with the striplings who rafted logs down rivers in a spate, drove a wagon over the Natchez Trace, pulled a fishing dory on the Grand Banks, or broke sod on the Nebraska prairies. Not long after he started shaving, my father went off alone to homestead a farm in what eventually became the state of Oklahoma. If he had been bothered by an "identity crisis"—something he couldn't even conceive—it would have evaporated long before he got his final papers.

Today of course the strenuous life, which Theodore Roosevelt thought essential for a healthy man, has all but vanished. Probably not 5 percent of our youngsters grow up to outdoor work, in farming, forests, or fisheries; and even for them, although the work may be hard, it is rarely either exciting or dangerous. (The modern cowboy does most of his work in a pickup truck, while Captain Ahab's successor goes to sea in a floating oil factory.) This final conquest of nature has had some results both comic and a little sad. Among the Masai tribesmen, for instance, when a boy comes of age it has always been customary for him to prove his manhood by killing a lion with a spear; but according to recent reports from Africa, there are no longer enough lions to go around.

In our tamer culture, we have shown remarkable ingenuity in inventing lion-substitutes. The most fashionable surrogates for violence are the strenuous and risky sports—skiing, skin diving, surfing, mountain climbing, drag racing, sailing small boats in rough weather—which have burgeoned so remarkably in recent years. When a middle-aged

Cleveland copy editor crosses the Atlantic alone in a twelve-foot sloop, nobody accuses him of suicidal impulses; on the contrary, millions of sedentary males understand all too well his yearning for at least one adventure in life, however self-imposed and unnecessary. (Women, of course, generally do not understand; most of the wives I've overheard discussing the Manry voyage wondered, not how he made it, but why Mrs. Manry ever let him try.)

But these devices serve only the middle class. For the poor, they ordinarily are too expensive. When Robert Benchley remarked that there was enough suffering in life without people tying boards on their feet and sliding down mountains, he missed the point; the real trouble with skiing is that slum kids can't afford it. Consequently, they try to get their kicks vicariously, by watching murder, football, boxing, and phony wrestling matches on television. When that palls, their next resort usually is reckless driving. That is why access to a car (his own, his family's, or a stolen one) is as precious to the adolescent male—rich or poor—in our culture as possession of a shield was in fifth-century Athens. It is a similar badge of manhood, the equipment necessary to demonstrate that he is a fearless and dashing fellow. (It also is the reason why insurance premiums are so high on autos driven by males under twenty-five years old.)

Such games are socially useful, because they absorb in a relatively harmless way some of our pent-up aggressions. But they all have one great drawback: they are merely games. They are contrived; they are artificial adjuncts to life, rather than the core of life itself. When our ancestors harpooned a whale, pillaged a city, or held the pass at Thermopylae, they knew they were playing for keeps. When our sons break their legs on a ski slope or play "chicken" on the highway, they know that the challenge is a made-up one, and therefore never wholly satisfying. They still yearn for a genuine challenge, a chance to prove their hardihood in a way that really means something.

Lacking anything better, some of them—a growing number, apparently—turn to crimes of violence. Gang fights, vandalism, robbery are, in an important sense, more "real" than any game. And for large groups of disadvantaged people, any form of antisocial violence is a way of striking back, in blind fury, at the community which has condemned them to disappointment and frustration. This is equally true, I suspect, of the Negro rioters in Watts and the poor whites of the South, who take so readily to the murders, church burnings, and assorted barbarities of the Klan.

This sort of thing may well continue, on a rising scale, until we can discover what James called a "moral equivalent for war." He thought he had found it. He wanted to draft "the whole youthful population" into a peacetime army to serve in "the immemorial human warfare against nature." What he had in mind was a sort of gigantic Civilian Conservation Corps, in which every youngster would spend a few years at hard and dangerous labor—consigned to "coal and iron mines, to freight trains, to fishing fleets in December . . . to road-building and tunnel-making." When he wrote, a half-century ago, this idea sounded plausible, because the need for such work seemed limitless.

Today, however, his prescription is harder to apply. In many parts of the globe, the war against nature has ended, with nature's unconditional surrender. Automation, moreover, has eliminated most dangerous and physically demanding jobs; our mines and freight trains are overmanned, our roads are now built with earth-moving machines rather than pick and shovel.

Nevertheless, so far as I can see James's idea is still our best starting point. And already an encouraging number of people are groping for ways to make it work, in the different and more difficult circumstances of our time.

A few have found personal, unofficial answers. The young people who join the civil-rights movement in the South, for example, are encountering hardship, violence, and occasionally death in a cause that is obviously genuine; they aren't playing games. But The Movement can accommodate only a limited number of volunteers, and presumably it will go out of business eventually, when the white Southerners reconcile themselves to rejoining the United States. In the North, civil-rights work has often turned out to be less satisfying, emotionally, because The Enemy is harder to identify and the goals are less clear. As a result its young partisans sometimes have drifted into a kind of generalized protest, carrying placards for almost anything from SNCC to Free Speech to World Peace: that is, they have ended up with another form of game playing.

President Kennedy, who understood thoroughly the youthful need for struggle and self-sacrifice, had the Jamesian principle in mind when he started the Peace Corps. It remains the most successful official experiment in this direction, and it led to the Job Corps and several related experiments in the domestic Antipoverty Program. How they will work out is still an open question, as William Haddad pointed out last month in *Harpers'*. At least they are a public recognition that the country has to do *something*. If we don't—if we continue to let millions of young men sit around, while the adrenalin bubbles and every muscle screams for action, with no outlet in sight but a desk job at best and an unemployment check at worst—then we are asking for bad trouble. Either we can find ways to give them action, in some useful fashion, or we can look forward to a rising surge of antisocial violence. In the latter case we may, a decade from now, remember the Fort Lauderdale beach riots as a mere boyish prank.

What I am suggesting, of course, is that all of us—especially our businessmen, sociologists, and political leaders—ought to invest a good deal more effort, ingenuity, and money in the search for acceptable substitutes for violence. How many industries have really tried to create interesting and physically demanding jobs for young people? Have the paper companies, for instance, figured out how many foresters they might use, if they were to develop their timber reserves for camping, hunting, and fishing, as well as for wood pulp? And are they sure such a venture would not be profitable?

To take care of the population explosion, we are going to have to duplicate all of our present college buildings within the next twenty years. Has any university looked into the possibility of using prospective students to do some of the building? Maybe every able-bodied boy should be required to labor on the campus for six months as a brick-layer or carpenter before he is admitted to classes?

Cleaning up our polluted rivers is a task worthy of Paul Bunyan, and one we can't postpone much longer. What governor has thought of mobilizing a state Youth Corps to do part of the job? Has Ladybird Johnson calculated how many husky youngsters might be deployed, axes in hand, to chop down billboards along our highways and replace them with trees?

The possibilities aren't as easy to spot as they were in William James's day, but even in our overcrowded and overdeveloped society some of them still exist. No single one of them will provide the kind of simple, large-scale panacea that James had in mind—yet if we can discover a few hundred such projects, they might add up to a pretty fair Moral Equivalent. In any case, the search is worth a more serious try than anyone has made yet.

Why, my wife asks me, is all that necessary? Wouldn't it be simpler for you men to stop acting like savages? Since you realize that belligerence is no longer a socially useful trait, why don't you try to cultivate your gentler and more humane instincts? Are you saying that You Can't Change Human Nature?

No, that isn't quite what I'm saying. I recognize that human nature changes all the time. Cannibalism, for example, is now fairly rare, and polygamy (at least in its more open form) has been abandoned by a number of cultures. Someday (I hope and believe) the craving for violence will leach out of the human system. But the reversal of an evolutionary process takes a long time. For a good many generations, then, the Old Adam is likely to linger in our genes; and during that transitional period, probably the best we can hope for is to keep him reasonably quiet with some variant of William James's prescription. □

BIBLIOGRAPHY

Abercrombie, M. L. J. *The Anatomy of Judgment*. Harmondsworth: Penguin, 1969.

Bechtel, Jean M. "Conversation, A New Paradigm for Librarianship?" *College and Research Libraries* 47 (1986): 219–224.

Borresen, C. Robert. "Success in Introductory Statistics with Small Groups." *College Teaching* 38 (1990): 26–28.

Bouton, Clark, and Russell Y. Garth, eds. *Learning in Groups*. San Francisco: Jossey-Bass, 1983.

Bruffee, Kenneth A. "Collaborative Learning and 'The Conversation of Mankind.'" *College English* 46 (1984): 635–652.

———. "Social Construction, Language, and the Authority of Knowledge: A Bibliographic Essay." *College English* 48 (1986): 773–790. *See also*, "Comment and Response," *College English* 49 (1987): 707–716.

Cooper, Marilyn M., and Cynthia L. Selfe. "Computer Conferences and Learning: Authority, Resistance, and Internally Persuasive Discourse." *College English* 52 (1990): 847–869. *Also*, "Comment and Response," *College English* 53 (1991), 950–955.

Elbow, Peter. *Sharing and Responding*. New York: McGraw Hill, 1989.

Fish, Stanley. *Is There a Text In This Class? The Authority of Interpretive Communities*. Cambridge: Harvard Univ. Press, 1980.

Gere, Anne Ruggles. *Writing Groups: History, Theory, and Implications*. Carbondale, IL: Southern Illinois Univ. Press, 1987.

Gergen, Kenneth J. "The Social Constructionist Movement in Modern Psychology." *American Psychologist* 40 (1985): 266–275.

Glidden, Jock, and Joanne Gainen Kurfiss. "Small-Group Discussion in Philosophy 101." *College Teaching* 38 (1990): 3–8.

Goodsell, Anne, Michelle Maher, and Vincent Tinto. *Collaborative Learning: A Source Book for Higher Education*. State College, PA: National Center on Postsecondary Teaching, Learning, and Assessment, 1992.

Hawkes, Peter. "Collaborative Learning and American Literature." *College Teaching* 39 (fall 1991): 140–144.

Holt, Mara. "Towards a Democratic Rhetoric: Self and Society in Collaborative Theory and Practice." *Journal of Teaching Writing* 8 (spring/summer 1989): 99–112.

Holt, Mara Dawn. "Collaborative Learning from 1911–1986: A Socio-Historical Analysis." Diss. Univ. of Texas, 1988.

Johnson, David W., Roger T. Johnson, and Karl A. Smith. *Cooperative Learning: Increasing College Faculty Instructional Productivity*. Washington, D.C.: ASHE-ERIC Higher Education Reports, 1992.

Kail, Harvey. "Collaborative Learning in Context: The Problem with Peer Tutoring." *College English* 45 (1983): 594–599.

Kail, Harvey, and John Trimbur. "The Politics of Peer Tutoring." *WPA: Journal of the National Council of Writing Program Administrators* (fall 1987): 5–12.

Lefevre, Karen Burke. *Invention as a Social Act*. Carbondale, IL: Southern Illinois Univ. Press, 1987.

Lundsford, Andrea, and Lisa Ede. *Singular Texts/Plural Authors: Perspectives on Collaborative Writing*. Carbondale, IL: Southern Illinois Univ. Press, 1990.

Miller, Judith E., and Ronald D. Cheetham. "Teaching Freshmen to Think—Active Learning in Introductory Biology." *BioScience* 40 (1990): 388–391.

Rau, William, and Barbara Sherman Heyl. "Humanizing the College Classroom: Collaborative Learning and Social Organization Among Students." *Teaching Sociology* 18 (1990): 141–155.

Reither, James A., and Douglas Vipond. "Writing as Collaboration." *College English* 51 (1989): 858–867.

Sprague, Elmer. "Using the 'Group Method' in Teaching Introductory Philosophy Courses." *APA Newsletter on Teaching Philosophy* 4 (1984): 1–2.

Steffens, Henry. "Collaborative Learning in a History Seminar." *The History Teacher* 21 (1988): 1–14.

Trimbur, John. "Collaborative Learning and Teaching Writing." In Don McClelland and Timothy Donovan, *Research and Scholarship in Composition*. New York: Modern Language Association, 1985.

_____. "Consensus and Difference in Collaborative Learning." *College English* 51 (1989): 602–616.

Wiener, Harvey S. "Collaborative Learning in the Classroom: A Guide to Evaluation." *College English* 48 (1986): 52–61.

ACKNOWLEDGMENTS

Passages from *A Roving Commission* by Winston Churchill (English title, *My Early Life*).Copyrighted by Odhams Press Ltd. Reprinted by permission of Charles Scribner's Sons and Odhams Books Ltd. (The Hamlyn Group).

"Sources for Book Reviews" prepared by Jackie Eubanks, Brooklyn College Library Occasional Publications, No. 2. Brooklyn College: CUNY, Brooklyn, NY. Reprinted by permission.

"Examsmanship and the Liberal Arts: A Study in Educational Epistemology" by William C. Perry, Jr. from *Examining in Harvard College: A Collection of Essays by Members of the Harvard Faculty*. Copyright © 1963 by the Harvard University Press. Reprinted by permission.

Excerpt from "The Indispensable Opposition" by Walter Lippman, from *The Atlantic Monthly*, August 1939. Copyright © 1939, 1967 by The Atlantic Monthly Company, Boston, MA. Reprinted with permission of the President and Fellows of Harvard College.

"Aerodynamic Whistles" by Robert C. Chanaud, from *Scientific American*, January 1970. Copyright © 1970 by Scientific American, Inc. All rights reserved. Reprinted by permission.

"Substitutes for Violence" by John Fischer from *Harper's Magazine*, January 1966. Copyright © 1965 by Harper's Magazine. All rights reserved. Reprinted by special permission.

Parts of "Teaching Peer Tutors" in Appendix C first appeared in "The Brooklyn Plan: Attaining Intellectual Growth through Peer-Group Tutoring," *Liberal Education 64* (December 1978), pp. 447–68. Reprinted by permission of the Association of American Colleges.

Excerpt from "Writing and Reading as Collaborative or Social Acts" by Kenneth A. Bruffee in *The Writer's Mind*, edited by Janice N. Hays, et al. Reprinted by permission of the National Council of Teachers of English, Urbana, IL.

"A Way of Learning," by Hung Chan, and "Tutoring as a Learning Experience," by Gail Olmstead, in *Writing Center: Points of View*, Brooklyn College: CUNY, 1977. Reprinted by permission.

INDEX OF COLLABORATIVE LEARNING TASKS